D1743213

Social Policy in Changing European Societies

Social Policy in Changing European Societies

Research Agendas for the 21st Century

Edited by

Kenneth Nelson,

Full Professor of Sociology, Swedish Institute for Social Research (SOFI), Stockholm University, Sweden

Rense Nieuwenhuis,

Associate Professor of Sociology, Swedish Institute for Social Research (SOFI), Stockholm University, Sweden

Mara A. Yerkes

Associate Professor of Interdisciplinary Social Science, Department of Interdisciplinary Social Science, Utrecht University, the Netherlands

Edward Elgar
PUBLISHING

Cheltenham, UK • Northampton, MA, USA

© Editors and contributors severally 2022

This is an open access work distributed under the Creative Commons Attribution-NonCommercial-NoDerivatives Unported (This is an open access work distributed under the Creative Commons Attribution-NonCommercial-NoDerivatives 4.0 Unported (https://creativecommons.org/licenses/by-nc-nd/4.0/). Users can redistribute the work for non-commercial purposes, as long as it is passed along unchanged and in whole, as detailed in the License. Edward Elgar Publishing Ltd must be clearly credited as the rights holder for publication of the original work. Any translation or adaptation of the original content requires the written authorization of Edward Elgar Publishing Ltd.). Users can redistribute the work for non-commercial purposes, as long as it is passed along unchanged and in whole, as detailed in the License. Edward Elgar Publishing Ltd must be clearly credited as the rights holder for publication of the original work. Any translation or adaptation of the original content requires the written authorization of Edward Elgar Publishing Ltd.

Published by
Edward Elgar Publishing Limited
The Lypiatts
15 Lansdown Road
Cheltenham
Glos GL50 2JA
UK

Edward Elgar Publishing, Inc.
William Pratt House
9 Dewey Court
Northampton
Massachusetts 01060
USA

A catalogue record for this book
is available from the British Library

Library of Congress Control Number: 2022937627

This book is available electronically in the **Elgar**online
Sociology, Social Policy and Education subject collection
http://dx.doi.org/10.4337/9781802201710

ISBN 978 1 80220 170 3 (cased)
ISBN 978 1 80220 171 0 (eBook)

Printed and bound by CPI Group (UK) Ltd, Croydon, CR0 4YY

Contents

Figures

Contributors

Jolanta Aidukaite is a Chief Researcher at the Institute of Sociology at the Lithuanian Centre for Social Sciences. She has published extensively on the topics of social policy, family policy, housing policy, and community mobilization. Her research has been published in the *Journal of European Social Policy, Social Policy and Administration, Social Inclusion, Journal of Baltic Studies, Communist and Post-Communist Studies, International Journal of Sociology and Social Policy*, and *East European Politics*. Jolanta edited the book *Challenges to the Welfare State: Family and Pension Policies in the Baltic and Nordic Countries* (2021, Edward Elgar Publishing) in the New Horizons in Social Policy Series.

Giuliano Bonoli is Professor of Social Policy at the Swiss Graduate School of Public Administration, University of Lausanne. He has been involved in several national and international research projects on social policies. His work has focused on pension reform, labour market, and family policies. He has published some 50 articles in journals such as *Politics and Society, Journal of European Public Policy, European Sociological Review*, and *Journal of European Social Policy*. He was a founding member of the European Social Policy Analysis Network (ESPAnet) board in 2003.

Karen N. Breidahl is Associate Professor at Department of Politics and Society of Aalborg University. She specializes in the study of comparative welfare state research and the fields of integration and migration studies. Her major projects have focused on how the welfare state and its institutions influence migrants' socio-cultural incorporation patterns and their attitudes towards the welfare state, work–family orientations, national identification, and trust in the welfare state. More recently, she has started a research project on asylum reception in Sweden and Denmark. These studies, utilizing both qualitative and quantitative methods, have contributed with new theoretical and empirical insights and have been published in recognized international scholarly journals.

Bea Cantillon is Professor of Social Policy and member of the Herman Deleeck Centre for Social Policy at the University of Antwerp. She has published widely on the topic of social policy in rich welfare states. Bea is a Fellow of the Royal Belgian Academy of Sciences and corresponding Fellow of the

British Academy. She was awarded a doctorate honoris causa by UCLouvain Saint-Louis Brussels and the Van Doorn Chair at the Erasmus School of Social and Behavioural Sciences in Rotterdam.

Jochen Clasen is Professor of Comparative Social Policy at the University of Edinburgh. His research interests include comparative social policy, labour market and social security policy, and welfare reform. Until 2006, he was Professor of Comparative Social Research at the University of Stirling, and held visiting positions at the Universities of Roskilde, European University Institute, Florence, Tübingen University, and the Hertie School of Governance, Berlin. He is co-founder and honorary president of ESPAnet.

Daniel Clegg is Senior Lecturer in Social Policy at the University of Edinburgh. He holds a PhD from the European University Institute and has previously held appointments at the University of Stirling, the University of Oxford, and Sciences Po. His research focuses on the comparative analysis of social policies addressed to labour market risks in advanced welfare states.

Mary Daly is Professor of Sociology and Social Policy at the Department of Social Policy and Intervention at the University of Oxford and a Governing Body Fellow of Green Templeton College, Oxford. Most of her work is comparative, in a European and international context. She is interested in and has published widely on the social policy areas of long-term care and care for children, gender inequality, family policy, poverty, and welfare. Mary Daly's research has been supported by, among others, the Economic and Social Research Council, the European Union, International Labour Organization, Council of Europe, UNWomen, and UNICEF.

Caroline De la Porte is Professor MSO at the Department of International Economics, Government and Business, Copenhagen Business School. Her research focuses on comparative welfare state reform, the Nordic welfare model, and the Europeanization of welfare states. Currently, she is involved in a Horizon-funded project, EUSocialCit, where she leads a working party on fair working conditions. Her recent publications include 'The next generation EU: An analysis of the dimensions on conflict behind the deal' in *Social Policy and Administration* (with Mads Dagnis Jensen) and 'The work–life balance directive: Towards a gender equalizing EU regulatory welfare state? Denmark and Poland compared' in *Annals of the American Academy of Political and Social Science* (with Trine Larsen and Dorota Szelewa).

Christopher Deeming is Senior Lecturer in Social Policy at the University of Strathclyde. Much of his research focuses on comparative and global policy issues, with his latest works being *The Struggle for Social Sustainability: Moral Conflicts in Global Social Policy* (2021, Policy Press), *Minimum*

Income Standards and Reference Budgets: International and Comparative Policy Perspectives (2020, Policy Press), and *Reframing Global Social Policy: Social Investment for Sustainable and Inclusive Growth* (2019, Policy Press).

Caroline Dewilde is Associate Professor at the Department of Sociology, Tilburg University. Her research interests concern the dynamics of social stratification, and resulting inequality and poverty, at different levels of analysis, from a comparative perspective. She publishes widely across the social sciences. In 2011, she received a European Research Council Starting Grant. In numerous HOWCOME publications she has analysed the interplay between trends in economic and social inequalities and changing housing regimes (housing markets, housing policies, and housing wealth). Her most recent work focuses on (changes in) housing as a driver of both increased poverty and affluence (housing wealth accumulation).

Bernhard Ebbinghaus is Professor of Sociology at the University of Mannheim. Previously, he was Professor of Social Policy at the University of Oxford, Head of the Department of Social Policy and Intervention, and also Senior Research Fellow of Green Templeton College, Oxford. In addition, he has been Co-Principal Investigator and Mercator Fellow at the Collaborative Research Centre Political Economy of Reform, University of Mannheim. His research studies the politics and outcomes of welfare state reforms, comparing pension systems, employment policies during crises, and the role of public attitudes and organized interests.

Emanuele Ferragina is Associate Professor of Sociology at Sciences Po, Paris. Prior to Sciences Po, he was a departmental lecturer at the University of Oxford, where he also received his DPhil. Emanuele is interested in the political economy of the welfare state, family policy, and social capital. Besides academia, he is a columnist for the Italian newspaper *Il Fatto Quotidiano*.

Bent Greve is Professor in Social Sciences with an emphasis on welfare state analysis at the University of Roskilde, Denmark. His research interest focuses on the welfare state and social and labour market policy, often from a comparative perspective. He has published extensively on social and labour market policy, social security, tax expenditures, public-sector expenditures, and financing of the welfare state. He is Editor of *Social Policy and Administration*. His recent books include *Rethinking the Welfare State* (2022, Edward Elgar Publishing), *Myths, Narratives and the Welfare State* (2021, Edward Elgar Publishing), *Austerity, Retrenchment and the Welfare State* (2020, Edward Elgar Publishing), *Routledge International Handbook of Poverty* (2020, Routledge), *Welfare, Populism and Welfare Chauvinism* (2019, Policy Press), and *Multidimensional Inequalities* (2021, De Gruyter).

Marietta Haffner is Assistant Professor at Delft University of Technology. She has more than 30 years has more than 30 years of experience in conducting European comparative studies in the field of housing and has close to a decade of teaching experience at Delft University of Technology, for two years as Assistant Professor. She is interested in the financial and economic aspects of housing, including topics such as the affordability and sustainability of housing costs, housing tenures, housing policy, housing equity release, and equity issues. She is Co-Editor-in-Chief of Housing Studies and Coordination Committee member of the European Network for Housing Research.

Troels Fage Hedegaard is Associate Professor in Political Science at the Department of Politics and Society, Aalborg University. His work has focused on describing how migrants perceive the Northern European welfare states and how inhabitants of Northern European welfare states perceive migrants. His latest published article is 'Attitudes to climate migrants: Results from a conjoint survey experiment in Denmark' in *Scandinavian Political Studies*.

Bjørn Hvinden was Professor of Sociology at the Norwegian University of Science and Technology, Trondheim (1995–2006) and at Norwegian Social Research, Oslo Metropolitan University until 2020. His main research areas have been work and organizational studies, public administration, marginality, comparative social policy, and more recently the interface between climate change and social welfare. He has been a visiting scholar at the universities of Edinburgh, Umeå, and Helsinki and guest professor at the universities of Bremen and Lund. He has been scientific coordinator of several cross-national and comparative projects funded by European, Nordic, and Norwegian sources.

Trudie Knijn is Emeritus Professor of Interdisciplinary Social Science at Utrecht University. Her research interests have been on comparative approaches to the relationship between the development and implementation of social policy in the field of work and care, family relationships, gender, and citizenship. More recently, she has published on solidarity, justice, and social welfare.

Tijs Laenen is Postdoctoral Researcher at the School of Social and Behavioral Sciences of Tilburg University and the Centre for Sociological Research of KU Leuven. His main research interest and expertise lies in studying popular attitudes towards differently targeted and differently designed welfare state policies.

Margarita León is Professor of Political Science at the Universitat Autònoma Barcelona. Between 2010 and 2015, she was a 'Ramón y Cajal' senior research Fellow at the Institute of Government and Public Policies of the same university.

From 2003 until 2010, she was a lecturer in European social policy, University of Kent. She has been a Marie Curie Post-doctoral Fellow at the European University Institute in Florence (2001–2003) and a Fulbright Visiting Scholar at the University of Berkeley (2018). Her main areas of research are comparative public policy and welfare state reform. She has published in numerous international peer-reviewed scientific journals, co-edited with A. Guillén *The Spanish Welfare State in European Context* (2011, Routledge), and edited *The Transformation of Care in European Societies* (2014, Palgrave Macmillan).

Ilaria Madama is Associate Professor of Political Science in the Department of Social and Political Sciences at the University of Milan, where she teaches European Union politics and policies and international political economy and the welfare state, and coordinates the academic minor programme in 'Diritti, Lavoro e Pari Opportunità' (Rights, work and equal opportunities). Her principal research areas are European Union social governance and comparative social policy, with an interest in the political and institutional dynamics behind the development and reform of benefits, regulations, and services across European countries in the fields of minimum income protection, social inclusion, and work–life balance.

Bart Meuleman is Professor of Sociology at the Centre for Sociological Research at KU Leuven. His research focuses on cross-national comparisons of value and attitude patterns, such as ethnic prejudice, egalitarianism, and support for the welfare state. He is the Belgian coordinator of the European Social Survey and member of the questionnaire design team that developed the welfare attitudes module included in round 8.

Katja Möhring is Assistant Professor for Sociology of the Welfare State at the University of Mannheim. She completed her PhD at the University of Cologne and worked as a postdoctoral researcher at the University of Bremen. She leads projects at the Collaborative Research Center SFB 884 'Political Economy of Reforms' and the Mannheim Centre for European Social Research. Her work focuses on life courses, pensions, welfare states, gender equality, and quantitative methods, and has been published in, among others, the *Journal of European Social Policy, Social Policy and Administration*, and *European Sociological Review*.

Jekaterina Navicke is Associate Professor at the Social Policy Department, Vilnius University. Her interests include poverty, social exclusion, inequalities, social policy evaluation, and social protection. She received her PhD in sociology from Vilnius University in 2015 and has been a national coordinator of the European Social Policy Network since 2019. Jekaterina collaborates with and provides expert services to the Joint Research Centre at the European Commission, the Organisation for Economic Co-operation and Development, and the Lithuanian Ministry of Social Affairs and Labour. Her papers have been published in international journals, for example *Social Indicators Research, Social Science Research, Journal of Baltic Studies*, and *Baltic Journal of Economics*.

Kenneth Nelson is Professor of Sociology at the Swedish Institute for Social Research, Stockholm University. His areas of interest include comparative social policy, income distributions research, wellbeing, and health. He is the principal director of the SPIN database (www.sofi.su.se/spin). Kenneth is one of the co-chairs of ESPAnet. He is also a board member of the Foundation for International Studies of Social Security and is the chair of the Swedish Sociological Association.

Rense Nieuwenhuis is Associate Professor in Sociology at the Swedish Institute for Social Research at Stockholm University. He studies how family diversity and social policy affect poverty and economic inequality. Typically, his research is country comparative and has a gender perspective. His recent focus was on single-parent families, how women's earnings affect inequality between households, and family policy outcomes. Together with Wim Van Lancker, he is the editor of the Palgrave Handbook of Family Policy (2020, Palgrave Macmillan). Rense is a board member and secretary of ESPAnet and associate editor of the *Community, Work and Family* journal.

Thomas Paster is Assistant Professor at the University of Roskilde, Department of Social Sciences and Business. He specializes in business–politics relations, corporate taxation, and the politics of the welfare state. He is author of the book *The Role of Business in the Development of the Welfare State and Labor Markets in Germany* (2012, Routledge) and his research has been published in journals such as *World Politics, Socio-Economic Review, New Political Economy, British Journal of Industrial Relations*, and *Comparative Political Studies*.

Femke Roosma is Assistant Professor in Sociology at Tilburg University. Her main research interests regard the social legitimacy of welfare states, the cross-national analysis of multiple dimensions of welfare attitudes, solidarity and deservingness perceptions, and the universal basic income.

Mi Ah Schoyen is Senior Researcher at NOVA Norwegian Social Research, Oslo Metropolitan University. She works in the field of comparative welfare state research. Her interests include the welfare mix, the politics and social consequences of welfare state reforms, intergenerational solidarity, and the interplay between climate and social policy.

Verena Seibel is Assistant Professor at Utrecht University. Next to migrants' labour market integration processes, Verena is interested in migrants' perceptions and knowledge of their host society and welfare state. In her current work, Verena focuses on the link between migrants' welfare knowledge and migrants' welfare behaviour in terms of welfare take-up and the role that social networks play in this regard. Her work has been published in, among others, the *Journal of International Migration and Integration, International Journal of Public Opinion Research, European Societies*, and the *Journal of Ethnic and Migration Studies*.

Minna van Gerven is Professor of Social Policy at the University of Helsinki. Her research interests include broad aspects of social policy research, e.g., comparative social policy, welfare states, social security and social services, European Union social policy, digitalization, and automation.

Wim Van Lancker is Assistant Professor in Social Work and Social Policy affiliated with the Centre for Sociological Research, KU Leuven. His research agenda focuses on the measurement and analysis of social and family policies and how these policies affect outcomes in terms of wellbeing, inequality, employment, and poverty. Together with Rense Nieuwenhuis, he is the editor of the *Palgrave Handbook of Family Policy* (2020, Palgrave Macmillan). More information can be found at www.wimvanlancker.be.

Wim van Oorschot is Emeritus Professor of Social Policy at the Centre for Sociological Research of KU Leuven. His main academic interests regard the cultural analysis of welfare states and social policies in a European comparative context. He was the initiator and (co-)coordinator of the Welfare Attitudes modules of the European Social Survey. He is an honorary president of ESPAnet.

Claus Wendt is Professor of Sociology of Health and Healthcare Systems at the University of Siegen. His research interests include international comparisons of welfare states and health-care systems, health policy and demographic change, and the sociology of health. Professor Wendt is a 2008–2009 Harkness/Bosch Fellow of Health Policy and Practice at Harvard School of Public Health and J. F. Kennedy Fellow at Harvard's Center for European Studies. Prior to joining the University of Siegen, he was Senior Researcher at the Mannheim Center for European Studies, University of Bremen, and the University of Heidelberg, where he received his PhD in 2003.

Mara A. Yerkes is Associate Professor of Interdisciplinary Social Science at Utrecht University. Her research centres on comparative social policy (including welfare states, industrial relations, and citizenship regimes) and social inequalities (related to work, care, communities, and families, in particular relating to gender, generations, and sexuality). Yerkes is one of the co-chairs of ESPAnet. She is also Principal Investigator of the European Research Council project CAPABLE, a comparative study on gender inequalities in work–life balance in eight European countries, and leads the longitudinal COVID-19 Gender (In)equality Survey Netherlands study.

Hannah Zagel is Senior Researcher in Sociology at Humboldt-Universität zu Berlin and Head of the Research Group at WZB Berlin Social Science Center. Her research looks at associations between family and reproductive processes with social inequalities in different policy contexts. She recently studied the role of policies for mothers' employment, single-mother poverty, and inequalities in contraceptive use, including publications in *Social Politics*, *Journal of European Social Policy*, and *Advances in Life Course Research*.

Preface

Twenty years ago, in August 2002, a meeting co-organized by Wim van Oorschot, Jon Kvist, and Jochen Clasen, and hosted in Tilburg, the Netherlands, gave life to the European Social Policy Analysis network (ESPAnet). The aim was to create an interdisciplinary platform for scholarship on social policy in Europe, and to be inclusive to (among others) junior scholars. This aim holds strong. To celebrate 20 years of ESPAnet, we aimed to bring together a selection of senior and junior members of the ESPAnet community to present their views on the past, present, and future of social policy research.

The editorial team for the book is made up of the two ESPAnet co-chairs (Kenneth Nelson and Mara Yerkes) and the ESPAnet secretary (Rense Nieuwenhuis). We took over as co-chairs and secretary in 2019, six months before Europe would be confronted with the COVID-19 pandemic. None of us could have foreseen the role social policy would take during the pandemic, or the impact the pandemic would have on society. The ESPAnet community has proven itself to be very resilient throughout this period. Despite the cancellation of the 2020 annual meeting, senior scholars worked together to provide online alternatives, particularly to support opportunities for junior scholars to present their work. In 2021, a very successful online version of the annual meeting was held. We are humbled to be part of this community in our current roles, and for having the opportunity to edit this volume in relation to the ESPAnet 20-year anniversary. We would like to acknowledge the work of many colleagues in making this book possible.

First, the ESPAnet board. The idea for this book came about in preparation for the 2020 ESPAnet annual meeting, and the board immediately supported our efforts. Our annual board meetings, traditionally held every year the day before the annual meeting (and now also another meeting each spring), have been a great source of inspiration, and we truly appreciate the hard work, academic enthusiasm, and friendship of the many board members who have served ESPAnet in the past, present, and those to come. Many board members provided supportive peer reviews of the draft chapters. We thank you for your time and effort throughout the editorial process. In particular, we wish to thank Janine Leschke and Birgit Pfau-Effinger for their detailed comments on the conclusion chapter of this book.

We would also like to thank the contributors to this volume, including many ESPAnet enthusiasts, several of whom previously served as ESPAnet board members or co-chairs. Even the founders of ESPAnet were willing to contribute to this endeavour. We thank all contributors for the high quality of their contributions and for their patience and efforts in meeting the intense work schedule required for putting this book together in just nine short months in the midst of a pandemic.

A final note of thanks goes to Anna Kahlmeter, the editorial assistant at Stockholm University, and to our editors at Edward Elgar, Catherine Elgar and Beatrice McCartney. Anna, we appreciate your flexibility and thoroughness, helping us through the final stages of the manuscript. Catherine and Beatrice, thank you for making this edited volume possible, and for working with us to ensure a timely publication for the 2022 meeting.

We have made a concerted effort to provide an overview of the key scholarly debates central to the past 20 years of research on social policy in Europe. We have undertaken great effort to ensure a representative overview of this research, and accept that each chapter represents necessary interpretations of vast volumes of work. We also have the ambition, together with the book's contributors, to suggest where social policy research in Europe is headed. None of us is clairvoyant, but clearly research about social policy will continue to play a vital role in European societies in the coming years. The views offered represent our understanding of what is most needed to ensure another 20 years of robust, lively scholarly debate. We hope that current and future ESPAnet scholars will find the book inspiring.

Kenneth Nelson, Rense Nieuwenhuis, and Mara A. Yerkes
Amsterdam / Stockholm, December 2021

1. Social policy research in changing European societies

Kenneth Nelson, Rense Nieuwenhuis, and Mara A. Yerkes

INTRODUCTION

Social policy is an essential element of European societies (Lendvai-Bainton & Kennett, 2017). Most European countries have elaborate systems of redistribution and services in place to regulate social risks (i.e., unemployment, sickness, lone parenthood, old age, and so forth; Taylor-Gooby, 2004). Social policy is the backbone of these systems, intervening in almost all aspects of social life and following us through the life course as we grow older. Given the importance of social policy, it is no surprise that research on social policy has grown tremendously. In a few European countries, social policy has even emerged as an academic topic in its own right. However, in most European countries it is truly a multidisciplinary (or even an interdisciplinary) subject that engages scholars in various broad fields of study, such as economics, history, political science, sociology, public administration, and more.

This edited volume takes stock of major developments in research about social policy in Europe from the last two decades and sets a research agenda for the future. The focus is on the past, present, and future of social policy *research* carried out by scholars of European social policies rather than the organization of European social policies *per se*. Although not the prime area of study, where relevant, social policy developments will of course be touched upon to characterize how research has changed. The volume addresses the following three broad questions: (1) What is the state of the art regarding research about social policy in Europe? (2) How has research about social policy in Europe evolved to this point? (3) Where should research about social policy in Europe be headed?

This introductory chapter sketches the conceptual framework of the book and motivates our European focus. We also provide a concise overview of the different chapters. The book is being published in celebration of 20 years of the European Social Policy Analysis Network (ESPAnet) and ESPAnet activities, including international conferences, workshops, and seminars. ESPAnet was established in 2002, with the aim of facilitating exchange and cooperation among social policy scholars in Europe, as well as providing a multidisciplinary scholarly forum for communication about social policy research and teaching. Promoting comparative social policy research is another, more specific, aim of the network, together with supporting the entry of young researchers into the field. See Clasen and Kvist (2021) for more on the history of ESPAnet. This book provides key insights from this ongoing ESPAnet endeavour to advance European social policy research. The research themes selected for analysis have been identified using central topics and debates that have attracted considerable attention in various ESPAnet events and communities over the years, as well as a few that have received substantial amounts of scholarly interest more recently.

EUROPEAN SOCIAL POLICY

The focus in this book is on the scholarship of European social policy, a choice which is motivated in part by Europe being home to the world's most advanced welfare states. It is also a region characterized by multiple approaches to social policy. There is no univocal definition of social policy, neither in academia nor in public discourse (cf. Alcock, 2008). Most people would probably agree that it includes government programmes and services that directly aim to improve living conditions and wellbeing (Dean, 2019). However, what precisely counts as social policy is continuously discussed. In this book, we pragmatically take a broad understanding of social policy and follow Béland's (2010: 9) suggestion of defining it as 'an institutionalized response to social and economic problems'.

We focus here on policies institutionalized or initiated by the state, whether at national, regional, or local levels. Even as international and supra-national organizations such as the European Union (EU), the Organisation for Economic Co-operation and Development (OECD), and the International Labour Organization gained more influence in social policymaking (e.g., Nieuwenhuis & Van Lancker, 2020; Razavi, 2020; White, 2020), much of this influence is still implemented through national legislation and policy. The exact role of the state may differ, across countries as well as areas covered by the welfare state and social policies. In many countries, governments not only legislate social policy, but also finance, administer, and implement it in full. However, it is not uncommon for governments to provide solely the legislative frameworks, while other tasks are performed outside the public sector. In many European welfare states, the role of the state has consistently declined in recent years and become more occupied by regulating private and/or not-for-profit actors, local governments, or other institutions such as the family (e.g., Kazepov, 2010; Martinelli et al., 2017; Szebehely & Meagher, 2018).

The prominent role of social policy in European countries is clearly visible in national expenditure, with European welfare states among the top social policy spenders in the world. Figure 1.1 shows public expenditures on cash and in-kind benefits (services) as a percentage of gross domestic product (GDP) in 38 OECD countries in 2017, prior to the COVID-19 pandemic. Despite widespread differences across individual countries, European countries spend, on average, 13.1 per cent of annual GDP on cash benefits, and 8.1 per cent of GDP on in-kind benefits (services). The corresponding percentages for the non-European OECD countries are 7.1 and 7.6 per cent, respectively. The prominence of social policy in European economies can clearly be illustrated by summing up the two spending categories. On average, European countries spend more than 20 per cent of GDP annually on social policy. It thus constitutes one of the single largest cost categories of national expenditures of most European countries.

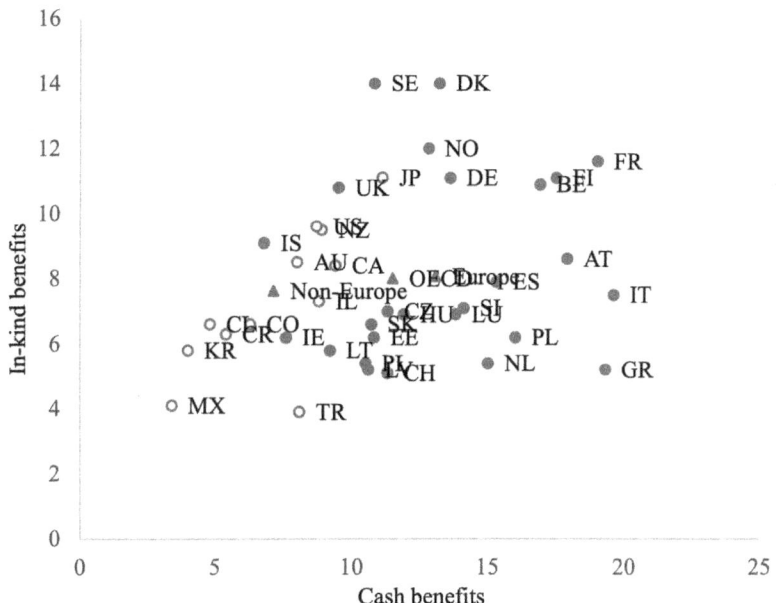

Source: OECD SOCX database.

Figure 1.1   *Public expenditures on cash and in-kind benefits (services) as a percentage of annual GDP*

Much social policy is financed from the public sector, but its financing has become more varied in recent decades. Besides the state, private actors like trade unions, employers, and employers' organizations also play key roles in social policy (Yerkes, 2011; Trampusch, 2013). In addition, the tax system in many countries is increasingly used for social policy purposes, for example, in the form of refundable child tax benefits (Ferrarini et al., 2013) and earned income tax credits. Meanwhile, social insurance benefits are taxable in some countries, thus parts of public social expenditures are reclaimed by the state via the fiscal system (Ferrarini & Nelson, 2003; Adema & Ladaique, 2005). Nonetheless, the characterization of European countries as big social policy spenders hardly changes if private expenditures are taken into account, or if we examine net social spending instead of gross public expenditures. Cross-country differences become somewhat more compressed after private social expenditures or taxes are included in the analyses, as individual countries (primarily the United States, which we do not take into account here) substantially change position.

Social policy expenditure in all its variations is a reflection of complex processes in society. Social policies are developed and implemented with the aim to address a variety of societal and economic issues and to ensure human wellbeing (Béland, 2010; Dean, 2019), such as supporting families, improving gender equality, investing in young generations, regulating fertility, stabilizing the economy, or raising political support. Social policies thus incorporate and set out a normative framework of what society looks like, and should look like (Goerne, 2010; Javornik, 2014; Yerkes & Javornik, 2019). What social policies achieve in practice may overlap with these standpoints, but not necessarily. Regardless of the state's initial aims in developing social policies, all social policies are likely to have redistributive consequences, even if these consequences are not foreseen or articulated by policymakers in the first place. This redistribution can pertain to redistribution between groups of people or redistribution across an individual's life course. Redistribution may not only involve money transfers, but may also take the form of services, such as those associated with health care, long-term care, and early childhood education and care.

Social policy models, or approaches to social policy, their aims, and outcomes, vary greatly across Europe. Broadly speaking, and in particular in relation to the protection of paid work, principles of universalism are strong in the Nordic countries, whereas much of continental Europe still organizes large parts of social policy on the basis of occupational categories (Palme et al., 2009). In the United Kingdom and Ireland, the reliance on market principles is widespread, as in other English-speaking capitalist societies (O'Connor et al., 1999). Many Southern European countries have introduced a clear division between labour market insiders and outsiders in their welfare states (Ferrera,

1996; Häusermann & Schwander, 2010), whereas parts of Central and Eastern Europe (CEE) still struggle to shape their own unique social models (e.g., Javornik, 2014).

The regional differentiation of European social policy may of course look very different if the classification of countries into different groups is based on factors other than protecting paid work, such as the emancipation of women (Pateman 1988; Hobson 1990; Lewis 1992; Orloff 1993; Sainsbury 1996), ethnic integration (Sainsbury, 2012; Van Der Waal et al., 2013), social investment (Iversen & Stephens, 2008; Morel et al., 2012), and so forth. We do not have the ambition in this introductory chapter to provide a complete analysis of the different social policy models that exist in Europe, nor to discuss in closer detail which factors should form the basis of such classifications. Rather, we wish to emphasize the vast institutional variation that is evident in European social policy, as it provides fertile ground for cross-country comparisons and in-depth case studies that are so central to research on European social policy.

Social policy is essential to the functioning of European societies. However, what role social policy is meant to play within these societies is continually evolving in response to external and internal reform pressures. Taking a historical perspective, the first three decades of the post-Second World War period marked the 'Golden Age' of social policy and the welfare state, when European economies grew and pre-war mass unemployment was replaced by what was assumed to be permanent full employment, albeit with employment and protection centred on the male breadwinner (Lewis, 1992). During this period, welfare states expanded, both in total expenditure and in the number of areas covered by social policy (Flora, 1987; Pierson, 1991; Huber & Stephens, 2001). After the mid-1970s, however, a period of turmoil set in with two-digit unemployment levels, stagflation, large-scale industrial restructuring, and accelerating economic internationalization (Bluestone & Harrison, 1982; Layard et al., 1991; Collins, 1998). From this period onwards, welfare states were simultaneously and increasingly confronted with the need to provide social protection for diverse groups of workers beyond the male breadwinner, including women, younger workers, and migrants (Taylor-Gooby, 2004).

Against this backdrop, European social policy was, in many ways, characterized by stagnation and decline from the 1980s onwards, with cutbacks particularly evident in cash benefits (Korpi & Palme, 2003; Nelson et al., 2007; Nelson, 2013). Perhaps the most notable exception that defies this pattern is developments in family policy (Eydal & Rostgaard, 2018; Nieuwenhuis & Van Lancker, 2020), including expansions in paid parental leave (Ferrarini, 2006; Ray et al., 2010) and childcare (Van Lancker & Ghysels, 2016). Overall, while aggregate social expenditures may not necessarily have declined, there have been gradual changes in their composition. Partly due to population ageing, larger shares of social expenditures are devoted to old-age pensions and health care, while the fraction of social spending going to out-of-work benefits has declined in many European countries (Castles, 2004; Obinger & Wagschal, 2010). The stagnation and decline that set in during the 1980s, with changes in the composition of social spending, have gone hand in hand with other major changes to European welfare states, including the fiscalization of social policy (Ferrarini et al., 2013), privatization or marketization of core public services (Peters, 2012), and a decentralization of social policies from national to local levels (Kazepov, 2010; Martinelli et al., 2017).

Today, European societies face multiple challenges to social policymaking. Demographic pressures such as declining fertility rates and ageing populations, combine with societal challenges (e.g., changing gender roles, growing family diversity, and new migration flows), political challenges (e.g., the rise of populism, extremism, and manipulative information, as well as adjustments to supra-national organizations such as the EU), and global challenges (e.g., sudden international financial crises, climate change, and more recently the COVID-19 pandemic). These challenges to social policymaking translate to challenges for research on social policy in Europe, an issue we return to in Chapter 19.

THE EVOLUTION OF SOCIAL POLICY RESEARCH

If social policy is about institutional responses to economic and social challenges that contribute to various aspects of human wellbeing, *research* about social policy studies all aspects of these institutions, including why they emerged in the first place, their design, and how they have developed over time, as well as their governance, structure, and effects. Inevitably, social policy research has evolved in alignment with how social policy itself has changed, but has also been facilitated by methodological and conceptual innovation.

The questions addressed in social policy research have naturally followed developments in, and societal debates about, social policy – just as the answers to these questions have, in some cases, informed the development of future social policy. As such, the different eras of welfare state and social policy development identified above have also inspired a significant body of research. Substantial scholarship in the last few decades was devoted to the crisis of the welfare state and social policy, its challenges, and sustainability. While the consequences of economic globalization and processes of deindustrialization used to be the prime focus of these crisis-induced analyses of social policy (Iversen & Cusack, 2000), research today also includes in-depth discussions of social policy in the context of environmental change (e.g., Koch, 2021), digitalization (e.g., Lindgren et al., 2019), and new migration patterns (e.g., Lafleur & Vintila, 2020), three prominent issues that are affecting various aspects of our societies today. An increasing amount of research is also devoted to the reorganization of welfare states and social policy to cope with future challenges.

Research has also become more multifaceted through a broadened focus beyond the driving forces of institutional diversity and change, towards outcomes such as low incomes and poverty, female labour force participation, fertility, child wellbeing, trust, political participation, health, and so forth. While much of this outcome-oriented research was, in large part, motivated by the reorganization and downsizing of the welfare state discussed above, it was also facilitated by more and better data on social policy and living conditions in European countries. Alongside improved national data in many countries, scholars have been directly involved in the establishment of several prominent social policy data infrastructures, including the Social Policy Indicator database (Nelson et al., 2020), the Comparative Welfare State Entitlements dataset (Scruggs et al., 2017), the Comparative Family Policy database (Gauthier, 2010), the OECD benefit and wages project, and the WORLD Policy Analysis Center Database (Heymann & Earle, 2010). Europe is also home to several widely used international socio-economic surveys, such as the European Social Survey, the European Union Statistics on Income and Living Conditions, and the European Union Labour Force Study, as well as the Luxembourg Income and Wealth Studies.

Today, social policy research includes both large-scale cross-country comparisons as well as more in-depth investigations of individual countries. There is also a tendency towards more thematically oriented studies of social policy, where particular policy areas (e.g., family policy or minimum income protection) or even specific policies (e.g., parental leave or social assistance) are in focus. This suggests a fundamental shift away from the study of regimes and holistic investigations of welfare states that emerged in social policy research during the 1990s. To some extent, we see European social policy research breaking up into different sub-fields of study, each with their own scholarly standards, international networks, communities, and sometimes publication outlets. These sub-fields are often defined in relation to the broad target groups of social policy, such as the family, the elderly, the unemployed, the sick and disabled, and so forth. Alternatively, new sub-fields of inquiry have emerged in relation to the diverse objectives of policy, such as gender equality, activation, social investment, and so on (Yerkes, 2019). In short, scholarship on European social policy is continuously evolving, similar to its main area of study.

OVERVIEW OF THE CHAPTERS

In this book, we showcase the diversity and evolution of European social policy research in the past 20 years by focusing on key themes in the litera-

ture, each with its own specific goals, achievements, and challenges (Part I).
A number of cross-cutting themes are also identified (Part II). In Part III, we
consider research related to broad social policy challenges, before concluding
with a chapter on key lessons learned, setting a research agenda for the future.

Part I includes seven chapters focused on care policies, family policy, health
care, housing policy, pensions and ageing, poverty and social exclusion, as
well as unemployment and activation policies. Important interplays exist
between welfare states and families, for instance in relation to care. In the first
two chapters of this part, authors Daly and León (Chapter 2) and Van Lancker
and Zagel (Chapter 3) outline the evolution of social policy research in these
areas. While care policy was initially absent from the early systematic studies
of welfare state regimes, it is now a core concept and subject of study. Daly and
León show how care became this core concept in social policy research from
the 1990s onwards thanks to gender scholars and others. The chapter considers
the evolution of social policy research in care and provides a critical overview
of the current state of affairs in the field of care studies from a comparative and
international perspective. In assessing where research on care policy is headed,
the authors consider its potential as an analytic framework, paying attention
to the ways in which care lies at the intersection of welfare, employment, and
migration. They further consider what the concept of care and its application
bring to major challenges such as the growth of inequality, climate change, and
changes in the world of employment.

In the chapter that follows, Van Lancker and Zagel show how family policy
research has shifted from a slowly developing field into a central field of state
intervention. Focusing on comparative family policy research, they highlight
the shift from typologizing and clustering, similar to the early days of comparative welfare state research, towards more outcome-oriented research, including women's employment, the economic wellbeing of families, and the impact
of work–family reconciliation policies. In doing so, they show the broad scope
of research on family policy, which encompasses labour markets, education,
housing policies, family law, and more. The chapter also considers the role of
research in uncovering changing motives behind family policy, from uphold-
ing the family as an institution towards supporting (mothers') employment
and investing in children. As they look towards the future of family policy
research, the authors demonstrate that while many countries have expanded
their family policies and increasingly included measures aimed at supporting
gender equality in work and care arrangements, research on these policies
points to persistent country differences in the generosity and design of family
policies. The authors also caution against too great a focus on outcomes and
single family policy areas in contemporary research, which risks losing sight
of the multidimensionality and complexity of family policy.

In Chapter 4, Wendt moves on to discuss the past, present, and future of health-care research. The focus is on comparative health-care system research, and how it relates to other fields, such as public health. Although research on health-care system types has improved in recent decades, particularly in terms of the indicators used for analyses, the chapter highlights the absence of evidence on best practices as well as how public health is challenged by new risks (such as those appearing with the COVID-19 pandemic) and increased vulnerability of particular population groups. Looking towards the future, Wendt argues we need to direct increased focus on the relationship between health care and other areas of social policy, such as major cash benefits and other forms of services, as public health is only partly influenced by the health-care system. Another topic of increasing concern is forms of coordination in health-care systems that are becoming more specialized and fragmented.

Following on from health-care policy, Dewilde and Haffner consider long-term developments in housing policy and research in Chapter 5. This chapter introduces the specific nature of housing as both a service fulfilling basic needs and a capital-intensive commodity, which has long complicated understandings of housing policy in relation to the analysis of social policy. It analyses how housing policy and scholarly understandings thereof have fared over the last two decades, elaborating on the idea that what happens in one housing market sector impacts on other sectors. Furthermore, the chapter reports on recent research, arguing that trends in housing policy are intricately related to changes in welfare states, but also to broader economic developments. Illustrations of this interrelationship include changes in tenure structure intersecting with changes in the characteristics of households typically living in different tenures. The conclusion addresses key challenges for policy and research.

Across ageing European societies, the fiscal, political, and social sustainability of pensions are major policy issues, and research on them is covered in Chapter 6 by Ebbinghaus and Möhring. This chapter reviews the interdisciplinary field of pension research, providing an overview of the design, reform politics, and challenges of current pension systems in Europe. Pension research has moved from a concern about economic sustainability and reform capability to the social consequences of reforms and the need to adapt to societal changes. Comparative research has focused on differences in pension tiers and pillars, and differences in pensions of the Beveridge and Bismarckian types. Although this research often assumed path dependence, there is a need for understanding how and why pension systems change. Research on the socio-economic outcomes of pension policies has shifted its focus towards the problems of maintaining living standards for the elderly, mitigating old-age poverty, and reducing social inequalities such as gender gaps. The chapter concludes with a new research agenda in response to social and economic change, such as the destandardization of careers and economic crises, including the COVID-19 pandemic.

In Chapter 7, Cantillon discusses two decades of poverty research and the role of minimum income benefits in alleviating poverty. While research shows that relative income poverty among the elderly has declined quite substantially in many European countries over the past decades, poverty among the working-age population has started to grow. Cantillon argues that this trend raises three sets of fundamental questions for research. First, why have welfare states not been successful in reducing poverty? Second, why are some policies, countries, and welfare regimes more successful in combatting poverty than others? Third, which policies are needed in order to be more successful in a future characterized by major transformations such as climate transition, ageing, and digitalization? Besides showing how research has responded to these questions, Cantillon also provides some suggestions for future research. The need for multidimensional perspectives in analyses of social policy and poverty is particularly highlighted, as well as whether disappointing poverty trends are systemic or due to failures in specific parts of social policy. Research should also devote more attention to alternative policy orientations beyond the strategies deployed today.

Chapter 8, the final chapter in this part, by Bonoli focuses on unemployment and activation. The idea that social policies should support disadvantaged groups by facilitating access to the labour market and promote self-sufficiency has been very influential in recent social policy debates. Bonoli traces the evolution of this activation paradigm in policy, and how it has influenced research. He outlines the shift away from early studies concerned with the role of activation policy in the process of welfare state transformation towards impact assessments of active social policy on employability and social cohesion. Following a discussion of the politics of activation, Bonoli suggests that research needs to focus more on possible Matthew effects in activation policy (i.e., situations in which policies are mostly used by well-off citizens), the role of activation in managing increasingly multicultural societies, and perceptions of deservingness in relation to active social policies.

Part II moves on to discuss six cross-cutting themes: research on European social policy, regional social policy, gender, labour markets, welfare attitudes, and comparative social policy methodologies. Social policy research often focuses on national-level policies, but also on supra-national and regional policy, as highlighted by Chapters 9 and 10. In Chapter 9, De la Porte and Madama discuss the evolution of research on European social policy, as well as key accompanying changes in the regulation and governance of EU social policy. The authors show how research initially focused on the role of the Court of Justice of the European Union in interpreting the legislative provisions of social policy related to the social rights of mobile citizens. They highlight lively debates in the field throughout this period and beyond, as research shifted towards new forms of EU regulation and governance, such as the open method of coordination. Research interest in EU governance and policy initiatives remains high today, with scholars investigating the interplay between EU policy and funding instruments and their influence on member state policies, regulatory initiatives, and new policy and fiscal instruments emerging during the COVID-19 pandemic. The chapter showcases the diversity of research topics in this field and the rich array of topics likely to be the focus of future research on European social policy, particularly emanating from the European Pillar of Social Rights.

Alongside research focused on the European level, many social policy scholars focus on particular regions. While studies of regional social policy encompass a wide variety of European regions, one particular region drawing significant scholarly attention is CEE. In Chapter 10, Aidukaite and Navicke highlight the evolution of social policy research in the CEE region, showing how the fall of communist regimes across CEE since 1989 resulted in a plethora of research stemming from the desire to place CEE countries into existing welfare state typologies. The ensuing debate on the emergence of the post-communist or Eastern European welfare state model focused on accounting for the rather different historical and economic development in former socialist countries compared to capitalist democracies. The chapter also highlights the rich comparative literature emerging from the region, showcasing the attention given to developments in family policy, pension insurance, and poverty. The authors suggest future research in the region would do well to focus on social investment and social rights, climate change and the development of the eco-social welfare state, and the consequences of the COVID-19 pandemic on social policy as well as the consequences for the wellbeing of the CEE population.

Chapter 11 shifts from a geographical focus to a substantive cross-cutting focus in social policy research: gender. When social policy research was in its infancy, gender was often ignored (e.g., Lewis, 1992; O'Connor et al., 1999). Now gender is a key dimension in social policy research across multiple fields. In this chapter, Knijn starts by looking back at feminist scholarship as well as what came out of European gender equality objectives, a dominant theme in European social policy since the 1980s and an important topic in social policy research. As she highlights, social policy research on gender focused on comparative studies of European societies and systemic gender divisions of productive and reproductive work, and their related social security systems (wages, pensions, welfare benefits). Her historical comparison of social policy research on gender shows that accents have shifted both empirically and theoretically. To start with the latter, she shows how the theoretical approach has moved from Marxist and structuralist approaches towards more social-cultural, socio-political, constructionist, and intersectional approaches. Empirically, new topics have been added to the once dominant focus on work and care to now also include, among others, body politics, identity-based policies, gender-based violence, and poverty. Knijn suggests future social policy research on gender can continue to make a meaningful contribution by remembering that equality and difference are not opposites. As she suggests, this seminal idea from Wollstonecraft can inspire research to explain the par-adoxical developments of European policymaking focused on gender equality alongside contemporary, parallel attacks on women's sexual and reproductive rights.

A further key substantive cross-cutting theme is research on labour market policy. In Chapter 12, Clasen and Clegg discuss the evolution of labour market research, and how it has helped us to understand how welfare states have responded to the increased precariousness of European labour markets. Their chapter reviews the state of the art in European social policy research on labour market change, focusing on the growth and politics of employment-friendly social policies (such as in-work benefits), as well as their impacts on employ-ment, incomes, and the lived experiences of people in precarious employment. Several new strands of research are suggested, particularly in relation to how social policy sets a framework for future labour market change.

The final two chapters in this part consider the growing body of research looking at welfare state attitudes (Chapter 13) and comparative methodologies for studying social policy (Chapter 14). In Chapter 13, van Oorschot, Laenen, Roosma, and Meuleman showcase how our knowledge about welfare attitudes in Europe has developed over the past 20 years. Welfare attitudes are impor-tant for the social legitimacy of social policy, and today the scientific study of welfare attitudes is a well-settled discipline. Van Oorschot and colleagues identify several major advancements in attitudinal social policy research. One is the increased focus on the multidimensionality of welfare attitudes. Others are the role of contextual factors, both in relation to contexts that influence welfare attitudes (e.g., cultural and institutional contexts) and in relation to so-called feedback loops (e.g., the ongoing, mutually reinforcing relationship between institutional context and welfare attitudes). Research on attitudinal change is also addressed, as well as perceptions of welfare deservingness for specific target groups. Finally, they discuss what research tells us concerning attitudes towards different parts of social policy. In terms of research gaps, the attitudinal position of various stakeholders and how prior knowledge or experience influence attitudes are highlighted. In terms of challenges, the need for continued investment in collecting preferably cross-national attitudinal data is underscored.

Chapter 14 takes stock of the methodologies employed in comparative social policy analysis. Ferragina and Deeming trace the evolution and development of comparative methodology, empirically analysing trends in the *Journal of European Social Policy* since the publication of the first issue in February 1991, while situating comparative analysis within broader theoretical trends and European social policy debates. They focus on both methods and substance, looking at how major techniques and approaches have been applied to comparative social policy to enlighten different key subject areas. Their chapter centres on three key questions: What is the scholarly use of comparative methods in social policy over the last three decades? How has comparative methodology helped us to better understand the role, nature, and outcomes of European social policy? Where is comparative methodology heading for the future? Their focus on publications in a leading European social policy journal offers interesting insights into social policy research. A key finding is that while scholarship seems to be increasingly geared towards studies based on causation and more sophisticated techniques, the case study approach is foundational and continues to occupy a prominent place in social policy scholarship.

Part III deals with the key challenges facing European societies, including climate change, technological change, migration, and recurring global crises, and concludes by highlighting the key lessons learned from 20 years of ESPAnet, discussing challenges for future social policy research. A first key challenge is climate change. Climate change is highly relevant to social policy and the welfare state for a number of reasons, as described by Hvinden and Schoyen in Chapter 15. It more and more frequently affects people in their everyday life, and is thus an important and growing source of social risk in the twenty-first century. Despite the many points of intersection between climate change and social policy, the research agenda on this topic remains in its infancy. Research has mostly focused on the social and welfare implications of the global climate crisis, and more recently on the actual and potential roles of social policy in contributing to the necessary transformation to a net-zero or low-emission world. Hvinden and Schoyen raise the most central points of debate in social policy research on climate change, and suggest areas in which new research is particularly eminent.

In Chapter 16, van Gerven discusses the evolving social policy research in the context of technological change. From the start of the twenty-first century, the emerging literature suggests the birth of a 'digital welfare state', where digitalization and automation have become an integral part of welfare benefit and service delivery. Emergent social policy literature shows that many technological innovations 'disrupt' existing welfare systems and practices and their impact goes beyond a transformation of the way the welfare state operates. Technological advancement also produces (new) social risks for the welfare states to manage and mitigate. In this chapter, a two-fold research agenda is proposed for studying digital welfare governance as well as its impact in the social policy domains of welfare and work in this new and quickly emerging field.

Chapter 17 shifts to challenges related to migration policy and research. Over the last decades, migration both to and within Europe has increased substantially. Wars and conflicts have pushed many migrants towards Europe's borders, culminating with the refugee crisis in 2015. Internally, the enlargement of the EU and its common market have caused work-related migration at an unprecedented scale. Consequently, migrants' rights to and use of social policies as well as their integration patterns have moved up the political agenda both nationally and within the EU. In Chapter 17, Breidahl, Hedegaard, and Seibel discuss key social policy developments influencing migration and integration patterns within European societies. They thereby highlight social policy scholars' interest in how immigration as a phenomenon influences welfare states and social policies, as well as the role social policies play in migrants' everyday life, wellbeing, life prospects, and attitudes. In particular, they discuss the more recent focus of research on migrants' rights to, usage of, and attitudes towards social policies. As shown by the authors, these studies provide crucial and nuanced insights but are still in development. Further research is needed, among others, on migrants' knowledge of the welfare state as well as geographical differences between Northern/Western European countries and Central/Eastern/Southern European countries, which have received much less attention.

The challenges discussed so far in Part III, as well as others, give way to (potentially) recurring crises. Initial social policy advancements were a response to the crisis of the period following the Second World War. Since then, the oil crises in the 1970s, the financial crisis starting in 2008–2009, and the COVID-19 crisis, among others, have illustrated the need for social policy in times of crisis. These crises have also shown variation in what kinds of policies are needed and adopted. Following the global financial crisis of 2008–2009, the focus in many, but not all European countries was mainly on reducing public spending, whereas during the COVID-19 crisis there has been a greater focus on investment and various forms of financial support for people affected by the crisis. These contradictory approaches reflect on the one hand a classical difference between a liberal and Keynesian-inspired approach to social policy, and, on the other hand, recent discussions about austerity, populism, and the legitimacy of welfare states. The development of social policies has seemingly focused more on social benefits for the citizens of the nation state, and to migrants only in a more limited fashion, which is an indication of exacerbated conflicts in a number of countries. At the same time, there has been a stronger focus on conditionality, which, in addition to welfare chauvinism, has been a continuation of the long-standing discussions about universalism and selectivism.

In Chapter 18, Greve and Paster consider whether social investment offers an ideational tool for overcoming both the legitimacy crisis of the welfare state as well as recurring economic crises. Even with social investment, welfare states will continue to be confronted by crises in the future. New challenges, like automation and the digitalization of work, will lead to the definition of additional social risks, requiring a further adaptation of social policies. Future research will need to focus on the extent to which welfare states are able to manage and mitigate these risks and other challenges to come.

In the final chapter (Chapter 19), we provide a conclusion to the volume that serves two aims. First, we highlight common developments in the research agendas that have been observed across social policy themes as highlighted in the different chapters. The emphasis is not on providing a complete summary of the content of each chapter, but rather on the overarching lessons to be learned. How has the broader social policy research agenda evolved, and what are the main drivers behind this change? Second, we formulate a number of recommendations for research that we believe would further increase our understanding of European social policy, thereby setting an agenda for the future of research on social policy in Europe.

REFERENCES

Adema, W., & Ladaique, M. (2005). Net social expenditure, 2005 edition: More comprehensive measures of social support. OECD.

Alcock, C. (2008). *Introducing Social Policy*. Routledge.

Béland, D. (2010). *What Is Social Policy?* (Vol. 1). Polity.

Bluestone, B., & Harrison, B. (1982). *Deindustrialization of America: Plant Closings, Community Abandonment and the Dismantling of Basic Industry*. Basic Books.

Castles, F. G. (2004). *The Future of the Welfare State: Crisis Myths and Crisis Realities*. Oxford University Press.

Clasen, J., & Kvist, J. (2021). Wim van Oorschot and the early years of ESPAnet. In T. Laenen, B. Meuleman, A. Otto, F. Roosma, & W. Van Lancker (Eds), *Leading Social Policy Analysis from the Front: Essays in Honor of Wim van Oorschot*. Centrum for Sociological Research.

Collins, S. M. (1998). *Imports, Exports, and the American Worker*. Brookings.

Dean, H. (2019). *Social Policy*. John Wiley & Sons.

Eydal, G. B., & Rostgaard, T. (Eds). (2018). *Handbook of Family Policy*. Edward Elgar Publishing.

Ferrarini, T. (2006). *Families, States and Labour Markets: Institutions, Causes and Consequences of Family Policy in Post-War Welfare States*. Edward Elgar Publishing.

Ferrarini, T., & Nelson, K. (2003). Taxation of social insurance and redistribution: A comparative analysis of ten welfare states. *Journal of European Social Policy, 13*(1), 21–33.

Ferrarini, T., Nelson, K., & Höög, H. (2013). From universalism to selectivity: Old wine in new bottles for child benefits in Europe and other countries. In I. Marx

& K. Nelson (Eds), *Minimum Income Protection in Flux* (pp. 137–160). Palgrave Macmillan.

Ferrera, M. (1996). The 'Southern model' of welfare in social Europe. *Journal of European social policy, 6*(1), 17–37.

Flora, P. (1987). Appendix: Synopses, bibliographies, tables. In P. Flora (Ed.), *Growth to Limits: The Western European Welfare States since World War II* (Vol. 4). de Gruyter.

Gauthier, A. H. (2010). Comparative family policy database, Version 3. www.demogr .mpg.de/cgi-bin/databases/fampoldb/index.plx

Goerne, A. (2010). *The Capability Approach in Social Policy Analysis: Yet Another Concept?* Edinburgh: University of Edinburgh, Publication and Dissemination Centre (PUDISCwowe). https://nbn-resolving.org/urn:nbn:de:0168-ssoar-198104

Häusermann, S., & Schwander, H. (2010, April). Explaining welfare preferences in dualized societies. 17th Conference of Europeanists, Montreal (pp. 1–33).

Heymann, J., & Earle, A. (2010). *Raising the Global Floor: Dismantling the Myth That We Can't Afford Good Working Conditions for Everyone*. Stanford University Press.

Hobson, B. (1990). No exit, no voice: Women's economic dependency and the welfare state. *Acta Sociologica, 33*(3), 235–250.

Huber, E., & Stephens, J. D. (2001). *Development and Crises of the Welfare State: Parties and Policies in Global Markets*. University of Chicago Press.

Iversen, T., & Cusack, T. R. (2000). The causes of welfare state expansion: Deindustrialization or globalization? *World Politics, 52*(3), 313–349.

Iversen, T., & Stephens, J. D. (2008). Partisan politics, the welfare state, and three worlds of human capital formation. *Comparative Political Studies, 41*(4–5), 600–637.

Javornik, J. (2014). Measuring state de-familialism: Contesting post-socialist exceptionalism. *Journal of European Social Policy, 24*(3), 240–257.

Kazepov, Y. (Ed.). (2010). *Rescaling Social Policies: Towards Multilevel Governance in Europe*. Routledge.

Koch, F. (2021). Cities as transnational climate change actors: applying a Global South perspective. *Third World Quarterly, 42*(9), 2055–2073.

Korpi, W., & Palme, J. (2003). New politics and class politics in the context of austerity and globalization: Welfare state regress in 18 countries, 1975–95. *American Political Science Review, 97*(3), 425–446.

Lafleur, J.-M., & Vintila, D. (2020). *Migration and Social Protection in Europe and Beyond* (Vol. 1). Springer Nature.

Layard, R., Nickell, S., & Jackman, R. (1991). *Unemployment: Macroeconomic Performance and the Labor Market*. Oxford University Press.

Lendvai-Bainton, N., & Kennett, P. (2017). Introduction: Trajectories and frictions of European social policy. In P. Kennett, & N. Lendvai-Bainton (Eds), *Handbook of European Social Policy*. Edward Elgar Publishing.

Lewis, J. (1992). Gender and the development of welfare regimes. *Journal of European Social Policy, 2*(3), 159–173.

Lindgren, I., Madsen, C. Ø., Hofmann, S., & Melin, U. (2019). Close encounters of the digital kind: A research agenda for the digitalization of public services. *Government Information Quarterly, 36*(3), 427–436.

Martinelli, F., Anttonen, A. A., & Mätzke, M. (Eds). (2017). *Social Services Disrupted: Changes, Challenges and Policy Implications for Europe in Times of Austerity.* Edward Elgar Publishing.

Morel, N., Palier, B., & Palme, J. (Eds). (2012). *Towards a Social Investment Welfare State? Ideas, Policies and Challenges*. Policy Press.

Nelson, K. (2013). Social assistance and EU poverty thresholds 1990–2008. Are European welfare systems providing just and fair protection against low income? *European Sociological Review, 29*(2), 386–401.

Nelson, K., Montanari, I., & Palme, J. (2007). Convergence pressures and responses: Recent social insurance development in modern welfare states. *Comparative Sociology, 6*(3), 295–323.

Nelson, K., Fredriksson, D., Korpi, T., Korpi, W., Palme, J., & Sjöberg, O. (2020). The social policy indicators (SPIN) database. *International Journal of Social Welfare*. https://doi.org/10.1111/ijsw.12418

Nieuwenhuis, R., & Van Lancker, W. (Eds). (2020). *The Palgrave Handbook of Family Policy*. Palgrave Macmillan.

O'Connor, J. S., Orloff, A. S., & Shaver, S. (1999). *States, Markets, Families: Gender, Liberalism and Social Policy in Australia, Canada, Great Britain and the United States*. Cambridge University Press.

Obinger, H., & Wagschal, U. (2010). Social expenditure and revenues. In F. G. Castles, S. Leibfried, J. Lewis, H. Obinger, & C. Pierson (Eds), *The Oxford Handbook of the Welfare State*. Oxford University Press.

Orloff, A. S. (1993). Gender and the social rights of citizenship: The comparative analysis of gender relations and welfare states. *American Sociological Review*, 303–328.

Palme, J., Nelson, K., Sjöberg, O., & Minas, R. (2009). European social models, protection and inclusion. Research report 2009/1. Stockholm: Institute for Future Studies.

Pateman, C. (1988). The patriarchal welfare state. In A. Gutman (Ed.), *Democracy and the State* (pp. 231–278). Princeton University Press.

Peters, J. (2012). Neoliberal convergence in North America and Western Europe: Fiscal austerity, privatization, and public sector reform. *Review of International Political Economy, 19*(2), 208–235.

Pierson, C. (1991). *Beyond the Welfare State? The New Political Economy of Welfare*. Polity.

Ray, R., Gornick, J. C., & Schmitt, J. (2010). Who cares? Assessing generosity and gender equality in parental leave policy designs in 21 countries. *Journal of European Social Policy, 20*(3), 196–216.

Razavi, S. (2020). What does the UN have to say about family policy? Reflections on the ILO, UNICEF, and UN Women. In R. Nieuwenhuis & W. Van Lancker (Eds), *The Palgrave Handbook of Family Policy* (pp. 87–115). Springer International.

Sainsbury, D. (1996). *Gender, Equality and Welfare States*. Cambridge University Press.

Sainsbury, D. (2012). *Welfare States and Immigrant Rights: The Politics of Inclusion and Exclusion*. Oxford University Press.

Scruggs, L, Jahn, D., & Kuitto, K. (2017). *Comparative Welfare Entitlements Dataset 2*. Version 2017-09. University of Connecticut and University of Greifswald.

Szebehely, M., & Meagher, G. (2018). Nordic eldercare: Weak universalism becoming weaker? *Journal of European Social Policy, 28*(3), 294–308.

Taylor-Gooby, P. (Ed.). (2004). *New Risks, New Welfare: The Transformation of the European Welfare State*. Oxford University Press.

Trampusch, C. (2013). Employers and collectively negotiated occupational pensions in Sweden, Denmark and Norway: Promoters, vacillators and adversaries. *European Journal of Industrial Relations, 19*(1), 37–53.

Van Der Waal, J., De Koster, W., & Van Oorschot, W. (2013). Three worlds of welfare chauvinism? How welfare regimes affect support for distributing welfare to immigrants in Europe. *Journal of Comparative Policy Analysis: Research and Practice*, *15*(2), 164–181.

Van Lancker, W., & Ghysels, J. (2016). Explaining patterns of inequality in child-care service use across 31 developed economies: A welfare state perspective. *International Journal of Comparative Sociology*, *57*(5), 310–337.

White, L. A. (2020). Do international organizations influence domestic policy outcomes in OECD countries? In R. Nieuwenhuis & W. Van Lancker (Eds), *The Palgrave Handbook of Family Policy* (pp. 69–86). Springer International.

Yerkes, M. A. (2011). *Transforming the Dutch Welfare State: Social Risks and Corporatist Reform*. Policy Press.

Yerkes, M. A. (2019). *Social Policy*. J. Baxter (Ed.). Oxford University Press. www.oxfordbibliographies.com

Yerkes, M. A., & Javornik, J. (2019). Creating capabilities: Childcare policies in comparative perspective. *Journal of European Social Policy*, *29*(4), 529–544.

PART I

Key themes in social policy research

2. Care and the analysis of welfare states

Mary Daly and Margarita León

INTRODUCTION

In this chapter, we cut through the voluminous scholarship on care to focus on the role of the state. With this lens, the overall aim of the chapter is to outline the main trajectory of the concept and its potential as an analytic framework for future research.

While care is now a widely used term and concept, it is important to clarify its meaning and core references. For the purposes of this chapter, care refers to the labour, resources, and relations involved in meeting the needs of those requiring assistance and help because of age, illness, or frailty of some kind. This understanding encompasses care for both children and adults, and it covers both the persons receiving care and those providing it. Care has arguably been one of the most original concepts in gender, welfare state, and social policy studies, especially in the sense of a concept emerging from practices and relations in real life. The associated scholarship is vibrant and diverse as well as being solidly comparative and increasingly global.

KEY FEATURES AND INTERESTS OF CARE AS A CONCEPT

In the first part of this chapter we briefly outline the main literatures within which the concept of care has developed. We then look more closely at how care has been utilized to analyse the welfare state. The two questions that guide us here are: What is care? And how has care been applied to analyse the welfare state?

What Is Care?

Care as a concept in academic work can be estimated to be some 30–40 years old. The concept has developed from a range of perspectives and roots, making it an interdisciplinary concept in key respects. Probably it is better thought of as a set of concepts rather than a single concept. When viewed from the perspective of the study of the welfare state and social policy, we can locate its historical origins in two main sets of work: on the one hand feminist and gender scholarship regarding the position of women and the organization of life inside and outside the home, and, on the other, analyses of the development of services for older people (and to a lesser extent children). We will look at the two literatures briefly in turn.

The first set of literature arose out of feminist and gender-oriented engagement. This is not only a large but also a very broad corpus of work, focusing over time on care as it encompasses care for older people and that for children. A perspective with a broad reach was sought. For our purposes and indeed for research and scholarship a core question was: What is care and how should we conceive of it?

In one originating school of thought, care is located within the domestic and interpersonal setting. Here, the concept is used to examine the day-to-day reproductive work that goes on in households and families, including both the material activities involved and the normative and ideological processes. Both are seen to confirm women as (for the most part unpaid) carers, and to define women in a family or home context (Finch & Groves, 1983; Graham, 1983). Uncovering the nature of the caring activity itself was especially important, because it was largely hidden from view. Thomas (1993), for example, identified seven dimensions to care. These pertain to the identity of the provider and of the recipient of care, the relationship between the two, the social content of the care, the economic character of the relationship and of the labour, and the social domain and institutional setting within which the care is provided. Analyses of the content of care work served to distinguish between different types of care. Graham (1991), for example, sought to include non-kin forms of home-based care (as well as kinship-based care), and she makes the important point that defining care in terms of home-based care for family members has served to centre the analysis around (white) women's reproductive work for kin while obscuring other forms of home-based work (paid domestic service, for example) and relations of class and race.

Care as a set of activities and relations was developed in another gender and feminist-oriented literature as well. Here, it was seen as a particular way of relating to others, much wider than but also including the activities of tending to the needs of others. In this expansive vision, caring is a basic form of human interconnection set within complex relations and moral commitments (Tronto, 1993; Held, 2005). This too moved care beyond the home. Indeed, in this perspective, care's limits and foci are endless; it can be applied everywhere, from our environment and experiences to the people we live with or alongside. Fisher and Tronto's (1990) work is a classic here in defining caring as a species activity involving four phases: caring about, caring for, caregiving, and care receiving. Drawing from moral theory, philosophy, and legal theory, this approach elucidates a vision of how individuals can 'be' with each other and how an ethics of care could seed profound change at a local, national, and especially global level. As well as challenging the notion of the isolated individual of liberal and social contract theory, it emphasizes the intrinsic value of care and of interdependence as the human condition rather than individualism.

In the second body of work, the concept of care emerged out of studies of health and eldercare. To answer the question of what care is, this work looked especially at the needs of older people and the responses to their needs. In order to pinpoint this focus of endeavour, the reader might consider such fields as 'health care' or 'health and care' or 'community care' or 'care of the elderly'. This work remained in the shadow of health scholarship for a long time, and its evolution is part of a critique of the relatively narrow focus of health research on care in a medical setting or of care as a response to medical need. Indeed, the dominance of the health and medical perspective is part of the reason why some scholars started to use the term 'social care' (which is now a widely accepted term in some countries, such as the United Kingdom, although in other countries and internationally the term 'long-term care' demarcates the field). In a social care framing, research began to examine the needs associated with care conceived of as more than a health-related condition, and the organizational and community responses to such needs, through personal social services, for example (Sainsbury, 1977). Frailty and reduced or declining competence were at the centre here. This was a literature located in both health and public services, but it also touched on the welfare state as a system of provision for need and the administration of this provision. The difficulties of meeting need in a context of pressures such as population ageing and the growing prevalence of dementia-related conditions and declining public resources have not just been underlined, but have often been a starting point for research and study as time has gone on (OECD, 2004).

In truth, the answer to the question of what care is has been taken for granted as self-evident. This, we suggest, is unacceptable. Perhaps the most serviceable definition for the present purpose – and one that is most widely used – is that of Daly and Lewis (2000: 285), for whom care signifies 'the activities and relations involved in meeting the physical and emotional requirements of dependent adults and children, and the normative economic and social frameworks within which these are assigned and carried out'.

How Has Care Been Applied to Analyse the Welfare State?

The application of care to analyse the welfare state has led to a very rich and vibrant body of work. Again, here, it is possible to identify a number of different strands of work but, we suggest, a helpful way of making sense of the literature is to think in terms of the care system and the state's role in it.

There are narrower and broader interpretations of the underlying 'system'. One of the concepts that early scholarship worked with was that of the welfare mix (Evers & Svetlik, 1993). This helped to bring together formal and informal provision into a broad-ranging understanding of the care system as spanning a range of fields and agency. From a social policy perspective, a key question was how the state engaged with different types or forms of care. This brought the service infrastructure centre stage (Jamieson & Illsley, 1990). In general, the literature on care is much more services-oriented as compared with the main body of work on the welfare state, which has tended to view the state in terms of cash transfers and income support generally. In the care literature, the evolution of particular service responses and the appropriate 'mix' became an enduring question posed of the welfare state (with 'mix' understood in a relatively broad way to encompass market-based, voluntary sector, public, and family-based provision) (e.g., Anttonen & Sipilä, 1996).

It is only a short step from this to system design and resource use. In this regard, both the longstanding elements of the system of care provision are revealed as are the innovations (Ranci & Pavolini, 2013). There is much to report in regard to the latter, as welfare states continuously reform their 'offer' around care. For example, among the innovations in long-term care policy, there is an increasing use of personal budgets for care to allow people to organize their own care, a focus on reablement and ageing in place, a greater use of a range of technologies, and the introduction of a support architecture (such as leaves and benefits) for informal carers. An increasingly reported trend is the general move of the state out of direct service provision, with the growing use of so-called 'cash-for-care' benefits (e.g., Da Roit & Le Bihan, 2019). These have the purpose of individualizing control of care and have roots in Italy and the United Kingdom; since the 1990s they have been expanded in Austria, France, Germany, the Netherlands, Spain, inter alia.

The feminist work has especially emphasized the matter of rights and entitlements and the political implications of the way states respond to care. From the perspective of individuals receiving or giving care, one question asked is about what states make available as entitlements and supports to people in either situation. This has sometimes been framed in terms of how care is recognized in citizenship (Knijn & Kremer, 1997; Anttonen & Zechner, 2011). What are the equivalences between the entitlements (if any) that people obtain as a result of caring compared to those accrued through employment? This has led to investigations and some comparisons of the entitlements of people who need care (typically those who are frail or vulnerable because of infirmity or age) and those who provide it. The rights and obligations of women (especially mothers, and in earlier studies, wives) have been a central topic here, in scholarship that unpacks women's citizenship. This has led to a host of work that has undertaken a rather fine-grained analysis of the policy packages associated with care (which, at least in European countries, typically combine interventions that provide time through leave schemes, financial assistance, and/or services to support caregivers and those in need of care).

But the studies have also moved beyond the individual level. From the start, comparative work on care and the welfare state from a feminist perspective insisted on the need to incorporate the interactions between and within the state, the market, and the family/community. Family-derived relations and obligations were seen to be especially interesting. The pioneering work of gender scholars (Lewis, 1992; Orloff, 1993) argued against constructions of welfare system typologies that were oblivious to the relevance of care in society. Much of this early work focused on the limitations of 'decommodification' as an indicator of welfare generosity, and argued for alternatives that would acknowledge both the relevance of the unpaid work of women for welfare state development, and the ways in which the welfare state treated women and care. In this space, the concept of familialization/defamilialization was developed. It was in origin derived from feminist work (Lister, 1994), although it is now used more broadly in comparative welfare state studies (e.g., Esping-Andersen, 2009). While it has different usages, through a feminist lens the concept seeks to theorize the role of social policy in affecting women's dependence on the family on the one hand, and the state's construction of family responsibilities and roles on the other. Both are measured by the degree to which policies redistribute the responsibility for and practice of care-related tasks and associated dependencies away from or to the family – for example, the extent to which the state substitutes the family as a service provider, 'socializes' or subsidises family-related tasks or functions, and treats family members as individuals (in terms of rights, status, obligations, and sources of support) and potential earners (Leitner, 2003). Kröger's (2011) concept of dedomestication offers interesting insights too. The concept is understood as the degree to which policies facilitate a certain degree of personal freedom from confinement to the domestic sphere. It is intended to be complementary to the concept of defamilialization in that it attempts to measure the capacity of welfare states to help people to participate in society and not just paid work. In a more explicit gender framing, Mathieu (2016) wants to shift the weight of analysis from families to mothers, arguing that the focus has been too much on the institution of the family, and that policies can affect the gender division of care labour without shifting it from the family (e.g., paternity leaves).

As the component elements of care provision came to be identified, systematic and configurational thinking became widespread. In fact, interrelations between the state, the market, and the family proved to be a magnet for researchers and subsequent years saw work on intergenerational regimes (Saraceno & Keck, 2010), care regimes (Bettio & Plantenga, 2004), and family policy regimes (Leitner, 2003), to name just a few. A second contribution was to use the typologies to identify trends and pinpoint emerging policy trajectories. The male breadwinner model was an analytic stalwart here, hosting many analyses that pointed out the 'private' arrangements of employed father/ home-based mother that benefit systems help shape and persist (Lewis, 1992). From this work, the notion of the 'adult worker model' as the alternative arrangement was born. Jane Lewis's contribution to this was key, naming it in the first instance and identifying a number of empirical features of the associated social policy template, such as policy's concern with 'work–life balance', the flexibilization of employment, and the emphasis on care leaves for parents and fathers (Lewis, 2001). Other attempts at classifying underlying models include those of Crompton (1999) and Daly (2011). Notably, this work did not engage in producing typologies based on race or ethnic origin or, indeed, other axes of inequality.

It will be obvious that there is no singular interpretation of 'the system'. And this is appropriate given its complexity. However, a constant limitation in studies of care has been on the one hand the lack of a shared common conceptual ground of what care means and how it can or should be applied and, on the other hand, the lack of data availability at the cross-national level. One matter that very much affects the interpretation of the system is whether care is interpreted to refer to long-term care or care for children (such as early childhood education and care), or both. Scholarship is quite diverse in this regard. The appeal of a broad version of the concept is understandable: it allows access to an ontological perspective on human life in general and the complex ethics involved, and it provides an overarching framework of analysis. There is an inherent life-course view in the more plural usage also (although this is not always explicit) which allows access to how care connects structures, processes, and relations across various points and stages of the life course (Daly, 2018). But common denominators notwithstanding, there are good grounds to differentiate care for adults from that for children. For example, the latter is far more embedded in the family than the former, and in many countries policy tends to frame long-term care very differently from that of care for children (especially in a social investment context).

LOOKING TOWARDS THE FUTURE: NEW AGENDAS IN CARE RESEARCH

New Directions in Care Research

It is incontrovertible that care as a field of research has expanded in a number of directions. Driven in key respects by the need to understand, measure, and tackle some of the most pressing problems in European societies such as declines in fertility and ageing populations, care policy has a more central position in today's welfare states. Cross-country examinations of care policies and the outputs of such policies have also grown and improved over the last two or three decades. New datasets have emerged, such as the Multilinks database on policies related to intergenerational obligations within the family; or the International Network on Leave Policies (www.leavenetwork.org). New theoretical and conceptual approaches have been applied. National and international institutions such as the European Union and the Organisation for Economic Co-operation and Development have played key roles in promoting and funding comparative research on care policy (Mahon, 2018; Spasova et al., 2018).

One major trend is for care policies to be studied through the lenses of novel theoretical frameworks within social sciences that allow for broader and more nuanced understandings of the significance of social policy in affecting personal wellbeing and autonomy. The capabilities approach (CA) is one of these more novel approaches. In the original formulation of Amartya Sen and Martha Nussbaum (Nussbaum, 2003), capabilities are opportunities to achieve the 'functionings' needed to live a good and meaningful life. This perspective has opened up discussions on ethical concerns regarding the actual delivery of care and not just the availability of resources for care. The CA allows research-ers to pose the important question of what the appropriate metric of justice is (Brighouse & Robeyns 2010). This includes perceptions of dignity and well-being felt by those at the receiving end of care services with clear implications for the everyday practice of social care (Pirhonen, 2014). Scholars interested in understanding the extent to which policies provide equal opportunities for chil-dren and families have also applied the CA to move beyond mere supply-side analyses (Orton, 2011; Yerkes & Javornik, 2018).

A second relatively novel orientation in care work is intersectionality, which when applied focuses on multiple inequalities and sees care as tying together race and ethnicity, gender and class. This work takes both a 'local' and a 'global' approach. It shows that the increased outsourcing of household/famil-ial care responsibilities in a neoliberal market context has created increased social and economic polarization among women along socio-economic, racial/ ethnic, and citizenship lines (Peng, 2019). There are several ways in which such inequalities are being investigated and explained. Lutz (2018) suggests 'transnational social inequality' as a concept that brings together key aspects, such as female care work as a social and gendered obligation across borders; the lack of social protection attached to care work performed by migrants; and the intersection of race and migration. Another leading idea here has been the concept of global care chains, which focuses on the flow of care-providing labour across countries and regions. This idea traces the implications for the providers (especially the individuals and their native countries) and the receiv-ers (usually higher-income people and countries) (Hochschild, 2000; Yeates,

2011). When the lens is turned towards policy, the work examines the interconnections between economic, social, employment, and migration policies to be considered (Williams, 2012; Michel & Peng, 2017). The perspective is much larger than the classic conception of care as domestic labour or nurture – its inherent critical international political economy approach in particular crafts an explanation centred upon power relations and clashes between nations (in their own right and in regard to how these are institutionalized in policy) and the economic and political forces of global processes and imperialism that reproduce gender and other inequalities in various forms (Parreñas, 2001; Fraser, 2016).

Another line of investigation places marketization at the centre of the analysis. Since the early 1990s at least, the care sector has been particularly affected by such development, due to strong demand pressure caused by population ageing and welfare state cutbacks (Brennan et al., 2012; León, 2014). In most countries, the development of care services 'happened in an era of markets and often through markets' (Gingrich, 2011: 175) and thus governments' responsibilities towards provision were not as well defined as in other public services such as health or education. We now know that there is great diversity in what marketization means in different contexts and for different population groups, especially in both the degree of introduction of market principles and mechanisms (such as competition and consumer choice) and the way for-profit institutions are located among other types of providers (Anttonen & Meagher, 2013). This work makes it clear that there is a steady growth in the recourse to market mechanisms and for-profit providers across welfare states, although arguably these trends are at their most extreme in the liberal countries as well as the familialistic countries of Southern Europe. There is considerable critique of the turn towards marketization, and how it is rooted in both new public management philosophies and a neoliberalization of the welfare state (Gingrich, 2011). Drawing such principles into care risks commodifying it.

Lessons from the COVID-19 Pandemic

The pandemic has exposed some major weaknesses of the social care sector in many countries, especially the extremely vulnerable situation of workers in nursing homes. The slow and inadequate reaction of governments to the high risk of COVID-19 in nursing homes is at least partly related to increased marketization and the erosion of public-sector regulation (Daly, 2020; Daly et al., forthcoming). Extremely high death tolls in nursing homes have catapulted discussions about the need to reorient the care sector in the political agenda. Undefined quality standards, poor working conditions, lack of public regulation and control, and poor governance mechanisms are an essential part of the discussions.

The 'social investment turn' (Morel et al., 2012; Hemerijck, 2017) has also given a role to research in care, especially out-of-home care for children. Under the rubric of social investment, work–life balance and childcare policies are now strategically supported as part of a more comprehensive agenda regarding economic growth and human capital formation (Hemerijck, 2013). This new paradigm is especially interested in early education and care as an investment in the human capital of children and as an enabler of higher female employment. A growing and more critical body of research is looking at the interaction of such social investment policies with their institutional, economic, and cultural contexts. Especially in highly dualized labour markets and unequal societies, the focus on activation and human capital formation may produce discrimination against the most vulnerable groups in society, since a number of 'Matthew effects' – whereby the well off in society tend to benefit more from policy – might operate (Cantillon & Van Lancker, 2013). Measuring the redistributive effects of care policies, in particular services for very young children, is an important contribution to broader understandings of comparative welfare analyses and a corrective to the long-standing tendency to consider the welfare state in terms of economic transfers and labour market policy.

The recent expansion of family and care policies following the social investment paradigm (Daly & Ferragina, 2017) – even in countries whose welfare regimes are considered conservative and familialistic – has also triggered relatively new comparative work which is centred around the political dynamics behind these trends (see for instance Palier et al., forthcoming). This scholarly work can be grouped into three main strands. First, there are the studies which analyse the introduction of family and care policies to attract new voter groups in the context of secularization, cultural change, and greater electoral volatility (Morgan, 2013). In a second stream the higher presence of women in politics is considered to be a reasonable, although somehow difficult to gauge, predictor of policies that address gender issues. Third, policies that foster the externalization of care work and those that support employment-oriented family policies are also responding to pressures for labour force reskilling (Fleckenstein & Lee, 2014).

In a further iteration, the mainstream welfare state literature is slowly starting to link debates about the welfare state to the environment (Gough, 2015), although care is not always present in these debates. The key question is whether an ethic of care can help rethink the relationship between growth and welfare which would, in turn, affect the ecological transition. Growth has allowed welfare state expansion, but it has also created greater demand for welfare state spending (Büchs, 2021). The 'relentless revolution' of capitalism (Appleby, 2011) has created great new opportunities but it has also generated bitter conflicts, the most important of which is the threat to our own survival. Arguments in favour of degrowth and the building of a green sustainable economy push us to question the very meaning of productive and reproductive work and the underpinnings of sustainable economic prosperity. In this respect, some renowned economists have been making the case for a fundamental change in the way in which we measure growth and progress to take into account considerations about equality, subjective wellbeing, and sustainability (Stiglitz et al., 2010). To be fair, the argument was already put forward by Marilyn Waring back in the 1980s when she analysed the roots of gender discrimination by going to the foundational practices of caring labour and demonstrating what was being missed by failing to account for it (Waring, 1988). After this seminal work, the bulk of feminist economics, including the important work of Nancy Folbre (1993), has been devoted to unveiling the ways in which the organization of social reproduction was not just unfair and inefficient, but also unsustainable.

Quests for sustainable futures inevitably need to address the question of how to organize and allocate time and resources. Ultimately, this becomes an issue of power and equality between the Global North and the Global South, between women and men, and people of different ages, classes, ethnicities, and sexual orientations. It is here that Joan Tronto (2015) proposes addressing the inequalities embedded in the handing out of care responsibilities through politics, recognizing the democratic goals of our caring practices. This is nothing new, since as we have shown earlier in this chapter, the ethics of care concept goes to the heart of notions of social justice, but it has not been realized. And the major global transformations that we face today, from the climate emergency to the rise of social inequalities, the ageing of populations, and the challenges of automation all lead to the politicization of care as a concept and critical line of analysis.

CONCLUSIONS

Although initially absent from the early systematic studies of welfare state variations, care has become a core concept and subject of study since at least the early 1990s. Thanks to this scholarship, care is today a focus of a broad and growing swathe of work in comparative social policy studies. In this chapter, we have first looked at the evolution of research on care to identify how the concept has been defined and applied and the kinds of analyses of social policy that it has led to. The second part of the chapter identified where research in this field is headed and its potential as an analytic framework. Attention has been paid to the ways in which care lies at the intersection of welfare, employment, and migration, and how the concept and its application can help our understanding of major challenges such as population ageing, the growth of inequality, the complexity of contemporary social diversity, rapid processes of digitalization, and the threat of climate change.

Population ageing is perhaps the issue that has been more centrally placed in discussions regarding care regimes given the immediate pressures it puts on public care systems. The need to control public budgets in a context of expansionary demand is one of the reasons behind the rapid expansion of care markets.

With regard to the problem of inequality, despite and in some ways perhaps because of the mass incorporation of women into the world of paid employment, caring work continues to play a major role in gender-based inequalities in the labour market and beyond. Whilst childrearing still explains to a large extent gender pay gaps in most countries, the externalization of care work to the low-paid service sector accounts for structural intersectional inequalities. As a matter of fact, much of the precarious conditions of what during lockdown was considered 'essential work' actually derives from the scarce value we attach to reproductive and care labour. Hence, although discussions around care are conspicuously absent in mainstream debates concerning rising inequality, it is hard to imagine any political response, at whatever scale, that will not seriously consider the systemic undervalue of care. Likewise, discussions around care work and policies are also relevant for broader socio-ecological transformations in post-growth contexts. The ecological crisis and the process of automation are both redefining the nature of the welfare–work nexus. These two major threats produce new societal and economic dynamics that, in the words of Nancy Fraser (2016), create to different degrees different strains on care. In one way or another, all these new developments raise important questions with regard to the very definition of human progress and the links between productivity, growth, and welfare. In fundamental ways, the COVID-19 pandemic has shown us in the hard way the urgency to rethink the overall public value we grant to care. As Tronto rightly envisaged back in 1998 'When our public values and priorities reflect the role that care actually plays in our lives, our world will be organized quite differently' (Tronto, 1998: 16). This is a conversation still pending in many respects but one we cannot afford not to have.

REFERENCES

Anttonen, A., & Meagher, G. (2013). Mapping marketisation: Concepts and goals. In G. Meagher & M. Szebehely (Eds), *Marketisation in Nordic Eldercare: A Research Report on Legislation, Oversight, Extent and Consequences* (pp. 13–22). Stockholm University Press.

Anttonen, A., & Sipilä, J. (1996). European social care services: Is it possible to identify models? *Journal of European Social Policy*, 6(2), 87–100.

Anttonen, A., & Zechner, M. (2011). 'Theorising care and care work'. In B. Pfau-Effinger & T. Rostgaard (Eds), *Care between Work and Welfare in European Societies* (pp. 15–34). Routledge.

Appleby, J. (2011). *The Relentless Revolution: A History of Capitalism*. Norton.

Bettio, F., & Plantenga, J. (2004). Comparing care regimes in Europe. *Feminist Economics*, *10*(1), 85–113.

Brennan, D., Cass B., Himmelweit, S., & Szebehely, M. (2012). The marketisation of care: Rationales and consequences in Nordic and liberal care regimes. *Journal of European Social Policy*, *22*(4), 377–391.

Brighouse, P., & Robeyns, I. (2010). *Measuring Justice: Primary Goods and Capabilities*. Cambridge University Press.

Büchs, M. (2021). Sustainable welfare: Independence between growth and welfare has to go both ways. *Global Social Policy*, 1–5.

Cantillon, B., & Van Lancker, W. (2013). Three shortcomings of the social investment perspective. *Social Policy and Society*, *12*(4), 553–564.

Crompton, R. (1999). *Restructuring Gender Relations and Employment: The Decline of the Male Breadwinner*. Oxford University Press.

Da Roit, B., & Le Bihan, B. (2019). Cash for long-term care: Policy debates, visions and designs on the move. *Social Policy and Administration*, *53*(4), 519–536.

Daly, M. (2011). What adult worker model? A critical look at recent social policy reform in Europe from a gender and family perspective. *Social Politics*, *18*(1), 1–23.

Daly, M. (2018). Generations, age and life course: towards an integral social policy framework of analysis. *Contemporary Social Science*, *15*(3), 291–301.

Daly, M. (2020). COVID-19 and care homes in England: What happened and why? *Social Policy and Administration*, *54*(7), 885–998.

Daly, M., & Ferragina, E. (2017). Family policy in high-income countries: Five decades of development. *Journal of European Social Policy*, *28*(3), 255–270.

Daly, M., & Lewis, J. (2000). The concept of social care and the analysis of contemporary welfare states. *British Journal of Sociology*, *51*(2), 281–298.

Daly, M., León, M., Pfau-Effinger, B., Ranci, C., & Rostgaard, T. (forthcoming). COVID-19 and policies for care homes in European welfare states: Too little, too late? *Journal of European Social Policy*.

Esping-Andersen, G. (2009). *The Incomplete Revolution: Adapting to Women's New Roles*. Polity Press.

Evers, A., & Svetlik, I. (Eds). (1993). *Balancing Pluralism: New Welfare Mixes in Care for the Elderly*. Avebury and European Centre.

Finch, J., & Groves, D. (Eds). (1983). *A Labour of Love: Women, Work and Caring*. Routledge.

Fisher, B., & Tronto, J. (1990). Toward a feminist theory of caring. In E. K. Abel & M. K. Nelson (Eds), *Circles of Care Work and Identity in Women's Lives* (pp. 36–54). State University of New York Press.

Fleckenstein, T., & Lee, C. (2014). The politics of postindustrial social policy: Family policy reforms in Britain, Germany, South Korea and Sweden. *Comparative Political Studies*, *47*(4), 601–630.

Folbre, N. (1993). Counting housework: New estimates of real product in the US 1800–1860. *Journal of Economic History*, *53*(2), 275–288.

Fraser, N. (2016). Contradictions of capital and care. *New Left Review*, *100*, 99–117.

Gingrich, J. R. (2011). *Making Markets in the Welfare State: The Politics of Varying Market Reforms*. Cambridge University Press.

Gough, I. (2015). Climate change and sustainable welfare: The centrality of human needs. *Cambridge Journal of Economics*, *39*(5), 191–214.

Graham, H. (1983). Caring: A labour of love. In J. Finch & D. Groves (Eds), *A Labour of Love: Women, Work and Caring* (pp. 13–30). Routledge & Kegan Paul.

Graham, H. (1991). The concept of caring in feminist research: The case of domestic service. *Sociology*, *25*(1), 61–78.

Held, V. (2005). *The Ethics of Care: Personal, Political, and Global*. Oxford University Press.

Hemerijck, A. (2013). *Changing Welfare States*. Oxford University Press.

Hemerijck, A. (2017). *The Uses of Social Investment*. Oxford University Press.

Hochschild, A. (2000). Global care chains and emotional surplus value. In A. Giddens & W. Hutton (Eds), *On the Edge: Living with Global Capitalism* (pp. 130–146). Vintage.

Jamieson, A., & Illsley, R. (Eds). (1990). *Contrasting European Policies for the Care of Older People*. Avebury.

Knijn, T., & Kremer, M. (1997). Gender and the caring dimension of welfare states: Towards inclusive citizenship. *Social Politics*, *4*(3), 328–361.

Kröger, T. (2011). Defamilisation, dedomestication and care policy: Comparing childcare services provisions of welfare states. *International Journal of Sociology and Social Policy*, *31*(7/8), 424–440.

Leitner, S. (2003). Varieties of familialism: The caring function of the family in comparative perspective. *European Societies*, *5*(4), 353–375.

León, M. (Ed.). (2014). *The Transformation of Care in European Societies*. Palgrave.

Lewis, J. (1992). Gender and the development of welfare regimes. *Journal of European Social Policy*, *2*(3), 159–173.

Lewis, J. (2001). The decline of the male breadwinner model: Implications for work and care. *Social Politics*, *8*(2), 152–169.

Lister, R. (1994). 'She has other duties': Women, citizenship and social security. In S. Baldwin & J. Falkingham (Eds), *Social Security and Social Change: New Challenges to the Beveridge Model* (pp. 31–44). Harvester Wheatsheaf.

Lutz, H. (2018). Care migration: The connectivity between care chains, care circulation and transnational social inequality. *Current Sociology*, *66*(4), 577–589.

Mahon, R. (2018). Through a fractured gaze: The OECD, the World Bank and transnational care chains. *Current Sociology*, *4*(2), 562–576.

Mathieu, S. (2016). From the defamilialization to the 'demotherization' of care work. *Social Politics*, *23*(4), 576–591.

Michel, S., & Peng, I. (2017). *Gender, Migration and the Work of Care*. Palgrave Macmillan.

Morel, N., Palme, J., & Palier, B. (Eds). (2012). *Towards a Social Investment Welfare State? Ideas, Policies and Challenges*. Policy Press.

Morgan, K. (2013). Path shifting of the welfare state: Electoral competition and the expansion of work-family policy in Western Europe. *World Politics*, *65*(1), 73–115.

Nussbaum, M. (2003). Capabilities as fundamental entitlements: Sen and social justice. *Feminist Economics*, *9*(2–3), 33–59.

OECD. (2004). *Long-Term Care Policies for Older People*. OECD.

Orloff, A. S. (1993). Gender and the social rights of citizenship: The comparative analysis of gender relations and welfare states. *American Sociological Review*, *58*(3), 303–328.

Orton, M. (2011). Flourishing lives: The capabilities approach as a framework for new thinking about employment, work and welfare in the 21st century. *Work, Employment and Society, 25*(2), 352–360.

Palier, B., Häusermann, S., & Garitzmann, J. (forthcoming). *The World Politics of Social Investment.* Oxford University Press.

Parreñas, R. (2001). *Servants of Globalization: Women, Migration and Domestic Work.* Stanford University Press.

Peng, I. (2019). *The Care Economy: A New Research Framework* (Sciences Po LIEPP Working Paper no 89). Sciences Po.

Pirhonen, J. (2014). Dignity and the capabilities approach in long-term care for older people. *Nursing Philosophy, 16*(1), 29–39.

Ranci, C., & Pavolini, E. (Eds). (2013). *Reforms in Long-Term Care Policies in Europe.* Springer Verlag.

Sainsbury, E. (1977). *The Personal Social Services.* Pitman.

Saraceno, C., & Keck, W. (2010). Can we identify intergenerational policy regimes in Europe? *European Societies, 12*(5), 675–696.

Spasova, S., Baeten, R., Costa, S., Ghailani, D., Peña-Casas, R., & Vanhercke, B. (2018). *Challenges of Long-Term Care in Europe: A Study of National Policies 2018.* European Commission.

Stiglitz, J., Sen, A., & Fitoussi, J. P. (2010). *Mis-measuring Our Life: Why GDP Doesn't Add Up.* The New Press.

Thomas, C. (1993). Deconstructing concepts of care. *Sociology, 27*(4), 649–669.

Tronto, J. C. (1993). *Moral Boundaries: A Political Argument for an Ethic of Care.* Routledge.

Tronto, J. C. (1998). An ethic of care. *Generations Journal of the American Society on Aging, 22*(3), 15–20.

Tronto, J. C. (2015). *Who Cares? How to Reshape a Democratic Politics.* Cornell Selects.

Waring, M. (1988). *If Women Counted: A New Feminist Economics.* Harper Collins.

Williams F. (2012). Converging variations in migrant care work in Europe. *Journal of European Social Policy, 22*(4), 363–376.

Yeates, N. (2011). Going global: The transnationalization of care. *Development and Change, 42*(4), 1109–1130.

Yerkes, A., & Javornik, J. (2018). Creating capabilities: Childcare policies in comparative perspective. *Journal of European Social Policy, 29*(4), 529–544.

3. Family policy research in Europe

Wim Van Lancker and Hannah Zagel

INTRODUCTION

Family policy has gained attention as an independent field of study since the 1970s (Gauthier & Koops, 2018). In the context of profound changes in labour markets, family structures, and gender arrangements, powerful narratives emerged, for example, about the need to boost women's labour market participation and to support children as human capital 'repositories' of future economic prosperity (Lister, 1994, 2006; Jenson, 2004). Family policies have increasingly been seen as instrumental for approaching such goals among other policy domains (Lewis, 2006). Family policy research has monitored and made sense of the developments in family policy and its outcomes (Daly, 2020). In this role, the field of family policy research itself has undergone large changes since its early days.

Family policy scholarship is diverse and rich. Researchers working in various disciplines contribute to family policy research, such as from sociology, political sciences, social work, economics, educational science, law, and public health. This diversity even applies to sub-strands within the field such as comparative family policy research, which is the focus of this chapter. Comparative family policy research is an established branch in the ESPAnet community since its inaugural conference in 2002 (Clasen & Kvist, 2021). It has strong routes in the welfare regime typologizing tradition, and in its feminist critique.

There is no general consensus about what the boundaries of family policy research are, which is arguably due to the nature of family policy as a policy area. Measures commonly considered 'family policy' cut across different policy fields such as labour market and social security policies, education, family law, and housing policies. In their pioneering 1978 work, Sheila Kamerman and Alfred Kahn distinguished between explicit and implicit family policies, the latter referring to all policy domains and decisions that have consequences for families with children. Indeed, it is sometimes said that the subject of family policy is less defined by the type of policy, but more by its virtue of intervening in family life (Kaufmann et al., 2002). A more concise definition views family policy 'as centered around the well-being, functioning and responsibilities of families with children' (Daly, 2020: 27). Comparative family policy research arguably converges in the analysis of a core of three areas of family policy: income supports to families (money), childcare (services), and parental leave rights (time).

In this chapter, we look back on the trajectory of 'the field' of family policy research roughly from the 1970s, map its current state (from 2003), and finally lay out emerging topics and those likely to occupy family policy research in the future. We take stock of these developments addressing four key questions: (1) Which family policy outcomes are studied? (2) Which policies are analysed? (3) What are the dominant methods? (4) What are the theoretical perspectives in family policy research in the respective periods?

CURRENT RESEARCH AGENDA

Looking at the period from the inaugural ESPAnet conference in 2002 until 2021, the agenda in family policy research is increasingly dominated by a conception of the family as a productive unit. This is in contrast to focusing on the impact of family policy for the family's reproductive functions, which has previously been more common (Gauthier & Hatzius, 1997). That means that in current research, family policies are predominantly analysed in terms of their implications for the role of families in securing labour supply, in particular women's employment (Daly & Ferragina, 2018). The focus on the impact of family policy on the productive function of families also implies that children's wellbeing is increasingly discussed in economic terms. Observers noted this trend already in the 2000s (Lister, 2003; Ostner, 2008).

A current example is the discussion of the role of childcare provision for building children's human capital resources, which is common in studies of the so-called 'social investment' approach to welfare (Esping-Andersen, 2002; Kersbergen & Hemerijck, 2012). Resources used for childcare services and for parental leave policies can be considered investment in children's life chances but also in those of parents whose negative employment consequences from care-related leave will be reduced.

Outcomes

Current family policy research has a strong focus on outcomes. This is fuelled by the ever-increasing availability of harmonized cross-national surveys which include detailed data on the living conditions of families, as well as by an increased policy focus on employment, poverty, work–life balance, and wellbeing. For the ESPAnet community, the European Union (EU) Statistics on Income and Living Conditions survey has been particularly instrumental here. A widespread focus of outcome-oriented comparative studies, which had already emerged in the 1990s (Gornick et al., 1997; Gornick & Meyers, 2003), is on the impact of family policies on parents' employment participation. Recent reform trends in family policy in European countries, as well as EU directives on working times, parental leaves, and work–life balance[1] spurred research interest in outcomes of family–employment reconciliation policies. The same holds for poverty and in particular child poverty, which is centre stage in European policy discourse, the European Platform for Investing in Children, and the European Child Guarantee being prominent examples.

Employment outcomes of family policies are studied on different dimensions, such as parents' employment participation, work hours, and earnings. The assumption is that parental leave policies provide different degrees of rights for job-protected leave, either paid (leave benefits) or unpaid, with differential effects for parents' freedom to care for children without risking job or earnings losses. One important focus of study is on differences in employment across different parental leave settings (Han et al., 2009; Misra et al., 2011; Nieuwenhuis et al., 2017). The provision of childcare services, by contrast, is thought to allow parents to pursue employment by outsourcing care responsibilities. Childcare is hence often considered the ideal-typical measure of work–family reconciliation. As a result, many comparative studies focused on the role of childcare services in facilitating women's employment, looking at childcare costs, availability or use, or spending on childcare. Ferragin (2020), for instance, documents a surge in cross-national studies from the 2000s onwards, many of these focusing on the outcomes of childcare policies.

Besides employment, research often studies poverty in light of different family policy settings. Current comparative family policy research asks how different policies reduce poverty for families or particular types of families. A focus of recent multicountry comparative studies has been on family policies' role in moderating poverty of single mothers (Brady & Burroway, 2012; Misra et al., 2012; Maldonado & Nieuwenhuis, 2015; Nieuwenhuis & Maldonado, 2018) or children (Bäckman & Ferrarini 2010; Van Lancker & Van Mechelen, 2015).

Recent comparative studies caution about the reach of family policies, suggesting that the benefits of family policies are unequally distributed across families. For example, use of childcare services varies among parents from different social backgrounds (Pavolini & Van Lancker, 2018; Van Lancker, 2018), which has implications for its effects on employment and poverty. Recent evidence also points to unequal benefits of childcare services and parental leave policies for the employment of mothers with different levels of education (Hook & Paek, 2020). In general, more attention is being devoted to heterogeneous effects of family policies on outcomes in terms of class, gender, and education (Keck & Saraceno, 2013).

Policies

The above-mentioned outcome orientation of the current family policy research agenda goes hand in hand with an increased focus on single family policy areas, and often comes at the cost of acknowledging the complexity and multidimensionality of family policy (Daly, 2020). Especially in multicountry comparisons, there is a tendency to analyse single policies rather than packages. Three types of policies are predominantly studied in current comparative family policy research: income supports to families (child benefits, family allowances), parental leave policies with a recently growing interest in leave policies for fathers, and childcare policies.

Income supports are granted in many different forms to families. A key distinction is whether they are provided as a universal benefit, for example to all families with children, or as targeted measures, for example to families with low incomes. While income supports to families has long been a key interest (see the third section below), research has arguably become more nuanced. The fiscalization of child benefits has been one topic (Daly & Ferragina, 2018). A more recent focus is on the design of child benefit systems in relation to the targeting versus universalism debate (Bárcena-Martín et al., 2018). This research benefited from advances in standard simulation and hypothetical household models, in which entitlements that run through the tax and benefit system are simulated for a range of household types. Recent research used this method to assess which types of child benefit system compensate best for the costs of children (Penne et al., 2020).

Parental leave policies take varied forms and shapes. The main types of leave are maternity leave (reserved for mothers), paternity leave (reserved for fathers), and parental leave (available to both parents; possibly same-sex parents as well) (Koslowski et al., 2020). In comparative family policy research, leave policy is mostly operationalized in terms of the time granted for job-protected leave rights and as to whether the leave time is paid or not, and the generosity of the benefit (Ray et al., 2010; Dobrotić & Blum, 2020). Empirically, studies also often employ social expenditures on parental leave schemes as a proxy of policy generosity or inclusiveness. It is now widely recognized that such proxy measures are usually ill-suited to operationalize actual policies (Otto & van Oorschot, 2019). In response, recent research ventures into the measurement of parental leave policies, and how policy designs can be operationalized for use in comparative studies (Otto et al., 2021), or whether survey microdata can be used to assess the actual entitlement to parental leave future parents have (Bártová & Emery, 2018).

Childcare policies (or: early childhood education and care), are also varied and complex, and comparative research faces even more limitations to study them comprehensively. Formal childcare is intrinsically difficult to conceptualize and measure in comparative perspective (Yerkes & Javornik, 2019). First, childcare is provided on many different levels of governance (local, municipal, national). Second, childcare providers range between fully statutory, fully private, fully third-sector based, and any combination of the three – both within and across countries. Third, it is particularly difficult to distinguish between outright provision (supply) and demand of childcare, let alone between different financing mechanisms. Finally, an important aspect of childcare provision is the pedagogical quality, which is critical for child development. Comparative indicators covering all of these aspects for a sufficient period of time are not available as of yet. As a result, comparative research on childcare too relies on measures of expenditures or coverage to operationalize childcare policies.

Theoretical Perspectives in Current Family Policy Research

Compared to earlier periods, the current agenda of comparative family policy research is less theoretically oriented. The comparison of quantitative indicators across countries is not usually embedded in a thick theoretical framework nor, it seems, is theory development among the key interests of the field today. Rather, concepts developed in prior theoretical work are commonly used to frame research interests, motivate comparisons, or for classifying family policies in quantitative studies.

Current comparative family policy research often uses previously developed concepts and ideas for framing an empirical research question. That means, concepts such as the male breadwinner model (Lewis, 1992, 2001), familialism (Saraceno, 1994; Leitner, 2003), or care regimes (Anttonen & Sipilä, 1996; Daly & Lewis, 2000) are discussed in background sections and inform new empirical puzzles. For example, common questions are how poverty rates developed for children across different breadwinner models, or how breadwinning is organized in households across different contexts of familialism. More recent conceptual approaches in the field of comparative family policy, which have been used in a similar way, are the social investment (Morel et al., 2011; Hemerijck, 2018) and life-course perspectives (Elder et al., 2003; Mayer, 2009). Both perspectives cannot be considered theories in a strict sense. But they reflect newer narratives in social research, which emphasize the processual nature of individual lives within policy contexts.

An area with some conceptual discussion in current comparative family policy research has been around the concept of defamilization. In its most common interpretation, defamilization refers to the degree to which welfare states reduce individuals' dependence on other family members. Distinctions between reducing economic or social dependencies made in the original use of the concept (Lister, 1994; McLaughlin & Glendinning, 1994) seem to have been washed out somewhat over time. Since its first mentions, the concept has been applied broadly in empirical studies and sometimes with diverging meaning attached (Lohmann & Zagel, 2016).

There have been several contributions to flesh out the multiple facets of defamilization for comparing family policies across countries (Leitner & Lessenich, 2007; Daly, 2011). However, recent discussions have spurred new concepts such as dedomestication (Kröger, 2011), degenderization (Saxonberg, 2013), and demotherization (Mathieu, 2016). This renewed conceptual debate of defamilization is a welcome contribution to theorizing in comparative family policy research, which has tended to take an increasingly narrow focus on sub-areas of family policy. In order to describe the field more comprehensively, multidimensional concepts such as defamilization are useful frameworks (Zagel & Lohmann, 2021).

Methods in Current Family Policy Research

Current comparative family policy research is methodologically diverse. There is a recently growing strand of empirical studies using multicountry designs with quantitative methods. Where outcomes of family policy are the research interest, studies commonly apply multilevel modelling strategies on large-scale comparative datasets. Another strand of comparative family policy research has used qualitative comparative analysis and fuzzy set methodology (Szelewa & Polakowski, 2008; Ciccia & Verloo, 2012).

Availability of comparative family policy data is an issue. In general, the tradition of mapping European policy landscapes with a regime lens has pushed the collection of comparative indicators in large-scale international datasets. And although family policy has not been at the centre of these projects, the availability of comparative family policy indicators has still improved overall (Lohmann & Zagel, 2018). However, such datasets are often limited in terms of the time period covered, the types of family policies measured, or the number of countries included. Researchers have hence heavily relied on social expenditure data (OECD, 2019), which is now available for long time periods and on a level of detail that allows to distinguish a number of different types of family policy.

EARLY DAYS AND TRAJECTORY OF FAMILY POLICY RESEARCH

Comparative family policy research arguably 'took off' as a field of study in the late 1970s. Earlier studies applied case-oriented approaches, often focusing on one country, others compiled international data on single indicators (Gauthier & Koops, 2018). A pioneer in comparative family policy research was the edition by Kamerman and Kahn (1978), which built on an earlier article by the same researchers (Kamerman & Kahn, 1976) and took the lack of a debate of policies for families in the United States as a starting point. The edition contributed to coining the term comparative family policy. In the 1990s, comparative family policy research developed in conversation with the broader welfare state literature, with a strong focus on typologizing and clustering (Lewis, 1992; Sainsbury, 1994). The emerging field of European comparative family policy was characterized by a strong focus on gender as an analytical lens on state–market–family relationships.

Outcomes

In the early period of the 1970s and 1980s, comparative family policy research did not have a strong focus on outcomes. Where outcomes were studied, child poverty and mothers' health were a likely focus. Since the 1990s, a further widely studied outcome of family policies has been the division of labour in heterosexual couples. This strand of comparative family policy research is closely linked to the theorizing of gender and welfare states (Orloff, 1993; Sainsbury, 1994, 1999; Lewis, 2001, 2009; Daly & Rake, 2003). Earlier studies commonly presented comparative tables of aggregate employment rates of women and men or the composition of family incomes across different welfare state contexts. This demonstrated the characteristic links between a particular institutional setting and a gendered division of labour outcomes. A wealth of empirical research on these links emerged throughout the 1990s and 2000s (e.g., Lewis & Giullari, 2005; Pettit & Hook, 2009; Cooke & Baxter, 2010; Korpi et al., 2013).

Fertility has also been studied as an outcome of family policies (e.g., Gauthier, 2007; Kalwij, 2010; Wesolowski & Ferrarini, 2018). The interest in family policy effects on fertility grew in the early 2000s when fertility rates across Europe fell below 'population replacement level', which was perceived as a threat to the future of the intergenerational contract underpinning the welfare state. Politically, family policy was increasingly discussed from an arguably neonatalist stance, and comparative research tested the associations between generous family policies and fertility, often with ambiguous outcomes (Neyer & Andersson, 2008).

Policies

Early family policy research picked up on the two major themes addressed by policies directed at families: securing mothers' health after birth (from the early twentieth century) and supporting the 'family wage' (from the 1950s). Hence, maternity leave regulations were among the first policies studied as family policy. Income support policies such as child benefit, initially considered more as a poor relief measure, were increasingly viewed as family policies. Other family allowances were also analysed.

Parental leave was emerging as a more important topic in comparative family policy research in the 1990s, when several countries adapted their maternity leave regulations. In the second half of the 1980s, the first comparative studies on childcare services emerged as well, fuelled by emerging interest at the EU (then European Community) policy level.[2]

Theory

The trajectory of comparative family policy research has been marked by a critical stance towards the consequences of welfare state intervention in family relationships. Critical social policy studies also engaged with family policies. Likewise, feminist scholarship has been influential in the field, highlighting the gendered nature of welfare state provision (Lewis, 1992; O'Connor, 1993; Orloff, 1993). That literature revealed the complexity of policies in general, and in those targeted towards the family in particular. Theories grappled with the multidimensional nature of policies for families, the different actors and power relationships involved. New ways of typologizing welfare regimes were proposed based on gender as an analytical framework (see also Chapter 11 by Knijn, this volume).

This literature contrasts with another theoretical orientation visible in comparative family policy research, which focuses more on the role of policies in supporting the functions of families. For example, Kaufmann et al.'s (2002) heuristic of modes of family intervention but also Kamerman and Kahn's (1978) approach can be seen in this light. Regime thinking was not the dominant focus, but rather the different aims and structures of policies and policy packages.

Methods

The bulk of the earlier studies in comparative family policy either used more case-oriented, small-N approaches or applied a multicountry design with primarily descriptive methodologies. Multicountry quantitative designs using statistical methods were becoming more common when data availability grew in the 1990s and 2000s.

EMERGING THEMES AND FUTURE DIRECTIONS IN FAMILY POLICY RESEARCH

Outcomes

Rather than embarking into the study of 'new' outcomes, future research on the outcomes of family policy should look more at outcomes across diverse family settings. Several factors are important dimensions to study, for example family policy effects by social background, ethnicity, status of migration, and across complex family structures, possibly approached from an intersectional perspective.

Beyond maternal health as a focus in early family policy research, health has not been studied as a common outcome for all family members. It should become a more important focus in the future, not least considering the context of the COVID-19 pandemic. Health may not be an obvious outcome of family policy, yet mental health is closely linked to mothers' workloads in terms of combining employment and care. In light of the pandemic, several new questions arise, for example questions around whether children's (in) ability to attend childcare centres through lockdown periods affected their socio-emotional wellbeing. A more general, systemic question also remains, namely how family policies, and the interaction between different family policy measures, can reinforce social security buffers to cushion income loss due to the economic consequences of the pandemic.

Policies

The three key areas of family policy – income supports, leave policies, and childcare – are likely to remain a focus of future family policy research. We note a number of issues within these categories that should be of greater interest in future comparative family policy research, either because they pre-viously received little attention or because they emerged as research topics due to policy reforms. These include taxation for families and child maintenance regulations as income support policies and leave rights to the second parent as parental leave policy.

Both child maintenance regulations (Skinner et al., 2017; Hakovirta et al., 2020) and fathers' leave policies (Smith & Williams, 2007; Eydal & Rostgaard, 2016; Ma et al., 2020) have been the subject of comparative research. Maintenance systems are, however, often studied as separate from family policy, arguably because they are entangled with legal systems in many countries. It can be fruitful to consider them more holistically, consid-ering institutional links. Fathers' leave policy is an upcoming theme because demand may be shifting and it may also become more politicized with progressing family change in many countries, and some countries' return to policy support of maternal home-care models.

Theory

We agree with Daly (2020) that much of the current research does not reflect the complexity inherent to the field of family policy. Especially the way different policies relate, affecting policy outcomes in varying domains, is an often overlooked issue or is discussed only in passing, especially in outcome-oriented multicountry quantitative studies (but see Thévenon, 2016).

Given the impact that social investment thinking has had on the field, a critical interrogation of its assumptions and core concepts is overdue as well. Social investment studies tend to be thin on theory, treating family policy in light of the economics of human capital formation and future return on investment. Bringing back critical perspectives on policies and the welfare state, which characterized early research in this field, seems a fruitful route. Moreover, a return to core fundamentals that take a critical view of the current state of family policy and its role in the broader societal context has the potential to account for its complex multilevel structure and the different actors involved.

Methods

The field of social sciences has been characterized by a turn towards causal inference, and in recent years many ESPAnet sessions explicitly dealt with methods to uncover causal effects as well. Family policy research is also benefiting from natural experiments in which policy changes are exploited to examine the causal impact of a given policy on a range of outcomes. Recent examples include studies of child benefit reforms, studies on childcare expansions, or studies on parental leave reforms (Lefebvre & Merrigan, 2008; Havnes & Mogstad, 2011; Ekberg et al., 2013; Kluve & Tamm, 2013; Bauernschuster & Schlotter, 2015; Bettendorf et al., 2015; Kleven et al., 2020).

A drawback of these methods is that it is difficult to compare policy changes across countries (external validity), and they risk losing sight of interaction effects and system complexity, or the political economy of policy implementation and change. While the field is moving towards causal inference, there is still, and perhaps even more so, a need for comparative studies focusing on the grander questions, underpinned by theoretical reasoning. A focus on the specific, such as with causal links between a small set of variables, risks losing sight of the general. Future research should strive to combine specific and general approaches, putting research findings and what can be learnt from them into the contexts of national and comparative policy settings.

CONCLUSION

Our review of the current, past, and emerging issues of the family policy research agenda shows a rich and dynamic research field with a remarkable trajectory since the 1970s. The field has moved towards assessing outcomes of family policies in multicountry studies, with a tendency to look at different types of family policy separately. Although many of the concepts developed in earlier research have been applied and adapted, we noted the lack of a deeper theoretical engagement. In short, much of the field is preoccupied with comparing outcomes across European family policy settings loosely described in terms of family support or breadwinner models, and increasingly using refined, causally oriented methodologies to uncover policy effects in ever greater detail. We suggest that a return to more theoretically oriented reasoning could benefit the research field, allowing for a greater contextualization of findings.

NOTES

1. Directive (EU) 2019/1158 of the European Parliament and of the Council of 20 June 2019 on Work–Life Balance for Parents and Carers and Repealing Council Directive 2010/18/EU, 2019.
2. The first comparative report on childcare in the European Community was published by the European Commission Childcare Network in 1985.

REFERENCES

Anttonen, A., & Sipilä, J. (1996). European social care services: Is it possible to identify models? *Journal of European Social Policy*, *6*(2), 87–100.

Bäckman, O., & Ferrarini, T. (2010). Combating child poverty? A multilevel assessment of family policy institutions and child poverty in 21 old and new welfare states. *Journal of Social Policy*, *39*(2), 275–296.

Bárcena-Martín, E., Blanco-Arana, M. C., & Pérez-Moreno, S. (2018). Social transfers and child poverty in European countries: Pro-poor targeting or pro-child targeting? *Journal of Social Policy*, *47*(4), 739–758.

Bártová, A., & Emery, T. (2018). Measuring policy entitlements at the micro-level: Maternity and parental leave in Europe. *Community, Work and Family*, *21*(1), 33–52.

Bauernschuster, S., & Schlotter, M. (2015). Public child care and mothers' labor supply: Evidence from two quasi-experiments. *Journal of Public Economics*, *123*, 1–16.

Bettendorf, L. J., Jongen, E. L., & Muller, P. (2015). Childcare subsidies and labour supply—Evidence from a large Dutch reform. *Labour Economics*, 36, 112-123.

Brady, D., & Burroway, R. (2012). Targeting, universalism, and single-mother poverty: A multilevel analysis across 18 affluent democracies. *Demography*, *49*(2), 719–746.

Ciccia, R., & Verloo, M. (2012). Parental leave regulations and the persistence of the male breadwinner model: Using fuzzy-set ideal type analysis to assess gender equality in an enlarged Europe. *Journal of European Social Policy*, *22*(5), 507–528.

Clasen, J., & Kvist, J. (2021). Wim van Oorschot and the early years of ESPAnet. Leading social policy analysis from the front. https://soc.kuleuven.be/ceso/spsw/publications/liber-amicorum-wim-van-oorschot/CH4%20Clasen%20and%20Kvist.pdf

Cooke, L. P., & Baxter, J. (2010). 'Families' in international context: Comparing institutional effects across Western societies. *Journal of Marriage and Family, 72*(3), 516–536.

Daly, M. (2011). What adult worker model? A critical look at recent social policy reform in Europe from a gender and family perspective. *Social Politics: International Studies in Gender, State and Society, 18*(1), 1–23.

Daly, M. (2020). Conceptualizing and analyzing family policy and how it is changing. In R. Nieuwenhuis & W. Van Lancker (Eds), *The Palgrave Handbook of Family Policy* (pp. 25–41). Springer International.

Daly, M., & Ferragina, E. (2018). Family policy in high-income countries: Five decades of development. *Journal of European Social Policy, 28*(3), 255–270.

Daly, M., & Lewis, J. (2000). The concept of social care and the analysis of contemporary welfare states. *British Journal of Sociology, 51*(2), 281–298.

Daly, M., & Rake, K. (2003). *Gender and the Welfare State*. Polity.

Dobrotić, I., & Blum, S. (2020). Inclusiveness of parental-leave benefits in twenty-one European countries: Measuring social and gender inequalities in leave eligibility. *Social Politics: International Studies in Gender, State and Society, 27*(3), 588–614.

Ekberg, J., Eriksson, R., & Friebel, G. (2013). Parental leave: A policy evaluation of the Swedish 'Daddy-Month' reform. *Journal of Public Economics, 97*, 131–143.

Elder, G. H., Johnson, M. K., & Crosnoe, R. (2003). The emergence and development of life course theory. In J. T. Mortimer & M. J. Shanahan (Eds), *Handbook of the Life Course* (pp. 3–19). Springer US.

Esping-Andersen, G. (2002). A child-centred social investment strategy. In *Why We Need a New Welfare State* (pp. 26–68). Oxford University Press.

Eydal, G. B., & Rostgaard, T. (2016). *Fatherhood in the Nordic Welfare States: Comparing Care Policies and Practice*. Policy Press.

Ferragina, E. (2020). Family policy and women's employment outcomes in 45 high-income countries: A systematic qualitative review of 238 comparative and national studies. *Social Policy and Administration, 54*(7), 1016–1066.

Gauthier, A. H. (2007). The impact of family policies on fertility in industrialized countries: A review of the literature. *Population Research and Policy Review, 26*(3), 323–346.

Gauthier, A. H., & Koops, J. (2018). The history of family policy research. In T. Rostgaard & G. B. Eydal (Eds), *Handbook of Child and Family Policy* (pp. 11–23). Edward Elgar Publishing.

Gauthier, A. H., & Hatzius, J. (1997). Family benefits and fertility: An econometric analysis. *Population Studies, 51*(3), 295–306.

Gornick, J. C., & Meyers, M. K. (2003). *Families That Work: Policies for Reconciling Parenthood and Employment*. Russell Sage Foundation.

Gornick, J. C., Meyers, M. K., & Ross, K. E. (1997). Supporting the employment of mothers: Policy variation across fourteen welfare states. *Journal of European Social Policy, 7*(1), 45–70.

Hakovirta, M., Skinner, C., Hiilamo, H., & Jokela, M. (2020). Child poverty, child maintenance and interactions with social assistance benefits among lone parent families: A comparative analysis. *Journal of Social Policy, 49*(1), 19–39.

Han, W.-J., Ruhm, C., & Waldfogel, J. (2009). Parental leave policies and parents' employment and leave-taking. *Journal of Policy Analysis and Management, 28*(1), 29–54.

Havnes, T., & Mogstad, M. (2011). Money for nothing? Universal child care and maternal employment. *Journal of Public Economics, 95*(11–12), 1455–1465.

Hemerijck, A. (2018). Social investment as a policy paradigm. *Journal of European Public Policy, 25*(6), 810–827.

Hook, J. L., & Paek, E. (2020). National family policies and mothers' employment: How earnings inequality shapes policy effects across and within countries. *American Sociological Review, 85*(3), 381–416.

Jenson, J. (2004). Changing the paradigm: Family responsibility or investing in children. *Canadian Journal of Sociology/Cahiers Canadiens de Sociologie, 29*(2), 169–192.

Kalwij, A. (2010). The impact of family policy expenditure on fertility in Western Europe. *Demography, 47*(2), 503–519.

Kamerman, S. B., & Kahn, A. J. (1976). Explorations in family policy. *Social Work, 21*(3), 181–186.

Kamerman, S. B., & Kahn, A. J. (1978). *Family Policy: Government and Families in Fourteen Countries*. Columbia University Press.

Kaufmann, F.-X., Kuijsten, A., Schulze, H.-J., & Strohmeier, K. P. (Eds). (2002). *Family Life and Family Policies in Europe* (Vol. 2). Oxford University Press.

Keck, W., & Saraceno, C. (2013). The impact of different social-policy frameworks on social inequalities among women in the European Union: The labour-market participation of mothers. *Social Politics, 20*(3), 297–328.

Kersbergen, K. V., & Hemerijck, A. (2012). Two decades of change in Europe: The emergence of the social investment state. *Journal of Social Policy, 41*(3), 475–492.

Kleven, H., Landais, C., Posch, J., Steinhauer, A., & Zweimüller, J. (2020). Do family policies reduce gender inequality? Evidence from 60 years of policy experimentation. No. w28082. National Bureau of Economic Research.

Kluve, J., & Tamm, M. (2013). Parental leave regulations, mothers' labor force attachment and fathers' childcare involvement: Evidence from a natural experiment. *Journal of Population Economics, 26*(3), 983–1005.

Korpi, W., Ferrarini, T., & Englund, S. (2013). Women's opportunities under different family policy constellations: Gender, class, and inequality tradeoffs in Western countries re-examined. *Social Politics: International Studies in Gender, State and Society, 20*(1), 1–40.

Koslowski, A., Blum, S., Dobrotić, I., Kaufman, G., & Moss, P. (2020). *16th International Review on Leave Policies and Related Research*. https://doi.org/10.18445/20200915-131331-0

Kröger, T. (2011). Defamilisation, dedomestication and care policy: Comparing child-care service provisions of welfare states. *International Journal of Sociology and Social Policy, 31*(7/8), 424–440.

Lefebvre, P., & Merrigan, P. (2008). Child-care policy and the labor supply of mothers with young children: A natural experiment from Canada. *Journal of Labor Economics, 26*(3), 519–548.

Leitner, S. (2003). Varieties of familialism: The caring function of the family in comparative perspective. *European Societies, 5*(4), 353–375.

Leitner, S., & Lessenich, S. (2007). (In-)dependence as dependent variable: Conceptualizing and measuring 'de-familization'. In J. Clasen & N. Siegel (Eds),

Investigating Welfare State Change: The 'Dependent Variable Problem' in Comparative Analysis (pp. 244–260). Edward Elgar Publishing.

Lewis, J. (1992). Gender and the development of welfare regimes. *Journal of European Social Policy*, *2*(3), 159–173.

Lewis, J. (2001). The decline of the male breadwinner model: Implications for work and care. *Social Politics*, *8*(2), 152–169.

Lewis, J. (2006). Work/family reconciliation, equal opportunities and social policies: The interpretation of policy trajectories at the EU level and the meaning of gender equality. *Journal of European Public Policy*, *13*(3), 420–437.

Lewis, J. (2009). *Work–Family Balance, Gender and Policy*. Edward Elgar Publishing.

Lewis, J., & Giullari, S. (2005). The adult worker model family, gender equality and care: The search for new policy principles and the possibilities and problems of a capabilities approach. *Economy and Society*, *34*(1), 76–104.

Lister, R. (1994). 'She has other duties': Women, citizenship and social security. In S. Baldwin & J. Falkingham (Eds), *Social Security and Social Change: New Challenges to the Beveridge Model* (pp. 31–44). Harvester Wheatsheaf.

Lister, R. (2003). Investing in the citizen-workers of the future: Transformations in citizenship and the state under New Labour. *Social Policy and Administration*, *37*(5), 427–443.

Lister, R. (2006). Children (but not women) first: New Labour, child welfare and gender. *Critical Social Policy*, *26*(2), 315–335.

Lohmann, H., & Zagel, H. (2016). Family policy in comparative perspective: The concepts and measurement of familization and defamilization. *Journal of European Social Policy*, *26*(1), 48–65.

Lohmann, H., & Zagel, H. (2018). Comparing family policies: Approaches, methods and databases. In T. Rostgaard & G. B. Eydal (Eds), *Handbook of Child and Family Policy* (pp. 48–65). Edward Elgar Publishing.

Ma, L., Andersson, G., Duvander, A.-Z., & Evertsson, M. (2020). Fathers' uptake of parental leave: Forerunners and laggards in Sweden, 1993–2010. *Journal of Social Policy*, *49*(2), 361–381.

Maldonado, L. C., & Nieuwenhuis, R. (2015). Family policies and single parent poverty in 18 OECD countries, 1978–2008. *Community, Work and Family*, *18*(4), 395–415.

Mathieu, S. (2016). From the defamilialization to the 'demotherization' of care work. *Social Politics: International Studies in Gender, State and Society*, *23*(4), 576–591.

Mayer, K. U. (2009). New directions in life course research. *Annual Review of Sociology*, *35*(1), 413–433.

McLaughlin, E., & Glendinning, C. (1994). Paying for care in Europe: Is there a feminist approach? In L. Hantrais & S. Mangen (Eds), *Family Policy and the Welfare of Women* (Vol. 3, pp. 52–69). Cross-National Research Group.

Misra, J., Budig, M., & Boeckmann, I. (2011). Work–family policies and the effects of children on women's employment hours and wages. *Community, Work and Family*, *14*(2), 139–157.

Misra, J., Moller, S., Strader, E., & Wemlinger, E. (2012). Family policies, employment and poverty among partnered and single mothers. *Research in Social Stratification and Mobility*, *30*(1), 113–128.

Morel, N., Palier, B., & Palme, J. (2011). Beyond the welfare state as we knew it? In N. Morel, B. Palier, & J. Palme (Eds), *Towards a Social Investment Welfare State? Ideas, Policies and Challenges* (pp. 1–32). Policy Press.

Neyer, G., & Andersson, G. (2008). Consequences of family policies on childbearing behavior: Effects or artifacts? *Population and Development Review*, *34*(4), 699–724.

Nieuwenhuis, R., & Maldonado, L. C. (2018). Single-parent families and in-work poverty. In H. Lohmann & I. Marx (Eds), *Handbook of Research in In-Work Poverty* (pp. 171–192). Edward Elgar Publishing.

Nieuwenhuis, R., Need, A., & Van der Kolk, H. (2017). Is there such a thing as too long childcare leave? *International Journal of Sociology and Social Policy*, *37*(1/2), 2–15.

O'Connor, J. S. (1993). Gender, class and citizenship in the comparative analysis of welfare state regimes: Theoretical and methodological issues. *British Journal of Sociology*, *44*(3), 501–518.

OECD. (2019). *Social Expenditure Database*. www.oecd.org/social/expenditure.htm

Orloff, A. (1993). Gender and the social rights of citizenship: The comparative analysis of state policies and gender relations. *American Sociological Review*, *58*(3), 501–518.

Ostner, I. (2008). Ökonomisierung der Lebenswelt durch aktivierende Familienpolitik? In A. Evers & R. G. Heinze (Eds), *Sozialpolitik* (pp. 49–66). VS Verlag für Sozialwissenschaften.

Otto, A., & van Oorschot, W. (2019). Welfare reform by stealth? Cash benefit recipiency data and its additional value to the understanding of welfare state change in Europe. *Journal of European Social Policy*, *29*(3), 307–324.

Otto, A., Bártová, A., & Van Lancker, W. (2021). Measuring the generosity of parental leave policies. *Social Inclusion*, *9*(2), 238–249.

Pavolini, E., & Van Lancker, W. (2018). The Matthew effect in childcare use: A matter of policies or preferences? *Journal of European Public Policy*, *25*(6), 878–893.

Penne, T., Hufkens, T., Goedeme, T., & Storms, B. (2020). To what extent do welfare states compensate for the cost of children? The joint impact of taxes, benefits and public goods and services. *Journal of European Social Policy*, *30*(1), 79–94.

Pettit, B., & Hook, J. L. (2009). *Gendered Tradeoffs: Women, Family, and Workplace Inequality in Twenty-One Countries*. Russell Sage Foundation.

Ray, R., Gornick, J. C., & Schmitt, J. (2010). Who cares? Assessing generosity and gender equality in parental leave policy designs in 21 countries. *Journal of European Social Policy*, *20*(3), 196–216.

Sainsbury, D. (1994). *Gendering Welfare States*. Sage Publications.

Sainsbury, D. (1999). *Gender and Welfare State Regimes*. Oxford University Press.

Saraceno, C. (1994). The ambivalent familism of the Italian welfare state. *Social Politics: International Studies in Gender, State and Society*, *1*(1), 60–82.

Saxonberg, S. (2013). From defamilialization to degenderization: Toward a new welfare typology. *Social Policy and Administration*, *47*(1), 26–49.

Skinner, C., Meyer, D. R., Cook, K., & Fletcher, M. (2017). Child maintenance and social security interactions: The poverty reduction effects in model lone parent families across four countries. *Journal of Social Policy*, *46*(3), 495–516.

Smith, A., & Williams, D. (2007). Father-friendly legislation and paternal time across Western Europe. *Journal of Comparative Policy Analysis*, *9*(2), 175–192.

Szelewa, D., & Polakowski, M. P. (2008). Who cares? Changing patterns of childcare in Central and Eastern Europe. *Journal of European Social Policy*, *18*(2), 115–131.

Thévenon, O. (2016). Do 'institutional complementarities' foster female labour force participation? *Journal of Institutional Economics*, *12*(2), 471–497.

Van Lancker, W. (2018). Reducing inequality in childcare service use across European countries: What (if any) is the role of social spending? *Social Policy and Administration*, *52*(1), 271–292.

Van Lancker, W., & Van Mechelen, N. (2015). Universalism under siege? Exploring the association between targeting, child benefits and child poverty across 26 countries. *Social Science Research, 50*, 60–75.

Wesolowski, K., & Ferrarini, T. (2018). Family policies and fertility: Examining the link between family policy institutions and fertility rates in 33 countries 1995–2011. *International Journal of Sociology and Social Policy, 38*(11/12), 1057–1070.

Yerkes, M. A., & Javornik, J. (2019). Creating capabilities: Childcare policies in comparative perspective. *Journal of European Social Policy, 29*(4), 529–544.

Zagel, H., & Lohmann, H. (2021). Conceptualising state–market–family relationships in comparative research: A conceptual goodness view on defamilization. *Journal of Social Policy, 50*(4), 852–870.

4. Comparative research on health and health care

Claus Wendt

INTRODUCTION

Never before has the issue of health and health care dominated the public and political debate as it has since the beginning of the COVID-19 epidemic in late 2019. And never before has a single health issue had such a severe impact on the economic and political systems and societies worldwide. The experiences from the 'corona years' 2020 and 2021 will have feedback effects on national and international health-care systems, public health systems, related social policy institutions, and health and social policy research. This chapter provides an overview of how health care and health research have evolved over the past 20 years and assesses the potential for innovative research in this field for the future. Both the review of past research and the assessment of avenues for future research provide only a snapshot, since related fields, such as medicine, health economics, health services research, and others cannot be covered. Furthermore, this chapter concentrates on comparative research and not on single case studies.

The main changes that have taken place in comparative health-care system research (excluding health economics, medicine, and health services research) over the last 20 years have been, first, the convergence towards research goals, methods, and use of quality criteria similar to comparative social policy research; second, a new focus on institutional change; and third, the combination of health-care system research and output research, such as an analysis of how health status and health inequalities are influenced by health-care and social policy systems. This focus, however, has not contributed sufficiently to providing high-quality information on best practice strategies to respond to the COVID-19 crisis or institutional settings that provide the best protection in a time in which the population and individual health are most at risk.

The huge crisis has shown that one of the main resources in times in which health is at high risk is trust. As with other social protection systems, the health-care system represents an institution that promises security in critical times. People want to believe that they will receive the necessary medical care in case of a serious sickness and that the costs of health-care provision will be covered. The pandemic may have weakened this trust. People have experienced, for instance, that many high-risk groups were not well protected and that health care was not provided sufficiently in all cases. They have also experienced that the health-care system as a single institution is not enough to protect the health of the population. In the next decades, population ageing will have the effect that monetary and health-care resources will be insufficient to serve all those in need and that the health-care system alone cannot cope with the demographically caused future health crisis.

Based on the scenario that personnel and financial resources will not be sufficient without structural changes, we identify the following four areas of innovation in comparative health policy research: the first two areas follow the path of the last 20 years. The second two require new data and methods as well as collaboration with other fields of research. First, it is important to adopt an international comparative perspective and to identify best practices in health-care provision when financial and personnel resources are scarce. Second, while progress has been made in better capturing and classifying the institutional structure and resources of health-care systems in an international perspective, we still need to improve our understanding of how health-care systems can protect and enhance health in collaboration with other welfare state institutions, in particular those for the elderly, such as long-term care. Third, we have seen that individual health cannot be separated from population health. Health-care systems that focus not only on individual health but also on population (or public) health are potentially better prepared to protect individual health than health-care systems that concentrate on providing services to the individual patient in the event of individual sickness. Therefore, comparative studies are required that analyse both health-care and public health systems. Fourth, digitalization processes have increased in developed health-care systems worldwide, and comparative studies are required to better understand the positive and potentially negative effects of such and further structures with the potential to improve collaboration between actors and institutions in health care, social policy, and public health.

COMPARATIVE HEALTH-CARE SYSTEM RESEARCH

Early health policy and health-care system research was dominated by single case studies such as those by Rudolf Klein (1992) and Chris Ham (1999) on the British National Health Service. At that time, in the 1980s and 1990s, hardly any comparative health policy papers were published in international journals and very often reviewers saw 'their own country' misrepresented. It took some time and new research methods before results from comparative health policy research were considered as innovations in their own right. Two developments contributed to increased attention to comparative studies in health care: first, the high attention towards comparative studies that followed Esping-Andersen's book *The Three Worlds of Welfare Capitalism*, published in 1990, spilled over to the field of health care. Second, both researchers and practitioners began to realize that new insights could be gained from examples of other countries that would also help to better understand their own country. In a contribution with Ted Marmor, we categorized comparative studies that were developed on the lee side of these two processes by analytically separating studies that focus on health policy actors and political institutions from those concentrating on the organizational structure of health-care systems (Marmor & Wendt, 2012). Second, we separated studies with a focus on the consequences from those without. In principle, all four areas of research are related, and we want to understand the values and constellations of actors and political institutions that contributed to certain institutional arrangements in health-care financing and provision that, in turn, contribute to a high quality of treatment in the case of sickness. However, for reasons of clarity, reduced complexity, and precision of measurement, it is often advisable to separate the different steps, and by doing so we arrived at the following areas of research in comparative health policy (Marmor & Wendt, 2012): (1) health policy actors and institutions, (2) health policy actors and institutions and their consequences, (3) health-care systems, and (4) health-care systems and outcomes.

Health Policy Actors and Institutions

One of the main works of reference in this field is still Ellen Immergut's (1992) seminal study *Health Politics: Interests and Institutions in Western Europe*, in which she compares veto positions with relevance for health policymaking in Germany, France, and Switzerland. She concludes that veto groups such as doctor associations are powerful but not all-powerful, and that in certain situations it is the constellation of the institutional veto position, such as a two-chamber system or direct voting, that makes the difference. Following this line of argument, Steinmo and Watts (1995) accentuate 'It's the Institutions, Stupid!' and argue that the particular institutional constellations of the United States political systems make large-scale health reforms almost impossible (see also Marmor & Wendt, 2011).

Comparative studies that seek to answer the question of how political insti-tutions and health policy actors are organized, and how they influence health reform processes and the development of health-care systems have to face the difficulty that there are no comparative datasets that cover such information. Health statistics such as the Organisation for Economic Co-operation and Development (OECD) Health Data or the World Health Organization (WHO)

Health for All database (see below) provide information about the number of health-care resources but not about the strength of health policy actors. The SOFI dataset that is used for welfare state comparison also provides some information on health care, or better health policy, but mainly regarding social rights. The new volume by Immergut et al. (2021) includes the Health Politics in Europe dataset, which will help analyse the influence of actor constellations on health reform processes (accessible through health reform tables in Immergut et al., 2021).

Since the 2000s, the main focus in the field of actors and institutions has been on health governance. Moran's (1999) book *Governing the Health Care State: A Comparative Study of the United Kingdom, the United States and Germany* can be seen as a starting point for this in comparative health politics research. He distinguishes health-care politics on the basis of three dimensions: 'consumption' captures patients' access to health care and the allocation of financial resources, 'provision' describes the control and regulation of hospitals and medical doctors, and 'production' includes medical innovation. On the basis of these dimensions, Moran (1999) identifies four types of health-care politics: the 'supply state' (e.g., the United States), with provider interests dominating in all three dimensions; the 'corporatist health-care state' (e.g., Germany, France), with public law bodies and doctors' associations being most powerful; the 'entrenched command-and-control state' (e.g., Nordic countries, Great Britain), with the state being dominant in all three areas; and the 'insecure command-and-control state' (e.g., Greece, Portugal), with the state being formally responsible but lacking administrative capacities (for further studies in this field, see Blank et al., 2017).

This concept has been further developed by Rothgang et al. (2010), who analyse the role of actors in health-care financing, provision, and regulation, distinguishing between state, private for-profit, and private non-profit actors. By combining these three types of actors with financing, provision, and regulation, they arrive at 27 types of health-care politics, three of which are ideal types: (1) a 'state health-care system', with the state being dominant in all dimensions; (2) a 'societal health-care system', with societal actors such as social health insurance being dominant in all dimensions; and (3) a 'private health-care system', in which private for-profit actors are key in regulation, financing, and health-care provision. At first glance, this is similar to the often quoted OECD typology of 1987 with a 'national health service', a 'social insurance', and a 'private insurance' model. The Rothgang et al. (2010) typology, however, also allows for classifying health-care systems that are not ideal types. Furthermore, it shows that in Germany, financing and regulation is dominated by corporatist actors (with a growing role of state and private for-profit actors), while health-care service is to a great extent provided in a private for-profit context. In most social health insurance systems in Central and

Eastern Europe, only financing is in the hands of corporate (or societal) actors and the state is still of great importance in regulation and service provision.

Using this conceptual framework, Böhm et al. (2013) identify six types of health-care politics in OECD countries: 'national health service', 'national health insurance', 'social health insurance', 'private health insurance', 'private health system', and 'etatist social health insurance'. Furthermore, Frisina et al. (2021) extend the actor-centred typology by analysing the role of state, societal, market, and global actors in key areas of the health-care system. In principle, therefore, the actor-centred approach can be used for health-care system comparison not only in OECD countries but also in the Global South.

Health Policy Actors and Institutions and Their Consequences

Different actor constellations in the health-care arena have different conse-quences, for instance, for health reform processes and the institutionalization of health-care systems, for the coordination of health-care systems with other fields of social policy, for the level and quality of health-care provision and the financial burden for those in need of health care, and for health and health inequalities. Again, we only refer to a few selected studies in this field (for an overview, see Marmor & Wendt, 2011; Kuhlmann et al., 2015; Blank et al., 2017; Hurrelmann et al., 2019).

Immergut et al.'s (2021) book on health politics in Europe, for instance, goes beyond her former focus on veto positions and asks to what extent and in which way certain actor constellations have contributed to health reform processes. It shows that, in Europe, different paths have resulted in universal health care and at the same time to highly diverse patterns of the public–private mix in the financing and delivery of health care. These patterns, such as private out-of-pocket payments, in turn, affect patients' access to health care and quality of services (for another actor-centred approach to health policy change, see Hassenteufel et al., 2010; for an analysis of partisan politics for health-care provision, see Montanari & Nelson, 2012). These comparative studies seek to understand the influence of actors on health-care systems, which implicitly is also the focus of the work by Moran (1999), Rothgang et al. (2010), and Böhm et al. (2013) discussed above. The labels, for instance the six types suggested by Böhm et al. (2013), stand for European health-care systems that are charac-terized by certain actor constellations. To understand how these actor-centred types influence the level and quality of health-care services, further indicators need to be included (see 'Health-Care Systems' section).

Another field of research brings us back to the question of governance (see Kuhlmann et al., 2015; Hurrelmann et al., 2019) but this time in combination with outputs, or better outcomes, such as access to health care, health, and health inequalities. To better understand how to respond to health inequalities,

Kuhlmann et al. (2015) suggest connecting governance and policy approaches and considering local as well as global roadmaps for reform. Hurrelmann et al. (2019) argue that patient-centred care, in particular in times of heavy demographic change, requires not only effective governance but also multi-professional health-care centres that enhance the coordination and cooperation of health-care providers. While governance mechanisms are often at hand, it requires the political will of actors at different political levels to implement such structural changes including public health measures for improving individual and population health and reducing health inequalities (see also Bambra, 2019; Besnier & Eikemo, 2019; Kickbusch & Liu, 2019).

Many comparative studies have repeatedly shown that socio-economic and behavioural factors such as income, education, work, nutrition, physical activity, and alcohol, tobacco, and substance abuse (Mackenbach et al., 2008; Bambra et al., 2010; Stringhini et al., 2017) have a high impact on health and health inequalities and that the welfare state (including health care) seems to have a low impact (Eikemo et al., 2008; Rydland et al., 2020). Neither the institution of health-care provision (see 'Health-Care Systems' section) nor the institutional context of the welfare state seem to be of major importance to health or health inequalities. Such empirical results, however, are questioned in new theoretical, methodological, and empirical studies. Beckfield et al. (2015) see the distribution of social determinants of health as a function of the institutional context such as collective bargaining, the welfare state, housing, health care, and education. Referring to institutional theory, they identify mechanisms (redistribution, compression, mediation, and imbrication) that produce and modify the effects of social determinants of health. Analysing potential interventions, Bambra et al. (2010) consider improvements in housing and the work environment effective in reducing health inequalities and improving the health of disadvantaged groups. Gkiouleka et al. (2018) emphasize the importance of intersectionality as an analytical tool for under-standing health inequalities. Layers of privilege and disadvantage such as ethnicity, gender, and sexuality, which in turn are institutionally bounded, are seen as central to the production of health inequalities. From this perspective, equal access to health care has not only direct but also indirect effects on the reduction of health inequalities by improving the situation of disadvantaged groups in our societies.

An attempt to directly measure institutional effects on health is made by Mackenbach and McKee (2015), who use more than 30 government and health policy indicators and potential confounders for 30 European countries from 1990 to 2010. The study shows that, in particular, the measures of quality, of democracy and of government are positively associated with health policy as well as with health indicators. Results regarding the distribution of power and political representation are more mixed with the share of women in parliament, which is particularly high in Nordic countries, having a strong positive effect on health policy and on health indicators. Regarding the health policy indicators, it has to be noted that government and other political indicators seem to be more associated with public health than with health-care system indicators. These findings replicate and specify the results by Immergut (1992) that interest groups and political power are important but not all-important and that the institutional design of democracy and the quality of government makes the difference in access to health care, individual and population health, and quality of life.

Health-care Systems

Comparative health-care system research, in the past 20 years, has approximated comparative welfare state research more generally. As with other fields of social policy, health care is included in the SPIN dataset (www.spin.su.se), which mainly covers social rights. While coverage and financial security in the case of sickness are important social rights, they only comprise a very narrow part of the overall health-care system. The role of health professions, health care and social services, and a respective health-care infrastructure is much more important than professions, services, and infrastructures are in other fields of social policy. Despite these restrictions, there have been attempts to transfer methods and indicators, in particular related to the concept of decommodification (Esping-Andersen, 1990), to health care. Bambra (2005) developed an index of 'health decommodification' to measure to what extent the provision of health care depends on the market and used the indicators of 'private financing', 'private provision', and 'private coverage'.

Since the 2000s, comparative studies on health-care systems have shared the goal to better characterize health-care systems and provide information not only about financing and health-care providers but also about the institutional structure. The OECD Health Database (https://stats.oecd.org) and the European Health for All database (https://gateway.euro.who.int/en/datasets/european -health-for-all-database) provide comparative data for an increasing number of countries. However, comparative institutional data on the organization of health care are still difficult to obtain. With its Health System in Transition (HiT) series, the European Observatory of Health Systems and Policies provides country studies that include information on the historical development, health reforms, and current institutional structure of European health-care systems and beyond. Using data from the HiT series and the MISSOC database (www.missoc.org), Reibling (2010) analyses – in line with Esping-Andersen's decommodification index – the institutional design of health-care systems with access to health care as the main institutional dimension. Wendt's (2009) approach to map European health-care systems focuses more on the central dimension of 'financing', 'provision', and 'regulation', but in contrast to Moran (1999) and Rothgang et al. (2010), not with an actor-centred concept but with the aim to unfold the institutional structures of developed health-care systems. Wendt (2009, 2014) and Reibling (2010) marked the beginning of the construction of health-care system typologies to better understand similarities and differences of developed health-care systems and as a tool for studying health-care system effects regarding patients' satisfaction, the take-up of health-care services, and population health (for an overview, see Burau et al., 2015; Toth, 2016; Wendt & Bambra, 2021).

Reibling et al. (2019) use the dimensions 'supply', 'public–private mix', 'access regulation', 'primary care orientation', and 'performance' to capture not only 'financing', 'service provision', and 'regulation' but also indicators of the quality of health-care provision. Furthermore, comparative studies, for instance, those by Starfield et al. (2005) and Groenewegen et al. (2013), demonstrate the importance of primary care for increasing efficiency, equity, and quality in health care, and Reibling et al. (2019) therefore include primary care indicators in the typology. On the basis of these dimensions, they identify five types of health-care systems: (1) a 'supply-and-choice-oriented public type' (e.g., Austria, Germany, France), with a medium to high level of financing (in particular public financing), a high level of health-care providers, extensive patient choice and access to providers, and low primary care orientation; (2) a 'supply-and-performance-oriented private type' (United States and Switzerland), characterized by high supply (in particular high levels of financing and a high share of private funding), low general access regulation but with access and choice being restricted in accordance with a respective private insurance plan; (3) a 'performance-and-primary-care-oriented public type' (e.g., Finland, Norway, Sweden), with a medium level of financial and personnel resources, high public funding, strong primary care orientation, and access to specialists and patient choice being regulated by gatekeeping systems and through further institutional regulations; (4) a 'regulation-oriented public type' (e.g., Canada, Denmark, United Kingdom), like the former type with a medium level of financial and personnel resources, in particular from public funding, the highest regulation of patients' access to care and limited provider choice, but eased availability of services through very low private out-of-pocket payment, and strong primary care orientation; and (5) a 'low-supply-and-low-performance mixed type' (e.g., Hungary, Poland), with both financial resources and numbers of health-care providers being low, health-care systems being financed by a high share of public funding but combined with a particularly high level of out-of-pocket payment, increasing inequity of care, and primary care orientation and performance being weak.

The findings suggest that the dividing line, mainly based on the principle of financing, between social insurance and national health service is of little relevance to the classification of health-care systems, and that other dimensions such as access regulation and primary care orientation are of much greater importance. The three largest system types identified by Reibling et al. (2019) comprise both social insurance and national health service countries. Health policy reforms of the past decades may have fractured old institutional logics and may have contributed to a hybridization of health-care systems (see also Rothgang et al., 2010; Immergut et al., 2021). Other classifications, e.g., by Ferreira et al. (2018), include additional indicators on health-care provision and performance such as 'hospital discharges' and suggest using such information to better understand differences in health-care systems concerning social inequalities and health outcomes.

Health-care Systems and Outcomes

Beckfield and Krieger's (2009) review of 45 studies on health inequities published from 1992 to 2008 shows that there was little collaboration between researchers studying health outcomes and those studying health-care systems. Only nine of these studies analysed the effects of health-care systems, and none of them was comparative. This research gap has been reduced over the past decade, in part related to new classifications of health-care systems (see 'Health-Care Systems' section), advanced methods to combine macro- and micro-level research, and better comparative data on health and health inequalities.

In the following, we refer to three types of comparative studies that analyse the consequences of different health-care systems: first, studies on public perception and patients' satisfaction with the health-care system; second, analyses of access to care and the utilization of health-care services; and third, the assessment of the link between health-care systems and health.

Most studies on public opinion have revealed a high level of public support and satisfaction with European health-care systems (Mossialos, 1998; Gelissen, 2002; Wendt et al., 2011). Satisfaction with the health-care system depends to a higher extent on the institutional context and personal experiences than the support of a strong role of the state in health care (Missinne et al., 2013). When analysing the macrocontext, the level of public expenditure as well as the amount of private out-of-pocket payments are positively related to a high public support for a strong role of the state and negatively with privatization processes in health care (Wendt et al., 2010, 2011). High public health expenditure, furthermore, has a positive effect on satisfaction with the overall health-care system. Gatekeeping and access regulation, in contrast, does not reduce satisfaction with the health-care system. A strong primary care orientation and the time health-care providers spend with their patients leads to a positive evaluation of the health-care system.

Public opinion data do not only show how health-care systems are perceived and evaluated but also reflect norms and values such as solidarity institutionalized in health-care systems (Immergut & Schneider, 2020). Burlacu and Roescu (2021) find the highest levels of solidarity in low-performing as well as in universal and generous health-care systems. But in contrast to the latter, low-performing health-care systems result in lower satisfaction. Immergut and Schneider (2020), furthermore, find that those exposed to inequality in health care are also more likely to accept inequality, which indicates that the institutional framework has an influence on the acceptance of inequalities within the health-care system and potentially also on the willingness to pay for redistribution.

Regarding access to health care, health-care systems with a stronger access regulation have been shown to have higher equality regarding health-care utilization of income and educational groups (Van Doorslaer et al., 2006; Reibling & Wendt, 2011). Strong gatekeeping, as in Denmark, reduces overall health utilization and increases equality in the take-up of health-care services but does not affect satisfaction with the health-care system (Wendt et al., 2011). Furthermore, Terraneo (2015) finds that, in health-care systems with higher health expenditure, higher-educated patients reduce specialist out-patient care and increase GP care. He suggests as a possible explanation that higher resources and a stronger primary care orientation increase quality in this sector and thus also confidence in primary health care, particularly among higher-educated groups. Focusing on migrants, O'Donnell et al. (2016) suggest that politics and policy effects have to be considered when analysing consequences for marginalized groups. They identify health-care system effects and find that strong primary care systems are key for improving migrants' access to health care. At the same time, changes in government are of greater importance to migrant health care than to other population groups.

There are also studies available that analyse the relationship between health-care systems and health. Schneider et al. (2021) consider access to health care as the main mediator of health-care system effects on health and health inequalities. They identify, for instance, that inequalities in self-rated health are significantly related to education and that this relationship is modified by the respective health-care system to a certain extent. Rydland et al. (2020) measured educational inequalities in mortality amenable to health care. Using the health-care system types introduced by Reibling et al. (2019), they conclude that high supply with a strong orientation towards primary health care and prevention is ideally suited for reducing health inequalities. Low supply and low performance systems, on the other hand, showed the largest relative and absolute health inequalities (Rydland et al., 2020).

Welfare state and health-care system typologies have also been used to analyse country responses to COVID-19, and Greener (2021) suggests that welfare state typologies are better suited for unfolding effective COVID-19 responses than health-care system typologies. The COVID-19 crisis has also shown that information on health-care supply is not sufficient to assess how well a health-care system protects its population in a severe health crisis. Denmark, for instance, has one of the lowest densities of hospital beds among the developed countries worldwide (OECD health data; https://stats.oecd.org) and also a particularly low level of intensive care beds (Rhodes et al., 2012). Instead of being overburdened, however, Danish health policy responded with effective regulation, preventive health care, digital health care, and effective public health governance.

FUTURE DIRECTIONS IN HEALTH-CARE SYSTEM RESEARCH

As a response to the health crisis, there will be huge investments both in health-care systems and in health-care system research in the next decades. Resources, however, in particular, available health-care providers, will not be sufficient to cope with the approaching health crisis related to demographic change, of which the COVID-19 crisis might be considered a precursor. Without institutional change, we expect that the current level and quality of health-care provision cannot be maintained. Institutional change to overcome the problem of providing good-quality care in periods of increasing demand and fiscal constraints requires comparative research and the possibility and willingness to learn from other countries' experiences, preferably best prac-tice experiences. Comparative health policy research has demonstrated that health-care supply, in particular primary health care and prevention, as well as governance measures that regulate patients' access to health-care services are key for outcomes such as equity in health care. However, this field of research should be improved with data capturing the quality of care as well as innova-tive methods that help identify what factors modify health-care system effects on health outcomes. Such research will require building up an international database with comparative institutional data to amend quantitative data from the OECD and WHO. Such information should also include, for instance, the structure and intensity of collaboration between health-care providers within primary care centres and other units of health-care delivery with more efficient management and collaboration than is possible in single-handed practices and other small-sized units. A new direction in comparative health-care system research is therefore to identify health-care systems with high-quality health care under conditions of low supply of health-care providers and, later, also of financial resources.

Collaboration is essential and needs to be studied and improved not only within the health-care system but also between health-care institutions and other welfare institutions. Health and health inequalities are influenced by a number of macro- and micro-level factors. Many of these factors do not only potentially protect health but, as work conditions and related stress, can also harm health. Research is needed to better understand how institutions in the areas of health care, employment, unemployment insurance, family policy, education, and other fields work together to protect and improve people's health. A central starting point for such research is the question whether institutions that take care of people's health are guided by consistent ideas and values or by different and competing ideas. Privatization processes and competition could result in lower collaboration and sharing of necessary information, which often has negative implications for health-care provision and health. Institutions that have proven essential during the COVID-19 crisis are education and long-term care. There is a critical need to study how these institutions are related to health-care and public health systems and how they can contribute to improving public and individual health and reducing health inequalities. Besides governance to enhance cooperation, better knowledge and health literacy is required to achieve better health. This might have the side effect of higher health inequalities, and good institutions are needed to achieve equal access to health care and to information relevant to health behaviour and health. Therefore, another new direction in health-care system research is to analyse how health-care systems can collaborate with other institutions to achieve better health outcomes.

Today, most health-care systems concentrate on individual health. The COVID-19 crisis has demonstrated that individual health and public health are closely related. Public health measures with regulations that in part restrict individual freedom have been introduced to not overburden the health-care system. Health-care systems, in turn, have contributed to a great extent to public health measures, not only through vaccination programmes but also by implementing further preventive health measures. In the future, limited resources for health-care supply, in particular of health-care providers, will require better population health. To achieve this aim, health-care systems need to increasingly implement public health measures (Lundberg et al., 2008), for instance based on health targets suggested by the WHO (www.euro.who.int/en/publications/abstracts/health21-the-health-for-all-policy-framework-for-the-who-european-region) and the United Nations Sustainable Development Goals (www.who.int/health-topics/sustainable-development-goals) and closely cooperate with public health institutions. Therefore, comparative studies that analyse health-care systems and public health systems, how they are related, and in what respect they contribute to public and individual health will presumably become a further important path of health-care system research.

Comparative studies have continuously emphasized the importance of collaboration in prevention and health-care provision. Health-care provision has experienced continuing specialization, which requires collaboration and makes it more difficult at the same time. There are three ways to improve collaboration in highly specialized health and welfare institutions. First, the implementation of larger units of health-care delivery; second, the set-up of actors and organizations with the task of coordinating specialized services in health care, long-term care, public health, and further areas; and third, digitalization in health care, welfare, and public health institutions. Especially the latter process requires innovative comparative research. Improvements in digitalization such as electronic medical records facilitate the real-time provision of necessary information, for instance in cases of emergency and exchange of information between involved health-care providers. The sharing of information also reduces unnecessary examinations, which in some cases, such as X-rays, may harm patients' health. Furthermore, digitalization and patients' access to their medical records might have positive effects on their health literacy and health behaviour. Digitalization processes in health care and public health and their effects on health behaviour, health, and health inequalities are therefore another important future direction of comparative health-care system research.

REFERENCES

Bambra, C. (2005). Cash versus services: 'Worlds of welfare' and the decommodification of cash benefits and health care services. *Journal of Social Policy, 34*(2), 195–213.

Bambra, C. (2019). Governing health inequalities. In K. Hurrelmann, M. Shaikh, & C. Wendt (Eds), (2019). *The Governance Report 2019: Health Governance* (pp. 51–66). Oxford University Press.

Bambra, C., Gibson, M., Sowden, A., Wright, K., Whitehead, M., & Petticrew, M. (2010). Tackling the wider social determinants of health and health inequalities: evidence from systematic reviews. *Journal of Epidemiology and Community Health, 64*(4), 284–291.

Beckfield, J., & Krieger, N. (2009). Epi + demos + cracy: Linking political systems and priorities to the magnitude of health inequities – evidence, gaps, and a research agenda. *Epidemiologic Reviews, 31*, 152–177.

Beckfield, J., Bambra, C., Eikemo, T., Huijts, T., & Wendt, C. (2015). A theory of welfare state effects on the distribution of population health. *Social Theory and Health, 13*, 227–244.

Besnier, E., & Eikemo, T. A. (2019). Health and well-being worldwide. In K. Hurrelmann, M. Shaikh, & C. Wendt (Eds), (2019). *The Governance Report 2019: Health Governance* (pp. 27–50). Oxford University Press.

Blank, R. H., Burau, V., & Kuhlmann, E. (2017). *Comparative Health Policy* (5th edn). London: Red Globe Press.

Böhm, K., Schmid, A., Götze, R., Landwehr, C., & Rothgang, H. (2013). Five types of OECD healthcare systems: Empirical results of a deductive classification. *Health Policy, 113*(3), 258–269.

Burau, V., Blank, R. H., & Pavolini, E. (2015). Typologies of health care systems and policies. In E. Kuhlmann, R. H. Blank, I. Bourgeault, & C. Wendt (Eds), *The Palgrave International Handbook of Health Care Policy and Governance* (pp. 101–115). Palgrave.

Burlacu, D., & Roescu, A. (2021). Public opinion and healthcare. In E. M. Immergut, K. Anderson, C. Devitt, & T. Popic (Eds), *Health Politics in Europe: A Handbook* (pp. 49–68). Oxford University Press.

Eikemo, T. A., Bambra, C., Judge, K., & Ringdal, K. (2008). Welfare state regimes and differences in self-perceived health in Europe: A multilevel analysis, *Social Science and Medicine*, *66*, 2281–2295.

Esping-Andersen, G. (1990). *The Three Worlds of Welfare Capitalism*. Polity Press.

Ferreira, P. L., Tavares, I. A., Quintal, C., & Santana, P. (2018). EU health systems classification: A new proposal from EURO-HEALTHY. *BMC Health Services Research*, *18*, 511.

Frisina Doetter, L., Schmid, A., Carvalho, G., & Rothgang, H. (2021). Comparing apples to oranges? Minimizing typological biases to better classify healthcare systems globally. *Health Policy OPEN*, *2*.

Gelissen J. (2002). *Worlds of Welfare, Worlds of Consent? Public Opinion on the Welfare State*. Brill.

Gkiouleka, A., Huijts, T., Beckfield, J., & Bambra, C. (2018). Understanding the micro and macro politics of health: Inequalities, intersectionality and institutions – a research agenda. *Social Science and Medicine*, *200*, 92–98.

Greener, I. (2021). Comparing country risk and response to COVID-19 in the first 6 months across 25 Organisation for Economic Co-operation and Development countries using qualitative comparative analysis. *Journal of International and Comparative Social Policy*, *37*(3), 211–225.

Groenewegen, P. P., Dourgnon, P., Gress, S., Jurgutis, A., & Willems, S. (2013). Strengthening weak primary care systems: Steps towards stronger primary care in selected Western and Eastern European countries. *Health Policy*, *113*(1–2), 170–179.

Ham, C. (1999). *Health Policy in Britain: The Politics and Organisation of the National Health Service* (4th edn). Palgrave.

Hassenteufel, P., Smyrl, M., Genieys, W., & Moreno-Fuentes, F. J. (2010). Programmatic actors and the transformation of European health care states. *Journal of Health Politics, Policy and Law*, *35*, 517–538.

Hurrelmann, K., Shaikh, M., & Wendt, C. (Eds). (2019). *The Governance Report 2019: Health Governance*. Oxford University Press.

Immergut, E. M. (1992). *Health Politics: Interests and Institutions in Western Europe*. Cambridge University Press.

Immergut, E. M., & Schneider, S. M. (2020). Is it unfair for the affluent to be able to purchase 'better' healthcare? Existential standards and institutional norms in health-care attitudes across 28 countries. *Social Science and Medicine*, *267*.

Immergut, E. M., Anderson, K., Devitt, C., & Popic, T. (Eds). (2021). *Health Politics in Europe: A Handbook*. Oxford University Press.

Kickbusch, I., & Liu, A. (2019). Global health governance. In K. Hurrelmann, M. Shaikh, & C. Wendt (Eds), *The Governance Report 2019: Health Governance* (pp. 83–101). Oxford University Press.

Klein, R. (1992). *The Politics of the NHS*. Longman Group.

Kuhlmann, E., Blank, R. H., Bourgeault, I. L., & Wendt, C. (Eds). (2015). *The Palgrave International Handbook of Healthcare Policy and Governance*. Palgrave Macmillan.

Lundberg, O., Kölegård Stjärne, M., Elstad, J. I., Ferrarini, T., Kangas, O., Norström, T., Palme, J., Fritzell, J., & NEWS Nordic Expert Group. (2008). The role of welfare state principles and generosity in social policy programmes for public health: An international comparative study. *The Lancet*, *372*(9650), 1633–1640.

Mackenbach, J. P., & McKee, M. (2015). Government, politics and health policy: A quantitative analysis of 30 European countries. *Health Policy*, *119*(10), 1298–1308.

Mackenbach, J. P., Stirbu, I., Roskam, A.-J. R., Schaap, M. M., Menvielle, G., Leinsalu, M., & Kunst, A. E., for the European Union Working Group on Socioeconomic Inequalities in Health. (2008). Socioeconomic inequalities in health in 22 European countries. *New England Journal of Medicine*, 358, 2468–2481.

Marmor, T. R., & Wendt, C. (Eds). (2011). *Reforming Healthcare Systems* (2 Vols). London: Edward Elgar Publishing.

Marmor, T. R., & Wendt, C. (2012). Conceptual frameworks for comparing healthcare politics and policy. *Health Policy*, *107*(1), 11–20.

Missinne, S., Meuleman, B., & Bracke, P. (2013). The popular legitimacy of European healthcare systems: A multilevel analysis of 24 countries. *Journal of European Social Policy*, *23*(3), 231–247.

Montanari, I., & Nelson, K. (2012). Social service decline and convergence: How does healthcare fare? *Journal of European Social Policy*, *23*(1), 102–116.

Moran, M. (1999). *Governing the Health Care State: A Comparative Study of the United Kingdom, the United States and Germany*. Manchester University Press.

Mossialos E. (1998). Citizens' views on health care systems in the 15 member states of the European Union. *Health Economics*, *6*, 109–116.

O'Donnell, C. A., Burns, N., Mair, F. S., Dowrick, C., Clissmann, C., Muijsenbergh, M. d., Weel-Baumgarten, E. v., Lionis, C., Papadakaki, M., Saridaki, A., Brun, T. d., & Mac Farlane, A., on behalf of the RESTORE Team. (2016). Reducing the health care burden for marginalised migrants: The potential role for primary care in Europe. *Health Policy*, *120*(5), 495–508.

Reibling, N. (2010). Healthcare systems in Europe: Towards an incorporation of patient access. *Journal of European Social Policy*, *20*(1), 5–18.

Reibling, N., & Wendt C. (2011). Regulating patients' access to healthcare services. *International Journal of Public and Private Healthcare Management and Economics*, *1*, 1–16.

Reibling, N., Ariaans, M., & Wendt, C. (2019). Worlds of healthcare: A healthcare system typology of OECD countries. *Health Policy*, *123*(7), 611–620.

Rhodes, A., Ferdinande, P., Flaatten, H., Guidet, B., Metnitz, P. G., & Moreno, R. P. (2012). The variability of critical care bed numbers in Europe. *Intensive Care Medicine*, *38*, 1647–1653.

Rothgang, H., Cacace, M., Frisina, L., Grimmeisen, S., Schmid, A., & Wendt, C. (2010). *The State and Healthcare: Comparing OECD Countries*. Palgrave Macmillan.

Rydland, H. T., Fjær, E. L., Eikemo, T. A., Huijts, T., Bambra, C., Wendt, C., Kulhánová, I., Martikainen, P., Dibben, C., Kalėdienė, R., Borrell, C., Leinsalu, M., Bopp, M., & Mackenbach, J. P. (2020). Educational inequalities in mortality amenable to healthcare. A comparison of European healthcare systems. *PLoS ONE*, *15*(7), e0234135.

Schneider, S. M., Roots, A., & Rathmann, K. (2021). Health outcomes and health inequalities. In E. M. Immergut, K. Anderson, C. Devitt, & T. Popic (Eds), *Health Politics in Europe: A Handbook* (pp. 32–48). Oxford University Press.

Starfield, B., Shi, L., & Macinko, J. (2005). Contribution of primary care to health systems and health, *Milbank Quarterly*, *83*(3), 457–502.

Steinmo, S., & Watts, J. (1995). It's the institutions, stupid! Why comprehensive national health insurance always fails in America. *Journal of Health Politics, Policy and Law, 20*, 329–372.

Stringhini, S., Carmeli, C., Jokela, M., Avendaño, M., Muennig, P., Guida, F. et al. (2017). Socioeconomic status and the 25 × 25 risk factors as determinants of premature mortality: A multicohort study and meta-analysis of 1.7 million men and women. *The Lancet, 389*(10075), 1229–1237.

Terraneo, M. (2015). Inequities in health care utilization by people aged 50+: Evidence from 12 European countries. *Social Science and Medicine, 126*, 154–163.

Toth, F. (2016). Classification of health care systems: Can we go further? *Health Policy, 120*(5), 535–543.

Van Doorslaer, E., Masseria, C., & Koolman, X. (2006). Inequalities in access to medical care by income in developed countries. *Canadian Medical Association Journal, 174*, 177–183.

Wendt, C. (2009). Mapping European healthcare systems: A comparative analysis of financing, service provision, and access to healthcare. *Journal of European Social Policy, 19*(5), 432–445.

Wendt, C. (2014). Changing healthcare system types. *Social Policy and Administration, 48*(7), 864–888.

Wendt, C., & Bambra, C. (2021). From ideal types to healthcare system typologies: Dimensions, labels, and country classifications. In C. Aspalter (Ed.), *Ideal Types in Comparative Social Policy* (pp. 169–186). Routledge.

Wendt, C., Kohl, J., Mischke, M., & Pfeifer, M. (2010). How do Europeans perceive their healthcare system? Patterns of satisfaction and preference for state involvement in the field of healthcare. *European Sociological Review, 26*(2), 177–192.

Wendt, C., Mischke, M., & Pfeifer, M. (2011). *Welfare States and Public Opinion: Perceptions of Healthcare Systems, Family Policy and Benefits for the Unemployed and Poor in Europe*. Edward Elgar Publishing.

5. Long-term developments in housing policy and research

Caroline Dewilde and Marietta Haffner

INTRODUCTION

The nature of housing as a service (fulfilling basic needs) and a capital-intensive commodity (houses and the 'underlying' land have exchange value) hampers comparative understandings of 'housing policy', and its relation to social policy research. On the one hand, housing is a pillar of social policy, addressing social problems in the urban slums under early industrial capitalism (Fahey & Norris, 2011). Housing was provided mainly through unregulated private renting, characterized by the extraction of 'super profits'. Following government regulation in the early years of the last century (rent control, quality standards) and in the post-war decades, the development of large-scale *social housing* programmes, as well as increasing affluence enabling *homeownership*, the *private rental sector* has shrunk more or less continuously over the course of time.

On the other hand, housing is qualified as the 'wobbly' pillar under the welfare state (Torgersen, 1987). While other social services are (re)distributed mainly by the state, the market is the main mechanism for the financing, production, and consumption of housing. Houses are built, sold, and bought on the market, while rental housing is allocated mostly via market contracts between landlords and tenants. Housing policy is hence 'unique', as 'European welfare states provide correctives to the market in order to ensure that people's social right to housing as a commodity is realized' (Bengtsson, 2001: 259).

Thus, when housing researchers define 'housing policy', they do not solely think about housing-related welfare benefits and social services. They conceptually include the market regulation of housing tenures (owning, private and social renting), even when such regulation is operationalized indirectly by referring to underlying 'housing systems/regimes' (e.g., Doling, 1997). Housing economics (analysing housing finance and development as economic sectors), fiscal policy, and monetary stabilization policy tend to be excluded by most 'non-economist' scholars. The latter fields nevertheless address an important context in which housing policy takes place. As discussed in our conclusion, the heightened integration of housing in the global economy, as well as the consequences thereof in terms of tenure restructuring, rising housing unaffordability (for 'housing market outsiders') and unequal housing wealth accumulation opportunities (for 'housing market insiders') call for an even broader integrative perspective.

The 'wobbly pillar' is by no means small: given the wide range of policy instruments targeting different tenures – fiscal support, 'implicit' subsidies such as social rents – it is virtually impossible to arrive at a conclusive measurement approach (e.g., user costs (Haffner, 2003) versus imputed rent (Verbist & Grabka, 2017)) and an estimate of public expenditure on housing. Reported trends over time mostly pertain to isolated elements. While social spending on housing-related benefits has tended to increase (compensating for declining social housing as well as 'automatic' spending related to the 2008–2009 Global Financial Crisis (GFC)) (Dewilde, 2021), the Organisation for Economic Co-operation and Development (OECD) (2021) recently approximated that public investments towards (affordable) housing development (relative to gross domestic product) declined with almost two-thirds on average across OECD countries between 2001 and 2018.

This chapter introduces the main concepts and relationships, and analyses how housing policy and scholarly understandings thereof have fared over the last two decades. Reflective of the 'division of work' in the broader field of housing studies – with most researchers specializing in policies and regulation pertaining to one tenure – we discuss substantive developments in research regarding the different tenures commonly found in European welfare states. We elaborate on the idea that what happens in one housing market sector impacts on other sectors. Furthermore, we report on recent research arguing that trends in housing policy are intricately related to changes in welfare states, but also to broader economic developments. We illustrate changes in tenure structure, intersecting with changes in the characteristics of households typically living in different tenures. Our conclusion addresses key challenges for policy and research.

HOUSING REGIMES AND TENURE STRUCTURES

The 'Esping-Andersen of housing research' is the somewhat mysterious Jim Kemeny, who wrote an evolving body of theoretical ideas (Kemeny, 1981, 1992, 1995, 2006) regarding the provision of housing, and relationships with society and the welfare state. While some stood the test of time, for instance the argument that homeownership preferences are socially constructed through ideology and policy, others were less long-lasting but nevertheless continue to inform recent debate (Stephens, 2020b). Akin to Esping-Andersen and also Varieties of Capitalism, Kemeny locates the origins of housing policy responses to the urban/social/housing question – in particular the nature of rental markets – in social structures of inequality. Specifically, countries with corporatist power structures, be they labour-led (e.g., Sweden, Denmark) or conservative (e.g., Germany, Netherlands), tend to be characterized by a *unitary rental market*. In these countries, private and not-for-profit housing providers operate in a common rental market. The competition between public and private, more strictly regulated but similarly subsidized providers, resulted in overall good-quality affordable housing and higher 'tenure neutrality': it matters less whether one rents or owns. Countries with a 'right-wing hegemonic coalition' (mostly liberal welfare states) ended up with a shielded, state-governed, social housing sector targeted at poorer households, alongside a more lightly regulated private rental sector characterized by higher rents but not necessarily higher quality – known as a *dual rental market*. Middle-income households in these countries (e.g., United Kingdom (UK), Belgium) gravitated towards the most 'rewarding' and ideologically supported tenure – homeownership.

Similar to the social division of 'welfare' along the lines of welfare regimes in social policy, in housing research the social production of 'housing welfare' is captured with the term 'housing regimes'. Following Stephens (2020a), such regimes arise from the interplay between the spheres of *production* (housing supply – analogous to labour *markets* in welfare regimes), *consumption* (mediated by tenure structures – analogous to the *distributional outcomes* of welfare states), and *exchange* (housing finance, e.g., debt-financed homeownership). Family support for housing or historically grown owner or renter cooperatives pertain to *civil society*. Housing regimes are concretized in policies and regulations ('housing systems') associated with different tenures. Precise meanings and qualities of concepts such as 'homeownership' or 'social renting' vary across institutional contexts, as do interrelationships between housing tenures (e.g., Dewilde, 2017).

Given the historical lack of comparative housing indicators and the focus in housing research on in-depth case studies, empirical applications of the housing regimes concept are more recently compared with the army of scholars that have engaged with Esping-Andersen's welfare regime typology. Though the limitations are similar, housing regimes help to make sense of cross-national variations pertaining to outcomes, such as young adults' transition to homeownership (Lersch & Dewilde, 2015); housing and financial wealth accumulation (Wind et al., 2017; Wind & Dewilde, 2019); housing conditions (Mandic & Cirman, 2012; Borg, 2015; Soaita & Dewilde, 2019); and welfare attitudes and political behaviour (Ansell, 2014; André & Dewilde, 2016; André et al., 2017). Though social surveys remain threadbare when it comes to housing indicators, socio-economic surveys such as European Union

Statistics on Income and Living Conditions (EUROSTAT) and the Household Finance and Consumption Survey (European Central Bank) are popular data sources informing comparative micro-level research. Given the heightened prominence of housing for the 'wealth of households and nations' following its incorporation in global capital and the ensuing GFC, OECD started to build macro-level data structures, e.g., the Affordable Housing Database and the Housing Policy Toolkit.

As we refer to commonly used housing regimes to present some empirical patterns later on, we briefly discuss them here. In Northern and Western Europe, mortgage markets are well developed, resulting in a marketized provision of debt-financed homeownership. Countries with unitary and dual rental markets are distinguished. In Southern Europe, the driving force behind a rapid transformation from 'private renting' to (outright) 'owning' during the post-war period was the absence of government support for rental housing. Gaps in housing provision were solved within extended families by older generations providing housing support to younger adults in return for assistance in old age (Allen et al., 2004). 'Informal' routes to self-provisioned homeownership were sustained by weak land use and building standard regulations until the 1980s (Cabré Pla & Módenes Cabrerizo, 2004; Poggio, 2011). Although in recent decades, mortgage credit has become more accessible, strong house price inflation combined with strict maximum loan-to-value ratios. There are few alternatives to homeownership. In Eastern Europe, the transition from planned to free-market economies brought extensive privatization of state-owned housing, including the restitution of property to pre-communist owners. As mortgage markets did not develop at the same pace, the family stepped in (Stephens et al., 2015). Housing shortages prevent young people from establishing independent households; units are redistributed within extended families (Zavisca & Gerber, 2017). Although outright homeownership is very high, the housing stock is of low quality (Mandic, 2010). In the Baltics, urban overcrowding typical for Soviet-style state-provided 'mass' housing combined with increased economic affluence and labour migration to produce better-than-expected housing conditions (Soaita & Dewilde, 2019).

HOW HAVE HOUSING REGIMES CHANGED IN PREVIOUS DECADES?

The recent rise of quantitative-deductive comparative research focusing on housing-related outcomes has spurred on a new wave of more in-depth institutionalist research investigating the thornier theoretical issue of housing regime change as both driver and outcome of welfare regime change. Ideas regarding such change resonate with the welfare reform literature in the wider social policy field (for a recent review, see Dewilde, 2020a). External pressures (mainly globalization resulting in labour market flexibilization) and demographic change challenge the viability of welfare states. Concepts such as 'dualization' (Rueda, 2014), or 'precariousness' (Kalleberg, 2018) not only refer to a growing divide between labour market 'insiders' and 'outsiders' (those in precarious work or unemployed), but also to larger welfare gaps arising from the erosion of social insurance for the latter groups (Palier & Thelen, 2010). The nature of such 'dualization' plays out differently across institutional contexts, depending on social policy design (i.e., the importance of contributory schemes), the relative balance of power (i.e., whether social policy reform is 'voted' in the political arena rather than 'negotiated' through collective bargaining), and the nature of collective bargaining (centralized or not, 'labour-led' versus 'conservative'/segmented) (Dewilde, 2020a). Such a political-economy perspective moves the focus from what goes on in welfare states to the relationship between welfare state restructuring and trends in labour markets. As we will discuss later, *analogies can be drawn when studying dynamic relationships between social policy and housing policy*. To this end, we first discuss how tenure structures have changed over the last decades.

WHAT HAPPENED TO TENURE STRUCTURES?

Social Housing

Blackwell and Bengtsson (2021: 2–3) define social rental housing as 'not-for-profit good-quality housing that is aimed at meeting housing needs and offers security of tenure'. They evaluate changes over time for three countries – Sweden, the UK, and Denmark. The trends discussed are, however, of wider relevance. Over the last decades, social housing has further lost market share (Stephens et al., 2008). Reductions were achieved by Right-to-Buy programmes (UK, starting in the 1970s) (Forrest & Murie, 1988) or by the 'privatization' of not-for-profit housing (Germany; Kofner, 2017). Recent declines have been spurred on by the sale of social housing to equity funds and institutional investors (Wijburg & Aalbers, 2017). Within the sector, there have been tendencies towards declining security of tenure, the introduction of market-linked 'affordable' (rather than 'social'/cost) rents and business-like principles such as the generation of surpluses. Commodification has been reinforced by an increasing reliance on non-government finance, as in the UK and the Netherlands (Aalbers et al., 2017).

Homeownership

Across Western Europe, homeownership expanded during the post-war decades and then stabilized, with higher rates in dual rental markets and lower rates in unitary rental markets. In Eastern Europe, 'super (outright) homeownership' was the result of mass privatization. Historically, in many countries 'private' homeownership has been supported by subsidies and favourable taxation, mostly by allowing cost deductions (e.g., mortgage interest) and exempting taxable income (e.g., capital gains) (Haffner & Winters, 2016; Fatica & Prammer, 2018). As such schemes are associated with house price increases or volatility, as well as regressive distributional outcomes (e.g., Heylen & Haffner, 2012), housing economists have repeatedly advised a more tenure-neutral taxation (OECD, 2010; European Commission, 2012). House price increases and volatility were, however, reinforced by enhanced access to debt-financed homeownership.

The so-called 'financialization' of mortgage, homeownership, and real estate markets originated from the deregulation of global capital and the creation of the European Monetary Union (Stephens, 2007; Scanlon et al., 2008). 'Financialized capitalism' as of the 1990s worked when historically low interest rates combined with the liberalization of mortgage finance (via the creation, from the United States, of a global chain of 'securitized' mortgage-related investment products), allowing more, but also lower-income, households to enter (sub-prime) homeownership (e.g., Bratt, 2012). When, however, house prices started declining in the United States, the collapse of securitization caused the GFC of 2008–2009, hitting the housing markets of several European countries (e.g., Ireland, Spain, the Netherlands) (Fuentes et al., 2013). House price decline, sometimes in combination with repossessions (e.g., Ireland, Spain, UK), resulted in declining completions and transactions (Van der Heijden et al., 2011). Following economic/house price recovery, financialization strategies resumed, particularly targeted at (residential) real estate and land in economically attractive cities (Haffner & Hulse, 2021). When financial capital is not used for new construction, but is mobilized instead to compete for the acquisition of existing dwellings, house price increases contribute to the wealth accumulation of 'housing market insiders' (Kohl, 2021).

Although 'overall' homeownership rates have remained fairly stable throughout the post-crisis period, the reregulation of housing finance, combined with sluggish new housing supply and increasing house price-to-income ratios (OECD, 2021), have restricted access to homeownership for selective groups. For instance, since the GFC, cross-European variation in deteriorating homeownership opportunities for young households is strongly associated with the extent of housing and mortgage market turmoil, presumably through risk mitigation and credit constraints. Young adult homeownership across Europe has also became increasingly stratified by education, indicating permanent income prospects and 'creditworthiness' (Dewilde, 2020b).

Private Renting

To understand developments in research on private renting, we start with some definitions (Haffner et al., 2009, 2018; Hoekstra et al., 2012). Private renting is usually approached from an ownership perspective. Rental housing is owned by private persons (the majority of landlords) and commercial or for-profit organizations (including institutional investors). However, as social landlords can own/let 'private rental' dwellings, while private landlords may own/let 'social rental' dwellings, an additional criterion pertains to allocation criteria. If criteria are not connected to a(n) (public) administrative system of allocation based on needs, but based on market criteria (is the tenant willing and able to pay the rent?), the dwelling functions as private renting. Private renting furthermore exists in various regulated forms, among which the distinction between rent price control by government and unregulated rents is important.

Private renting in its most extreme 'unregulated' form relatively quickly lost ground in the early decades of the twentieth century, following strict (later less strict) rent price control in most Western European countries. The tenure further lost terrain as it often remained 'unsubsidized' in comparison with the large post-war social housing programmes launched by North-Western European countries (e.g., Austria, France, Netherlands, UK), and with (tax)-subsidized homeownership (e.g., Belgium, Ireland, Southern European countries, UK; Denmark and France to a lesser extent). At the turn of the twenty-first century, in many countries, private renting counted for less than 20 per cent of the housing stock.

The 'resurrection of private renting' in this century – accompanied by a renewed research interest in this sector – came as a surprise, but can be explained by the changing housing (economy) context. In England, for example, private renting has doubled over the last two decades. This 'success' hinges on several demand and supply positives, combined with the deregulation of private renting under the Thatcher government. The sector offers 'pass-through' housing for starters, given reduced access to homeownership and social renting (Kemp & Kofner, 2010).

Given continued low interest rates following the GFC, particularly urban real estate itself (rather than financial derivatives) is valued as an asset class, contributing towards a changing ownership profile of the housing stock. Supplying private renting became more attractive because of low alternative returns on investment, whilst offering a regular income stream. Across several countries and spurred on by so-called 'Buy-to-Let' mortgages, multiproperty ownership by middle-class 'investor households' has increased (Australia: Pawson & Martin, 2020; Ireland: Byrne, 2020; UK: Ronald et al., 2015). Across Europe, rental market regulation has declined (contributing to profitability), mostly during the last two decades of the previous century, with more diverse developments after the GFC – e.g., tightening up in Ireland and Germany versus 'tremendous deregulation' in Spain and Portugal (e.g., Weber, 2017: 15).

This revival coincides with the renewed interests of European policymakers in the potential of private renting as a solution to housing scarcity (Haffner et al., 2018), particularly in cities. This potential is, however, compromised by competition from other players, especially in urban growth centres (see e.g., speculative foreign direct investment by (transnational) wealth elites or equity funds (e.g., Fernandez et al., 2016; Fields & Uffer, 2016; Kitzmann, 2017)). These players are generally interested in the financial value represented by private rental housing, with little interest in the people housed in these assets.

A Gradual Process of Tenure Restructuring

The housing market is like an oil tanker: changes take place very slowly, as demolition and new construction amount to only a small share of total stock. However, in the past two decades some fundamental, even 'regime-converging', structural changes seem to have taken place in the tenure structure – who owns and lives in what part of the housing stock, combining with tenure conversions affecting certain types of the housing stock.

This slow-moving process of restructuring is documented in Figure 5.1 for 29 European countries (2005–2019), averaged by 'housing regime'. Although the overall first impression is one of striking stability, under the surface subtle but likely durable changes are taking place with regard to the characteristics of households typically living in different tenures.

In this chapter, we look firstly at the intersection with household income (lowest income tertile). Averaged across country groups, from 2005 to 2019, the share of households in social housing has remained fairly stable across Western Europe, though targeting towards low-income households has increased, more so in dual rental markets. In Southern and Central and Eastern Europe, social housing has declined more strongly. Stronger declines occurred in the Netherlands, Malta, Latvia, and the Czech Republic. While in Central and Eastern Europe homeownership rates increased even further, there were small to larger declines in all other country groups. These declines were clearer for low-income households, particularly in the North-West European countries with higher homeownership rates and dual rental markets. Decreased access to homeownership and social renting leaves only one option for many new housing market entrants: private renting. Across Europe, there is a quasi-universal tendency towards an increasing number of households living in the private rental sector, and this trend is clearer for lower-income households. The latter is particularly the case in Southern Europe and the North-West European countries with a dual rental market.

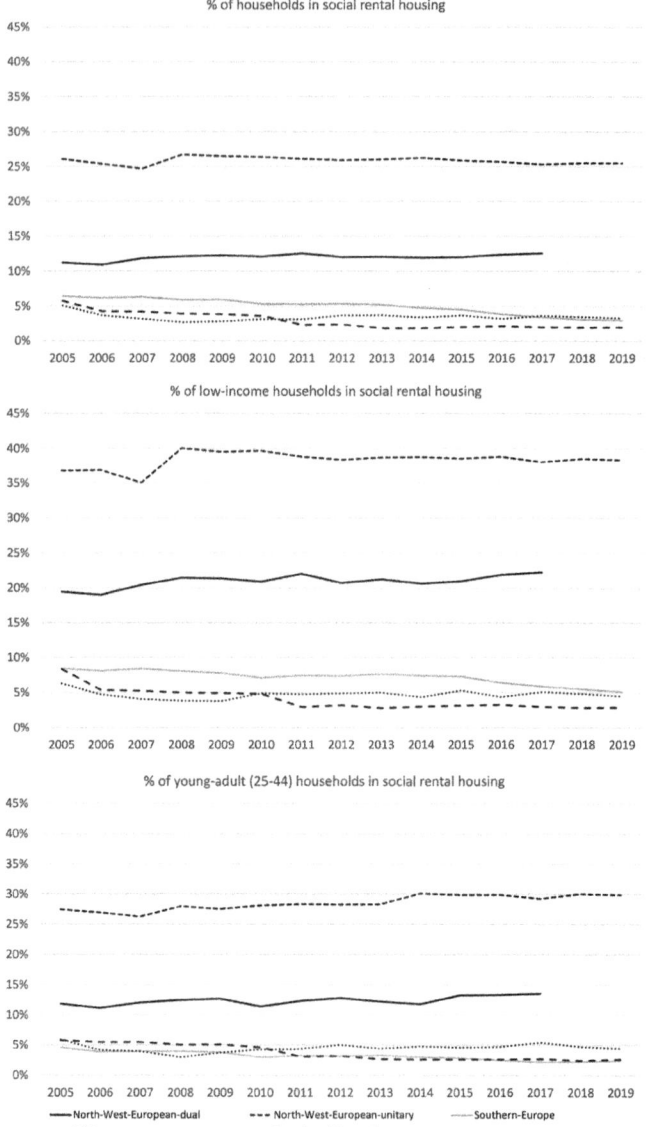

% of households in social rental housing

% of low-income households in social rental housing

% of young-adult (25-44) households in social rental housing

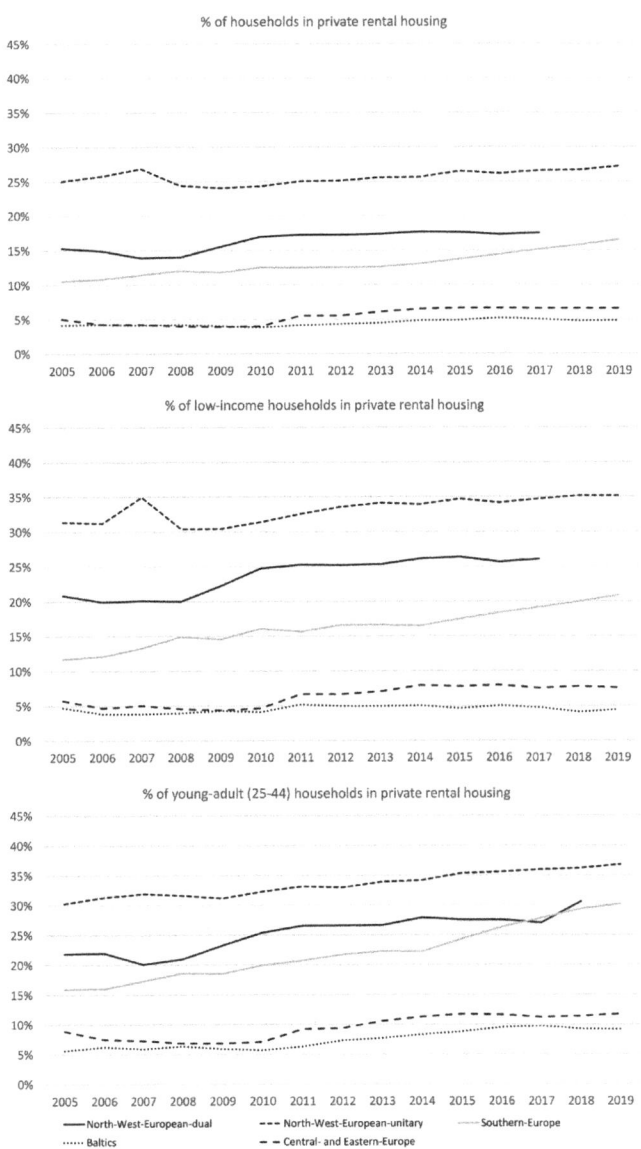

% of households in private rental housing

% of low-income households in private rental housing

% of young-adult (25-44) households in private rental housing

An emerging literature has focused on the declining opportunities of young adults to access independent housing, particularly homeownership (e.g., McKee, 2012; Lennartz et al., 2016; Coulter, 2017; Dewilde, 2020b). Post-crisis declines in young adult homeownership are rather large: hardly any

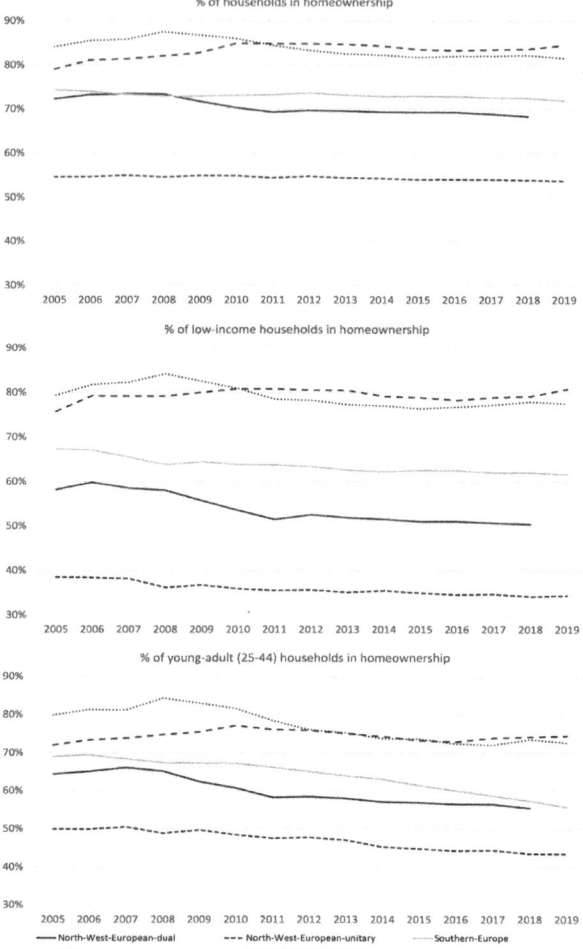

Source: Own calculations
Note: Social rental housing operationalized as 'renting at reduced rate', private rental housing
operationalized as 'renting at market rate'. In Denmark and Sweden, all renting households
were recoded as 'renting at reduced rate'. In the Netherlands, rental housing above the
so-called 'liberalization'-threshold is classified as private rental housing. 2019-data not
available for the United Kingdom and Iceland. Furthermore, as of November 2017 Housing
Associations in the UK are no longer classified by ONS as social housing providers, but as
'private non-financial cooperations'. For this reason, the trendline is truncated at 2017 for the
'North-West-European-dual' countries, as the average for 2018 is distorted by this change.

Figure 5.1   *Trends in tenure structure, and in the social characteristics*
                    of households living in different tenures, 2005–2019
                    (EU-SILC, 29 countries, household level)

18–24 year olds are independent homeowners, with sizeable declines in the older cohort. In Eastern Europe the pattern is more varied, as for some countries we note large increases (Poland) as well as larger decreases (Slovenia). Overall, declines in homeownership of young adult households translate into similarly sized increases in private renting. In most countries, over time, young adults are also somewhat less likely to be found in social renting.[1]

TWO KEY CHALLENGES STRETCHING BEYOND SOCIAL POLICY

We conclude by referring to Chapter 1, where it is noted that social policy research has become ever more 'specialized', focusing on smaller topics in sub-fields (e.g., childcare). This development, however, results in a loss of overview regarding recent trends in 'overall' welfare provision. For instance, even though social spending keeps increasing, it is entirely possible that such spending increasingly benefits some more than others. It also hampers a broader understanding of relationships between social policy and developments in other domains of capitalist regulation. We already pointed at relationships between labour market flexibilization and the restructuring of social insurance, particularly in conservative-corporatist welfare states, where 'dualization' between 'insiders' and 'outsiders' is more evident (e.g., Palier & Thelen, 2010). Regarding housing, we argue for an even broader, more interdisciplinary perspective, pertaining to two key challenges for research: (1) the inclusion of 'changes in housing' (markets, regulation, policy) into analyses of welfare state restructuring; and (2) the analysis of social outcomes.

The first challenge pertains to the type of research needed in order to truly grasp developments in housing (policy). The second challenge pertains to the adverse social outcomes of tenure restructuring and changes in housing provision, in the context of global economic developments, changes in labour markets, and population change. Both challenges relate to the complex positioning of housing as a welfare state pillar, a pillar that hardly figures in 'mainstream' social policy research. Not only is the majority of housing produced and distributed by 'the market', housing itself is a commodity. The salience of 'owned' housing as an asset, an investment-generating (complementary) income, or a 'privatized' welfare resource, has increased.

Key Challenge 1: A Dynamic Relationship between Housing and the Welfare State?

A broader perspective on the relationship(s) between housing policy and social policy takes into account that the analysis of so-called 'institutional complementarities' (Matznetter, 2020) between diverse housing and other welfare regime arrangements is intricate, as they are embedded in multiple institutional contexts that have been subject to (re)commodification in their own specific ways. Recent historical-institutionalist comparisons are re-engaging with the reconceptualization of housing and welfare regime change. Stephens (2020a: 584, 2020b), for instance, proposes a multilayered framework where 'theories of the middle range are extended upwards to capture high-level forces of convergence (e.g. financialization) and downwards to capture institutional variations and market pressures (e.g. regional and metropolitan housing markets) that produce intra-regime variations of outcomes'. From this research (often based on comparative case studies, hence harder to generalize from), the impression arises that potentially recommodification and financialization of the 'wobbly' housing pillar has supported trends in other domains. Various studies locate instances of such processes across tenures. Stephens (2020a, 2020b) argues that particularly in unitary rental markets, the decay of 'social' housing has come from both 'within and outwith'. External factors such as labour market precarity, welfare reform, and rising poverty undermined the ability of cost-rental sectors to operate as social markets, leading to changes in the nature of social housing. Moreover, stock sales and subsidy withdrawal were used to extract and redirect resources from housing to other welfare state purposes. In his view, the decline of cost-rental housing is driven by broader welfare regime change.

Other studies point at the opposite dynamic: from housing (wealth) to welfare state restructuring. Increased take-up of (mortgage) credit, combined with housing asset inflation, was argued to compensate for declining wages and social protection at the bottom (Crouch, 2009). The limitations of such 'asset-based welfare strategies' for lower-income households, however, became apparent throughout the GFC. Although several studies have demonstrated that house price inflation mobilizes housing market insiders against welfare state redistribution (Ansell, 2014; André & Dewilde, 2016; André et al., 2017), it remains unclear how such welfare attitudes consequently affect actual welfare reforms. Lennartz (2017) put forward the more complex argument that in social-democratic welfare states (including the Netherlands), higher levels of 'post-industrial' female labour market participation in tandem with generous social protection 'enabled' increased take-up of mortgage credit in highly financialized mortgage markets, and possibly a redirection of compensatory social spending towards social investment-type spending. Put differently, the 'successful decommodification of human lives leads to generalised creditworthiness which stimulates asset price inflation and new wealth and risk inequalities' (Tranøy et al., 2020: 1). It would seem, therefore, that not just the economy but also welfare state restructuring has come to rely on wealth creation through housing markets. In this process, however, market inequalities will eventually be reproduced in one way or another.

Key Challenge 2: The Rising Housing Unaffordability Problem?

Developments discussed in this chapter are combining to produce adverse social outcomes, which perhaps are best illustrated by referring to the rise of (urban) housing unaffordability (Haffner & Hulse, 2021). While better-placed households have been able to absorb increasing house-price-to-income ratios (OECD, 2021) and accumulate housing wealth through capital gains (Dewilde & Flynn, 2021), low-income households and housing market entrants have found it much harder to access homeownership (e.g., Dewilde & De Decker, 2016; Lennartz et al., 2016). While before the GFC 'financialization research' focused on mortgage market deregulation, recent work focuses on the financial exploitation of 'physical' housing assets targeted by global capital, particularly in economically successful urban locations. At the same time, (affordable) housing supply has been sluggish.

Enhanced competition for scarce land and housing, for different purposes than housing itself, particularly affects private renters, as this tenure is the only option for an increasing number of vulnerable households. Increased demand for (affordable) private rental housing exceeds increased supply. Across Western Europe, housing market financialization has been associated with declined affordability of housing for (low-income) private renters, mainly through increased rents (Dewilde, 2018). More recent OECD data (2021: 50–51) showed that house prices and rents in 2019/2020 were higher than in 2005, particularly affecting the bottom quintile of the income distribution. Higher house prices and price volatility have also been shown to increase living conditions deprivation for renters and low-income owners (Dewilde, 2021): when more is spent on housing, less can be spent on other basic needs. Growing problems of affordability, security, and quality contribute towards emerging housing precariousness (Clair et al., 2019).

FUTURE RESEARCH

In such a complex context, juggling 'housing as investment' and 'housing as social right' is no easy task. Subsidizing demand of different disadvantaged groups, e.g., higher housing allowances, will simply increase demand pressure. Solutions may very well need to go beyond social policy, given the investment character of housing, and links with global financial markets and monetary policies. Wider-reaching proposals include reducing favourable taxation of homeownership and debt finance (Fatica & Prammer, 2018; OECD, 2021); reforming financial markets and banking systems by reducing stimuli for financial capitalism (Ryan-Collins, 2019; Wijburg, 2020); exploring alternative (collaborative) housing tenures (Archer, 2020; Wijburg, 2020); reforming land policy and taxation to curb speculative tendencies (Ryan-Collins, 2019;

OECD, 2021); reinvigorating public investments in affordable/social housing, simultaneously offering opportunities to promote environmental sustainability (OECD, 2021).

Our key message is that changes in housing policy and regulation, as well as trends in 'social policy-type' indicators (i.e., housing allowances) and social outcomes, certainly in comparative perspective, can only be understood when analysed in the context of fundamental changes in the political economy of housing.

ACKNOWLEDGEMENTS

European Union Statistics on Income and Living Conditions data were accessed via Tilburg University (RPP50/2018).

NOTE

1.   A seemingly small increase in the North-Western European countries with a unitary rental market is due to increases for Denmark and Sweden, for which we classified all renting households as 'social rental'.

REFERENCES

Aalbers, M. B., Van Loon, J., & Fernandez, R. (2017). The financialization of a social housing provider. *International Journal of Urban and Regional Research, 41*(4), 572–587.

Allen, J., Barlow, J., Leal, J., Maloutas, T., & Padovani, L. (2004). *Housing and Welfare in Southern Europe*. Blackwell Publishing/RICS Foundation.

André, S., & Dewilde, C. (2016). Home-ownership and support for government redistribution. *Comparative European Politics, 14*(3), 319–348.

André, S., Dewilde, C., & Luijkx, R. (2017). The tenure gap in electoral participation: Instrumental motivation or selection bias? Comparing homeowners and tenants across four housing regimes. *International Journal of Comparative Sociology, 58*(3), 241–265.

Ansell, B. (2014). The political economy of ownership: Housing markets and the welfare state, *American Political Science Review, 108*(2), 383–402.

Archer, T. (2020). The mechanics of housing collectivism: How forms and functions affect affordability. *Housing Studies, 37*(1), 73–102.

Bengtsson, B. (2001). Housing as a social right: Implications for welfare state theory. *Scandinavian Political Studies, 24*(4), 255–275.

Blackwell, T., & Bengtsson, B. (2021). The resilience of social rental housing in the United Kingdom, Sweden and Denmark. *Housing Studies*, 17 February.

Borg, I. (2015). Housing deprivation in Europe: On the role of rental tenure types. *Housing, Theory and Society, 32*(1), 73–93.

Bratt, R. G. (2012). Home ownership risk and responsibility before and after the US mortgage crisis. In R. Ronald & M. Elsinga (Eds), *Beyond Home Ownership: Housing, Welfare and Society* (pp. 146–169). Routledge.

Byrne, M. (2020). Towards a political economy of the private rental sector. *Critical Housing Analysis*, *7*(1), 103–113.

Cabré Pla, A., & Módenes Cabrerizo, J. A. (2004). Home ownership and social inequality in Spain. In K. Kurz & H. P. Blossfeld (Eds), *Home Ownership and Social Inequality in Comparative Perspective* (pp. 233–254). Stanford University Press.

Clair, A., Reeves, A., McKee, M., & Stuckler, D. (2019). Constructing a housing precariousness measure for Europe. *Journal of European Social Policy*, *29*, 13–28.

Coulter, R. (2017). Social disparities in private renting amongst young families in England and Wales, 2001–2011. *Housing, Theory and Society*, *34*(3), 297–322.

Crouch, C. (2009). Privatised Keynesianism: An unacknowledged policy regime. *British Journal of Politics and International Relations*, *11*(3), 382–399.

Dewilde, C. (2017). Do housing regimes matter? Assessing the concept of housing regimes through configurations of housing outcomes. *International Journal of Social Welfare*, *26*(4), 384–404.

Dewilde, C. (2018). Explaining the declined affordability of housing for low-income private renters across Western Europe. *Urban Studies*, *55*(12), 2618–2639.

Dewilde, C. (2020a). Poverty and access to welfare benefits. In B. Greve (Ed.), *Routledge International Handbook of Poverty* (pp. 268–284). Routledge.

Dewilde, C. (2020b). Exploring young Europeans' homeownership opportunities. *Critical Housing Analysis*, *7*(1), 86–102.

Dewilde, C. (2021). How housing affects the association between low income and living conditions across Europe. *Socio-Economic Review*, 28 February.

Dewilde, C., & De Decker, P. (2016). Changing inequalities in housing outcomes across Western Europe. *Housing, Theory and Society*, *33*(2), 121–161.

Dewilde, C. & Flynn, L. B. (2021). Post-crisis developments in young adults' housing wealth. *Journal of European Social Policy*, 9 December.

Doling, J. (1997). *Comparative Housing Policy. Government and Housing in Advanced Industrialized Countries*. Houndmills: Macmillan.

European Commission. (2012). *European Economy. Possible Reforms of Real Estate Taxation. Criteria for Successful Policies* (Occasional Papers, No. 119). European Commission, Directorate-General for Economic and Financial Affairs.

Fahey, T., & Norris, M. (2011). Housing in the welfare state: Rethinking the conceptual foundations of comparative housing policy analysis. *International Journal of Housing Policy*, *11*(4), 439–452.

Fatica, S., & Prammer, D. (2018). Housing and the tax system: How large are the distortions in the Euro area? *Fiscal Studies*, *39*(2), 299–342.

Fernandez, R., Hofman, A., & Aalbers, M. B. (2016). London and New York as a safe deposit Box for the transnational wealth elite. *Environment and Planning A*, *8*(12), 2443–2461.

Fields, D., & Uffer, S. (2016). The financialization of rental housing: A comparative analysis of New York City and Berlin. *Urban Studies*, *53*(7), 1486–1502.

Forrest, R., & Murie, A. (1988). *Selling the Welfare State: The Privatisation of Public Housing*. Routledge.

Fuentes, G. C., Etxezarreta Etxarri, A., Dol, K., & Hoekstra, J. (2013). From housing bubble to repossessions: Spain compared to other West European countries. *Housing Studies*, *28*(8), 1197–1217.

Haffner, M. (2003). Tenure neutrality, a financial-economic interpretation. *Housing, Theory and Society*, *20*(2), 72–85.

Haffner, M., & Hulse, K. (2021). A fresh look at contemporary perspectives on urban housing affordability. *International Journal of Urban Sciences*, *25*(1), 59–79.

Haffner, M., & Winters, S. (2016). Homeownership taxation in Flanders: Moving towards 'optimal taxation'? *International Journal of Housing Policy*, *16*(4), 473–490.

Haffner, M., Hegedüs, J., & Knorr-Siedow, T. (2018). The private rental sector in Western Europe. In J. Hegedüs, M. Lux, & V. Horváth (Eds), *Private Rental Housing in Transition Countries: An Alternative to Owner Occupation?* (pp. 3–40). Macmillan.

Haffner, M., Hoekstra, J., Oxley, M., & Van der Heijden, H. (2009). *Bridging the Gap between Market and Social Rented Housing in Six European Countries*. IOS Press BV.

Heylen, K., & Haffner, M. (2012). The effect of housing expenses and subsidies on the income distribution in Flanders and the Netherlands. *Housing Studies*, *27*(8), 1142–1161.

Hoekstra, J., Haffner, M., Van der Heijden, H., & Oxley, M. (2012). Private rental landlords: Europe. In S. J. Smith et al. (Eds), *International Encyclopedia of Housing and Home* (pp. 387–392). Elsevier.

Kalleberg, A. L. (2018). *Precarious Lives: Job Insecurity and Well-Being in Rich Democracies*. Polity.

Kemeny, J. (1981). *The Myth of Home Ownership. Private versus Public Choices in Housing Tenure*. Routledge and Kegan Paul.

Kemeny, J. (1992). *Housing and Social Theory*. Routledge.

Kemeny, J. (1995). *From Public Housing to the Social Market: Rental Policy Strategies in Comparative Perspective*. Routledge.

Kemeny, J. (2006). Corporatism and housing regimes. *Housing, Theory and Society*, *23*(1), 1–18.

Kemp, P. A., & Kofner, S. (2010). Contrasting varieties of private renting: England and Germany. *International Journal of Housing Policy*, *10*(4), 379–398.

Kitzmann, R. (2017). Private versus state-owned housing in Berlin: Changing provision of low-income households. *Cities*, *61*, 1–8.

Kofner, S. (2017). Social housing in Germany: An inevitably shrinking sector? *Critical Housing Analysis*, *4*(1), 61–71.

Kohl, S. (2021). Too much mortgage debt? The effect of housing financialization on housing supply and residential capital formation. *Socio-Economic Review*, *19*(2), 413–440.

Lennartz, C. (2017). Housing wealth and welfare state restructuring: Between asset-based welfare and the social investment strategy. In C. Dewilde & R. Ronald (Eds), *Housing Wealth and Welfare* (pp. 108–131). Edward Elgar Publishing.

Lennartz, C., Arundel, R., & Ronald, R. (2016). Young adults and homeownership in Europe through the Global Financial Crisis. *Population, Space and Place*, *22*(8), 823–835.

Lersch, P. M., & Dewilde, C. (2015). Employment insecurity and first-time homeownership: Evidence from twenty-two European countries. *Environment and Planning A*, *47*(3), 607–624.

Mandic, S. (2010). The changing role of housing assets in post-socialist countries. *Journal of Housing and the Built Environment*, *25*(2), 213–226.

Mandic, S., & Cirman, A. (2012). Housing conditions and their structural determinants: Comparisons within the enlarged EU. *Urban Studies*, *49*(4), 777–793.

Matznetter, W. (2020). Integrating varieties of capitalism, welfare regimes, and housing at multiple levels and in the long run. *Critical Housing Analysis*, *7*(1), 63–73.

McKee, K. (2012). Young people, homeownership and future welfare. *Housing Studies*, *27*(6), 853–862.

OECD. (2010). *Tax Policy Reform and Economic Growth* (Tax Policy Studies, no. 20). OECD.

OECD. (2021). *OECD Housing Policy Toolkit: Synthesis Report. Brick by Brick: Building Better Housing Policies*. OECD.

Palier, B., & Thelen, K. (2010). Institutionalizing dualism: Complementarities and change in France and Germany. *Politics and Society*, *38*(1), 119–148.

Pawson, H., & Martin, C. (2020). Rental property investment in disadvantaged areas: The means and motivations of western Sydney's new landlords. *Housing Studies*, *36*(5), 621–643.

Poggio, T. (2011). The housing pillar of the Mediterranean welfare regime: Relations between home ownership and other dimensions of welfare in Italy. In R. Ronald & M. Elsinga (Eds), *Beyond Home Ownership: Housing, Welfare and Society* (pp. 51–67). Routledge.

Ronald, R., Kadi, J., & Lennartz, C. (2015). Homeownership-based welfare in transition. *Critical Housing Analysis*, *2*(1), 52–64.

Rueda, D. (2014). Dualization, crisis and the welfare state. *Socio-Economic Review*, *12*, 381–407.

Ryan-Collins, J. (2019). Breaking the housing-finance cycle: Macroeconomic policy reforms for more affordable homes. *EPA: Economy and Space*, *53*(3), 480–502.

Scanlon, K., Lunde, J., & Whitehead, C. (2008). Mortgage product innovation in advanced economies: More choice, more risk. *International Journal of Housing Policy*, *8*(2), 109–131.

Soaita, A. M., & Dewilde, C. (2019). A critical-realist view of housing quality within the post-communist EU states: Progressing towards a middle-range explanation. *Housing, Theory and Society*, *36*(1), 44–75.

Stephens, M. (2007). Mortgage market deregulation and its consequences. *Housing Studies*, *22*(2), 201–220.

Stephens, M. (2020a). Towards a multi-layered housing regime framework: Responses to commentators. *Housing, Theory and Society*, *37*(5), 584–596.

Stephens, M. (2020b). How housing systems are changing and why: A critique of Kemeny's theory of housing regimes. *Housing, Theory and Society*, *37*(5), 521–547.

Stephens, M., Elsinga, M., & Knorr-Siedow, T. (2008). The privatisation of social housing: Three different pathways. In K. Scanlon & C. Whitehead (Eds), *Social Housing in Europe II: A Review of Policies and Outcomes* (pp. 105–129). London School of Economics and Political Science.

Stephens, M., Lux, M., & Sunega, P. (2015). Post-socialist housing systems in Europe: Housing welfare regimes by default? *Housing Studies*, *30*(8), 1210–1234.

Torgersen, U. (1987). Housing: The wobbly pillar under the welfare state. In B. Turner, J. Kemeny, & L. J. Lundqvist (Eds), *Between State and Market: Housing in the Post-Industrial Era* (pp. 116–126). Almqvist & Wiksell.

Tranøy, B. S., Stamsø, M. A., & Hjertaker, I. (2020). Equality as a driver of inequality? Universalistic welfare, generalised creditworthiness and financialised housing markets. *West European Politics*, *43*(2), 390–411.

Van der Heijden, H., Dol, K., & Oxley, M. (2011). Western European housing systems and the impact of the international financial crisis. *Journal of Housing and the Built Environment*, *26*(3), 295–313.

Verbist, G., & Grabka, M. M. (2017). Distributive and poverty-reducing effects of in-kind housing benefits in Europe: With a case study for Germany. *Journal of Housing and the Built Environment*, *32*(2), 289–312.

Weber, J. P. (2017). The regulation of private tenancies: A multi-country analysis. Universitätsbibliothek Regensburg, International Real Estate Business School. https://epub.uni-regensburg.de/36228/1/Weber%20%282017%29_The%20Regulation%20of%20Private%20Tenancies%20A%20Multi-Country%20Analysis.pdf

Wijburg, G. (2020). The de-financialization of housing: Towards a research agenda. *Housing Studies, 36*(8), 1276–1293.

Wijburg, G., & Aalbers, M. B. (2017). The alternative financialization of the German housing market. *Housing Studies, 32*(7), 968–989.

Wind, B., & Dewilde, C. (2019). In which European countries is homeownership more financially advantageous? Explaining the size of the tenure wealth gap in 10 countries with different housing and welfare regimes. *International Journal of Housing Policy, 19*(4), 536–565.

Wind, B., Lersch, P., & Dewilde, C. (2017). The distribution of housing wealth in 16 European countries: Accounting for institutional differences. *Journal of Housing and the Built Environment, 32*(4), 625–647.

Zavisca, J. R., & Gerber, T. P. (2017). Experiences of home ownership and housing mobility after privatization in Russia. In C. Dewilde & R. Ronald (Eds), *Housing Wealth and Welfare* (pp. 214–235). Edward Elgar Publishing.

6. Studying the politics of pension reforms and their social consequences

Bernhard Ebbinghaus and Katja Möhring

INTRODUCTION

From a social policy perspective, social protection against income loss due to old age, death of the main breadwinner, and age-related disability is one of the fundamental social rights. Old age, survivor, and disability pensions are together the largest social benefit programmes accounting for about 15 per cent of gross domestic product and nearly 50 per cent of social protection expenditure across Europe. Most older people rely on pensions for their income, while working people usually pay their contributions and expect to fully retire when they are old. Statutory pension ages (and any early retirement options) structure the final transition into retirement (Kohli, 2007), a phase in which the living situation in old age, including poverty and inequality, but also societal participation and subjective wellbeing, warrant consideration by social research (Jürges & van Soest, 2012).

Around the millennium's turn, European social policy research on pensions faced a double tension: claiming the need for change in the face of global and internal challenges, while studying the difficulties of reform but also their consequences. At the time, European welfare states were seen as 'elephants on the move' (Hinrichs, 2000), reacting rather slowly to an ever more unsustainable environment of demographic ageing. This reluctance to reform was in stark contrast to the austerity calls by economists (Feldstein & Siebert, 2002). Ageing societies were seen as a 'time bomb' as longer life expectancy and ever smaller cohorts due to lower birth rates burdened pension funding on ever fewer shoulders. Economists pointed to financial unsustainability, calling for a shift from public pay-as-you-go pensions towards more private savings (Leimgruber, 2012). Moreover, the reversal of early retirement and an increase in pension age was advocated to redress financial imbalances (Ebbinghaus, 2006).

European research on pensions and retirement can broadly be divided into two threads: on the one hand, *policy studies*, which analyse reform politics, leading to changes in pension systems, and on the other hand, *impact studies* of their consequences on retirement transitions, retirement income and living conditions, civic participation, and subjective wellbeing of older people. The first, *policy-related* research agenda is concerned with the cross-national variations in pension systems and their institutional change, discussing the societal challenges, political dynamics, and policy options for pension reforms (Immergut et al., 2007; Ebbinghaus, 2011; Natali, 2017). The approach includes comparative analyses of European pension systems, or historical case studies with process tracing of reform dynamics (Häusermann, 2010; Vanhuysse & Goerres, 2013; Ebbinghaus & Naumann, 2018). The second, *outcome-related* research focuses on the social consequences of the ongoing societal and policy changes on living conditions of older people, such as old age poverty, working pensioners, and gender inequalities. Also, flexibilization of employment will create future retirement income problems (Hinrichs & Jessoula, 2012), while gender wage gaps, interruptions due to childcaring, and part-time employment among women translate into gender inequalities in retirement (Möhring, 2015).

This chapter outlines the main analytical approaches and key areas of European research on pension and retirement over the last two decades. The chapter begins with the multidisciplinary perspectives on pensions, before discussing demographic ageing, pension reform dynamics, and changing pension systems. While these analyses are mainly at the macrocomparative policy level, the subsequent sections address more individual-level data analyses, analysing the societal consequences of pension reforms and the societal inequalities. The outlook draws some lessons for the study of pensions and retirement in the future.

SOCIAL SCIENCE APPROACHES

Different disciplines inform pension and retirement analyses, ranging across a spectrum of social sciences (including also gerontology). *Demography* (Harper & Hamblin, 2014) provides an understanding of the long-term trends in ageing societies, the continued rise in life expectancy (including gender and social inequalities), the decline in birth rates, the increase of the older population (and its composition), and forecasts of population development for several decades. Differences in life expectancy between men and women but also social inequalities imply equity issues in respect to pension benefits without or with actuarial adjustment. Related migration studies have also informed our understanding of whether an influx of migrants provides relief for ageing societies (Karl & Torres, 2015).

Economics analyses the trade-off between work and leisure, seeing pensions (and early retirement options) as disincentives for working longer (Gruber

& Wise, 1999). Demographic ageing is seen as a threat to the financial sustainability of pensions and a shift from pay-as-you-go to funded pensions as prominently proposed by the World Bank (Holzmann, 2000). The political economy argument that people near or in retirement have a self-interest in maintaining generous pensions has been influential. While economists study the optimal design of pension policies from a financial sustainability view, only some of the political economy studies take into account the actual reform hurdles (Boeri et al., 2002) and few take a critical view (Barr, 2002; Barr & Diamond, 2009).

Political science has added to the political economy perspective by analysing the political dynamics of ageing electorates (Goerres & Vanhuysse, 2021; Vlandas et al., 2021). The most important influence has been the New Politics thesis (Pierson, 2001) in respect to reform dynamism, studying the obstacles to systemic reform and the path-dependent, gradual change of welfare states. The main argument is that pensions are popular and that the grey vote is weighty, thus politicians use 'blame avoidance' to not get punished at the voting booth. Shunning long-term problems, they focus on current problems and their feasible immediate mediation. Political studies thus focus on the conditions of policy change and whether public opinion is changing given ongoing reform efforts (Svallfors, 2010).

Sociology has contributed research that explores the social consequences of welfare state reforms in the context of societal challenges. Combining the life-course perspective, gender and social inequality concerns, and micro-level longitudinal analyses, such research has provided insights into changes in retirement patterns, old age living conditions, and wellbeing (Settersten et al., 2011).

Overall, research on pensions and retirement is thus still segmented by disciplinary focuses and approaches. Nevertheless, topic-related conference themes, specialized journals, and funding initiatives provide opportunities for exchange across disciplines. National networks such as FNA, the German public pension insurance, Netspar in the Netherlands, or pension research institutes largely focus on national developments. Some European funding schemes provide opportunities (e.g., European Union research funding, Norface). ESPAnet has played an important role in training doctoral researchers and bringing scholars from different disciplines together both internationally and in some countries nationally.

DEMOGRAPHIC AGEING CHALLENGES

Demographic ageing has been given as a rationale for reform, particularly with reference to the financial sustainability of pay-as-you-go pensions. Demographic studies show that population ageing occurs due to falling birth mortality, increasing life expectancy, and declining birth rates. From a financial perspective, old age dependency, commonly measured as share of older people (65+) in relation to the working-age population (16–64), is crucial for burden sharing: while about four persons of working age in Europe supported one elderly in the 2000s, the burden will be less than two for one older person in the 2050s (Rowland, 2009). Demographic ageing will thus remain a pressing political issue for several decades, thereafter it would become a steady state of slowly declining and ageing societies. Moreover, as retirement age increases and labour force participations expand, the age dependency indicator needs to be reconceptualized.

The trend towards early retirement has also added to the cost of pensions, disability, and other pre-retirement benefits (including unemployment in old age). While life expectancy increased, the actual age of retirement, measured as withdrawal from work, has been declining since the 1970s when mass unemployment led to labour-shedding policies among older workers (Ebbinghaus, 2006). The European Union after its Lisbon Agenda increased employment (above 50 per cent) for those 55–64 by 2010. The reversal of early retirement has been a topic since the late 1990s, when governments in countries like Denmark, Germany, and the Netherlands changed from passive labour market policies to activation and active ageing (Ebbinghaus & Hofäcker, 2013). The phasing out of early retirement pathways and the increase in statutory pensions became the new policy mix to rebalance time in work and retirement given increased life expectancy. Active ageing policies were developed to increase not only economic employment but also voluntary participation and healthy living in old age; this is reflected in the Active Age Index (Zaidi et al., 2018) developed by gerontologists and used in international policy circles.

Whether migration would help to relieve demographic pressure has been widely discussed. The argument that new migrants are younger than the host society was for instance used during the refugee wave of 2015 in Germany (with a net migration of about 1 million), though there were also concerns about the costs of integration. The counterargument is that first-generation migrants also need pensions during retirement and the non-native age profile quickly converges along with the host society, including birth rates. Hence, migration might be a short-term relief in respect to demographic ageing but it comes with its own welfare challenges, e.g., considering the pension rights for migrants (Frericks, 2012; Heisig et al., 2018; Bridgen & Meyer, 2019).

The political consequences of demographic ageing have been a common argument: while increasing old age dependency leads to financial sustainability problems, the 'grey vote' increases as those near or in retirement represent a substantial share of the vote. Indeed, according to recent data (European Social Survey, 2018), the voter share of individuals aged 60 and older reaches around 40 per cent across the European Union and United Kingdom (UK);

in French, Swedish, and Swiss elections as well as in several Central Eastern European countries the 'grey vote' exceeds this threshold. Younger voters are less likely to vote or more likely to be ineligible as non-citizens as first- or second-generation migrants. The argument that the interests of pensioners are strong in electoral politics and interest organizations remains powerful, though there are important cross-national variations.

PENSION REFORM POLITICS

Pension reforms have been on the political and academic agenda for many decades. With the 1980s 'conservative turn', Reagan's United States administration and Thatcher's UK government aimed at 'retrenchment' but only achieved partial pension reform (Pierson, 1994). The New Politics approach (Pierson, 1996, 2001) shaped the research agenda on welfare state reforms, particularly on pensions. Pierson argued that 'policy feedback', the social rights bestowed on beneficiaries, feeds into their support of the status quo. Attitudes towards pension policy show support for government intervention and more spending, nearly as much as for health services, but much higher than for unemployment benefits (van Oorschot et al., 2017; Ebbinghaus & Naumann, 2018). Therefore, politicians afraid of electoral backlash shun systemic reforms and instead aim for 'blame avoidance' (Weaver, 1986).

Large-scale reforms prove difficult, particularly since politicians face the 'double payer' challenge (Myles & Pierson, 2001) if they alter the 'intergenerational contract' of pay-as-you-go pensions (Myles, 2003). This financial distribution from those contributing to those receiving pensions is a prime example of path dependency. It institutionalizes the expectation of retirees to receive a pension based on their past contributions, while the working population expects the same when retiring given their contributions. A sudden transition from pay-as-you-go to funded pensions would put a double responsibility on current contributors, honouring the pensions of past contributors and also saving for their own pensions. Political feasibility therefore requires a gradual shift towards funded pensions, through a voluntary additional funded pension, or exempting those close to retirement through 'grandfathering' (Pierson, 2000).

European scholars explored the impact of institutions, the role of organized interests, and government strategies in pension reforms across Europe (Bonoli, 2000; Marier, 2008; Natali, 2008). Although Pierson (1996) initially expected the New Politics to be a break with 'old' power resource arguments about the strength of labour (Scarbrough, 2000), the European experience showed that unions were successfully mobilizing against major reforms such as in Italy and France during the 1990s (Natali & Rhodes, 2004). Comparative and country studies of interest organizations in pension reform used elite interviews and document analysis to map the position of political and societal actors on major reforms (Häusermann, 2010; Naczyk & Seeleib-Kaiser, 2015).

Some important reforms, however, did occur, partially advanced through European and transnational drivers. Across Europe, pension reforms were on the agenda since the 1990s, not least given the Maastricht limits on public borrowing for those countries joining the euro (Natali and Rhodes, 2004). Also in the late 1990s, the post-socialist transition economies in Central and Eastern Europe followed World Bank recommendations to adopt mandatory funded pensions to lower public pension liabilities and boost their economies (Müller, 1999; Orenstein, 2008). Across countries, governments were embracing reform as part of the Lisbon process, advancing a more reform-oriented agenda in respect to active ageing. Political scientists thus also explored the conditions under which governments were willing to risk reforms, if not even claim credit for redirecting resources to new social risks while cutting benefits for less deserving groups (Giger & Nelson, 2011; Bonoli, 2012; Vis, 2016).

TYPOLOGIES OF PENSION SYSTEMS

Institutions matter for pension reform (Bonoli, 2000). Comparative analysis, often based on collaborative projects with country studies by expert teams (Immergut et al., 2007; Ebbinghaus, 2011; Natali, 2017), revealed the path dependence along two legacies: Bismarckian social insurance versus Beveridgean basic security (Bonoli, 2003). Social insurance, common in conservative regimes, was aiming at status maintenance through contributory pensions, putting off the financial sustainability problems of pay-as-you-go funding. Beveridgean systems, ranging from the UK to Nordic countries but also the Netherlands and Switzerland, had already evolved into multipillar systems. While Bismarckian pensions initially 'crowded out' private funded pensions, they were slowly but belatedly emerging, whereas to fill the income gaps of public basic pensions, pension fund capitalism grew fast in Beveridge systems (Ebbinghaus, 2015).

Bismarckian systems were seen as slow reformers, given multiple political veto points and the intergenerational contract (Schludi, 2005; Palier & Martin, 2008; Palier, 2010). Although the demographic pressures were acute, governments engaged first in parametric reforms by phasing out early retirement options, gradually increasing (and equalizing) statutory pension age, extending contributory periods, and finally introducing demographic formula in benefit calculations. In addition, governments introduced or expanded voluntarily funded pensions. Prominently, Germany's left-green government introduced a subsidized Riester pension in 2003 as a voluntary funded pillar to compensate for cutbacks in the public pension value – a case of institutional 'layering', adding voluntary savings with only partial change of the core pillar

(Berner, 2006). Several countries opted for notional defined benefits, including Sweden's change towards a mixed multipillar model and Italy's multiple reforms in the 1990s (Schoyen & Stamati, 2013; Guardiancich et al., 2019).

Among the transition economies in Central and Eastern Europe, most had maintained their pension insurances with wide coverage and pay-as-you-go funding, but introduced mandatory funded pensions during the 1990s on the recommendation of the World Bank and before joining the European Union (Müller, 2008; Orenstein, 2008). However, as research on these countries showed, the high transition costs led to a partial reversal in contributions (and a nationalization of private funds in Hungary) following the financial market crash in 2008 and the European Union sovereign debt crisis in the 2010s (Cerami, 2011; Drahokoupil & Domonkos, 2012).

In Beveridge multipillar systems, there have been different reform dynamics for the minimum income protection and the private funded pension pillars. In liberal welfare states, austerity politics led to some cut-backs but also improvements (Bridgen, 2019). Recently, British state pensions were reformed (ending state earning-related pensions) and automatic enrolment of workplace pensions was enacted to nudge working people to save, following the recommendations of the Turner Commission (Pearce & Massala, 2020). In addition to the British Isles, the Dutch and Swiss multipillar systems include a universal basic pension, large coverage through occupational pensions negotiated by unions and employers or firm-sponsored plans, and private personal saving plans (Ebbinghaus, 2011). The Scandinavian welfare states rely on basic security, while occupational funded pensions or group insurance plans co-evolved (albeit Finland has collective schemes with funded elements). The anglophone, Dutch, Swiss, and Nordic countries all have multipillar systems with growing pension fund capitalism (Ebbinghaus, 2015); indeed, assets exceed annual national income in several Nordic countries, the Netherlands, Switzerland, and the UK.

SOCIAL CONSEQUENCES OF POLICY REFORMS

In European social policy analysis, the concept of new social risks has gained much attention since the 2000s (Taylor-Gooby, 2004; Armingeon & Bonoli, 2006), refocusing the concern from 'old' social risks such as old age to 'new' risks such as low skills in a knowledge society and family–work reconciliation. However, new social risks also have long-term consequences in respect to work–retirement transitions and social inequalities in pension income. The low skilled, with often flexible if not precarious jobs and frequent unemployment, will receive insufficient contribution-based pensions (Bravo & Herce, 2020). First- and second-generation migrants have also been seen as groups particularly affected by difficult employment trajectories and subsequent pension prospects (Frericks, 2012; Heisig et al., 2018). Women with interruptions or part-time jobs due to caring duties for children or relatives tend to have lower pensions despite care credits in public systems (Frericks et al., 2009; Madero-Cabib & Fasang, 2016; Möhring, 2021).

Linking the changes in the world of work with the long-term retirement consequences requires longitudinal analysis of employment trajectories and retirement incomes. Such research faces challenges given long working lives and variable retirement transitions, but also given the complexities of pension rules. There are at least three possible research strategies: the study of long-term labour market trends on today's retirement income; life-course analysis through retrospective surveys, panels, or administrative records; or forecasting with the help of typical agent simulation of pension outcomes. In labour market research, the trends towards flexibilization, deregulation, and dualization (Emmenegger et al., 2012) have been well established and their potential consequences for retirement income have been discussed (Meyer et al., 2007; Hinrichs & Jessoula, 2012), though more research is needed.

The ongoing pension reforms may induce changes in retirement age norms (Radl, 2012), though older workers have hardly adapted their retirement preferences (Hofäcker, 2015) but have updated their expectation of actual exit from work (Hess, 2017). While there is little indication that many would prefer to retire later, there are many who have been forced to retire early due to health issues or being laid off (Ebbinghaus & Radl, 2015). The increased 'marketization' of public and private pension benefits through tighter contribution linkage and actuarial principles will be problematic for flexible, precarious, and interrupted employment trajectories unless welfare states compensate by providing credits for childcare or long-term care or crediting unemployment years. The coverage of occupational pensions and personal pensions depends on whether it is mandated, collectively negotiated, or voluntary and whether there are incentives to nudge increases in coverage (Wiß, 2015). Moreover, the shift from end-of-career defined benefit to defined contribution systems will lead to an individualization of risks. While the compensatory role of public pensions is crucial, the study of private pensions across different social risk groups and sectors is more difficult.

While the post-war expansion of welfare states led to a decline in old age poverty, there are indications of a rise of poverty and inequality in old age income in some European countries and for specific risk groups. While European Union pension reports now focus on 'pension adequacy' (EU-Com., 2021), social policy research has studied old age inequality and poverty comparatively (Vliet et al., 2012; Ebbinghaus, 2021; Kuitto et al., 2021). Studies use individual and household (panel) data such as the Luxembourg Income Study, European Union Survey of Income and Living Conditions, or national panel sources. Two central indicators show the cross-national variations (1) vertically: the at-risk-of-poverty rate measured as share of people (adjusted for household size) living with less than 60 per cent of median disposable income, and (2) horizontally: the income spread (between top and bottom 20 per cent) among older people (aged 65 and older). As Figure 6.1 (see Ebbinghaus, 2021) shows, poverty rate and inequality levels vary across Europe from generous basic pensions, as in Denmark and The Netherlands as well as in some core Central and Eastern European countries, to those with high levels such as Switzerland and more peripheral countries.

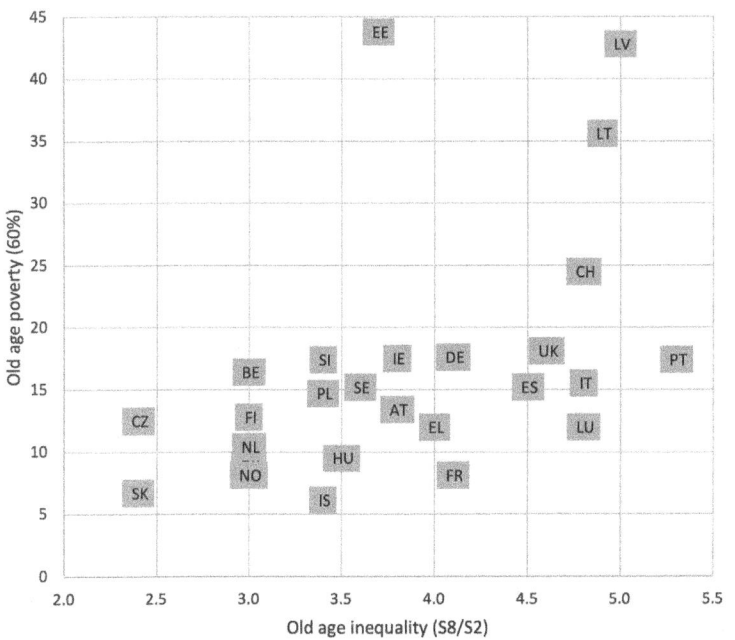

Figure 6.1   Old age inequality and at-risk-of-poverty rate, Eurostat 2010s

The explanations for such cross-national differences are complex, including the labour market attachment over past decades (such as gender employment and earnings gaps) and their interaction with public minimum income provision and the multipillar architecture. Poverty prevention is mainly due to state intervention, either through generous basic pensions and/or income-tested supplements so that retirement income is above the poverty line, while social insurance systems provide either social pensions (minimum benefits for those with a minimum contribution period) or means-tested social assistance. Anyone with incomplete years of residence or contributions are at poverty risk. Inequality among pensioners is due to both reproduced market inequality during working lives and the amplification through unequal access to or incomplete savings and high risks of supplementary funded pensions. Inequality can be high in both Bismarckian and Beveridge systems; the best record in Europe is among central transition economies with social insurance due to less work-related inequality. Also, Danish and Dutch multipillar pension systems achieve low poverty and inequality (Ebbinghaus, 2021).

LIFE-COURSE ANALYSIS

Over the last few years, a growing strand of research at the interface of social policy analysis and sociology has studied the relationship of pension policies and financial wellbeing in retirement from a life-course perspective, linking developments in the employment and fertility history to pensions and later-life inequalities. This research mostly takes an empirical quantitative approach and uses detailed life-course information from country-specific or comparative datasets in small-N (e.g., Sefton et al., 2011; Fasang et al., 2013) or large-N studies (e.g., Höppner, 2021; Möhring, 2021). The former type of studies also makes use of rich register data (Riekhoff & Järnefelt, 2018; Möhring & Weiland, 2021). These studies have advanced our knowledge of inequalities in old age by trying to disentangle the complex relationship of life courses and social policy that determines wellbeing in old age. Most importantly, they have integrated labour market and family policies and shown that, apart from pension systems, the incentive structure for life-course decisions in earlier life stages matters for old age inequalities. By taking a life-course perspective, these studies also study the impact of 'new' social risks on later-life wellbeing as they empirically model the consequences of life-course events and phases such as divorce, lone parenthood, and unemployment (Bravo & Herce, 2020; Muller et al., 2020).

Many of these studies take a gender perspective in studying the distribution of paid work and unpaid care work as well as fertility history as major determinants of gender inequality in pensions. In fact, gender pension gaps in Europe are more clearly related to labour market inequalities than to pension systems (Hammerschmid & Rowold, 2019), and level measures of pension care entitlements are rather related to higher gender inequality (Möhring, 2018). Further research will need to explore if and how changing life courses across women and men, but also intersecting social inequalities and ongoing pension reforms, have increased the trend towards more inequality and poverty in old age in Europe.

OUTLOOK

Pension and retirement have been on the political and academic agenda for more than the last two decades. While often a specialized policy field for pension experts, it has gained through the New Politics thesis crucial importance for theoretical and empirical advancements in research on welfare state reform politics. Today, excitement about the contradiction between the need and capacity to reform has given way to a more sober and differentiated analysis of various reform trajectories. Some of the commonly held beliefs of an intergenerational conflict have been disproven, while nudging people to save has become a fashionable policy.

There has been some myth busting on the funded pension strategy, not least advanced by the financial market crash of 2008, the considerable risk of asset depreciations, and the partial backtracking of some funded systems. Indeed, there has been cross-fertilization between political economy and pension policy research around financialization (van der Zwan, 2014). The governance of funded pensions, including sovereign funds, in particular in respect to social, green, and ethical investment strategies, is of growing importance (Vitols, 2011). Also, social and self-owned housing, a specialized topic in social policy as well as in political economy, are of relevance for understanding retirement in context (Delfani et al., 2014).

That financial sustainability needs to be in line with social aims has also been a major concern, not only in research. The increased attention to studies on social outcomes is of policy relevance – how can pension systems be adapted to meet the needs of those most vulnerable and how can a fair system be established for all? Moreover, old age pensions cannot be studied in isolation. The increase of the statutory pension age might require changes in unemployment, active labour market, and disability policies.

A further extension is to understand from a life-course perspective how retirement and pension income are shaped by societal trends and policy changes before retirement, early education and training and working life. Moreover, the tripartite life course has become more fluid as the working pensioner (Scherger, 2015) is gaining in importance. There need to be more studies looking at the interaction of health and long-term care with pension income and retirement patterns. Pension income is insufficient to pay for health and long-term care. The COVID-19 pandemic has decreased life expectancy due to age-related risks, while social inequalities also matter: both issues require further rethinking in respect to equity.

While European or other countries in the Organisation for Economic Co-operation and Development have been the main focus of much of ESPAnet research, there are also increasing efforts to extend the analysis to the Global

South (Böger & Leisering, 2020). Do these countries follow similar trends as in Europe while their demographics age, or will the North depend on these countries for their pension savings? Thus, pension and retirement studies would profit from a more encompassing comparative approach and cross-fertilization with political economy, while there is a need to link policy studies to more evaluation-based analysis of the socio-economic changes and social outcomes of these policy changes. Pension and retirement research is not new, but there are important upcoming topics to pursue in future research.

REFERENCES

Armingeon, K., & Bonoli, G. (2006). *The Politics of Postindustrial Welfare States: Adapting Postwar Social Policies to New Social Risks*. Routledge.

Barr, N. (2002). Reforming pensions: Myths, truths, and public choices. *International Social Security Review, 55*(2), 3–36.

Barr, N., & Diamond, P. (2009). Reforming pensions: Principles, analytical errors and policy directions. *International Social Security Review, 62*(2).

Berner, F. (2006). Riester pensions in Germany: Do they substitute or supplement public pensions? *German Policy Studies, 3*(3), 492–534.

Boeri, T., Boersch-Supan, A., & Tabellini, G. (2002). Pension reforms and the opinions of European citizens. *American Economic Review, 92*(2), 396–401.

Böger, T., & Leisering, L. (2020). A new pathway to universalism? Explaining the spread of 'social' pensions in the global South, 1967–2011. *Journal of International Relations and Development, 23*, 308–338.

Bonoli, G. (2000). *The Politics of Pension Reform: Institutions and Policy Change in Western Europe*. Cambridge University Press.

Bonoli, G. (2003). Two worlds of pension reform in Western Europe. *Comparative Politics, 35*, 399–416.

Bonoli, G. (2012). Blame avoidance and credit claiming revisited. In G. Bonoli & D. Natali (Eds), *The Politics of the New Welfare State in Europe* (pp. 93–110). Oxford University Press.

Bravo, J. M., & Herce, J. A. (2020). Career breaks, broken pensions? Long-run effects of early and late-career unemployment spells on pension entitlements. *Journal of Pension Economics and Finance*, 1–27.

Bridgen, P. (2019). The retrenchment of public pension provision in the liberal world of welfare during the age of austerity – and its unexpected reversal, 1980–2017. *Social Policy and Administration, 53*(1), 16–33.

Bridgen, P., & Meyer, T. (2019). Divided citizenship: How retirement in the host country affects the financial status of intra-European Union migrants. *Ageing and Society, 39*(3), 465–487.

Cerami, A. (2011). Ageing and the politics of pension reforms in Central Europe, South-Eastern Europe and the Baltic states. *International Journal of Social Welfare, 20*(4), 331–343.

Delfani, N., De Deken, J., & Dewilde, C. (2014). Home-ownership and pensions: Negative correlation, but no trade-off. *Housing Studies, 29*(5), 657–676.

Drahokoupil, J., & Domonkos, S. (2012). Averting the funding-gap crisis: East European pension reforms since 2008. *Global Social Policy, 12*(3), 283–299.

Ebbinghaus, B. (2006). *Reforming Early Retirement in Europe, Japan and the USA.* Oxford University Press.

Ebbinghaus, B. (Ed.). (2011). *The Varieties of Pension Governance: Pension Privatization in Europe.* Oxford University Press.

Ebbinghaus, B. (2015). The privatization and marketization of pensions in Europe: A double transformation facing the crisis. *European Policy Analysis, 1*(1), 56–73.

Ebbinghaus, B. (2021). Inequalities and poverty risks in old age across Europe: The double-edged income effect of pension systems. *Social Policy and Administration, 55*(3), 440–455.

Ebbinghaus, B., & Hofäcker, D. (2013). Reversing early retirement in advanced welfare economies: A paradigm shift to overcome push and pull factors. *Comparative Population Studies, 38*(4), 807–840.

Ebbinghaus, B., & Naumann, E. (Eds). (2018). *Welfare State Reforms Seen from Below: Comparing Public Attitudes and Organized Interests in Britain and Germany.* Palgrave.

Ebbinghaus, B., & Radl, J. (2015). Pushed out prematurely? Comparing objectively forced exits and subjective assessments of involuntary retirement across Europe. *Research in Social Stratification and Mobility, 40*, 115–130.

Emmenegger, P., Häusermann, S., Palier, B. et al. (Eds). (2012). *The Age of Dualization: The Changing Face of Inequality in Deindustrializing Societies.* Oxford University Press.

EU-Com. (2021). *The 2021 Pension Adequacy Report: Current and Future Income Adequacy in Old Age in the EU.* Brussels: EU Commission.

European Social Survey (2018). Data file edition 3.1. NSD – Norwegian Centre for Research Data, Norway, Data Archive and Distributor of ESS data for ESS ERIC, Round 9 Data. doi:10.21338/NSD-ESS9-2018.

Fasang, A. E., Aisenbrey, S., & Schömann, K. (2013). Women's retirement income in Germany and Britain. *European Sociological Review, 29*(5), 968–980.

Feldstein, M., & Siebert, H. (2002). *Social Security Pension Reform in Europe.* University of Chicago Press.

Frericks, P. (2012). Funded pensions and their implications for women and migrant workers. *Global Social Policy, 12*(3), 342–344.

Frericks, P., Knijn, T., & Maier, R. (2009). Pension reforms, working patterns and gender pension gaps in Europe. *Gender, Work and Organization, 16*(6), 710–730.

Giger, N., & Nelson, M. (2011). The electoral consequences of welfare state retrenchment: Blame avoidance or credit claiming in the era of permanent austerity? *European Journal of Political Research, 50*(1), 1–23.

Goerres, A., & Vanhuysse, P. (2021). *Global Political Demography: The Politics of Population Change.* Palgrave.

Gruber, J., & Wise, D. A. (1999). *Social Security and Retirement around the World.* University of Chicago Press.

Guardiancich, I., Weaver, R. K., Demarco, G. et al. (2019). *The Politics of NDC Pension Scheme Diffusion.* World Bank Social Protection and Jobs Discussion Papers 1927.

Hammerschmid, A., & Rowold, C. (2019). Gender pension gaps in Europa hängen eindeutiger mit Arbeitsmärkten als mit Rentensystemen zusammen. *DIW Wochenbericht, 25*(1).

Harper, S., & Hamblin, K. (2014). *International Handbook of Ageing and Public Policy.* Edward Elgar Publishing.

Häusermann, S. (2010). *The Politics of Welfare State Reform in Continental Europe: Modernization in Hard Times.* Cambridge University Press.

Heisig, J. P., Lancee, B., & Radl, J. (2018). Ethnic inequality in retirement income: A comparative analysis of immigrant–native gaps in Western Europe. *Ageing and Society, 38*(10), 1963–1994.

Hess, M. (2017). Rising preferred retirement age in Europe: Are Europe's future pensioners adapting to pension system reforms? *Journal of Aging and Social Policy, 29*(3), 245–261.

Hinrichs, K. (2000). Elephants on the move: Patterns of public pension reform in OECD countries. *European Review, 8*(3), 353–378.

Hinrichs, K., & Jessoula, M. (2012). *Labour Market Flexibility and Pension Reform: Flexible Today, Secure Tomorrow?* Basingstoke: Palgrave.

Hofäcker, D. (2015). In line or at odds with active ageing policies? Exploring patterns of retirement preferences in Europe. *Ageing and Society, 35*(7), 1529–1556.

Holzmann, R. (2000). The World Bank approach to pension reform. *International Social Security Review, 53*(1), 11–24.

Höppner, J. (2021). How does self-employment affect pension income? A comparative analysis of European welfare states. *Social Policy and Administration, 55*(5), 921–939.

Immergut, E., Anderson, K., & Schulze, I. (2007). *The Handbook of West European Pension Politics.* Oxford University Press.

Jürges, H., & van Soest, A. (2012). Comparing the well-being of older Europeans: Introduction. *Social Indicators Research, 105*(2), 187–190.

Karl, U., & Torres, S. (2015). *Ageing in Contexts of Migration.* Routledge.

Kohli, M. (2007). The institutionalization of the life course: Looking back to look ahead. *Research in Human Development, 4*(3–4), 253–271.

Kuitto, K., Madia, J. E., & Podesta, F. (2021). Public pension generosity and old-age poverty in OECD countries. *Journal of Social Policy,* 7 July.

Leimgruber, M. (2012). The historical roots of a diffusion process: The three-pillar doctrine and European pension debates (1972–1994). *Global Social Policy, 12*(1), 24–44.

Madero-Cabib, I., & Fasang, A. E. (2016). Gendered work–family life courses and financial well-being in retirement. *Advances in Life Course Research, 27,* 43–60.

Marier, P. (2008). *Pension Politics: Consensus and Social Conflict in Ageing Societies.* Routledge.

Meyer, T., Bridgen, P., & Riedmüller, B. (2007). *Private Pensions versus Social Inclusion? Non-State Provision for Citizens at Risk in Europe.* Edward Elgar Publishing.

Möhring, K. (2015). Employment histories and pension incomes in Europe. *European Societies, 17*(1), 3–26.

Möhring, K. (2018). Is there a motherhood penalty in retirement income in Europe? The role of lifecourse and institutional characteristics. *Ageing and Society, 38*(12), 2560–2589.

Möhring, K. (2021). The consequences of non-standard working and marital biographies for old age income in Europe: Contrasting the individual and the household perspective. *Social Policy and Administration, 55*(3), 456–484.

Möhring, K., & Weiland, A. (2021). Couples' life courses and women's income in later life: A multichannel sequence analysis of linked lives in Germany. *European Sociological Review,* 26 October.

Muller, J. S., Hiekel, N., & Liefbroer, A. C. (2020). The long-term costs of family trajectories: Women's later-life employment and earnings across Europe. *Demography*, *57*(3), 1007–1034.

Müller, K. (1999). *The Political Economy of Pension Reform in Central-Eastern Europe*. Edward Elgar Publishing.

Müller, K. (2008). The politics and outcome of three-pillar pension reforms in Central and Eastern Europe. In C. Arza & M. Kohli (Eds), *Pension Reform in Europe* (pp. 87–106). Routledge.

Myles, J. (2003). What justice requires: Pension reform in ageing societies. *Journal of European Social Policy*, *13*(3), 264–269.

Myles, J., & Pierson, P. (2001). The comparative political economy of pension reform. In P. Pierson (Ed.), *The New Politics of the Welfare State* (pp. 305–333). Oxford University Press.

Naczyk, M., & Seeleib-Kaiser, M. (2015). Solidarity against all odds: Trade unions and the privatization of pensions in the age of dualization. *Politics and Society*, *43*(3), 361–384.

Natali, D. (2008). *Pensions in Europe, European Pensions: The Evolution of Pension Policy at National and Supranational Level*. PIE Peter Lang.

Natali, D. (2017). *The New Pension Mix in Europe: Recent Reforms, Their Distributional Effects and Political Dynamics*. PIE Peter Lang.

Natali, D., & Rhodes, M. (2004). Trade-offs and veto players: Reforming pensions in France and Italy. *French Politics*, *2*, 1–23.

Orenstein, M. A. (2008). Out-liberalizing the EU: Pension privatization in Central and Eastern Europe. *Journal of European Public Policy*, *15*(6), 899–917.

Palier, B. (2010). *A Goodbye to Bismarck? The Politics of Welfare Reforms in Continental Europe*. Amsterdam University Press.

Palier, B., & Martin, C. (2008). *Reforming the Bismarckian Welfare Systems*. Blackwell.

Pearce, N., & Massala, T. (2020). Pension reforms in the UK: 1997 to 2015. Report.

Pierson, P. (1994). *Dismantling the Welfare State? Reagan, Thatcher, and the Politics of Retrenchment*. Cambridge University Press.

Pierson, P. (1996). The new politics of the welfare state. *World Politics*, *48*(2), 143–179.

Pierson, P. (2000). Increasing returns, path dependence, and the study of politics. *American Political Science Review*, *94*(2), 251–267.

Pierson, P. (Ed.). (2001). *The New Politics of the Welfare State*. Oxford University Press.

Radl, J. (2012). Too old to work, or too young to retire? The pervasiveness of age norms in Western Europe. *Work, Employment and Society*, *26*(5), 755–771.

Riekhoff, A.-J., & Järnefelt, N. (2018). Retirement trajectories and income redistribution through the pension system in Finland. *Social Forces*, *97*(1), 27–54.

Rowland, D. T. (2009). Global population aging: History and prospect. In P. Uhlenberg (Ed.), *International Handbook of Population Aging* (pp. 37–65). Springer.

Scarbrough, E. (2000). West European welfare states: The old politics of retrenchment. *European Journal of Political Research*, *38*, 225–259.

Scherger, S. (Ed.). (2015). *Paid Work beyond Pension Age: Comparative Perspectives*. Palgrave.

Schludi, M. (2005). *The Reform of Bismarckian Pension Systems: A Comparison of Pension Politics in Austria, France, Germany, Italy and Sweden*. Amsterdam University Press.

Schoyen, M. A., & Stamati, F. (2013). The political sustainability of the NDC pension model: The cases of Sweden and Italy. *European Journal of Social Security*, *15*(1), 79–101.

Sefton, T., Evandrou, M., Falkingham, J., & Vlachantoni, A. (2011). The relationship between women's work histories and incomes in later life in the UK, US and West Germany. *Journal of European Social Policy*, *21*(1), 20–36.

Settersten, J., Richard, A., & Angel, J. L. (Eds). (2011). *Handbook of Sociology of Aging*. Springer.

Svallfors, S. (2010). Public attitudes. In F. G. Castles, S. Leibfried, J. Lewis et al. (Eds), *The Oxford Handbook of the Welfare State* (pp. 241–251). Oxford University Press.

Taylor-Gooby, P. (2004). New social risks and welfare states: New paradigm and new politics? In P. Taylor-Gooby (Ed.), *New Risks, New Welfare: The Transformation of the European Welfare State* (pp. 209–238). Oxford University Press.

van der Zwan, N. (2014). Making sense of financialization. *Socio-Economic Review*, *12*(1), 99–129.

van Oorschot, W., Roosma, F., Meuleman, B. et al. (2017). *The Social Legitimacy of Targeted Welfare: Attitudes to Welfare Deservingness*. Edward Elgar Publishing.

Vanhuysse, P., & Goerres, A. (2013). *Ageing Populations in Post-Industrial Democracies: Comparative Studies of Policies and Politics*. Routledge.

Vis, B. (2016). Taking stock of the comparative literature on the role of blame avoidance strategies in social policy reform. *Journal of Comparative Policy Analysis*, *18*(2), 122–137.

Vitols, S. (2011). European pension funds and socially responsible investment. *Transfer*, *17*(1), 29–41.

Vlandas, T., McArthur, D., & Ganslmeier, M. (2021). Ageing and the economy: A literature review of political and policy mechanisms. *Political Research Exchange*, *3*(1).

Vliet, Ov., Been, J., & Caminada, K. (2012). Pension reform and income inequality among older people in 15 European countries. *International Journal of Social Welfare*, *21*(S1), 8–29.

Weaver, K. R. (1986). The politics of blame avoidance. *Journal of Public Policy*, *6*(4), 371–398.

Wiß, T. (2015). From welfare states to welfare sectors: Explaining sectoral differences in occupational pensions with economic and political power of employees. *Journal of European Social Policy*, *25*(5), 489–504.

Zaidi, A., Harper, S., Howse, K. et al. (2018). *Building Evidence for Active Ageing Policies: Active Ageing Index and Its Potential*. Palgrave.

7. Poverty, social policy and the welfare state: a research agenda

Bea Cantillon

INTRODUCTION

Poverty reduction should be at the heart of the social policy research agenda. Taking Rawls's theory of justice as an ethical compass, the primary mission of social policy is to improve, to the extent possible, the living conditions of the most vulnerable (Rawls, 1971). However, the empirical evidence suggests that, while relative income poverty among the elderly has declined quite substantially in many countries over the past decades, poverty among the working-age population has started to grow. From the Rawlsian perspective that social and economic inequality is only justified if the least advantaged in society benefit from it, the disquieting simultaneous increase in many European countries of inequality and poverty raises three sets of fundamental questions. First, why, in general, have welfare states in the past decades not been successful in reducing poverty, especially among the working-age population? Second, why are some policies, countries, and welfare regimes more successful in combating poverty than others? Third, which policies are needed in order to be more successful in a future characterized by major transformations such as climate transition, ageing, and digitalization?

This chapter offers a critical review of what social policy research has learned about poverty reduction in Europe. Poverty can be conceptualized in different ways, and in this chapter the focus is on relative income poverty as commonly applied in research on rich countries today (Atkinson et al., 2002). The chapter starts with a brief conceptualization of the time–scale–space relationships between the welfare state, social policy, and poverty and what this means for research strategies to be successful. Then, without pursuing completeness, major research advancements in social policy and poverty research from the past two decades are reviewed. The chapter continues with a critical account of social policy research and presents some recommendations for a deepened research agenda. We argue that, while social policy research in the past could limit itself to studying the impact of individual policies in order to come to recommendations on best practices, research shows that more systemic, forward-looking, and problem-solving approaches are increasingly needed. Due to considerations of space, most of the research cited in this chapter is primarily (but not exclusively) selected from the 2000–2020 issues of the *Journal for European Social Policy*.

POVERTY, SOCIAL POLICY, AND THE WELFARE STATE: A SYSTEMIC APPROACH

The study of the relationship between the welfare state, social policy, and poverty is complex. First, poverty is an ambiguous concept: it essentially refers to a relative, gradual, and multidimensional problem (Atkinson et al., 2002). The dependent variable therefore places great conceptual and methodological demands on the researcher who wants to empirically assess the impact of anti-poverty strategies. Second, poverty trends are typically 'slow trends': sudden changes in the composition and the level of poverty occur only occasionally, as a result of major economic shocks, for example. Observing and explaining slow trends implies great data requirements: long and comparable time series are needed of both the dependent and the many independent variables at play. Third, poverty is the outcome of complex interactions between individual policies, underlying policy paradigms, and the basic architecture of welfare states.

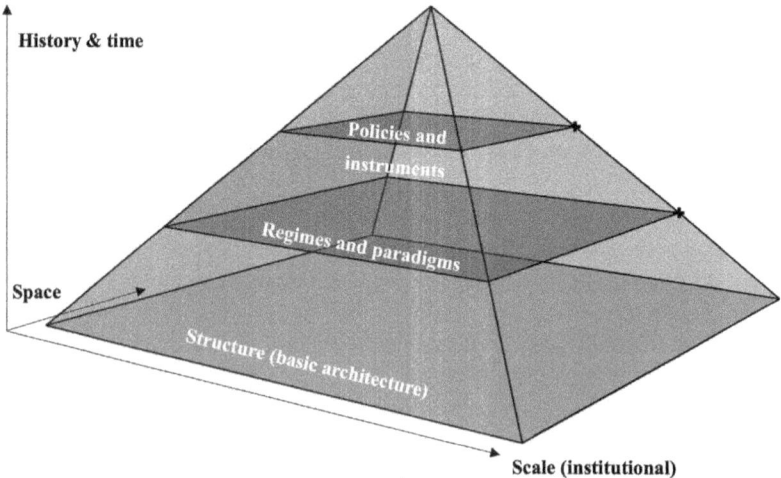

Figure 7.1   Social policy and the welfare state: a systemic approach

Figure 7.1 shows the relationships between social policies and the welfare state in three dimensions (time, space, and scale, to be understood as the extent to which different policy instruments are considered, such as social security, taxation, and education) and three layers (individual policies, policy paradigms, and basic welfare state architecture).[1]

At the top layer of the pyramid, *individual policy interventions* are located. For example, minimum income policy during the pandemic differed from country to country, from region to region, and was time-specific. Such policy interventions are to a certain extent path-dependent and thus linked to previous policies (time); they take place in a broader institutional context, of sometimes long-standing minimum income schemes and other regulations, for example on social security, activation, or minimum wages (scale), while, certainly in Europe, they are also taking place in a broader space than the national welfare state (space). Specific social interventions need therefore to be evaluated as part of a broader institutional context that originated in a more distant past and are dependent or at least influenced by experiences elsewhere.

The second layer of the pyramid representing *welfare regimes and associated policy paradigms* is broader in both time and space, but also in scale. The institutional context and poverty outcomes at this level of analysis represent different policy regimes (or paradigms) that display – although in constant flux – a certain degree of stability over time (for example, in Scandinavian welfare states minimum incomes are typically higher than in liberal regimes). Paradigm changes and their translation into policies occur over many years, involve a whole range of instruments, and their impact on poverty are most likely visible only after a long time.

At the third level of the pyramid, in the broadest time–scale–space dimension, *the basic architecture of the welfare state* characterized by the interplay between capitalist markets, the state, and families is situated. At this level of analysis, social progress in the post-war welfare state rests on the assumptions of full employment, wage growth, better social protection, and expansion of collective goods and services.

To understand the effects of social policy on poverty, contemporary research indicates that it is necessary to go through the three layers of the research pyramid. Let us take minimum income protection as an example. At the top, the theoretical impact of minimum income policies on poverty can be studied using simulation models. Standard simulations suggest, for example, that means-tested minimum incomes are inadequate in most countries (Marchal, 2017), while empirical simulations of more generous social assistance benefits suggest that this would be a more effective route to reducing poverty than, for example, increasing minimum wages (Leventi et al., 2019).

A broader time, space, and scale perspective reveals, however, more nuanced but no less disquieting insights. Cross-country comparisons shed light on, for example, positive associations between the size of social assistance and high poverty rates (space). Or to take yet another example, by studying the relationship between minimum income protection and minimum wages, it appears that more generous minimum benefits might create unemployment traps with a potentially negative impact on the employment of low-skilled workers (scale; see, e.g., Carone et al., 2004). Such findings qualify the outcome of simulation models predicting that increasing the generosity of social assistance is the most efficient path to poverty reduction. Comparisons across time and space might, moreover, show that the inadequacy of the social floor is a long-standing and fairly universal problem in welfare states which might point in the direction that there is more to it than just individual policy (non-)interventions (time; see, e.g., Marchal, 2017). This might suggest that there are factors at play that transcend policy options in the upper zone of the pyramid.

The poverty-reducing effect of minimum income protection is clearly more complex than what might be inferred from approaches that focus only on what happens at the top of the pyramid. To understand the structural nature of the inadequacy of minimum income protection we must descend to the base of the pyramid. For example, the 'productivity pay gap' which has become a major focus of research might support the hypothesis that the inadequacy of the social floor is related to the decoupling in many countries of wages and productivity so as to put a 'glass ceiling' on minimum incomes (Cantillon, 2011). Another structural explanation that also relates to the bottom layer of the pyramid might refer to the impact of social-demographic changes on the evolution of the poverty line itself. The spread of dual earnership may have exerted an upward effect on the poverty line, making it more difficult to maintain adequate social protection for single-earner families (Marx & Nolan, 2012). Both trends might point to a *systemic* feature of the inadequacy of the social floor in post-war welfare democracies.

Solutions can look very different depending on the time–scale–space perspective of the analysis. Social policy research shows that too narrow a focus risks heavily restricted or even wrong solutions. When studying the impact of social policy on poverty, researchers need a broader lens. In the case of minimum income protection, not only interventions in the minimum income schemes as such need to be evaluated but also (1) policy packages (for example, the effect of minimum incomes on poverty cannot be studied in isolation from low wages); (2) policy paradigms and associated bundles of policies (for instance, restrictions on the generosity of social minima may be part of and compensated by work-related welfare reforms that effectively reduce unemployment among the low skilled); and (3) the structure of the welfare state itself in the broader macroeconomic and social context (for example, restrictions on the generosity of social minima may *not* be compensated by work-related welfare reforms because of a simultaneous drop in minimum wages or a skewed distribution of work).

SOCIAL POLICY AND POVERTY: THE KNOWS, DON'T KNOWS, AND NEED TO KNOWS

In recent decades we have seen strong investment – both in Europe and elsewhere in the world – in the collection of data on the material and immaterial living conditions of individuals and households. Back in the 1980s, the Luxembourg Income Study was the first project to allow cross-country comparison of such data from national sources. Thanks to the European Union Statistics on Living Conditions, there are now European data series based on largely harmonized survey methods and administrative databases. Thanks to the Eurosystem Household Finance and Consumption Survey, wealth and debt can also be taken into account in the measurement of poverty within and across countries.

Innumerable studies have relied on these data in trying to chart and understand the phenomenon of poverty and social exclusion in a cross-national perspective. Across countries, large differences have been found in poverty levels but, invariably, lone parents, low-skilled persons, households with a low work intensity, migrants, and benefit claimants are at greater risk.[2] Strikingly, many countries have seen a steady decline in poverty among older persons, but low incomes lag behind the median, especially among working-age individuals and their children (Cantillon & Vandenbroucke, 2014; Nolan, 2018; Cantillon et al., 2019; Fischer & Strauss, 2020).

In Europe, between 2004 and 2007, trends combined three patterns: stability in at-risk-of-poverty rates for the non-elderly population in the majority of countries, increasing poverty rates in some countries, and decreasing poverty rates in yet another set of countries. Overall, the verdict on the anti-poverty ambitions of the Lisbon strategy was unequivocal: poverty had not decreased in most European nations (Cantillon & Vandenbroucke, 2014). In the aftermath of the 2008 financial crisis, the picture had become truly negative, not in the least due to strong diverging trends within the European Union. Decreasing employment rates in the recession brought increasing poverty rates in different degrees: at-risk-of-poverty increased dramatically in some of the Southern European countries whereas in other countries trends were less disappointing (Cantillon et al., 2019). In the decade that followed, in Southern European countries the bottom of the distribution fell away. The new member states did relatively well, mainly due, however, to falling severe material deprivation among non-poor households, while in the old member states poverty and inequality increased (Fischer & Strauss, 2020).

As a general trend, since the second half of the 1990s, relative income poverty started to grow in many countries, especially among the working-age population, low skilled, and jobless households, while child poverty began to rise, pointing to what might be referred to as a precarization of poverty. Also, in-work poverty is a cause for concern because in many countries trends have been upward (Marx & Nolan, 2012; Crettaz, 2013; Halleröd et al., 2015). This occurred in Europe but also elsewhere in rich welfare states, albeit at different levels and speed. What has social policy research learned about the role of social policies and the impact of welfare states' social fabrics?

Without striving for completeness, in the following the many relevant research findings on the impact of social policies on poverty are organized according to the different layers of the research pyramid proposed in Figure 7.1. What has social policy research learned about the impact of (bundles) of policies? What do we know about the effect of different welfare regimes and of changing policy paradigms? And what do we know about the effectiveness of the modus operandi of the welfare state itself in a changing social, economic, and demographic environment?

The Impact of Policies

Anti-poverty policies, broadly defined, are aimed at (a) reducing market income poverty and increasing social promotion through labour market regulation, activation, and capacitating services; (b) redistributing income through taxation and at social protection; and (c) social intervention within local communities.

Pre-distribution and social promotion

The relationship between social policies, market income inequality, and poverty is a complex one. Social policy reduces market income distribution through labour market and minimum wage regulations, activation, investment in human capital, childcare, etc., while, on the other hand, too generous social benefits might cause unemployment traps, especially for the low skilled, and reduce job opportunities which might lead to a more unequal pre-distribution (Mayes, 2002; Vandelannoote & Verbist, 2019). These issues lie at the heart of recent social policy research also because of the paradigmatic shift that has taken place in many countries since the second half of the 1990s towards work-related welfare reforms and social investment having the reduction of market income poverty as their goal. In general it has been shown that more 'pre-distribution equality' goes hand in hand with less poverty (see, e.g., Kammer et al., 2012).

Given the importance of income from work for most people of working age, employment and wage distribution are of obvious importance in reducing market income poverty. However, research has pointed at several reasons why employment gains do not necessarily translate into lower poverty rates. These include the growth of in-work poverty (Halleröd et al., 2015; Lohmann & Marx, 2019); the 'inefficient allocation' of employment, when the additional jobs do not go to the poor, low work-intensity households (Vandenbroucke & Corluy, 2014); and inadequate social protection for those who do not benefit from job growth. Dealing with all three of these factors is important in any strategy to reduce poverty but research suggests that doing so brings conflict. Achieving both employment growth, especially among the low skilled, and adequate social protection requires important efforts in terms of both the budgets involved and the construction of a coherent policy package (see, e.g., Vandelannoote & Verbist, 2019). While research on how to design efficient in-work benefits and tax credits is well developed (see, e.g., Kenworthy, 2019), research on how to pursue a better allocation of jobs among households and on strategies to create job opportunities for the low skilled is scarcer.

In recent decades, a shift in policies from (a) 'protection' to 'activation' and (b) transfers to services (e.g., childcare) has been witnessed and is referred to by some authors as a 'social investment turn' (Hemerijck, 2017) in the wake of which social policy research has increasingly focused on the impact of ena-bling policies, such as childcare and life-long learning. Investigations of such strategies suggest that they are at least in the short term subject to Matthew effects (Parolin & Van Lancker, 2021). However, once indirect effects on poverty (for example, via employment) are taken into consideration, and anal-yses are made more long term, the effects of social investment might be found to be more (Plavgo & Hemerijck, 2021) or less pro-poor (Havnes & Mogstad, 2011;[3] Parolin & Van Lancker, 2021). Measuring these effects thus require analyses with a broad time perspective that also takes into account the wider social and economic context in which these policy interventions take shape (see the second and third layers of the research pyramid).

The reduction of market income poverty is related to the broader issue of equality of opportunity and equality of outcomes which is central to the debate over the potential of social investment strategies. Influential authors such as Giddens (1998)[4] have argued for a shift in policy focus from 'equality of outcome' to 'equality of opportunity' and from 'protecting' to 'activation and empowerment'. Research has, however, pointed to the persistence of traditional stratification cleavages (Pintelon et al. (2013), which admittedly differs greatly in different welfare regimes; Esping-Andersen, 2014; Bukodi & Paskov, 2018). It has also been shown that capacitating services whose purpose is to increase equality of opportunity tend to generate Matthew effects, referring to strong inequalities in the take-up. The use of these services might thus jeopardize the potential equalizing effects of childcare services on the future life chances of vulnerable children (Parolin & Van Lancker, 2021).

Research on the effects of income poverty on children's developmental opportunities has also given support to the idea that inequality of outcome directly affects inequality of opportunity.

Wealth is another important issue related to the pre-distribution of economic wellbeing. Research has pointed to the unequal distribution of gifts and inheritances and to the fact that the poor have generally few assets (Kuypers & Marx, 2021). The relation between wealth and anti-poverty strategies is, however, still in its infancy and needs to be further deepened, especially in terms of problem-solving strategies (see Marx & Nolan, 2012). Interestingly, Morelli et al. (2018) suggest making the link between income and wealth poverty on the one hand and the concentration of wealth at the top on the other. Research on anti-poverty strategies that goes beyond the focus on poverty alone should embrace such essential and broadening issues both theoretically and empirically, and also indicate avenues along which further policy-oriented research may proceed.

Redistribution and protection
Vertical solidarity through progressive taxation and targeted social assistance redistributes from the rich to the poor. Horizontal 'piggy bank' solidarity redistributes between persons who are in different phases in their life cycle, for example from the healthy to the sick. Social spending levels suggest that the welfare state is mainly a collective piggy bank (Barr, 2001) designed for horizontal and life-course redistribution. Consistent with the universalism thesis, the late John Hills articulated the virtue of horizontal redistribution as follows:

> As a result of all this variation in circumstances over our lives between good times and bad times, most of us get back something at least close to what we pay in over our lives towards the welfare state. When we pay more than we get out, we are helping our parents, our children, ourselves at another time. (Hills, 2014)

Generally, a negative relationship is found between targeting and universality (see Korpi & Palme, 1998), although recent research indicates a significant weakening of the relationship. Marx et al. (2012), among others, found that the relationship between the extent of targeting and redistributive impact has in fact become a very weak one. Today, targeting tends to be associated with higher levels of redistribution, especially when overall effort in terms of spending is high. Further fundamental research needs to be done on the causes and drivers of this important research that calls into question a hitherto generally accepted hypothesis in social policy research. One of the possible causes may refer to a systemic weakening of the poverty-reducing effect of horizontal redistribution which we will address now.

The strong poverty-reducing effect of the 'piggy bank' has to do with the size of the budgets involved but also with the fact that horizontal redistribution generates considerable vertical redistribution too. Because low-income groups face higher risks of unemployment or sickness than high-income groups, the horizontal solidarity implied in social insurance systems effectuates significant vertical redistribution from the rich to the poor. Social security benefits are usually also more generous and more effective than targeted social assistance.[5]

While social security remains crucial, recent research shows that, although spending levels kept rising (Greve, 2020), the poverty-reducing capacity of social protection systems for the working-age population declined in many countries (Immervoll & Knotz, 2018; Nolan et al., 2018; Causa & Hermansen, 2019). Social policy researchers have linked this phenomenon with a 'dual transformation' (Bleses & Seeleib-Kaiser, 2004; Cantillon, 2011; Emmeneger et al., 2012) which retrenched earnings-related benefits for the long-term unemployed and atypically employed people and expanded social security to so-called 'new social risks' (Bonoli, 1997) that benefit two-earner families in higher income groups more (Pavolini & Van Lancker, 2018). Fleckenstein et al. (2011) pointed to functional underpinnings – the changed skill requirements of deindustrialized economies – for the evaporation of comprehensive unemployment protection on the one hand and the expansion of family policies on the other. This element refers, at least in part, to structural constraints on the poverty-reducing capacity of horizontal redistribution in contemporary welfare states.

Partly for that reason, in the past decades, social assistance has become increasingly more important. Social policy research has, however, pointed out that social assistance faces important inherent problems. The first problem refers to non-take-up (Van Oorschot, 2002; Bargain et al., 2012; De Wilde et al., 2016). The second problem relates to the fact that it is, by design, not preventative as is to a certain extent the case with social insurance.[6] The third problem refers to the structural inadequacy of benefit levels. In Europe, compared to the 60 per cent poverty threshold, even in the most generous settings, minimum income protection for jobless households falls short, in particular for families with children. This seems to be, at least in part, a *structural* problem because in many welfare states the wage floor, too, is inadequate (Marchal, 2017). So conceived, the increase in dependency on social assistance in a large number of countries is worrying, an issue that remains, however, underexposed in social policy research.

Place-based social action
In disconcerting circumstances, from the late 1970s onward, as spontaneous responses to growing social needs, a wide range of local social action emerged on the margins of the welfare state. Gradually, social innovation became

a third pillar of the welfare state (Ferrera, 1996; Oosterlynck et al., 2019; Kazepov et al., 2021), which can hardly be overestimated, as with the support received from Europe (think of the Social Funds) (Greiss et al., 2021). The role of civil society, social entrepreneurs, and local governments is important, but the impact on poverty is difficult to measure. If well designed, local social action can help to empower and capacitate individuals who are insufficiently supported by traditional social policy and improve their capacity to participate in society (Oosterlynck et al., 2019). Although one should not expect these actions alone to have a direct and significant impact on at-risk-of-poverty rates, by alleviating hardship, by forcing public authorities to recognize emerging needs, by strengthening the underlying social fabric, and by fortifying society from inside out, place-based social innovation can help to create the social and political conditions for more enduring poverty reduction. Research is needed here on the interplay between place-based social innovation on the one hand and the institutions of the welfare state on the other: How can best practices be identified? Under which conditions is upscaling possible? Do local initiatives penetrate the institutions of the welfare state and how can different levels reinforce each other (Kazepov et al., 2021)?

About the impact of policy regimes and policy paradigms

From the foregoing, it appears that success in combating poverty is related to multiple factors, such as the extent to which the institutions of the welfare state succeed in reducing market income inequality, in redistributing resources by means of social and fiscal transfers, and in providing access to services such as health care, education, childcare, and lifelong learning. Poverty outcomes can only be understood as the outcome of the whole of these interventions, which might be referred to as the 'social fabric' of the welfare state.

Between the multiple functions of the welfare state there are many positive interactions but also difficult trade-offs, for instance, between work and poverty or between horizontal and vertical solidarity. Different types of welfare states deal with these trade-offs in different ways, resulting in structurally different poverty outcomes. For instance, the performance of the Scandinavian welfare states is structurally – considered over the longer term – better than that of the liberal welfare states, although policy changes appear to have altered this general statement, as evidenced by the dramatic rise in poverty in Sweden over the past 20 years (Cronert & Palme, 2019). In a study of the social outcomes of different welfare regimes, Kammer et al. (2012) replicated the established welfare typology (as suggested by Esping-Andersen (1990) and Ferrera (1996)) focusing on distributional outcomes. They identified the Nordic welfare regime (plus the Netherlands and Belgium), where pre-distribution inequality is low and redistribution high, on the one hand

and the conservative, liberal, and Southern model typically combining higher market income inequality and less redistribution on the other hand.

From a similar perspective, considering the relationship between wage inequality, service employment, and public spending, in the late 1990s, Iversen and Wren (1998) identified three policy routes: the Scandinavian route, combining high employment, high public expenditure, and low poverty; the Anglo-Saxon route, with high employment, low public expenditure, and high poverty; and the continental route, characterized by a constellation of low employment, high social expenditure, and low poverty. Based on these observations, they came to the conclusion that 'governments and nations confront a three-way choice, or "trilemma", between budgetary restraint, income inequality and employment growth' (Iversen & Wren, 1998: 508). As evidenced by the previous discussion of the relationship between employment and poverty, on the inadequacy of the social minima and on the decrease of the poverty-reducing capacity of social spending, while it seems possible to pursue two of these goals simultaneously, subsequent research has confirmed that it might have become difficult to achieve all three (Collado et al., 2019). Almost 25 years after Iversen and Wren's social trilemma publication just about all rich welfare states combine, on the one hand, (almost) full employment (at least among the high skilled) and historical high social spending with, on the other hand, rising poverty among the low skilled (Cantillon et al., 2019).

In the second half of the 1990s, in trying to overcome difficult choices between spending, jobs, and poverty, all hope was placed on employment-centred welfare reform and, more generally, on 'social investment strategies'. The impact of these strategies on poverty has been the subject of much scholarly discussion to which we have already referred. Providing an assessment of social investment policies is a task of crucial importance but has proven to be a challenging one (think of childcare as part of social investment strategies, the impact of which can only be assessed after many years, partly because the impact on the opportunities of children in poor households will only become apparent in later stages of children's lives and partly because the investment in childcare should be viewed as part of broader policy packages, e.g., in the sphere of social protection and employment[7]). While it is difficult to empirically pinpoint the causes of rising poverty in recent decades (a trend that *preceded* the roll-out of social investment policies and therefore cannot be linked directly, or at least not exclusively, to it) it is certain that in many countries poverty has continued to rise among the working-age population, children, and the low educated despite the reorientation of the social policy paradigm. Conceptually, one can contrast a 'high road' to employment creation, based on training, education, and decent jobs, with a 'low road' to employment creation, pushing unemployed people into low-paid jobs or into inadequate benefit systems. The simultaneous increasing in-work poverty and poverty for work-poor households signals that in a number of rich countries the 'low road' has dominated in recent decades. The question is whether this was inevitable: Would the high road have been possible and, if so, under what conditions? To answer this fundamental question, social policy researchers must penetrate deeper into the third layer of the research pyramid.

The impact of the structure of the post-war welfare state and the changing nature of needs

What do we know about the structural causes of disappointing poverty trends in rich welfare states? As a starting point for presenting research findings, it is good to start from Atkinson's simple but thoughtful assertion:

> the welfare state and the expansion of transfers, the rising share of wages, the reduced concentration of personal wealth, and the reduced dispersion of wages are candidate explanations for the period of falling European income inequality while the main reason that equalization came to an end appears to be ... that these factors have gone to the reverse or come to an end. (Atkinson, 2015: 75)

This list referring to the basic architecture of the post-war welfare state provides a good summary of the factors that social policy research has identified as structural causes of disappointing poverty trends.

At a systemic level, although there were wide variations, in many countries three major mechanisms were found to be crucial (Cantillon & Vandenbroucke, 2014; Atkinson, 2015; Nolan, 2018; Cantillon et al., 2019). First, post-war full employment for men evolved to a dual labour market in which full employment for the higher-skilled men and women goes together with structural underemployment for low-skilled men and women. Even in the best years of the active welfare state and in the best-performing countries, the activity rate among the low skilled remained well below 60 per cent, leaving 40 per cent of them structurally behind. This has to do with the so-called polarization of jobs but also with what skills are required within occupations (Nolan, 2018). Second, because of shifting demands for labour toward higher-skilled and higher-wage occupations, since the 1990s, in many countries low wages began to lag behind productivity growth and median incomes. As a result also of unemployment in low-skilled households, low wages became increasingly less protective against in-work poverty, especially among lone-parent families (Marx & Nolan, 2012; Halleröd et al., 2015). Third, declining or sluggish growth in earnings for low-wage workers and work-related welfare reforms created downward pressure on the levels of minimum income protection for jobless households. Minimum wages serve as a 'glass ceiling' to the social floor of the welfare state, for reasons of both equity and efficiency. When the wage floor drops below the poverty line, so does social protection (Cantillon et al., 2020).

More generally, despite wide variations, a weakening of the poverty-reducing capacity of social spending has been a common experience in rich welfare states. Fleckenstein et al. (2011) pointed to functional underpinnings – the changed skill requirements of deindustrialized economies and changing family structures – for the evaporation of comprehensive unemployment protection on the one hand and the expansion of family policies on the other.

Much of social policy research is concerned with the assessment of individual measures and practices to accommodate the new context, for example through activation, in-work benefits, more effective social assistance, etc. This work is very important and has provided many useful insights. But, with the aim of framing productive responses, more fundamental reflections on deeper and forward-looking questions are needed: To what extent are disappointing poverty trends linked with macroeconomic policies? How can the wage floor be raised?[8] How can the poverty-reducing capacity of social spending be increased? How can jobs be created for people with a low level of education? How can adequate social floors be guaranteed without creating unemployment traps? Is a focus on affordability (services) rather than adequacy (income protection) part of the answer?

Of course, such fundamental questions place great challenges for research, theoretically and empirically. It is therefore no coincidence that few publications penetrate this fundamental layer of questions. There is also far too little attention paid to fundamental issues relating to poverty policy in the light of future developments, most notably climate transition. In the introduction of a special issue on climate change of the *Journal of European Social Policy*, the editors wrote, 'the linkages between these two issues – climate change and its policy corollaries, and the "traditional" domain of social policies – seem to us so strong and salient that they should be aired in a social policy journal' (Gough et al., 2008). Unfortunately, few studies have subsequently appeared in the journal on the relationship between poverty and climate policy.

In the issues of the *Journal of European Social Policy* of the last 20 years there are also few papers dealing with anti-poverty strategies in the broader macroeconomic context. In a seldom-cited paper, Mayes (2002) assessed, for example, whether macroeconomic developments in Europe would assist the reduction of social exclusion under the Economic and Monetary Union. Mayes concluded that the objectives of the Lisbon Council would be difficult to meet and he was proved right. He predicted that rapid structural change would have adverse asymmetric effects on average and regional unemployment and that increased public spending would have disincentive effects echoing the above-mentioned Iversen and Wren's social trilemma. He concluded that combating exclusion needs to focus on building 'capabilities' to participate in society and economic activity. But here his prediction did not (yet?) come true: the 'social investment turn' that had exactly that in mind also failed. Was this due to a flawed implementation of the new paradigm? Is it simply too early to tell? Or were disappointing poverty trends the result of structural obstacles (for instance, limits on the extent to which class mobility can be equivalized, downward pressures on low wages, or unemployment of low-skilled workers)?

Favouring the least advantaged should be the priority of social policy, for ethical reasons and also because poverty has adverse consequences for the people affected and societies as a whole (see, e.g., Wilkinson & Pickett, 2010). The sobering conclusions of social policy research on poverty discussed in this chapter raises therefore fundamental questions: Which transformations of political economies are needed, if any (see for a critical account Nolan, 2018)? Which alternative policy orientations beyond the strategies deployed today are conceivable (for instance a partial basic income, support for social entrepreneurship, wealth taxation, etc.)? What should and could be the role of Europe? These questions should feature prominently on the social policy research agenda of the future.

CONCLUSION

Social policy research on poverty has made great progress in terms of conceptualization and measurement (Atkinson et al., 2002). Central conclusions from research are that (a) social policies, if well designed, are decisive in preventing and alleviating poverty; (b) some countries and welfare regimes are structurally better equipped than others; (c) the paradigmatic 'social investment turn' and associated work-related welfare reforms could not prevent poverty to increase among the working-age, less educated, and workless families throughout. This sobering conclusion raises three fundamental issues.

First, are the disappointing poverty trends similar when social progress is assessed from a *multidimensional* perspective? Scholarship on poverty and policies has, after all, an overwhelmingly one-sided focus on inequalities in income and wealth.

Second, to what extent is the rise of poverty among the working-age population *systemic*, that is (a) consistent with the basic characteristics of the post-war national welfare state and (b) encompassing the organization of the welfare state as a whole? Social policy research suggests that the fairly universal experience of rising income poverty among the working-age population accompanied by growing inequalities may *not (only) be the result of failing social policy intervention here and there.*

Third, is there a need to consider *alternative policy orientations beyond the strategies deployed today* and what form should or could these strategies take against the backdrop of ageing, digitalization, and climate transition? Here questions arise, for example, about the potential of a basic income to lift the social floor or about the role of Europe in strengthening the poverty-reducing capacity of national welfare states, e.g., through regulations on minimum wages.

Whereas social policy research in the past could limit itself to studying the impact of individual policies in order to come to recommendations on best practices, now more systemic, forward-looking, and problem-solving approaches are needed. To that end, social policy research should take a wider time, scale, and space perspective, looking not only at individual policies but also at bundles of policies, how these bundles are tied to the architecture of welfare states, how welfare states interact with each other, and how they respond to changing social, economic, and ecological needs. The role of Europe should also appear more prominently on the research agenda.

To a large extent, social policy research remains stuck in the upper reaches of the analytical research pyramid which we proposed in the first section of this contribution. However important it is to understand the impact of individual policies, against the backdrop of decades of failure in making progress in the fight against poverty and inequality, with the view on the major economic, demographic, and ecological changes that lie ahead of us, it must be our ambition to penetrate further into the functioning of the welfare state in order to understand the arguably structural nature of unsolved poverty problems. Only then will we be able to understand the non-fulfilment of the mission of the welfare state, to identify promising new policy practices and to study alternatives.

ACKNOWLEDGEMENTS

I am grateful to Sarah Marchal, Anton Hemerijck, Kenneth Nelson, Martin Seeleib-Kaiser, Karel Vandenbosch, Wim Van Lancker, and an anonymous referee for helpful comments. I also thank Heleen Delanghe, Anna Lemmens, and Ingrid Vanzele for their excellent assistance.

NOTES

1. I thank Pieter Leroy for the inspiration for Figure 7.1, which he used in a slightly different version as part of an analysis of policies and climate transition (Leroy, 2021).
2. See the Eurostat social exclusion indicators (2021). Interestingly, the same risk categories emerged from a study that also took into account assets and debt (Kuypers & Marx, 2021).
3. Havnes and Mogdtad (2011) analysed the impact of subsidized childcare in Norway and found little, if any, causal effect of subsidized childcare on maternal employment, despite a strong correlation.
4. It would be a misconception that social investment scholars by and large prioritize capacitation over poverty alleviation. Esping-Andersen et al. (2001) were

adamant – against the Third Way – that strong income protection is needed for an effective social investment strategy.
5. Public opinion research suggests that this is related with greater public legitimacy (Van Oorschot, 2002). Research also pointed to the fact that social insurance is more resistant to retrenchment, inter alia because social partners are usually more directly involved in social security systems than in social assistance (Nelson, 2007).
6. This refers to the strongly debated crowding-out hypothesis (see, e.g., Vandenbroucke & Vleminckx, 2011).
7. See interesting reflections on this in Nolan (2018).
8. See for interesting work Lévay et al. (2020).

REFERENCES

Atkinson, A. B. (2015). *Inequality: What Can Be Done?* Harvard University Press.
Atkinson, A. B., Cantillon, B., Marlier, E., & Nolan, B. (2002). *Social Indicators: The EU and Social Inclusion*. Oxford University Press.
Bargain, O., Immervoll, H., & Viitamäki, H. (2012). No claim, no pain. Measuring the non-take-up of social assistance using register data. *Journal of Economic Inequality, 10*, 375–395.
Barr, N. (2001). *The Welfare State as Piggy Bank: Information, Risk, Uncertainty, and the Role of the State*. Oxford University Press.
Bleses, P., & Seeleib-Kaiser, M. (2004). *The Dual Transformation of the German Welfare State*. Palgrave Macmillan.
Bonoli, G. (1997). *Classifying Welfare States: A Two-Dimension Approach*. Cambridge University Press.
Bukodi, E., & Paskov, M. (2018). Income inequality, living standards, and intergenerational social mobility. In B. Nolan (Ed.), *Generating Prosperity for Working Families in Affluent Countries* (p. 352). Oxford University Press.
Cantillon, B. (2011). The paradox of the social investment state: Growth, employment and poverty in the Lisbon era. *Journal of European Social Policy, 21*(5), 432–449.
Cantillon, B., & Vandenbroucke, F. (2014). *Reconciling Work and Poverty Reduction: How Successful Are European Welfare States?* Oxford University Press.
Cantillon, B., Goedemé, T., & Hills, J. (2019). Decent Incomes for All: Improving Policies in Europe. Oxford University Press.
Cantillon, B., Parolin, Z., & Collado, D. (2020). A glass ceiling on poverty reduction? An empirical investigation into the structural constraints on minimum income protections. *Journal of European Social Policy, 30*(2), 129–143.
Carone, G., Immervoll, H., Paturot, D., & Salomäki, A. (2004). *Indicators of Unemployment and Low-Wage Traps* (Marginal Effective Tax Rates on Employment Incomes). OECD.
Causa, O., & Hermansen, M. (2019). *Income Redistribution through Taxes and Transfers across OECD Countries* (Economics Department Working Papers no. 1453). OECD.
Collado, D., Cantillon, B., Van den Bosch, K. et al. (2019). The end of cheap talk about poverty reduction: The cost of closing the poverty gap while maintaining work incentives. In B. Cantillon, T. Goedemé, & J. Hills (Eds), *Decent Incomes for All: Improving Policies in Europe* (p. 314). Oxford University Press.

Crettaz, E. (2013). A state-of-the-art review of working poverty in advanced econo-mies: Theoretical models, measurement issues and risk groups. *Journal of European Social Policy*, *23*(4): 347–362.

Cronert, A., & Palme, J. (2019). Social investment at crossroads: 'The third way' or 'the enlightened path' forward? In B. Cantillon, T. Goedemé, & J. Hills (Eds), *Decent Incomes for All*. Oxford University Press.

De Wilde, M., Cantillon, B., Vandenbroucke, F., & De Bie, M. (2016). *40 jaar OCMW en bijstand*. Acco.

Emmeneger, P., Hausermann, S., Palier, B., & Seeleib-Kaiser, M. (2012). *The Age of Dualization: The Changing Face of Inequality in Deindustrializing Societies*. Oxford Scholarship, May.

Esping-Andersen, G. (1990). *The Three Worlds of Welfare Capitalism*. Princeton University Press.

Esping-Andersen, G. (2014). Welfare regimes and social stratification. *Journal of European Social Policy*, *25*(1), 124–134.

Esping-Andersen, G., Gallie, D., Hemerijck, A., & Myles, J. (2001). *A New Welfare Architecture for Europe?* Report submitted to the Belgian Presidency of the European Union. September.

Eurostat. (2021). *Social Exclusion Indicators*. https://ec.europa.eu/eurostat/web/employment-and-social-inclusion-indicators/social-protection-and-inclusion/social-inclusion.

Ferrera, M. (1996). The 'Southern model' of welfare in social Europe. *Journal of European Social Policy*, *6*, 17–37.

Fischer, G., & Strauss, R. (Eds). (2020). *Europe's Income, Wealth, Consumption, and Inequality*. Oxford University Press.

Fleckenstein, T., Saunders, A. M., & Seeleib-Kaiser, M. (2011). Comparing Britain and Germany: The dual transformation of social protection and human capital. *Comparative Political Studies*, *44*(12), 1622–1650.

Giddens, A. (1998). *The Third Way: The Renewal of Social Democracy*. Polity Press.

Gough, I., Meadowcroft, J., Dryzek, J., Gerhards, J., Lengfeld, H., Markandya, A., & Ortiz, R. (2008). JESP symposium: Climate change and social policy. *Journal of European Social Policy*, *18*(4), 325–344.

Greiss, J., Cantillon, B., & Penne, T. (2021), The fund for European aid to the most deprived: A Trojan horse dilemma? *Social Policy and Administration*, *55*(4), 622–636.

Greve, B. (2020). *Austerity, Retrenchment and the Welfare State: Truth or Fiction?* Edward Elgar Publishing.

Halleröd, B., Ekbrand, H., & Bengtsson, M. (2015). In-work poverty and labour market trajectories: Poverty risks among the working population in 22 European countries. *Journal of European Social Policy*, *25*(5), 473–488.

Havnes, T., & Mogstad, M. (2011). No child left behind: Subsidized child care and children's long-run outcomes. *American Economic Journal: Economic Policy*, *3*(2), 97–129.

Hemerijck, A. (Ed.). (2017). *The Uses of Social Investment*. Oxford University Press.

Hills, J. (2014). *Good Times, Bad Times: The Welfare Myth of Them and Us*. Policy Press.

Immervoll, H., & Knotz, C. (2018). *How Demanding Are Activation Requirements for Jobseekers* (IZA DP No. 11704). Institute of Labor Economics.

Iversen, T., & Wren, A. (1998). Equality, employment and budgetary restraint: The trilemma of the service economy. *World Politics*, *50*(4), 507–546.

Kammer, A., Niehues, J., & Peichl, A. (2012). Welfare regimes and welfare state outcomes in Europe. *Journal of European Social Policy, 22*(5), 455–471.

Kazepov, Y., Cucca, R., Barberis, E., & Mocca, E. (2021). *Handbook of Urban Social Policy*. Edward Elgar Publishing.

Kenworthy, L. (2019). *Social Democratic Capitalism*. Oxford University Press.

Korpi, W., & Palme, J. (1998). The paradox of redistribution and strategies of equality: Welfare state institutions, inequality, and poverty in the Western countries. *American Sociological Review, 63*(5), 661–687.

Kuypers S., & Marx, I. (2021). *Poverty in the EU Using Augmented Measures of Financial Resources: The Role of Assets and Debt* (CSB Working Paper No. 21/02). Herman Deleeck Centre for Social Policy, University of Antwerp.

Leroy, P. (2021). Klimaat en sociale verandering: Valt de U-turn te sturen? in *UCSIA, the U-turn: Naar een nieuw sociaal contract*, Universitair Centrum Sint-Ignatius Atwerpen, pp. 169–188.

Lévay, P. Z., Vanhille, J., Goedemé, T., & Verbist, G. (2020). *The Association between the Carbon Footprint and the Socio-Economic Characteristics of Belgian Households* (CSP Working Paper 20/05). Herman Deleeck Centre for Social Policy, University of Antwerp.

Leventi, C., Sutherland, H., & Tasseva, I. V. (2019). Improving poverty reduction in Europe: What works best where? *Journal of European Social Policy, 29*(1), 29–43.

Lohmann, H., & Marx, I. (2019). *Handbook on In-Work Poverty*. Edward Elgar Publishing.

Marchal, S. (2017). *The Social Floor: Essays on Minimum Income Protection*. Doctoral thesis, University of Antwerp.

Marx, I., & Nolan, B. (2012). In-work poverty. In B. Cantillon & F. Vandenbroucke (Eds), *Reconciling Work and Poverty Reduction: How Successful Are European Welfare States?* (pp. 60–93). Oxford University Press.

Marx, I., Vandenbroucke, P., & Verbist, G. (2012). Can higher employment levels bring down relative income poverty in the EU? Regression-based simulations of the Europe 2020 target. *Journal of European Social Policy, 22*(5), 472–486.

Mayes, D. G. (2002). Social exclusion and macro-economic policy in Europe: A problem of dynamic and spatial change. *Journal of European Social Policy, 12*(3), 195–209.

Morelli, S., Nolan, B., & Van Kerm, P. (2018). Wealth inequality. In B. Nolan (Ed.), *Generating Prosperity for Working Families in Affluent Countries*. Oxford University Press.

Nelson, K. (2007). Universalism vs targeting: The vulnerability of social insurance and means-tested minimum income protection in 18 countries, 1990–2002. *International Social Security Review, 60*(1), 33–58.

Nolan, B. (2018). *Generating Prosperity for Working Families in Affluent Countries*. Oxford University Press.

Nolan, B., Leventi, C., Sutherland, H., & Tasseva, I. (2018). Strengthening redistribution. In B. Nolan (Ed.), *Generating Prosperity for Working Families in Affluent Countries*. Oxford University Press.

Oosterlynck, S., Novy, A., Kazepov, Y., Cools, P., Saruis, T., Leubolt, B., & Wukovitsch, F. (2019). Improving poverty reduction. In B. Cantillon, T. Goedemé, & J. Hills (Eds), *Decent Incomes for All: Improving Policies in Europe* (p. 314). Oxford University Press.

Parolin, Z., & Van Lancker, W. (2021). What a social investment 'litmus test' must address: A response to Plavgo and Hemerijck. *Journal of European Social Policy*, *31*(3), 297–308.

Pavolini, E., & Van Lancker, W. (2018). The Matthew effect in childcare use: A matter of policies or preferences? *Journal of European Public Policy*, *25*(6), 878–893.

Pintelon, O., Cantillon, B., Van den Bosch, K., & Whelan, C. (2013). The social stratification of social risks: The relevance of class for social investment strategies. *Journal of European and Social Policy*, *23*(1), 52–67.

Plavgo, I., & Hemerijck, A. (2021). The social investment litmus test: Family formation, employment and poverty. *Journal of European Social Policy*, *31*(3), 282–296.

Rawls, J. (1971). *A Theory of Justice*. Harvard University Press.

Van Oorschot, W. J. H. (2002). Targeting welfare: On the functions and dysfunctions of means testing in social policy. In P. Townsend & D. Gordon (Eds), *World Poverty: New Policies to Defeat an Old Enemy*. Policy Press.

Vandelannoote, D., & Verbist, G. (2019). *The Design of In-Work Benefits: How to Boost Employment and Combat Poverty in Belgium*. ImPRovE Working Paper, WP16/15, Herman Deleeck Centre for Social Policy, University of Antwerp.

Vandenbroucke, F., & Corluy, V. (2014). Individual employment, and risk of poverty in the European Union. A decomposition analysis. In B. Cantillon & F Vandenbroucke (Eds), Reconciling Work and Poverty Reduction: How Successful Are European Welfare States? (pp. 94–130). Oxford University Press.

Vandenbroucke, F., & Vleminckx, K. (2011). Disappointing poverty trends: Is the social investment state to blame? *Journal of European Social Policy*, *21*(5), 450–471.

Wilkinson, R., & Pickett, K. (2010). *The Spirit Level*. Penguin Books.

8. Research on active social policy

Giuliano Bonoli

INTRODUCTION

Academic interest on active social policy goes back to the late 1990s. At the time, most debates and attention focused on retrenchment and on the putative dismantling of European welfare states. However, some scholars pointed out that retrenchment was not the only relevant development going on in European social policy. Welfare states were also being reoriented and were taking up a new function, i.e., the promotion of labour market participation, as a way to fight disadvantage. The process of welfare state transformation came to be conceptualized as a two-dimensional process: retrenchment in relation to the traditional dimension of social policies, i.e., income replacement for individuals and households unable to obtain an income from the market; and expansion in relation to the new social policies that were meant to increase the labour market participation of those who needed state help. This two-dimensional process was identified by a few authors at the time and referred to with different terms, such as 'recalibration' (Ferrera & Rhodes, 2000), 'adaptation' (Bonoli, 2001), or a more colourful 'turning vice into virtue' (Levy, 1999).

In subsequent years, academic interest for active social policy intensified. On the one hand, interest was driven by developments in politics. The early 2000s saw the installation of centre-left progressive governments in several European countries. Referring to a 'Third Way', several of these governments promoted a social policy reform agenda that combined retrenchment in traditional social policies with expansion in the new ones. In short, new policies aimed at facilitating access to the labour market and at increasing employment rates in general, such as active labour market policies and childcare, were being developed, while old age pensions were cut (Bonoli & Powell, 2004; Huo, 2009).

On the other hand, academics were realizing that the Nordic welfare states were resisting particularly well to the twin pressures of globalization and population ageing (Scharpf & Schmidt, 2000; Esping-Andersen, 2002). And unlike much of continental Europe, these countries had been practising active social policy long before the 1990s. This was especially true of Sweden, which had introduced a system of active labour market policy as early as in the 1950s (Swenson, 2002).

By the 2000s, active social policy had become mainstream, and a key theme in both policy and research. Researchers were initially concerned with issues of definitions and classification. Is active social policy really something new? Is it different from retrenchment? More recent years have witnessed the development of two interesting lines of research on active social policy, which will be discussed in more detail below. Interestingly, this development has provided opportunities for the social policy research community to engage in a dialogue with other disciplines, mostly economics and political science. The first line of research concerns impacts. One key question is whether or not active social policy can deliver levels of social cohesion and reductions in inequality that are comparable to those achieved by the redistribution-heavy welfare states of the post-war years. The second recent line of research concerns the politics of active social policy, which has coincided with a change of terminology as reference is made increasingly to the notion of social investment. Research on the politics of active social policy or of social investment has focused on the processes (Bonoli, 2013), on patterns of coalition formation (Häusermann, 2010), and, more recently, on public opinion (e.g., Busemeyer & Garritzmann, 2017).

While we have witnessed major advances in our ability to understand its impact and its politics, active social policy remains a vibrant sub-field of social policy research. Key questions concern, for example, perceptions of deservingness to social investment interventions, understanding better Matthew effects and how to limit them, and the role that active social policy and social investment can play in emerging multicultural societies.

The chapter follows a loosely chronological line, starting with discussing early concerns in relation to definitions and qualifications of active social policies. It then moves on to consider research on the impact of active social policy and its politics. It concludes by highlighting open questions and areas in which further research is needed.

DEFINITIONS AND INTERPRETATIONS

With the emergence of active social policy across countries, the initial efforts of the research community were geared towards developing a definition and, perhaps more crucially, an interpretation of what the activation turn meant for Western welfare states.[1] Was it an improvement in relation to the mostly passive benefits that were dominant in much of the post-war years? Or was it instead a departure from the post-war settlement? The debate was intense, and concerned also how the shift in policy should be labelled.

One critical line of analysis of active social policy used the term 'workfare'. In this perspective, the shift to active social policy is largely seen as a departure from the welfare state of the post-war years. Emphasis is put on conditionality, time limits on recipiency, and use of sanctions against jobseekers as a tool to put pressure on them (Shragge, 1997; Lødemel & Trickey, 2001; Peck, 2001). Workfare is definitely considered as a normative departure from the post-war settlement, and as a return to a more punitive approach in social policy, which was a common feature in the old poor relief systems of the pre-modern era (Lødemel & Trickey, 2001).

Others pointed out the fundamental ambiguity of active social policy (Clasen, 2000; Barbier, 2001, 2004; Clegg, 2005) and argued that active social policies cannot be subsumed under a traditional one-dimensional view of social policy, referring to expansion and retrenchment. In order to deal with this problem, various authors have tried to develop a more multifaceted categorization, based on the identification of different types of active policies. These classifications tend to draw a line between the 'good' activation policies, which are about improving human capital, and the 'bad' ones, which use essentially negative incentives to move people from welfare programmes into employment. Examples of such classifications are found in Torfing (1999), who distinguishes between 'offensive' and 'defensive' workfare. Offensive workfare, which is the term used to describe the Danish variant of activation, relies on improving skills and empowering jobless people rather than on sanctions and benefit reduction, which is the 'defensive' variant found in the United States. Taylor-Gooby (2004) makes the same point using instead the terms of 'positive' and 'negative' activation.

In a similar vein, Barbier distinguishes between 'liberal activation' (characterized by stronger work incentives, benefit conditionality, and the use of sanctions) and 'universalistic activation', which is found in the Nordic countries and relies on extensive investment in human capital essentially through training (Barbier, 2004; Barbier & Ludwig-Mayerhofer, 2004). Barbier also hypothesizes the existence of a third type, found within continental Europe. This third type of activation emphasizes '*insertion sociale*', referring more to full participation in society and less to the fact of actually having a job. Its tools are job creation programmes in the public or non-profit sector (Barbier, 2001; Enjolras et al., 2001).

Dichotomies between human investment and incentive-based approaches to activation are a useful starting point in making sense of an ambiguous concept. However, they probably constitute an oversimplification of the real world and run the risk of carrying value judgements. The recent debate on social investment is no exception (Morel et al., 2012; Hemerijck, 2017). Social investment typically refers to a variant of active social policy that emphasizes the strengthening of human capital, and is less concerned with reinforcing work incentives (Esping-Andersen, 2002, 2009; Jenson, 2002; Jenson & Saint-Martin, 2006; Jenson, 2009; Morel et al., 2012). The term social investment is often used in a prescriptive, normative way. For example, Esping-Andersen (2002) calls for a new 'social investment' welfare state, whereas Vandenbroucke et al. (2011) advocate for a social investment pact for Europe, which in periods of harsh fiscal constraints should prioritize policies that support children, lifelong learning, work and family reconciliation, and so forth. Similarly, Hemerijck (2012) asks for 'affordable social investment' (i.e., policies that can be developed in spite of the dire state of public finances).

I have elsewhere developed a two-dimensional classification of active policies based on the degree to which emphasis is placed on (1) promotion of labour market participation and (2) investment in human capital (Bonoli, 2010). Next, I will discuss what we know about the impacts and politics surrounding these policies.

THE IMPACT OF ACTIVE SOCIAL POLICY

Research on the impact of active social policy can be divided into three sub-strands. First, several evaluation studies have tried to assess the impact of individual interventions. A large number of studies are available on the impact of individual interventions in the field of active labour market policies, as well as a few meta-analyses. In addition, one can also find a few studies on the impact of interventions targeted at children, on outcome variables such as child development and educational achievement. The second strand concerns broader studies on the overall impact of the turn to active social policy in terms of the ability to fight poverty and reduce inequality. Finally, a third strand of analysis has focused on the existence of access bias in active social policies. Referring to 'Matthew effects', these studies help in understanding the limits of active social policy as a universalist approach.

Studies on the impact of active social policies have seen the social policy community engaging in a dialogue with other disciplines, most notably labour economics, which is dominant in the evaluation literature. On other topics, such as the Matthew effect, the contribution of social policy scholars has been more substantial. Overall, the study of the impact of active social policies is a clearly interdisciplinary endeavour.

Active Labour Market Policy

Individual labour market programmes have been evaluated for the past few decades in nearly all countries in the Organisation for Economic Co-operation and Development. The result is that we can rely on a large number, a few hundred, of evaluation studies to understand what the potential of labour market policy is and what are the most promising types of interventions.

Fortunately, the knowledge contained in this vast corpus of research has been synthesized in a small number of literature reviews and meta-analyses.

Martin and Grubb (2001) are among the first to attempt to summarize the knowledge generated in these evaluation studies. Among the most effective types of interventions for gainful employment were programmes designed to help jobseekers in their job search efforts, while job creation schemes in the public sector seemed to be the least effective ones. This finding has been largely confirmed by subsequent studies.

Other important contributions are by Jochen Kluve and various colleagues, who have published several meta-analyses based on a growing corpus of literature (Kluve, 2006, 2010; Card et al., 2010, 2017). Given the fact that with time more studies have become available, the meta-analyses have also become more sophisticated in terms of methods and measurements used. The early meta-analyses simply distinguished between effective and non-effective programmes. They found that relative to training, the interventions categorized as 'services and sanctions' were more likely to help jobseekers find a job. In contrast, job creation programmes in the public sector were found to be clearly inferior to training (Kluve, 2006). Subsidies to private-sector jobs were also found to be an effective intervention.

The most recent work by this group of researchers confirms these findings. Job creation schemes are found to be mostly ineffective, even counter-productive in some cases. Job search assistance schemes and subsidies to private-sector jobs are found to be rather effective, and training is also found to be effective, but mostly in the medium to long run (Card et al., 2017). In another meta-analysis, researchers have tried to estimate the size of the impact of labour market programmes (Filges et al., 2015). They found an overall positive impact of participation and an average post-programme impact on employment probability of seven percentage points (but with great variation among programmes).

Overall, active labour market policies seem to be able to deliver positive outcomes in terms of facilitating access to the labour market for non-working individuals. However, the findings of this strand of research also point out that the effects are rather limited in size, in the sense that only a small minority of participants benefit from the programme. Using a metric borrowed from the medical sciences, Filges et al. (2015) point out that in order to allow one jobseeker to find employment, 15 jobseekers have to be treated.

Early Childhood Education and Care

The idea that investments in children and particularly in child development are an effective way to fight disadvantage has been made prominent in the work of James Heckman (e.g., Heckman, 2006), and subsequently emphasized in other important contributions to the debate on social policy (Esping-Andersen, 2009). Early childhood education and care (ECEC) can support child development in various ways. First, by directly investing in children's human capital and thus stimulating the development of both cognitive and non-cognitive skills (Kautz et al., 2014). Second, by improving the parental work–family balance and thus creating a better family context for children to grow up in (Kulic et al., 2019).

In general, studies of the impact of ECEC on child development have found positive impacts. In some cases, impacts are extremely favourable. This is the case, for example, of the well-known Perry pre-school study in which returns on investment of a magnitude of 600 per cent were estimated (Barnett & Masse, 2007). Apparently, the gains were essentially due to improvements in non-cognitive skills (Heckman & Kautz, 2012).

Other studies which have focused on the impact of participation in standard formal childcare have found less spectacular results, but still positive in general. For one of the German states, Felfe and Lalive (2018) find limited impact of participation in childcare overall, but a positive effect for immigrant children and for children of low-educated mothers in terms of language and socio-emotional wellbeing. Studying also Germany, but on the basis of a larger dataset, Cornelissen et al. (2018) find the same result, i.e., a clear positive effect of participation only for disadvantaged children. Kaiser and Bauer (2019) find that immigrant children who have experienced centre-based childcare display higher levels of overall wellbeing. The same conclusion is reached by Felfe et al. (2015) for Spain, where children of socially disadvantaged parents benefit from participation. For Norway, Havnes and Mogstad (2015) also find a positive effect of participation in childcare for children living in households in the lower and middle part of the income distribution. Finally, Datta-Gupta and Simonsen (2010), using Danish data, find a positive impact of centre-based childcare on non-cognitive skills at age seven, and also among children from disadvantaged backgrounds. No effects were found for home care.

Overall, the literature on the impact of ECEC services on child development is consistent in finding mostly positive effects for children from disadvantaged backgrounds. Well-targeted programmes can contribute to reduce the achievement gap among children of different socio-economic backgrounds (Kulic et al., 2019).

Overall Impact on Inequality

Micro-level impact studies of active social policies show modest but positive effects on both access to employment and child development. Is there evidence of a macro-level impact of these interventions? Of course, this question is considerably more difficult to answer, for want of a counterfactual and because some of the interventions that go under the rubric of active social policy will take decades to produce measurable impacts on macrosocial indicators, such as levels of inequality and poverty. As a result, the evidence on the impact of the shift to active social policy is at best tentative.

One line of argument on the impact of the activation and social investment turn in European social policy is that it has been mostly detrimental to the fight against poverty and inequality. This is because the policies that have been put in place have benefitted mostly individuals living in less disadvantaged households. On the other hand, the expansion of the active welfare state has gone hand in hand with reductions in cash benefits. The net result is a loss for the most disadvantaged. This view has been most forcefully put forward by Bea Cantillon, who has shown that the employment gains of pre-crisis 2000 have concerned essentially households with a relatively high level of labour market participation (Cantillon, 2011). Jobless households, in contrast, did not gain to any significant extent. Van Vliet and Wang (2015) found that increases in spending on social investment policies are associated with increases in poverty rates (though not in the Nordic countries). These macro-level studies suggest that social investment policies may be failing to reach those who need them the most.

A more optimistic view has been put forward by Plavgo and Hemerijck (2021), who show an association between family and children's living conditions and the degree of development of social investment policies. Their argument is not so much one of a direct relationship between social investment policies and improved family wellbeing, but more one that makes reference to configurations of policies, economic structures, labour market practices, and possibly societal values, a notion that is reminiscent of Esping-Andersen's 'regime' (1990). This position, however, implies that the selective development of specific social investment policies may be insufficient to achieve the desired social outcomes. This view resonates with the argument put forward by Kazepov and Ranci (2016), that social investment policies to be effective require a favourable context, in terms of institutions, the labour market, and possibly societal values (Parolin & Van Lancker, 2021).

Matthew Effects

How do we reconcile the mostly positive, if modest, effects of active social policies at the programme level, with absence of clear evidence at the macro level? One possible explanation lies in the access bias observed in relation to most active or social investment policies. In the social policy literature, this bias is often referred to as a 'Matthew effect' (Gal, 1998). This notion refers to the fact that it is often not the most disadvantaged who profit most from given social policies, but individuals who already possess some resources. Matthew effects have been identified in public services such as health and education (Le Grand, 1982) or family benefits (Deleeck et al., 1983), but also in typical social investment policies, such as subsidized childcare (e.g., Bonoli et al., 2017; Pavolini & Van Lancker, 2019) or active labour market policy (Bonoli & Liechti, 2018).

Matthew effects may be inevitable in active labour market policies. Since the ultimate objective of active social policy is to promote access to the labour market, and the labour market is by definition a selective institution, the selectivity of the labour market will likely trickle down into the policies that promote participation. Examples are training programmes that improve the human capital of jobless individuals. These can be rather effective, but in order to be enrolled participants often need to have some basic cognitive and non-cognitive skills. Those who don't, are likely to be excluded from participation. Hence, we observe a bias in terms of access to good-quality labour market training programmes (Heckman & Smith, 2003; Bonoli & Liechti, 2018; Pisoni, 2018).

Things may be different for childcare services, even though a strong Matthew effect has been observed also in relation to access to formal childcare (Ghysels & Van Lancker, 2011; Abrassart & Bonoli, 2015; Pavolini & Van Lancker, 2019). With regard to childcare, we can expect that appropriate policy design will drastically reduce the observed Matthew effects. Increasing supply and reducing the cost for parents, particularly low-income parents, as well as allowing access to children of unemployed parents, are likely to make an important contribution to reducing the extent of the Matthew effect. As a matter of fact, in Sweden, a country with a large supply of heavily subsidized childcare places, childcare participation is not related to parental socio-economic status (Van Lancker & Ghysels, 2012).

The existence of Matthew effects has been widely documented in a large corpus of the literature. Matthew effects are thus likely to be an inherent feature of active social policies. The focus on the promotion of labour market participation often affects access to these policies. Improved design may reduce potential access biases, possibly more in the field of childcare than in relation to policies for adults.

THE POLITICS OF ACTIVE SOCIAL POLICY

With the emergence of a political debate on active social policy, political scientists took an interest in the politics of the new social policies. Support or opposition to active social policy is generally conceptualized as a second dimension of contention in social politics, which is orthogonal to the main one, i.e. the vertical dimension of more versus less welfare effort. The idea that social policy in the twenty-first century is a two-dimensional political game was put forward in several early contributions on the politics of active social policy (Bonoli, 2001; Häusermann, 2010; Bonoli & Natali, 2012; Häusermann, 2012).

The view that social policymaking is a two-dimensional game offers scope for explaining change as the result of complex interactions among actors, who can trade gains and losses across dimensions. This means that the outcome of reform processes is difficult to predict, and depends on the preferences and power resources of the various actors involved (Häusermann, 2012, 2018). In the political game, promoting active social policy can be attractive for at least some political actors. At times of 'permanent austerity', social policymaking tends to revolve around retrenchment in most social policy fields, which makes it difficult for governments to engage in credit claiming. Relative to the traditional risk and income redistributive policies, active social policies offer high visibility at a comparatively low cost, and constitute as a result an opportunity for 'affordable credit claiming', which may help to explain the vast expansion of active social policies over the last three decades (Bonoli, 2012).

The political idea of 'affordable credit claiming' resonates with analyses of active social policies embraced by the Third Way governments who were in power at the turn of the century. A commitment to budgetary responsibility combined with a wish to modernize the welfare state provided a good fit with active social policies (Huo, 2009). However, the support-generating capacity of active social policy was a short-lived phenomenon. The social democratic parties who followed the Third Way approach in social policy lost the support of many of their traditional working-class voters and found themselves marginalized in subsequent years (Arndt, 2013).

A more recent and promising line of research on the politics of active social policies has focused on individual preferences. In general, public opinion tends to be rather favourable to increasing public spending on policies like education or childcare, which encompass clear elements of social investment. However, the support diminishes dramatically when respondents are made aware that increased spending may require tax increases or cuts in other areas of the welfare state (Busemeyer, 2017; Busemeyer & Garritzmann, 2017; Neimanns et al., 2018).

Research on public opinion suggests that active social policy appeals mostly to the middle and upper classes. Support for the more incentive-based forms of active social policies comes mostly from high-income groups holding conservative values. Active social policies with a stronger emphasis on investment in human capital are instead mostly supported by the highly educated and by people holding left-libertarian values. Low-income and low-educated people have clear preferences for traditional passive cash transfer policies (Garritzmann et al., 2018).

The politics of active social policy is complex, but thanks to the research carried out in the last few decades, it is relatively well understood. Active social policy has some broad appeal with large sections of the electorate. However, it is unlikely to generate strong popular support. This is likely to be true regardless of whether the emphasis is on the more aggressive workfare-based approaches or on the 'tranquil composure' (Hemerijck, 2015) of social investment. As a result, political actors will not be able to turn an active social policy agenda into a vote winner.

CONCLUSION: NEW RESEARCH AVENUES

Over the last three decades, research on active social policies by sociologists, economists, and political scientists has helped improve our understanding of this type of social intervention. Advances in research have been substantial, and we now understand these policies quite well. However, some blind spots remain. In this last section, I will try to outline some avenues that will be worth exploring over the next few years.

First, access biases and Matthew effects are crucial limitations to any reform strategy based on active social policy. We need to better understand the sources of this access bias, so as to be able to design policies that minimize them. Arguably, Matthew effects are inevitable in active and social investment policies. However, appropriate policy design can limit them. Matthew effects can have different origins. This may be due to shortage of supply (as in child-care), to the fact that target groups may lack the required skills, or to imple-mentation processes driven by a rigid bureaucratic logic (Pisoni, 2018). Some of these sources of Matthew effects may be easier to get rid of than others.

Second, active social policy is likely to play a crucial role as a tool to manage emerging multicultural societies (see Bonoli, 2020). How suitable is active social policy to this endeavour? In addition to the access bias, which is obviously relevant for immigrants, other questions deserve attention. One such question is how active social policy intersects with labour market discrimination.

Third, research is needed on perceptions of deservingness and active social policy (Heuer & Zimmermann, 2020). Perceptions of deservingness are likely to gain in importance in emerging multicultural societies, as country of birth and ethnicity are central criteria in this regard (e.g., van Oorschot 2006; Petersen et al., 2010; Reeskens & Van der Meer, 2019). Is this true also for active social policy, and is there a difference in perceptions of deservingness for immigrant groups between programmes aimed at labour market participa-tion versus human capital investment? As this short list of avenues for future research shows, active social policy remains a vibrant sub-field of social policy analysis. We can expect some exciting developments over the next few decades.

NOTE

1.   This section draws on research published in Bonoli (2013), chapter 2.

REFERENCES

Abrassart, A., & Bonoli, G. (2015). Availability, cost or culture? Obstacles to childcare services for low income families. *Journal of Social Policy*, *44*(4), 787–806.
Arndt, C. (2013). *The Electoral Consequences of Third Way Welfare State Reforms: Social Democracy's Transformation and Its Political Costs*. Amsterdam University Press.
Barbier, J.-C. (2001). *Welfare to Work Policies in Europe: The Current Challenges of Activation Policies*. Centre d'études de l'emploi.
Barbier, J.-C. (2004). Systems of social protection in Europe: Two contrasted paths to activation, and maybe a third. In J. Lind, H. Knudsen, & H. Jørgensen (Eds), *Labour and Employment Regulation in Europe* (pp. 233–254). Peter Lang.
Barbier, J.-C., & Ludwig-Mayerhofer, W. (2004). Introduction: The many worlds of activation. *European Societies*, *6*(4), 424–436.
Barnett, W. S., & Masse, L. N. (2007). Comparative benefit-cost analysis of the Abecedarian program and its policy implications. *Economics of Education Review*, *26*(1), 113–125.
Bonoli, G. (2001). Political institutions, veto points, and the process of welfare state adaptation. In P. Pierson (Ed.), *The New Politics of the Welfare State* (pp. 238–264). Oxford University Press.
Bonoli, G. (2010). The political economy of active labour market policies. *Politics and Society*, *38*(4), 435–457.
Bonoli, G. (2012). Credit claiming and blame avoidance revisited. In G. Bonoli & D. Natali (Eds), *The Politics of the New Welfare State*. Oxford University Press.
Bonoli, G. (2013). *The Origins of Active Social Policy: Active Labour Market Policy and Childcare in a Comparative Perspective*. Oxford University Press.
Bonoli, G. (2020). Immigrant integration and social investment. *Journal of European Social Policy*, *30*(5), 616–627.
Bonoli, G., & Liechti, F. (2018). Good intentions and Matthew effects: Access biases in participation in active labour market policies. *Journal of European Public Policy*, *25*(6), 894–911.
Bonoli, G., & Natali, D. (2012). Multidimensional transformations in the early 21st century welfare states. In G. Bonoli & D. Natali (Eds), *The Politics of the New Welfare State*. Oxford University Press.
Bonoli, G., & Powell, M. (Eds). (2004). *Social Democratic Party Policies in Contemporary Europe*. Routledge.
Bonoli, G., Cantillon, B., & Van Lancker, W. (2017). Social investment and the Matthew effect. In A. Hemerijck (Ed.), *The Uses of Social Investment*. Oxford University Press.

Busemeyer, M. R. (2017). Public opinion and the politics of social investment. In A. Hemerijck (Ed.), *The Uses of Social Investment* (pp. 358–367). Oxford University Press.

Busemeyer, M. R., & Garritzmann, J. L. (2017). Public opinion on policy and budgetary trade-offs in European welfare states: Evidence from a new comparative survey. *Journal of European Public Policy*, *24*(6), 871–889.

Cantillon, B. (2011). The paradox of the social investment state: Growth, employment and poverty in the Lisbon era. *Journal of European Social Policy*, *21*(5), 432–449.

Card, D., Kluve, J., & Weber, A. (2010). Active labor market policy evaluations: A meta-analysis. *The Economic Journal*, *120*.

Card, D., Kluve, J., & Weber, A. (2017). What works? A meta analysis of recent active labor market program evaluations. *Journal of the European Economic Association*, *16*(3), 894–931.

Clasen, J. (2000). Motives, means and opportunities: Reforming unemployment compensation in the 1990s. *West European Politics*, *23*(4), 89–112.

Clegg, D. (2005). Activating the multi-tiered welfare state: social governance, welfare politics and unemployment policies in France and the United Kingdom. Doctoral thesis, European University Institute.

Cornelissen, T., Dustmann, C., Raute, A., & Schonberg, U. (2018). Who benefits from universal child care? Estimating marginal returns to early child care attendance. *Journal of Political Economy*, *126*(6), 2356–2409.

Datta-Gupta, N., & Simonsen, M. (2010). Non-cognitive child outcomes and universal high quality child care. *Journal of Public Economics*, *94*(1–2), 30–43.

Deleeck, H., Huybrechs, J., & Cantillon, B. (1983). *Het Mattüseffect*. Kluwer.

Enjolras, B., Laville, J.-L., Fraisse, L., & Trickey, H. (2001). Between subsidiarity and social assistance. The French Republican route to activation. In I. Lødemel & H. Trickey (Eds), *An Offer You Can't Refuse: Workfare in International Perspective* (pp. 71–104). Policy Press.

Esping-Andersen, G. (1990). *The Three Worlds of Welfare Capitalism*. Polity Press.

Esping-Andersen, G. (Ed.). (2002). *Why We Need a New Welfare State*. Oxford University Press.

Esping-Andersen, G. (2009). *The Incomplete Revolution: Adapting to Women's New Roles*. Polity Press.

Felfe, C., & Lalive, R. (2018). Does early child care affect children's development? *Journal of Public Economics*, *159*, 33–53.

Felfe, C., Nollenberger, N., & Rodríguez-Planas, N. (2015). Can't buy mommy's love? Universal childcare and children's long-term cognitive development. *Journal of Population Economics*, *28*, 393–422.

Ferrera, M., & Rhodes, M. (2000). Recasting European welfare states: An introduction. *West European Politics*, *23*(2), 1–10.

Filges, T., Smedslund, G., Knudsen, A.-S. D., & Jørgensen, A.-M. K. (2015). Active labour market programme participation for unemployment insurance recipients: A systematic review. *Campbell Systematic Reviews*, *2*.

Gal, J. (1998). Formulating the Matthew principle: On the role of the middle classes in the welfare state. *Scandinavian Journal of Social Welfare*, *7*(1), 42–55.

Garritzmann, J. L., Busemeyer, M. R., & Neimanns, E. (2018). Public demand for social investment: New supporting coalitions for welfare state reform in Western Europe? *Journal of European Public Policy*, *25*(6), 844–861.

Ghysels, J., & Van Lancker, W. (2011). The unequal benefits of activation: An analysis of the social distribution of family policy among families with young children. *Journal of European Social Policy, 21*(5), 472–485.

Häusermann, S. (2010). *The Politics of Welfare State Reform in Continental Europe.* Cambridge University Press.

Häusermann, S. (2012). The politics of new and old social risks. In G. Bonoli & D. Natali (Eds), *The Politics of the New Welfare State* (pp. 111–134). Oxford University Press.

Häusermann, S. (2018). The multidimensional politics of social investment in conservative welfare regimes: Family policy reform between social transfers and social investment. *Journal of European Public Policy, 25*(6), 862–877.

Havnes, T., & Mogstad, M. (2015). Is universal child care leveling the playing field? *Journal of Public Economics, 127*, 100–114.

Heckman, J. J. (2006). Skill formation and the economics of investing in disadvantaged children. *Science, 312*, 1900–1902.

Heckman, J. J., & Kautz, T. (2012). Hard evidence on soft skills. *Labour Economics, 19*(4), 451–464.

Heckman, J. J., & Smith, J. A. (2003). The determinants of participation in a social program: Evidence from a prototypical job training program. *Journal of Labor Economics, 22*(2), 243–298.

Hemerijck, A. (2012). *Changing Welfare States.* Oxford University Press.

Hemerijck, A. (2015). The quiet paradigm revolution of social investment. *Social Politics: International Studies in Gender, State and Society, 22*(2), 242–256.

Hemerijck, A. (2017). Social investment and its critics. In A. Hemerijck (Ed.), *The Uses of Social Investment* (pp. 3–42). Oxford University Press.

Heuer, J.-O., & Zimmermann, K. (2020). Unravelling deservingness: Which criteria do people use to judge the relative deservingness of welfare target groups? *Journal of European Social Policy, 30*(4), 389–403.

Huo, J. (2009). *Third Way Reforms: Social Democracy after the Golden Age.* Cambridge University Press.

Jenson, J. (2002). *From Ford to Lego: Redesigning Welfare Regimes.* Annual Meeting of the American Political Science Association.

Jenson, J. (2009). Redesigning citizenship regimes after neoliberalism: Moving towards social investment. In N. Morel, B. Palier, & J. Palme (Eds), *What Future for Social Investment?* (pp. 27–44). Institute for Future Studies.

Jenson, J., & Saint-Martin, D. (2006). Building blocks for a new social architecture: The LEGO(TM) paradigm of an active society. *Policy and Politics, 34*(3), 429–451.

Kaiser, M., & Bauer, J. M. (2019). Preschool child care and child well-being in Germany: Does the migrant experience differ? *Social Indicators Research, 144*(3), 1367–1390.

Kautz, T., Heckman, J. J., Diris, R., Weel, B. t., & Borghans, L. (2014). *Fostering and Measuring Skills: Improving Cognitive and Non-Cognitive Skills to Promote Lifetime Success.* National Bureau of Economic Research Working Paper 20749.

Kazepov, Y., & Ranci, C. (2016). Is every country fit for social investment? Italy as an adverse case. *Journal of European Social Policy, 27*(1), 90–104.

Kluve, J. (2006). *The Effectiveness of European Active Labour Market Policy.* IZA Discussion Paper No. 2018.

Kluve, J. (2010). The effectiveness of European active labor market programs. *Labour Economics, 17*(6), 904–918.

Kulic, N., Skopek, J., Triventi, M., & Blossfeld, H.-P. (2019). Social background and children's cognitive skills: The role of early childhood education and care in a cross-national perspective. *Annual Review of Sociology*, *45*(1), 557–579.

Le Grand, J. (1982). *The Strategy of Equality: Redistribution and the Social Services*. Allen and Unwin.

Levy, J. (1999). Vice into virtue? Progressive politics and welfare reform in continental Europe. *Politics and Society*, *27*(2), 239–273.

Lødemel, I., & Trickey, H. (Eds). (2001). *An Offer You Can't refuse: Workfare in International Perspective*. Policy Press.

Martin, J., & Grubb, D. (2001). What works and for whom: A review of OECD countries' experiences with active labour market policies. *Swedish Economic Policy Review*, *8*, 9–56.

Morel, N., Palier, B., & Palme, J. (Eds). (2012). *Towards a Social Investment Welfare State? Ideas, Policies and Challenges*. Policy Press.

Neimanns, E., Busemeyer, M. R., & Garritzmann, J. L. (2018). How popular are social investment policies really? Evidence from a survey experiment in eight Western European countries. *European Sociological Review*, *34*(3), 238–253.

Parolin, Z., & Van Lancker, W. (2021). What a social investment 'litmus test' must address: A response to Plavgo and Hemerijck. *Journal of European Social Policy*, *31*(3), 297–308.

Pavolini, E., & Van Lancker, W. (2019). The immigrant penalty in childcare use: An empirical exploration for 22 European countries. Unpublished paper.

Peck, J. (2001). *Workfare States*. Guildford Press.

Petersen, M. B., Slothuus, R., Stubager, R., & Togeby, L. (2010). Deservingness versus values in public opinion on welfare: The automaticity of the deservingness heuristic. *European Journal of Political Research*, *50*(1), 24–52.

Pisoni, D. (2018). Activating the most disadvantaged youth in Switzerland: Administratively too risky, politically too costly? *International Social Security Review*, *71*(4), 51–70.

Plavgo, I., & Hemerijck, A. (2021). The social investment litmus test: Family formation, employment and poverty. *Journal of European Social Policy*, *31*(3), 282–296.

Reeskens, T., & Van der Meer, T. (2019). The inevitable deservingness gap: A study into the insurmountable immigrant penalty in perceived welfare deservingness. *Journal of European Social Policy*, *29*(2), 166–181.

Scharpf, F. W., & Schmidt, V. A. (Eds). (2000). *Welfare and Work in the Open Economy*. Oxford University Press.

Shragge, E. (1997). *Workfare: Ideology for a New Under-Class*. Garamond Press.

Swenson, P. A. (2002). *Capitalists against Markets: The Making of Labor Markets and Welfare States in the United States and Sweden*. Oxford University Press.

Taylor-Gooby, P. (2004). New risks and social change. In P. Taylor-Gooby (Ed.), *New Risks, New Welfare?* (pp. 1–27). Oxford University Press.

Torfing, J. (1999). Workfare with welfare: Recent reforms of the Danish welfare state. *Journal of European Social Policy*, *9*(1), 5–28.

Van Lancker, W., & Ghysels, J. (2012). Who benefits? The social distribution of subsidized childcare in Sweden and Flanders. *Acta Sociologica*, *55*(2), 125–142.

van Oorschot, W. (2006). Making the difference in social Europe: Deservingness perceptions among citizens of European welfare states. *Journal of European Social Policy*, *16*(1), 23–42.

Van Vliet, O., & Wang, C. (2015). Social investment and poverty reduction: A comparative analysis across fifteen European countries. *Journal of Social Policy, 44*(3), 611–638.

Vandenbroucke, F., Hemerijck, A., & Palier, B. (2011). *The EU Needs a Social Investment Pact*. OSE, Opinion Paper No. 5.

PART II

Cross-cutting research themes

9. Researching social Europe on the move

Caroline De la Porte and Ilaria Madama

INTRODUCTION

From the 1990s onwards, developments occurring at the supra-national level have prompted a lively scholarly debate about the nature and impact of social Europe, which has evolved together with changes in the regulation and governance of the social sphere within the European Union (EU) multilevel setting. While domestic politics and processes remain determinants for social policy, the result of decades of furthering European integration is that member states have become increasingly semi-sovereign with regard to their welfare states and labour markets (Ferrera, 2005; Pierson & Leibfried, 2005).

In the early phase of the integration process, when it was only through regulation that the EU influenced welfare states and labour markets, research tended to focus extensively on social rights for mobile EU citizens (Börner, 2020). Relying on the principle of equal treatment within the framework of the coordination of social security regimes, this literature primarily emphasized the role of the Court of Justice of the European Union (CJEU) in interpreting the legislative provisions of social policy (cf. Leibfreid, 2005; Martinsen, 2015). In this period and up to the 1990s, EU initiatives in the social sphere have been conceived as 'encapsulated federalism', that is, a strong direct impact of the EU but limited to narrow areas – i.e., gender equality and health and safety at work – that were not connected with the core redistributive function of welfare states (Streeck, 1995). Other scholars, however, have argued that even many early initiatives often embodied market-correcting goals and had far-reaching consequences, enhancing equality and with it fundamental social rights for citizens in the EU, even beyond mobile citizens (Falkner, 1998, 2010).

Later, following the Maastricht Treaty in 1992, new forms of indirect and direct mechanisms of governance have come into play, and through hard and soft policy coordination, the EU has started to influence core redistributive areas, such as pensions and health care, unemployment schemes, and labour market regulation (Radaelli, 2000; Zeitlin & Pochet, 2005; Graziano & Vink,

2007). In this phase, and especially from the early 2000s, a new bulk of studies dealing more specifically with the open method of coordination (OMC) and its influence on domestic labour market and social policy reform flourished (De la Porte & Pochet, 2002; Heidenreich & Zeitlin, 2009; Barcevičius et al., 2014).

The onset of the financial crisis prompted a renewed interest in the indirect influence of the EU on welfare states, via the newly strengthened Economic and Monetary Union (EMU) governance procedures (Costamagna, 2013; De la Porte & Heins, 2016); whereas research on soft coordination processes entered a new phase, by investigating more deeply the interplay between EU policy and funding instruments and their influence on member states' policies, shedding light on the functioning of hybrid governance modes (Jessoula, 2015; Jessoula & Madama, 2019). Overall, in the past few years, scholars interested in the interactions between the EU and member states in social policy have focused on multiple different issues, including EMU governance and its consequences on pensions and labour market reforms, policy coordination and funding, and regulatory initiatives led by the European Pillar of Social Rights (EPSR).

More recently, the outbreak of the COVID-19 pandemic has stimulated a new stream of studies interested in EU responses to the unprecedented crises scenario, in particular via the new fiscal instruments that are likely to relate to welfare states, and novel social and labour market programmes, such as support to short-term work schemes, as well as recovery and resilience funds (Armingeon et al., 2021; De la Porte & Jensen, 2021).

Drawing from these partly intertwined branches of the literature, this chapter aims to investigate the long-term trajectory of scholarly research on social Europe, roughly from the 1990s to its current state, identifying key emerging topics. To this end, we propose a preliminary periodization in the uneven path of social Europe, distinguishing four main phases: the early phase until the mid-1990s; the EMU and the Lisbon era (mid-1990s–2008); the Great Recession decade (2008–2019); and finally the current times led by the COVID-19 pandemic, whose transformations are likely to dominate the research agenda in the future. In what follows, for each broad phase we identify key developments, together with the prevailing modes of governance in core social policy fields, and provide a discussion of the major findings of the academic debate.

THE EARLY PHASE: MARKET MAKING THROUGH SOCIAL SECURITY COORDINATION AND FREE MOVEMENT

In the early phase of European integration, due to the lack of competences at the supra-national level to decide upon national social security – the design of social security systems, including access and level of generosity of social benefits and services, were decided at the national level – the EU developed legislation in narrow areas, captured by the notion of 'encapsulated federalism' (Streeck, 1995: 400), a concept which reflects the strong impact of the EU in areas such as gender equality and health and safety at work, that are not connected with the core redistributive function of welfare states. At the same time, market making facilitated the freedom of movement of workers, whereby social security systems were coordinated, enabling mobile workers to be protected by the social security systems of their host countries. From the 1970s onwards, the CJEU's interpretation of various principles, such as equality of treatment (access to benefits), exportability (the right for individual workers to export social benefits), and additionality (the right to add periods of social security, especially pensions), has led to wide-ranging consequences for national social security systems for mobile EU citizens. This has resulted in the extension of the material scope of coordination of social security over time, ranging from areas such as family allowances to student grants. This led Pierson and Leibfried (2005) to assess that welfare states had become 'semi-sovereign'; the CJEU has had a prominent role in interpreting core EU principles, especially regarding access to social rights and the social security of workers in host countries (Bell, 2012; Martinsen, 2015).

Parallel to the growing jurisprudence, the literature addressing the role of the CJEU in social policy integration flourished. While some scholars warned against the risk of overestimation (Wincott, 2001), others have emphasized the crucial role played by the CJEU as an 'engine of integration' (Leibfried & Pierson, 2000; Kelemen, 2012). The CJEU's expansive jurisprudence has been identified as a step towards making Europe more social (Caporaso & Tarrow, 2009). Other scholars have been sceptical about the role of the CJEU for the same reasons, arguing that it is political and activist (Rasmussen, 1986). What is clear is that 'free movement and increasing competition have prompted court cases and thus expanded the bite of European law on national social provisions' (Leibfried & Pierson, 2000: 270). From a different perspective, the asymmetry in the balance between judicial powers and political decision making in the EU multilevel polity prompted a debate about the possible impact of the CJEU's activism on the political autonomy and democratic legitimacy of member states (cf. Scharpf, 2009).

More recently, the literature on the role of the CJEU in incrementally interpreting social policy principles has taken another turn. In contrast to an emphasis on the view of the CJEU as political and activist (Rasmussen, 1986; Leibfried, 2005), there has been a shift to focus on the limitations of its activity (Davies, 2014; Martinsen, 2015), emphasizing the possible deep political and social tensions driven by the expansion of citizenship rights (Geddes & Hadj-Abdou, 2016). While free movement has been a cornerstone of European integration and is celebrated as one of the major achievements of the integration process, the rise of Euroscepticism and of anti-EU sentiment has largely revolved around intra-EU migration and cross-border access to national welfare systems. Recent studies examine the weight of net contributors and benefit recipients among migrants in their host countries, finding that EU migrants are net contributors, not net beneficiaries, of welfare states. This is not surprising, since the large part of citizens living in countries other than their country of origin are workers, whose reason to move to another country is to work (cf. Martinsen & Pons Rotger, 2017).

EMU AND THE LISBON ERA: BETWEEN HARD AND SOFT POLICY COORDINATION

Since the institutionalization of EMU in 1992, it has become evident that the influence of EU action on welfare states and labour markets takes place not only through regulation but also via other modes of governance. From the 1990s onwards, the EU has, in fact, started to influence core redistributive areas – such as pensions and health care, unemployment schemes, and labour market regulation – more pervasively through hard and soft policy coordination.

On the side of hard, yet indirect, policy coordination, one key pillar has come with the adoption of the Stability and Growth Pact (SGP) in 1997, developed to ensure continuous member state compliance with EMU aims. In the framework of EU policies of budgetary restraint, entailing benchmarks and surveillance, member states are required to run budgets that do not jeopardize the functioning of EMU. As social spending makes up the biggest share of public expenditure, the pressure on national welfare states exerted by the SGP has been considerable, especially during economic recessions. Scholarly research has documented the impact of EMU on welfare state reform, especially in the case of states whose public budgets were deemed to be perilous for macroeconomic stability (De la Porte & Natali, 2014). For countries under the 'excessive deficit procedure', through EMU, the EU acquired indirect influence on core redistributive areas, notably pensions, whereas in the field of labour market policy, deregulation and flexibilization were promoted as a way to boost growth. In this respect, the main mechanism of influence in EMU governance has been defined as 'EU-facilitated learning, in the shadow of coercion' (De la Porte, 2017: 146).

On the side of soft, non-binding forms of policy coordination, the reference to the 'European Social Model' became prominent in this phase (Jepsen & Pascual, 2005). Meant as a complement to monetarism, flexibilization of labour markets, and maintaining stable public finances, the label refers to the fact that although welfare states are organized within the boundaries of national borders, the EU level plays a role in promoting social benchmarking and policy coordination – to maintain, but also to foster the modernization of welfare policies. Concretely – in the wake of the Amsterdam Treaty of 1997 – the EU developed new forms of institutionalized policy coordination. In particular, the European Employment Strategy, which mimicked EMU governance but with no hard sanctions, focused on the social side of the labour market and employment policies, for example, encouraging not only increases in employment rates, but also in job quality. Parallel to this, the launch of the Lisbon Strategy in 2000 marked a further milestone for social Europe extending policy coordination to other areas – like pensions, health care, and combatting poverty – via OMC processes. This ensure policies in these areas would not only be economically sustainable, but also socially sustainable, entailing broad access to social rights. While being expected to move towards commonly agreed EU policies and benchmarks (Lopez-Santana, 2007), in line with the principle of subsidiarity and the non-binding nature of commitments, in this coordination framework, member states set their own aims and quantitative targets.

Prompted by such developments, and with an analytical focus on the potential, and the limits, of policy coordination mechanisms based on non-binding indicators, the intense academic debate that followed has produced contrasting assessments of the effectiveness of OMC processes to boost national social policy developments and adaptation in line with common objectives and/or supra-national guidelines and recommendations (cf. Armstrong, 2006; Jessoula & Madama, 2019). Some authors have emphasized the weakness of the social OMCs, suggesting that both their non-binding nature and lack of sanctions have hampered the attainment of commonly agreed objectives (i.e., Barbier, 2005). In contrast, others have interpreted the lack of coercion as a fruitful condition for the unfolding of experimentations and policy learning, while respecting member state heterogeneity and sovereignty (for a review, cf. Heidenreich, 2009; Heidenreich & Zeitlin, 2009). Turning to causal mechanisms at play, through which soft governance processes may affect institutional change at the national level, the literature has identified a number of key factors (cf. Jessoula & Madama, 2019). Mutual learning and socialization processes, jointly with soft sanctions in the form of 'naming, shaming, and faming' got resonance (Kok, 2004). Most studies rely on some form of actor-centred institutionalism; and thus, some studies underline the importance of national political actors' uses of the various European resources (cf. Jacquot & Woll, 2003; Armstrong, 2006; Graziano et al., 2011), by emphasizing the importance of domestic politics as a key filter for the EU's influence on member states' policy trajectories. Although mediated by other factors – including national elite and public attitudes towards Europe and the degree of policy fit/misfit (Graziano et al., 2011) – the use of European resources by national political and social actors has been the means through which OMCs have influenced member states

(Zeitlin, 2009: 231). Yet, as noted by Amandine Crespy (2020), the processes have been highly bureaucratic, and thus not embedded in national public spheres. The areas where the OMC has had some – even if indirect – influence include social investment type policies, in particular childcare and active labour market policy (see Chapter 8 by Bonoli, this volume). Thus, the OMC has supported the activation turn of welfare states, although mainly through ideas and socialization, and especially when they are in line with the political agendas in member states. Yet, implementation of OMC policies are uneven across member states, to a great extent shaped by welfare state configuration (De la Porte & Pochet, 2012).

THE GREAT RECESSION DECADE: ENTRENCHING HARD AND SOFT REGULATION THROUGH HYBRID GOVERNANCE

With the onset of the Great Recession in 2008, the EU agenda shifted dramatically to austerity policies and EMU governance became more constraining. Changes entailed reinforced *ex ante* monitoring and *ex post* surveillance of member states' economies and budgets, of which pensions and health care are important components. These new initiatives tightened the monetarist policy aims and increased the actual EU-level authority to enforce policy in member states. Hard coordination has also been enhanced by more focus on public debt, which has been high on the agenda due to the sovereign debt crisis that affected countries severely hit by the Great Recession. Meanwhile, EU social policies remained soft but were more directly linked to funding programs. 'Europe 2020', that replaced the Lisbon Strategy, became the new overarching institutional setting for the coordination of economic and social processes at the EU level (Sabato & Vanhercke, 2017).

Drawing from these changes which deeply reshaped the institutional framework, the literature started to consider not only the impact of soft social OMCs but also the joint effects of the EMU criteria and softer recommendations, as well as tougher types of conditionality on welfare reforms (Hassenteufel & Palier, 2014; Pavolini et al., 2014; Sacchi, 2014; Theodoropoulou, 2014; Moury et al, 2021). Thus, there was a shift from focusing on individual OMCs and their impact to considering the impact of joint EU processes on welfare states, including pensions and labour market policy (especially through EMU constraint), but also childcare and family policies (through softer social processes).

Many reforms were undertaken during this period, although mostly decided through domestic politics, were conditioned by EU budgetary constraints, particularly EU policy advice in country-specific recommendations and/or excessive deficit procedures (De la Porte & Natali, 2014; Hassenteufel & Palier,

2014; Pavolini et al., 2014). Prominently, research on the influence of EMU's monetarist regime and the convergence criteria has shown that the EU has helped to put pension reform high on the domestic agenda, and that the indirect pressure of EU-induced learning via the strengthened SGP, with iterative monitoring and surveillance backed up by strong enforcement mechanisms, has had a tangible impact on the direction of the reforms. Although it is through domestic politics that decisions about pension reform were made, a country's economic vulnerability has been an important condition enabling decision making (De la Porte & Natali, 2014; Hassenteufel & Palier, 2014). Domestic actors made decisions in the shadow of financial markets and the threat of negative ratings by credit-rating agencies, which represented important intervening factors in reform politics (Pavolini et al., 2014; Sacchi, 2014; Dukelow, 2015; Moury et al., 2021). Even in countries subject to the agreements signed with the 'Troika',[1] domestic politicians were able to negotiate which reforms to pursue. Yet, some were considered fundamental structural reforms, especially labour market flexibilization and pension reforms (Theodoropoulou, 2014; Crespy & Vanheuverzwijn, 2019; Moury et al., 2021).

During this phase, assessments about the salience of the social dimension in the European Semester framework offered two opposite readings: some studies have emphasized the gradual 'socialization' of the Semester (cf. Zeitlin & Vanhercke, 2018), whereas others have pointed to the persistent asymmetry and unbalance in favour of the economic dimension (e.g., Copeland & Daly, 2014; De la Porte & Heins, 2016; Maricut & Puetter, 2018). These views, however, are not mutually exclusive (Jessoula & Madama, 2019). On the one hand, the governance mechanisms in the social (policy) domain remain structurally and legally weaker than in 'core' EU policy fields. On the other hand, in the anti-poverty domain some evidence suggests that after a weak start, supra-national institutions – especially the Commission – have become more vocal, through adapting their strategies and recommendations to member states' domestic conditions and policy priorities; and in some cases the Commission has actually acted as a 'social policy advocate' in order to, at least partly, orient member state anti-poverty strategies (cf. Eihmanis, 2018; Jessoula & Madama, 2019).

Overall, the literature on the OMC became increasingly specialized from 2000 to 2020, looking for causal mechanisms and evidence of change. But the crux of interest, i.e., policy learning and welfare state reform, has remained central throughout. In the literature on the OMC, small-n analyses using qualitative methodology and data have focused on conditions of OMC influence, including institutional capability (Ferrera & Sacchi, 2005), political priorities, and receptiveness of each member state to aims in one policy area (Jessoula & Madama, 2019). Case study-based research using qualitative methods and data theorizes and analyses mechanisms of influence, mainly focusing on socialization, policy learning, and with these, the diffusion of ideas, framing of policy issues, and policy transfer (Lopez-Santana, 2007). This literature – focusing on processes – primarily uses actor-centred institutionalism to examine why, how, and with what consequences governments and non-governmental organizations strategically use the OMC. The findings examine how policy-specific OMCs have led to successful policy change (Büchs, 2007; Armstrong, 2010; Barčevicius et al., 2014). In this respect, the conceptualization of 'hybrid governance' modes (Armstrong, 2010; Jessoula, 2015; Bekker, 2017) – combining supra-national/national hard targets, governance tools relying on iterated interactions between EU institutions and national actors, and financial resources linked to the EU's targets and national strategies – such as 'Europe 2020' are deemed to be able to prompt a wider impact of the EU, also in social policy (Jessoula, 2015; Jessoula & Madama, 2019). In contrast, analyses by economists, using quantitative data, have focused on whether EMU governance, which is legally binding, is effective in terms of outcomes (Efstathiou & Wolf, 2019). Their findings are generally more pessimistic.

Finally, the research on social Europe in the aftermath of the financial crisis saw the emergence of a wider debate on the nature of the EU's polity and the deep legitimacy challenges ahead. Many commentators, not only scholars but also public intellectuals, have acknowledged that Europe had come to a crossroads, which required fundamental choices to tackle the risk of disintegration (cf. Dinan et al., 2017; Ferrera, 2017; Vandenbroucke et al., 2017). Drawing from the EU's social deficit diagnosis (Armingeon & Baccaro, 2012; Ferrera, 2017), improving the EU's social dimension was deemed to be a route to enhance the EU's legitimacy by public intellectuals (Ferrera, 2017). In line with these arguments, Jessoula and Madama (2019) claim that within a wider relaunch of the social dimension of the EU – or, the 'European Social Union' to use the effective definition coined by Vandenbroucke (2015) – strengthening the anti-poverty component of the EU toolkit could serve, then, not merely a normative rationale backed by social justice principles, but also a political rationale worth pursuing, considering that 'the poor', low-skilled, and less-educated Europeans are generally less supportive of the integration project and more likely to be Eurosceptic. Yet, there is not unilateral support for deepening the EU's social dimension. In particular, small richer countries in the North are hesitant about more EU social integration, as evidenced in their sceptical stance on Next Generation EU (NGEU) (De la Porte & Jensen, 2021). However, countries at the periphery of Europe that were hit hard by the financial crisis tend to welcome a more social Europe. It is in this context that EPSR was launched.

THE CURRENT STATE OF THE DEBATE AND THE COVID-19 PANDEMIC: A REINVIGORATION OF THE REGULATORY TURN OF EU SOCIAL POLICY?

The EPSR marks a new period for EU social policy, where the EU explicitly aims to improve the social situation for individual citizens, despite having limited competencies at the social–labour market nexus. This is leading to various different research agendas, as the EPSR builds on the EU's social policy legacy, comprising a regulatory framework in labour law, equality of treatment, and health and safety at work, as well as soft policy coordination (previously OMCs), centred on social investment.[2] The EPSR covers diverse areas, ranging from gender equality, where the EU has a strong legal base, through areas that are between welfare states and labour markets, which represent a legal grey zone between the national and EU levels (such as paid parental leave), to areas of exclusive national decision making, notably social protection, governed at the EU level through social benchmarking and policy coordination, now integrated in the European Semester. The emphasis on formal rights in the discourse of the EPSR, in particular via EU-level regulation, contrasts sharply with the Lisbon era, when the main EU-level instrument to tackle policy challenges was voluntary policy coordination (OMC) (De la Porte & Palier, forthcoming). As the EPSR comprehensively covers policies related to labour markets and welfare states, there is an interest in the extent to which the different rights, whether derived from nation states or the EU level, are taken up by citizens, in an approach focusing on the normative, instrumental, and enforcement aspects of EU social rights (Vandenbroucke et al., 2021). Relying on a novel resource-based conceptualization of social rights, this strand of research has brought evidence about existing multilevel interactions between the European, national, and regional plans in the construction of social rights, shedding light on the complex intersection between binding provisions, financing, and soft coordination processes, whose European dimension has become relevant and pertinent for all citizens, not just mobile ones (Ferrera et al., 2021; Vandenbroucke et al., 2021).

Thus far, the EPSR has, first, been examined from a normative perspective, where it is presented as a milestone for proponents of social Europe, including academics. It is seen as providing the EU with a novel, highly symbolic social manifesto, and a possible key step towards a fully fledged social union (Ferrera, 2019; Vandenbroucke, 2019). Politically, high hopes are placed on the EPSR to address the dualizations and inequalities that have crystallized since Lisbon. Some studies have mainly focused on the politics behind the decision making of the EPSR, especially the role of the European Commission

(Vesan et al., 2021), or the political tensions underlying the EPSR (Corti & Vesan, 2020).

Second, there is a focus on specific initiatives in the EPSR, with a growing interest in specific soft programmes, including (co-)funding initiatives such as the Youth Guarantee (Vesan & Lizzi, 2017; Tosun et al., 2019; Ferrera et al., 2021), and the Fund for the Most Deprived (Madama, 2016; Greiss et al., 2021).

Third, there is a revival of scholarly interest in the regulatory dimension of social Europe, because of legislative initiatives. EU social regulation is seen as a threat that could potentially undermine national institutions, especially where regulation is the prerogative of the social partners, as in the Nordic countries. Regulatory tensions could also emerge regarding the financing of new social rights because EU social regulation aimed at upward social convergence entails a financial cost. These tensions with regard to subsidiarity and financial constraints can be captured by the notion of an 'EU regulatory welfare state'. The EU as a regulatory welfare state can impinge upon national modes of policymaking at the welfare state–labour market nexus (Obinger et al., 2005; De la Porte et al., 2020), where top-down regulation without redistribution can impose significant costs at a lower level of governance (member state level) (Levi-Faur, 2014). This cost – or financial constraint – must in practice be carried by the (welfare) state, employers and employees (in collective agreements), or social insurance schemes (Falkner & Leiber, 2004; De la Porte et al., 2020). On the work–life balance directive, there is also a focus on earmarked parental level from a feminist perspective, as a means of degenderizing gender roles; and some studies focus on issues, such as carer days and flexible work (Waddington & Bell, 2021), that are particularly relevant in the context of the COVID-19 pandemic. Future research is likely to focus on other directives as well, in particular the Commission's proposed minimum wage directive, which is seen as particularly controversial, for instance in the Nordics where there is no statutory minimum wage. Yet, other countries and unions, especially at the periphery of the EU, welcome the initiative. But the high hopes for social Europe may work out differently on the ground, due to distinct political priorities as well as differences in financial resources and institutional capabilities.

Another focus related to social rights that is receiving attention from scholars is on how EU legislation has created differentiated citizen regimes, *de jure* and *de facto*. For instance, there has been a focus on posted workers, temporarily posted for a job in another country but with working conditions and wages that are below the standards in host countries (Arnholtz, 2021). Even beyond posted workers, there is a focus on workers from Eastern Europe that are self-employed or seasonally employed, undertaking jobs in Western Europe, who are exposed in terms of their occupation. The condition of such workers, especially in terms of health exposure, has been tougher during the COVID-19 pandemic (Szelewa & Polakoski, forthcoming). Another related line of research focuses on how EU migrant workers are included or excluded from citizenship rights in host societies via administrative hurdles (Bruzelius, 2021).

Fourth, there is a new research agenda on how social funds have actually been distributed, and whether they have decreased inequality. Up to now, research has shown that of the recipient regions, those that are richer benefit more from the funds, partly because they can contribute more in terms of co-funding, but also because these countries have weaker institutional capabilities. Thus, they are unlikely to be able to implement them in line with EU intentions (see also Dellmuth, 2021). Consequently, there may be an increase rather than a decrease in inter-EU inequality. There is likely to be further research on this topic, as there are more funding instruments including funds associated with the COVID-19 pandemic. More specifically, this includes the short-term work schemes and the recovery and resilience funds, which have been developed to help member states recover from the COVID-19 pandemic.

Fifth, in conjunction with the EPSR and the EU agenda to develop more EU social policy, there is an emerging body of research on public support for social Europe, carried out through a variety of methodologies, including surveys and survey experiments. The findings are that, at a general level, there is support for EU activity in social policy, yet more fine-grained micro-level analyses suggest that citizens are more sceptical about extensive social policies developed at the EU level (Baute, 2020; Katsanidou et al., 2022). In this respect, some studies investigating mass elites' differences in pro-EU solidaristic attitudes show that citizens are generally more keen on the introduction of EU-wide solidarity mechanisms than elites, even in core countries like Germany, suggesting that pro-European electoral and social constituencies seem to lack political leaders able to give a voice to these silent majorities (Ferrera & Pellegata, 2019). Further, the spread of the populist right and discourses that are hostile to migrants (including EU migrants) has led to a host of studies on whether EU migrants are net contributors or net beneficiaries from the welfare state. The studies, which are juxtaposed claims of the populist right in some countries, show that migrants, overall, are net contributors, rather than net beneficiaries from the welfare states in their host countries (for instance, Martinsen & Pons Rotger, 2017).

Finally, the impact of the COVID-19 pandemic on European solidarity and especially the fiscal components are being examined. The literature so far has documented how the adoption of NGEU was made possible thanks to a shift in the Council, from a position against risk sharing and common public debt to a position where member states supported a common fund to dampen the economic impact of the lockdowns and health crisis caused by the effect of the

COVID-19 pandemic (Bulmer, 2020; Schmidt, 2020; De la Porte & Jensen, 2021). Yet, the fund also sought to repair 'the economic and political imbalances left over from the Eurozone crisis', because pre-existing vulnerabilities, rather than the impact of the pandemic, have been key in the allocation of NGEU resources (Armingeon et al., 2021). Irrespective of political tensions underlying the decision (De la Porte & Jensen, 2021), and the continued tensions around issues such as rule-of-law, there is no doubt that this fiscal instrument, especially the grants component, of which the first tranche has already been allocated, on the basis of member state plans, could be a game changer. It enables member states to make investments, including in social policy, which are future-oriented. From a social policy perspective, there is an interest in the extent to which this fiscal instrument could not only support investments in the green economy, but also social policy initiatives, in particular in line with the social investment agenda, i.e., training, childcare, and other policies closely related to labour market investments (Busemeyer et al., 2020).

CONCLUSION

This chapter provided an overview of the long-term trajectory of scholarly research on social Europe, distinguishing four main phases: the early phase until the mid-1990s; the EMU and the Lisbon era (mid-1990s–2008); the Great Recession decade (2008–2019); and the current times led by the COVID-19 pandemic. Although the investigation of the transformations occurring in the last phase and their implications are likely to dominate the future research agenda, there is currently a lively scholarly interest in the politics, policies, and distributional implications of EU social rights related to the EPSR and beyond. This includes the impact for different welfare states of the multiple different initiatives emanating from the EPSR, including targeted funding (Youth Guarantee, Fund for the Most Deprived), but also regulatory initiatives (work–life balance directive, proposal for directive on minimum wage). The research on the EPSR builds on previous literature, but in a context where there is more political polarization within countries, and more pronounced political interests between EU countries. The fiscal instruments that have been developed to respond to the economic downturn in conjunction with the COVID-19 pandemic, including support to short-term work schemes and NGEU, are expected to shape the research agenda on EU social policy in years to come. These issues are being examined using various approaches, to tap into public opinion on EU social policy, the politics of EU social policy at EU level and in member states, as well as the policy and regulatory impact of EU initiatives. Whether new regulatory initiatives under the EPSR and fiscal instruments related to NGEU could lead to upwards social convergence, or at least mitigate social differences, or in contrast, whether inequalities will persist, or perhaps even be exacerbated by EU social policy, remain open questions: questions which research on the role of Europe is well poised to address.

NOTES

1. The term 'Troika' refers to the three institutions – European Commission, European Central Bank, and International Monetary Fund – which signed bailouts with Eurozone countries in need of financial aid during the financial crisis, relying on the Memoranda of Understanding, a three-year financial aid programme subject to strict conditionality.
2. Social investment entails human capital development throughout the life course, and includes active labour market policy, high-quality early childhood education and care, and education and life-long learning (Kvist, 2014).

REFERENCES

Armingeon, K., & Baccaro, L. (2012). Political economy of the sovereign debt crisis: The limits of internal devaluation. *Industrial Law Journal, 41*, 254–275.

Armingeon, K., De la Porte, C., Heins, E., & Sacchi, S. (2021). *Voices from the Past: Economic and Political Vulnerabilities in the Making of Next Generation EU Forthcoming in Comparative European Politics*. University of Edinburgh Press.

Armstrong, K. A. (2006). The 'Europeanisation' of social exclusion: British adaptation to EU co-ordination. *British Journal of Politics and International Relations, 8*, 79–100.

Armstrong, K. A. (2010). *Governing Social Inclusion*. Oxford University Press.

Arnholtz, J. (December 2021). The embedded flexibility of Nordic labor market models under pressure from EU-induced dualization: The case of posted work in Denmark and Sweden. DSE Conference.

Barbier, J. C. (2005). The European employment strategy: A channel for activating social protection? In J. Zeitlin & P. Pochet (Eds), *The Open Method of Coordination in Action: The European Employment and Social Inclusion Strategies* (pp. 417–446). Peter Lang.

Barcevičius, E., Weishaupt, T., & Zeitlin, J. (2014). *Assessing the Open Method of Coordination: Institutional Design and National Influence of EU Social Policy Coordination*. Palgrave.

Baute, S. (2020). *L'opinion publique envers l'Europe sociale*. KU Leuven.

Bekker, S. (2017). The European Semester process: Adaptability and latitude in support of the European Social Model. In F. Vandenbroucke, C. Barnard, & G. De Baere (Eds), *A European Social Union after the Crisis* (pp. 251–270). Cambridge University Press.

Bell, M. (2012). Between flexicurity and fundamental social rights: The EU Directives on atypical work. *European Law Review, 37*(1).

Börner, S. (2020). Marshall revisited: EU social policy from a social-rights perspective. *Journal of European Social Policy, 30*(4), 421–435.

Bruzelius, C. (2021). Taking emigration seriously: A new agenda for research on free movement and welfare. *Journal of European Public Policy, 28*(6), 930–942.

Büchs, M. (2007). *New Governance in European Social Policy: The Open Method of Coordination*. Palgrave Macmillan.

Bulmer, S. (2020). *The Member States in the European Union.* Oxford University Press.

Busemeyer, M. R., De la Porte, C., Garritzman J. L., & Pavolini, E. (Eds). (2020). *The Future of the Social Investment State: Politics, Policies and Outcomes.* Routledge.

Caporaso, J. A., & Tarrow, S. (2009). Polanyi in Brussels: Supranational institutions and the transnational embedding of markets. *International Organization, 63*(4), 593–620.

Copeland, P., & Daly, M. (2014). Poverty and social policy in Europe 2020: Ungovernable and ungoverned. *Policy and Politics, 42*(3), 351–365.

Corti, F., & Vesan, P. (2020). Social democracy, social Europe, and the 'post-Third Way agenda': From the European Pillar of Social Rights to the COVID-19 pandemic. *Constellations, 27*(14), 608–620.

Costamagna, F. (2013). The European Semester in action: Strengthening economic policy coordination while weakening the social dimension? LPF-WEL Working Paper.

Crespy, A. (2020). The EU's socioeconomic governance 10 years after the crisis: Muddling through and the revolt against austerity. *Journal of Common Market Studies, 58*(1), 133–146.

Crespy, A., & Vanheuverzwijn, P. (2019). What 'Brussels' means by structural reforms: Empty signifier or constructive ambiguity? *Comparative European Politics, 17*, 92–111.

Davies, G. (2014). Legislative control of the European Court of Justice. *Common Market Law Review, 51*(6), 1579–1607.

De la Porte, C. (2017). EU governance of welfare states and labour markets. In P. Kennett & N. Lendvai-Bainton (Ed.), *Handbook of European Social Policy* (pp. 141–154). Edward Elgar Publishing.

De la Porte, C., & Heins, E. (Eds). (2016). *The Sovereign Debt Crisis, the EU and Welfare State Reform.* Palgrave Macmillan.

De la Porte, C., & Jensen, M. D. (2021). The next generation EU: An analysis of the dimensions of conflict behind the deal. *Social Policy and Administration, 55*, 388–402.

De la Porte, C., & Natali, D. (2014). Altered Europeanisation of pension reform in the context of the Great Recession: Denmark and Italy compared. *West European Politics, 37*(4), 732–749.

De la Porte, C., & Palier, B. (forthcoming). The politics of European Union social investment initiatives. In J. Garritzman, S. Hauserman, & B. Palier (Eds), *World Politics of Social Investment.* Oxford University Press.

De la Porte, C., & Pochet, P. (Eds). (2002). *Building Social Europe through the Open Method of Co-ordination.* Peter Lang.

De la Porte, C., & Pochet, P. (2012). Why and how (still) study the OMC? *Journal of European Social Policy, 22*(2), 336–349.

De la Porte, C., Larsen, T. P., & Szelewa, D. (2020). A gender equalizing regulatory welfare state? Enacting the EU's work–life balance directive in Denmark and Poland. *ANNALS of the American Academy of Political and Social Science, 691*(1), 84–103.

Dellmuth, L. (2021). *Is Europe Good for You? EU Spending and Well-Being.* Policy Press.

Dinan, D., Nugent, N., & Paterson W. E. (Eds). (2017). *The European Union in Crisis.* Palgrave Macmillan.

Dukelow, F. (2015). 'Pushing against an open door': Reinforcing the neo-liberal policy paradigm in Ireland and the impact of EU intrusion. *Comparative European Politics*, *13*(1), 93–111.

Efstathiou, K., & Wolff, G. B. (2019). *What Drives National Implementation of EU Policy Recommendations?* Bruegel Working Paper Series. www.bruegel.org/wp -content/uploads/2019/04/WP4-final-2.pdf.

Eihmanis, E. (2018). Cherry-picking external constraints: Latvia and EU economic governance, 2008–2014. *Journal of European Public Policy*, *25*(2), 231–249.

Falkner, G. (1998). *EU Social Policy in the 1990s*. Routledge.

Falkner, G. (2010). The European Union. In F. G. Castles (Ed.), *Oxford Handbook of the Welfare State*. Oxford University Press.

Falkner, G., & Leiber, S. (2004). Europeanization of social partnership in smaller European democracies? *European Journal of Industrial Relations*, *10*(3), 245–266.

Ferrera, M. (2005). *The Boundaries of Welfare European Integration and the New Spatial Politics of Social Protection*. Oxford University Press.

Ferrera, M. (2017). Mission impossible? Reconciling economic and social Europe after the euro crisis and Brexit. *European Journal of Political Research*, *56*(1), 3–22.

Ferrera, M. (Ed.). (2019). *Towards a European Social Union: The European Pillar of Social Rights and the Roadmap for a fully-fledged Social Union: A Forum Debate*. Centro di Ricerca e Documentazione Luigi Einaudi, 2019, pp. 2–11, SSRN. https:// ssrn.com/abstract=3493749.

Ferrera, M., & Pellegata, A. (2019). Can economic and social Europe be reconciled? Mass-elite differences in attitudes toward integration and solidarity. Working Paper 1/2019, Department of Social and Political Science, University of Milan.

Ferrera, M., & Sacchi, S. (2005). The open method of co-ordination and national institutional capabilities: The Italian experience. In J. Zeitlin & P. Pochet (Eds), *The Open Method of Coordination in Action: The European Employment and Social Inclusion Strategies* (pp. 137–172). Peter Lang.

Ferrera, M. Miró, J., & Ronchi, S. (2021). Walking the road together? EU polity main-tenance during the COVID-19 crisis. *West European Politics*, *44*, 5–6, 1329–1352.

Geddes, A., and Hadj-Abdou, L. (2016). An unstable equilibrium: Freedom of move-ment and the welfare state in the European Union. In G. P. Freeman and N. Mirilovic (Eds), *Handbook on Migration and Social Policy* (pp. 222–238). Edward Elgar Publishing.

Graziano, P., & Vink, M. (2007). *Europeanization: New Research Agendas*. Palgrave Macmillan.

Graziano, P., Jacquot, S., & Palier, B. (Eds). (2011). *The EU and the Domestic Politics of Welfare State Reforms*. Palgrave Macmillan.

Greiss, J., Cantillon, B., Marchal, S., & Penne, T. (2021). *Europe as Agent That Fills the Gaps? The Case of FEAD*. Working Paper no. No 1903. Herman Deleeck Centre for Social Policy, University of Antwerp, 26 November. https://econpapers.repec .org/paper/hdlwpaper/1903.htm.

Hassenteufel, P., & Palier, B. (2014). Still the sound of silence? Towards a new phase in the Europeanisation of welfare state policies in France. *Comparative European Politics*, *13*(1), 112–130.

Heidenreich, M. (2009). The open method of coordination: A pathway to the gradual transformation of national employment and welfare regimes? In M. Heidenreich & J. Zeitlin (Eds), *Changing European Employment and Welfare Regimes: The Influence of the Open Method of Coordination on National Reforms* (pp. 10–36). Routledge.

Heidenreich, M., & Zeitlin, J. (Eds). (2009). *Changing European Employment and Welfare Regimes: The Influence of the Open Method of Coordination on National Reforms*. Routledge.

Jacquot, S., & Woll, C. (2003). Usage of European integration: Europeanisation from a sociological perspective. *European Integration Online Papers, 7*.

Jepsen, M., & Pascual A. S. (2005). The European social model: An exercise in deconstruction. *Journal of European Social Policy, 15*(3), 231–245.

Jessoula, M. (2015). Europe 2020 and the fight against poverty: Beyond competence clash, towards 'hybrid' governance solutions? *Social Policy and Administration, Europeanization of Welfare Regional Issue, 49*(4), 490–511.

Jessoula, M., & Madama, I. (2019). *Fighting Poverty and Social Exclusion in the EU: A Chance in Europe 2020*. Routledge.

Katsanidou, A., Reinl, A. K., & Eder, C. (2022). Together we stand? Transnational solidarity in the EU in times of crises. *European Union Politics*, 14651165211035663.

Kelemen, R. D. (2012). The political foundations of judicial independence in the European Union. *Journal of European Public Policy, 19*(1), 43–58.

Kok, W. (2004). *Facing the Challenge: The Lisbon Strategy for Growth and Employment*. High Level Group Report. European Commission.

Kvist, J. (2014). A framework for social investment strategies: Integrating generational, life course and gender perspectives in the EU social investment strategy. *Comparative European Politics, 13*(1), 131–149.

Leibfried, S. (2005). Social policy: Left to the judges and the markets? In H. Wallace, M. A. Pollack, & A. R. Young (Eds), *Policy-Making in the European Union*. Oxford University Press.

Leibfried, S., & Pierson, P. (2000). Social policy: Left to courts and markets? In H. Wallace, M. A. Pollack, & A. R. Young (Eds), *Policy-Making in the European Union* (pp. 273–293). Oxford University Press.

Levi-Faur, D. (2014). The welfare state: A regulatory perspective. *Public Administration, 92*(3), 599–614.

Lopez-Santana, M. (2007). *Soft Europeanisation? How the Soft Pressure from Above Affects the Bottom (Differently): The Belgian, Spanish and Swedish Experiences*. Working Paper EUI MWP, 2007/10.

Madama, I. (2016). The fund for European aid to the most deprived: Contested, contentious, yet successful. A case of 'supranational incrementalism' at work. Working Paper RescEu, no. 9/2016.

Maricut, A., & Puetter, U. (2018). Deciding on the European Semester: The European Council, the Council and the enduring asymmetry between economic and social policy issues. *Journal of European Public Policy, 25*(2), 193–211.

Martinsen, D. S. (2015). *An Ever More Powerful Court?* Oxford University Press.

Martinsen, D. S., & Pons Rotger, G. (2017). The fiscal impact of EU immigration on the tax financed welfare state: testing the 'welfare burden' thesis. *European Union Politics, 18*(4), 620–639.

Moury, C., Ladi, S., Cardoso, D., & Gago, A. (2021). *Bailout Politics in Eurozone Countries*. Manchester University Press.

Obinger, H., Leibfried S., & Castles, F. G. (2005). Bypasses to a social Europe? Lessons from federal experience. *Journal of European Public Policy, 12*(3), 545–571.

Pavolini, E., León, M., Guillén, A. M., & Ascoli, U. (2014). From austerity to permanent strain? The EU and welfare state reform in Italy and Spain. *Comparative European Politics, 13*(1), 56–76.

Pierson, P., & Leibfried, S. (2005). Social policy. In H. Wallace, W. Wallace, & M. A. Pollack (Eds), *Policy-Making in the European Union.* Oxford University Press.

Radaelli, C. (2000). Whither Europeanization? Concept stretching and substantive change. *European Integration Online Papers, 4.* https://doi.org/10.2139/ssrn .302761.

Rasmussen, H. (1986). *On Law and Policy in the European Court of Justice.* Martinus Nijhoff.

Sabato, S., & Vanhercke, B. (2017). Towards a European Pillar of Social Rights: From a preliminary outline to a Commission Recommendation. In B. Vanhercke, S. Sabato, & D. Bouget (Eds), *Social Policy in the European Union: State of Play 2017* (pp. 73–98). Etui/OSE.

Sacchi, S. (2014). Conditionality by other means: EU involvement in Italy's structural reforms in the sovereign debt crisis. *Comparative European Politics, 13*(1), 77–92.

Scharpf, F. W. (2009). Legitimacy in the multilevel European polity. *European Political Science Review, 1*(2), 173–204.

Schmidt, V. A. (2020). Theorizing institutional change and governance in European responses to the COVID-19 pandemic. *Journal of European Integration, 42*(8), 1177–1193.

Streeck, W. (1995). Neo-voluntarism: A new European social policy regime? *European Law Journal: Review of European Law in Context, 1*(1) 31–59.

Szelewa, D., & Polakowski, M. (forthcoming). European solidarity and 'free movement of labour' during the pandemic: Exposing the contradictions amid East–West migration. *Comparative European Politics, 20*(2).

Theodoropoulou, S. (2014). National social and labour market policy reforms in the shadow of EU bail-out conditionality: The cases of Greece and Portugal. *Comparative European Politics, 13*(1), 29–55.

Tosun, J., Hörisch, F., & Marques, P. (2019). Youth employment in Europe: Coordination as a crucial dimension. *International Journal of Social Welfare, 28*(4), 350–357.

Vandenbroucke, F. (2015). The case for a European social union: From muddling through to a sense of common purpose. In B. Marin (Ed.), *The Future of Welfare in a Global Europe* (pp. 489–520). Aldershot.

Vandenbroucke, F. (2019). The European Pillar of Social Rights: From promise to delivery. In M. Ferrera (Ed.), *Towards a European Social Union: The European Pillar of Social Rights and the Roadmap for a Fully-Fledged Social Union: A Forum Debate* (pp. 2–11). Centro di Ricerca e Documentazione Luigi Einaudi, SSRN. https://ssrn.com/abstract=3493749.

Vandenbroucke, F., Barnard, C., & De Baere, G. (2017). *A European Social Union After the Crisis.* Cambridge University Press.

Vandenbroucke. F., Keune, M., Ferrera, M., & Corti, F. (2021). *The Nature and Rationale for European Social Rights.* Deliverable 2.1, EusocialCit Project. www .eusocialcit.eu/published-our-working-paper-on-the-nature-and-rationale-for -european-social-rights/.

Vesan, P., & Lizzi, R. (2017). The Youth Guarantee in Italy and the 'new policy design' approach. *World Political Science Review, 13*(2), 57–84.

Vesan, P., Corti, F., & Sabato, S. (2021). The European Commission's entrepreneurship and the social dimension of the European Semester: From the European Pillar of Social Rights to the COVID-19 pandemic. *Comparative European Politics, 19*(6), 277–295.

Waddington, L., & Bell, M. (2021). The right to request flexible working arrangements under the work–life balance directive: A comparative perspective. *European Labour Law Journal*, 1–21, https://doi.org/10.1177/20319525211038270

Wincott, D. (2001). The Court of Justice and the European policy process. In J. Richardson & S. Mazey (Eds), *European Union, Power and Policy-Making*. Routledge.

Zeitlin J. (2009). The open method of co-ordination and reform of national and social policies: Influences, mechanisms, effects. In M. Heidenreich & J. Zeitlin (Eds), *Changing European Employment and Welfare Regimes: The Influence of the Open Method of Coordination on National Reforms* (pp. 214–245). Routledge.

Zeitlin, J., & Pochet, P. (2005). *The Open Method of Coordination in Action: The European Employment and Social Inclusion Strategies*. Peter Lang.

Zeitlin, J., & Vanhercke, B. (2018). Socializing the European Semester: EU social and economic policy co-ordination in crisis and beyond. *Journal of European Public Policy*, 25(2), 149–174.

10. The evolution of social policy research in Central and Eastern Europe

Jolanta Aidukaite and Jekaterina Navicke

INTRODUCTION

The fall of the communist regimes across Central and Eastern Europe (CEE) since 1989 has opened a plethora of welfare state and social policy research in this part of the world. Welfare state theories, typologies, and approaches excluded from their analysis former socialist countries, which had a rather different historical and economic development as compared to the capitalist democracies. Nevertheless, the former socialist countries had extensive social policies, which, in some cases, were just as developed as those in the West (Inglot, 2008; Aidukaite, 2009; Kuitto, 2016). After the fall of the various communist regimes, many of the CEE countries went through dramatic changes and all of them have experienced social policy reform. This chapter aims to review the evolution of welfare state and social policy research in the CEE region since the 1990s across several selected social policy areas, highlighting the current state of affairs and presenting suggestions for future research.

The focus is on primarily comparative research carried out in the CEE region, which includes ten EU member states (Bulgaria, Czech Republic, Estonia, Hungary, Latvia, Lithuania, Poland, Romania, Slovakia, Slovenia). These countries form three more or less similar clusters distinguished by a number of scholars (Bohle & Greskovits, 2007; Aidukaite, 2011; Jahn & Kuitto, 2011; Kuitto, 2016; Jahn, 2017) according to their socio-economic indicators (the Human Development Index, the shadow economy, Gini coefficient of equivalized disposable income, minimum wage, mean monthly earnings, severe material deprivation, and social policy expenses): Slovenia, the Czech Republic, and Hungary as the best performers; Bulgaria and Romania at the bottom; and the Baltic countries, Poland, and Slovakia in the middle.

We start our discussion with the review of debates on the desire to place CEE countries into the existing welfare state typologies, the emergence of the post-communist or Eastern European welfare state model, and how this debate has evolved. A number of studies confirm that the welfare state in CEE evolved in a similar way as in the West, except the distinct interaction of the communist period, which, however, was also marked by extensive and generous social policies comparable with those in the West (see e.g., Inglot, 2008, 2016; Aidukaite, 2009; Cerami & Vanhuysse, 2009; Szikra & Tomka, 2009). Nevertheless, the CEE region is currently quite diverse (Cerami, 2006, 2011; Aidukaite, 2011; Kuitto, 2016). Hence, this chapter asks about the place of new EU member state countries in the broader 'family' of welfare systems of old member states.

We then focus on the evolution of research in selected social policy areas in the CEE. Much of this research is relatively recent because prior to the collapse of the various communist regimes in the CEE region (in 1989–1991), social issues such as poverty, unemployment, and social inequalities were considered non-existent in the communist world (Matkovic et al., 2007). The chapter aims to review the evolution of social policy research since the 1990s in three social policy areas attracting the most scholarly attention in the region: family policy, pension insurance, and poverty.

WELFARE STATE REGIME/MODEL OF CEE: INCLUSION IN WESTERN TYPOLOGIES

At the beginning of the 1990s, social policy research evolved around the desire to place the CEE countries into existing welfare state regimes and typologies (see Deacon, 1992; Aidukaite, 2006; Cerami, 2006; Fenger, 2007). The changes in the social policy systems of the CEE were explained by the economic affordability of those countries' programmes, global pressures from the International Monetary Fund and the World Bank, the legacy of the past, the political leanings of the government, weak civil society, and low trade union membership (Deacon, 1997, 2000; Ferge, 2001; Aidukaite, 2009; Cerami & Vanhuyssen, 2009; Orenstein 2009). However, there were no clear agreements or clear empirical evidence in the scientific literature on whether radical welfare state cutbacks took place in CEE. It was also not clear whether CEE had developed a new welfare state type of its own, or whether it was developing one of the variants of the ideal-typical welfare state regimes delineated by Esping-Andersen (1990) (for details see Deacon, 1992; Abrahamson, 1999; Aidukaite, 2011).

Earlier studies have seen welfare state development in the post-communist region as falling within the liberal or residual regime (see Standing, 1996; Ferge, 1997, 2001), in which welfare is based on a mix of social insurance and social assistance, and a partial privatization of social policy. As those studies underlined, attempts at reform have come up against a legacy of what was essentially comprehensive social policy. However, it should be pointed out that some of those studies tended to overgeneralize and insufficiently accounted for the variety within the CEE region (see Fodor et al., 2002; Aidukaite, 2011; Javornik, 2014 on this point). Thus, other studies focused on highlighting these differences, suggesting CEE countries may not easily fit existing regime typologies.

Deacon (1992), for instance, predicted that Eastern European countries would develop their future social policies into distinct regimes that may even lie outside the three worlds of welfare capitalism described by Esping-Andersen. The comparative studies that followed also highlighted emerging differences among the Eastern European countries. Fajth (1999) emphasized that most of the post-communist countries have been moving away from collective solutions to individualized ones regarding social security. However, they have not necessarily followed the same paths when reforming their institutional arrangements. In his comparative study of institutions and their consequences for the social policy of several Western and transitional countries, Kangas (1999) concluded that to place the post-communist countries in the prevailing welfare state typologies is rather problematic as neither the Western nor the post-communist countries form a single homogenous group. There was, and still is, large variation when it comes to the institutional set-ups of social security programmes between them. Manning (2004) came to similar conclusions. In a comprehensive overview of changes since 1989 based on the main social indicators and social policies in eight East-Central European countries, he found that there were variations between these societies not only in the policies that they have developed, but also in their social and economic performances.

Many scholars have therefore logically emphasized emerging differences among Eastern European countries as well (Aidukaite, 2006; Bohle, 2007; Lendvai, 2008), although categorizations differ depending upon the countries being studied. Bohle demonstrated that the Baltic states' welfare regime can be characterized as neoliberal, with low social spending and a low degree of decommodification. In contrast, the Slovenian welfare state comes closer to encompassing the West European model, while the Visegrad countries (Czech Republic, Hungary, Poland, and Slovakia) exhibit something in-between the conservative and liberal welfare states. Lendvai (2008) has grouped Estonia, Latvia, Lithuania, and Slovakia as closely falling into the neoliberal model based on macroeconomic indicators of welfare state spending, income inequality, and minimum wage. In contrast, Lendvai's study suggests the Czech Republic and Slovenia were the most 'socially conscious' welfare states according to their highest social spending levels and lowest poverty levels compared to the other eight new European Union (EU) countries. Poland and Hungary were seen to occupy a middle ground. In short, scholars differ in their classification of CEE countries and the variation evident among them. It has further been suggested that differences exist not only within the CEE region but even within smaller regions (e.g., the three Baltic states when examining social security programmes in more detail, see for example Aidukaite, 2006).

In contrast to studies emphasizing variation within the region, another strand of research tried to group Eastern European countries into a distinct regime unaccounted for in Esping-Andersen's typology (see for example Wehner et al., 2004; Golinowska et al., 2008; Aidukaite, 2011). This regime was called the Eastern European or post-communist regime and is defined as sharing characteristics of both the liberal and conservative corporatist regimes as well as having some distinct post-communist features. These features include a high take-up rate of social security, but relatively low benefit levels, the identification of the social policy system with the Soviet past, and having citizens with a low level of trust in the state institutions.

Similarly, other studies (Cerami, 2006; Haggard & Kaufman, 2008; Inglot, 2008) have emphasized parallels among the CEE countries in their welfare state systems rather than variation, including characteristics such as universalism, corporatism, and egalitarianism, and the commitment to insure against a fairly wide range of risks. Such a system of social insurance appears, in principle, closer to the broad European conception of social insurance enshrined in the International Labour Organization than more liberal models. However, according to Cerami (2006), CEE countries also implemented some readjustments to the new post-communist consensus, such as market-based schemes, private pension insurance, and means-tested benefits. The implementation of these measures would suggest a shift away from the broad European conception of social insurance.

Despite these shared characteristics of an ideal-typical post-communist regime type, most social policy research would suggest key differences remain. The most recent literature (Jahn & Kuitto, 2011; Kuitto, 2016; Jahn, 2017) focused on social policy performance in CEE countries (often in comparison with Western ones) concludes that CEE countries do not form their own welfare state regime type. Instead, they form either hybrid cases (Kuitto, 2016) or simply fall into different regimes (Jahn, 2017). Similar conclusions about variation within smaller regions can be made. For example, when it comes to the three Baltic states, they do not necessarily fall into the same category. According to the level and source of welfare financing, Estonia has more in common with Slovakia and the Czech Republic than with Latvia and Lithuania. The former countries rely heavily on contribution financing, while in the latter countries, together with Bulgaria and Romania, the relationship between contribution financing and tax financing is somewhat more balanced. Yet, the generosity of social insurance benefits measured as a composition of replacement rates, eligibility criteria, and the coverage rate is higher in Latvia and Estonia (together with Slovenia and the Czech Republic) than in Lithuania. Lithuania falls together with Poland, Slovakia, and Hungary into a cluster of less generous countries (Kuitto, 2016). A further study by Aidukaite (2019) based on a detailed examination of social policy development in the three Baltic states also highlighted emerging differences among three countries. This is especially remarkable for family policy, pension insurance, and unemployment protection.

To sum up, the development of the welfare state in the CEE region has provoked a plethora of social policy research which tried to delineate the ideal-typical features and place these new democracies into the 'old' welfare state regimes and typologies. Research then emerged highlighting differences between CEE countries both in studies developed at the turn of the twenty-first century as well as in more recent studies. At present it is clear that the CEE region is diverse, and that the welfare state in this region has neither evolved into an Esping-Andersen regime type, nor into a distinct welfare regime type, but rather into a mixed/hybrid model. Alongside attention to welfare state similarities and differences within the CEE region, research on social policy increasingly focused on specific social policy fields, in particular family policy, pensions, and poverty, which we now turn to.

THE EVOLUTION OF RESEARCH ON FAMILY POLICY

Family policy reforms in CEE countries have attracted considerable attention from social scientists since the 1990s seeking to explain changes, outcomes, and future development pathways of family policy in the CEE region (see, e.g., Pascall & Manning, 2000; Fodor et al., 2002; Szikra & Tomka, 2009; Javornik, 2014; Inglot, 2016; Aidukaite, 2021). The main factors influencing the trajectories of research in this area have been demographic pressures (e.g., population ageing), the global financial crisis of 2008, and conceptual influences such as the (de)familialization discussion.

There has been considerable attention of research on family policy in the CEE region directly related to the collapse of the communist regimes across CEE and the dramatic impact on children's wellbeing, women's labour market participation, and family formation patterns. Among the most debated outcomes of the post-communist transformation were and still are declining fertility rates, which, over a period of more than 25 years, never recovered to the pre-transformation period (see Eurostat, 2020). Therefore, demographic pressures such as the ageing of the population, low fertility rates, and emigration have stimulated the scientific debate throughout the CEE region (Ainsaar & Stankuniene, 2010; Oláh, 2015; Ainsaar & Rootalu, 2016; Frejka & Gietel-Basten, 2016; Ainsaar, 2019).

The demographic pressure imposed by declining fertility rates, ageing of the population, and the population decline caused by emigration was particularly strong in the Baltics (see Ainsaar & Stankuniene, 2010; Ainsaar & Rootalu,

2016; Ainsaar, 2019). This stimulated social policy research in this area, with numerous studies documenting the reconfigurations of family policy systems (see, e.g., Aidukaite, 2006, 2019; Ainsaar, 2019). These countries were also hit dramatically by the global financial and economic crisis of 2008, which impacted family policies, especially in Lithuania (Aidukaite, 2019; Ainsaar, 2019). Specifically, the universal child allowance payable for all children suffered significant cutbacks in Lithuania, while means-tested benefits were expanded.

The impact of the financial and economic crisis on the family support systems in the CEE region was also researched by scholars focusing on the Czech Republic and Slovenia (Blum et al., 2014; Saxonberg & Sirovátka, 2014). Saxonberg and Sirovátka (2014) show, for example, how the crisis opened a window of opportunity for the centre-right governments in power (2007–2013) to carry out family policy reforms, such as making birth benefits means tested or introducing greater freedom of choice in the parental leave system. Such changes have contributed to a strengthening of the liberal path according to the authors. In Slovenia, crisis-related reforms were also directed towards family policy. While the right-wing governments in 2012 did not change the family policy path, the number of family benefit recipients was reduced by making some universal family benefits means tested and benefit levels were reduced for many families. All this was done using the austerity argument (Blum et al., 2014).

Another factor influencing research on family policies in the CEE region is the development of familialization-defamilialization typologies (see Leitner, 2003; Lohmann & Zagel, 2016; Saraceno, 2016; see also Chapter 3 by Van Lancker and Zagel, this volume), which stimulated the discussion on how to place the CEE countries into these typologies. Studies on the CEE countries showed emerging differences in their childcare and parental leave policies (see Javornik, 2014; Aidukaite, 2021). For instance, Javornik (2014), focusing on parental leave and childcare policies (from birth to mandatory schooling age), showed significant variation in the degree of familialization-defamilialization among eight CEE countries of the EU (Estonia, Latvia, Lithuania, Slovenia, the Czech Republic, Hungary, Poland, and Slovakia). Grounded in Leitner's (2003) familialism typology, Javornik distinguished three policy types: (1) Slovenian and Lithuanian systems were assigned as supporting defamilialism since states seek to incentivize women's continuous employment and active fatherhood through parental and paternity leave policies and available public childcare; (2) support to family systems in the Czech Republic, Hungary, and Estonia appeared to support explicit familialism with an emphasis on familial childcare and gendered parenting; and (3) the state in Poland, Slovakia, and Latvia leaves parents without public support, thus maintaining implicit familialism. In short, similar to social policy research placing the CEE region within or outside existing welfare regime types, research on family policy suggests this variation is just as considerable when taking a more detailed look at a given social policy field.

This variation extends to the within-region variation discussed earlier. For example, Aidukaite (2021) highlights the emerging differences in the evolution of family support systems in the Baltic states (Estonia, Latvia, and Lithuania) between 2004 and 2019. The Lithuanian family support system is the most defamilializing, however, with some hidden familialism in childcare practice, where informal childcare is provided by extended family members. The Latvian public support system for families and children was attributed to implicit familialism as the state supported working parents during the period 2004–2019; however, support was provided at a relatively low replacement rate. At the same time, flat-rate childcare benefits cannot ensure adequate well-being, which has to be sought through either the family or market. A detailed examination of the Estonian system showed a development from explicit familialism to optional familialism during this period, particularly with the introduction of a generous parental leave benefit in 2006.

A number of case studies suggest that in some CEE countries, such as Poland and Hungary, an increasing trend of familialization and a return to traditional gender views is taking place in family policy (Szelewa, 2020). In Poland, for instance, one can find a stronger maternalist direction in public discourse on childbearing which emerged especially during the right-wing coalition in office since November 2015 (Szelewa, 2016). The latter maternalist direction in Poland was in contrast to the mainstream trend and research on the increased role of fathers in childcare in the CEE (e.g., Hobson et al., 2011; Takács, 2019; Aidukaite & Telisauskaite-Cekanavice, 2020; Maslauskaitė & Tereškinas, 2020).

Overall, research on family policy in the CEE region mirrored the general policy developments in this area, driven by demographic pressures, the impact of the financial and economic crisis on family policy systems, the development of the familialization-defamilialization typologies, and the transformation of the father's role in childcare. As with research on welfare regime typologies in the CEE region, these studies suggest more variation than similarity.

THE EVOLUTION OF RESEARCH ON PENSIONS

A second strand of social policy research emerged in the CEE region related to pension insurance reforms, which attracted particular attention given the threat posed by ageing populations (see also Chapter 6 by Ebbinghaus and Möhring, this volume). Primarily, research on pension reforms in the CEE region focuses on the relationship between globalization and Europeanization, outlining how world-regional (EU) and global (World Bank, United Nations,

International Monetary Fund, International Labour Organization) institutions/ organizations have shaped policy by spreading their ideas, in part by providing consultancy, policy, and technical advice (Yeates, 2008).

Social policy research on the CEE region provides strong evidence that because of their economic vulnerability, CEE countries are rather susceptible to the influence of globalization, thereby impacting pension reform. For instance, Casey (2004) has argued that Latvia and Estonia and partly Lithuania have implemented the World Bank's so-called 'three pillar' model of privatization of pension insurance, not least because they were recipients of substantial World Bank loans. The same could be true for Hungary and Poland (Orenstein, 2009). Another significant reason why some CEE societies were more susceptible to globalization could be explained by the desire of these countries to join Euro-Atlantic organizations. That made their political elite more likely to accept advice from global organizations (Chandler, 2001).

Similarly, the implementation of the partial privatization of pension provisions in some East-Central European countries and the Baltic states has also been a broad subject for debate and research. Studies show that the role of international actors propagating new ideas and discourses has indeed played an important role in these reforms (Cerami, 2011; Inglot, 2016). However, these studies also emphasized path dependency in the process of pension transformation and the important role played by national actors and their understanding of how pension insurance should be organized.

Comparing these two strands of literature on the CEE region, the influence of Europeanization is not so visible and straightforward compared to the influence of globalization and international actors (see Rys, 2001a, 2001b; Wehner et al., 2004). This is because 'the EU does not impose on member countries any specific hard law rules on social policy' (Rys, 2001b: 185). It is therefore not surprising that research establishes more of an influence from the World Bank than Europeanization with regards to pension insurance, particularly in the Baltic countries (Casey, 2004). Nevertheless, some indirect evidence on the influence of the Europeanization in the sphere of pensions can be detected. For example, in the comparative study of pension insurance reform in Latvia and Russia, Chandler (2001) provided evidence that the implementation of pension insurance reform in Latvia was easier to achieve compared to Russia, although in both countries, pension reform proved to be politically unpopular. Chandler claims that Latvia's greater international orientation and its commitment to return to 'Western' Europe and Western European values were important in influencing its government's commitment to pursue pension reform. In contrast, Russian leaders tended to perceive few advantages from Western-oriented reforms. More recent studies on the region have looked at the results of implemented pension privatization reforms in the CEE and how

these reforms are likely to affect income inequalities among the retired population (e.g., Medaiskis & Eirošius, 2021; Piirits, 2021).

THE EVOLUTION OF RESEARCH FOCUSED ON POVERTY

The CEE region is diverse, with poverty being prevalent to a different extent
(Alam et al., 2005; Argatu, 2018). In this section we aim to provide an
overview of the main factors influencing poverty research in the CEE since
the 1990s, including the legacy effects of the socialist era, post-communist
liberalization, the influence of international agencies, and the process of euro
integration.

For more than half a century, social issues such as poverty, unemployment,
and inequalities were considered non-existent in the Soviet Union (Sipos,
1992; Matkovic et al., 2007) and were a taboo topic for researchers (Stubbs
et al., 2019). It was assumed that all social problems, including poverty, were
solved in communist societies, largely by means of full employment, universal
access to education and health care, enterprise-based social security, subsidized prices for many essential goods and services, and the provision of social
housing (Stubbs et al., 2019). Hence, poverty in the Soviet block was portrayed
as an individualized 'pathology' – an attribute of the lazy, unmotivated, those
lacking self-discipline, deviating from social norms or those unwilling to work
due to vicious moral predispositions and unproductive habits.

In practice, vulnerable groups included the rural poor, large families,
oppressed minorities, older people, and 'anyone living outside the rigid
work eligibility' (Stubbs et al., 2019: 16). The gaps in social provision meant
a lack of goods and services to satisfy the basic needs of people (Šileika
& Zabarauskaitė, 2006). Hence, the absolutist tradition of conceptualizing
poverty as a basic need problem was strong in the CEE and arguably to at least
some degree rooted in the Soviet legacy (Sipos, 1992).

While hidden under socialism, poverty became increasingly visible in the
CEE region in the 1990s (UNICEF, 1994; Milanovic, 1996; Simai, 2006;
Berend, 2009). After the collapse of the Soviet system, large groups of the
population were exposed to poverty, making it impossible to ignore. In the
meantime, the field of poverty research in the CEE region was scarce and
underfinanced. The predominant understanding of poverty as largely rooted in
individual pathological behaviour was further strengthened in the post-socialist
era by free market neoliberalist ideology, where the very idea of a welfare state
or a social state 'was judged as, at best, "premature" and at worst, a legacy of
socialism which had to be shrunk, residualized, and responsibilized so as not
to be an obstacle to economic reform' (Stubbs et al., 2019: 14).

With the lack of funding and political attention to a social policy agenda, scientific research was unable to keep pace with the rapid changes in the social conditions across the region in the 1990s (Stubbs et al., 2019). As the main source of research funding came from international agencies such as UNICEF, UNDP, the International Labour Organization, and World Bank, at the time, many policy reports echoed the main ideas of these organizations, including those on poverty alleviation, safety nets, and a need for reform (Stubbs et al., 2019). The United Nations agencies also played an important role in promoting a capability approach to poverty and its multidimensional measurement in the CEE region, especially with regards to human development indicators and research (see, e.g., Horvath et al., 2012).

The economic growth of the 2000s and the ambition of the CEE countries to join the EU brought about important changes in the way poverty was perceived and analysed. The post-communist transformations in the CEE coincided with important developments in the sphere of poverty research and policy in the EU. While poverty reduction was not among the initial primary EU aims – the focus was rather on economic development and cooperation – the Lisbon process put the issue of poverty firmly on the political agenda in the EU in the late 1990s (Daly, 2010). The influence of the EU discourse on poverty research intensified around the accession of the CEE countries into the EU during the late 1990s and mid-2000s and remained important thereafter. This influence was facilitated both by the open method of coordination in social policy and as the EU now provides an important source of funding for research and social policy development in the region.

A shift in the research on poverty in the CEE region was the official adoption of relative at-risk-of-poverty measures, which occurred in the context of implementation of the Lisbon Strategy launched in 2000. While there were previous reports on a sharp increase of relative poverty in the CEE between 1989 and the mid-1990s (Milanovic, 1996; UNICEF, 1994), the euro integration process put pressure on the CEE countries to mainstream the relative notion of poverty and to shift towards its measurement using a common methodology, including the use of income rather than consumption data. This transition did not happen without academic debate. The economies of scale used to equivalize disposable income when estimating at-risk-of-poverty rates were argued to be lower in Central-Eastern European countries than in their Western counterparts (Mysikova & Zelinsky, 2019). Moreover, relative poverty statistics were criticized for not reflecting the true levels of poverty and deprivation in countries where incomes and expenditures were relatively low due to high informality and in-kind production and consumption (Šileika & Zabarauskaitė, 2006).

Poverty research, including in the CEE region, was also fuelled by reconceptualizing poverty as social exclusion in the EU in early 2000s; the two terms were often used interchangeably in political discourse (Atkinson & Davoudi, 2000). In the context of implementation of the 'Europe 2020' strategy, the notions of social inclusion and social investment started shaping political and academic debates (see e.g., Cantillon, 2011; Kvist, 2014). Both approaches call for a multidimensional and intertemporal understanding of poverty and its measurement. However, it should be noted that there is low availability of longitudinal data in the CEE region, which is important for the analysis of the long-term and intergenerational effects of poverty and its dynamics.

The latest EU social policy strategy is the EU Pillar of Social Rights, which includes an ambitious goal of reducing the number of people at risk of poverty or social exclusion by at least 15 million by 2030. The strategy aims at promoting equal opportunities, access to the labour market, and fair working conditions. In addition, it is distinguished from the previous EU strategies by explicitly focusing on social protection and inclusion, including children's right to protection from poverty and a right to adequate minimum income benefits, effective access to enabling goods, services, and housing for those in need at all stages of life. It is, however, too early to evaluate to what extent the notion of social rights will penetrate the academic and political debates and poverty research in the CEE.

CONCLUSIONS

This chapter has reviewed the evolution of welfare state research in the CEE region and its development since the 1990s in three selected social policy areas common to CEE regional research: family policy, pension insurance, and poverty. This overview shows that the CEE, which was treated as a unified region by earlier social policy scholars, has evolved into different welfare state trajectories with varying social policy outcomes. However, the trajectories of social policy research followed similar patterns throughout the region and were driven by similar processes and factors. These processes included demo-graphic pressures and familialization-defamilialization processes in the sphere of family policies, and the influence of international agencies and the EU in the spheres of pension insurance and poverty research. In welfare state research, the desire to place CEE countries into existing welfare state typologies has particularly stimulated analytical discussions among social policy scholars.

This chapter, however, has limitations. It provided a fragmentary look at the most important aspects of research development in the CEE area and focused on selected international publications, mostly comparative studies. Research on the welfare state and social policy is, undoubtedly, much broader in its scope and depth, covering other areas of social policy research, which were not discussed.

Future research on social policy in the CEE region will likely provide new evidence and insights on the relevant issues discussed in this chapter. There will still be discussions about which directions welfare state models are heading in the CEE countries, especially in relation to social policy privatization (e.g., pensions), demographic concerns over the ageing of the population, changing family patterns (single parenthood, divorce), and changing gender roles (fathers' involvement in child upbringing) and family forms. Changing migration processes are also likely to affect research in the CEE region. Since the 1990s, the CEE countries have experienced massive outward labour migration (especially Lithuania, see on this point Genelyte, 2019). In recent years, these countries began attracting migrants from neighbouring countries and experiencing inflows of refugees. These changed patterns will provoke a plethora of research on migration, the integration of ethnic minorities and refugees and their access to social security in the region. Family policy research in the region is likely to follow 'Western' patterns in placing greater attention on work–life balance and shared parental roles within the family. Yet, the emphasis should be placed on long-term care as part of family policy measures, especially familial care. In many CEE countries, women are overburdened with care responsibilities (public or private), and critical questions remain in both family policy and pension research: How should family policy be reformed to solve the problems of child poverty and ensure gender equality in the region? Should pension systems be reformed so as to increase the influence of the private pension funds or should pay-as-you-go systems be maintained? In the sphere of poverty research, the analysis of the multidimensional, long-term, and intergenerational effects of poverty and its dynamics should be stimulated by the increasing availability of administrative longitudinal data. There is also an increasing pressure for developing new methodologies for conducting distributional impact assessments of policy measures, including that of poverty risks in the region.

Other important research themes remain. These include the need to advance research in the CEE region on social investment and social rights, climate change and the development of the eco-social welfare state, and the consequences of the COVID-19 pandemic on the social policy development and wellbeing of the CEE population.

ACKNOWLEDGEMENTS

For particularly useful comments in developing this chapter we would like to thank Mara Yerkes.

REFERENCES

Abrahamson, P. (1999). The welfare modelling business. *Social Policy and Administration, 33*(4), 394–415.

Aidukaite, J. (2006). The formation of social insurance institutions of the Baltic states in the post-socialist era. *Journal of European Social Policy, 16*(3), 259–270.

Aidukaite, J. (2009). Old welfare state theories and new welfare regimes in Eastern Europe: Challenges or implications. *Journal of Communist and Post-Communist Studies, 42*(1), 23–39.

Aidukaite, J. (2011). Welfare reforms and socio-economic trends in the ten new EU member states of Central and Eastern Europe. *Journal of Communist and Post-Communist Studies, 44*(3), 211–219.

Aidukaite, J. (2019). The welfare systems of the Baltic states following the recent financial crisis of 2008/2010: Expansion or retrenchment? *Journal of Baltic Studies, 50*(1), 39–58.

Aidukaite, J. (2021). Support to families with children in the Baltic states: Pathways of expansion and retrenchment from 2004 to 2019. In B. Greve (Ed.), *Handbook on Austerity, Populism and the Welfare State* (pp. 221–242). Edward Elgar Publishing.

Aidukaite, J., & Telisauskaite-Cekanavice, D. (2020). The father's role in child care in Lithuania and Sweden: Experts' views and citizens' evaluation of parental leave policies. *Social Inclusion, 8*(4), 81–91.

Ainsaar, M. (2019). Economic crisis, families, and family policy in the Baltic states, 2009–2014. *Journal of Baltic Studies, 50*(1), 59–77.

Ainsaar, M., & Rootalu, K. (2016). European demographic change and welfare challenges. In K. Schubert, P. de Villota, & J. Kuhlmann (Eds), *Challenges to European Welfare Systems* (pp. 793–807). Springer.

Ainsaar, M., & Stankuniene, V. (2010). Demographic cost of transition and the future of the Baltics. In M. Lauristin & M. Ainsaar (Eds), *Estonian Human Development Report: Baltic Way(s) of Human Development: Twenty Years On* (pp. 44–51). Eesti Koostoo Kogu.

Alam, A., Murthi, M., Yemtsov, R., Murrugarra, E., Dudwick, N., Hamilton, E., & Tiongson, E. (2005). *Growth, Poverty, and Inequality: Eastern Europe and the Former Soviet Union*. International Bank for Reconstruction and Development and World Bank.

Argatu, R. (2018). Analysis of social models in Central and Eastern Europe: A focus on poverty and social exclusion. *Proceedings of the International Conference on Business Excellence, 12*(1), 80–92.

Atkinson, R., & Davoudi, S. (2000). The concept of social exclusion in the European Union: Context, development and possibilities. *Journal of Common Market Studies, 38*(3), 427–448.

Berend, T. I. (2009). *From the Soviet Bloc to the European Union: The Economic and Social Transformation of Central and Eastern Europe since 1973*. Cambridge University Press.

Blum, S., Formánková, L., & Dobrotić, I. (2014). Family policies in 'hybrid' welfare states after the crisis: Pathways between policy expansion and retrenchment. *Social Policy and Administration, 48*(4), 468–491.

Bohle, D. (2007). The new great transformation: Liberalization and social protection in Central Eastern Europe. Paper prepared for presentation at the second ESRC seminar: '(Re) distribution of Uncertainty', Warwick Business School, 2 November.

Bohle, D., & Greskovits, B. (2007). Neoliberalism, embedded neoliberalism, and neo-corporatism: Paths towards transnational capitalism in Central-Eastern Europe. *West European Politics*, *30*(3), 443–466.

Cantillon, B. (2011). The paradox of the social investment state: Growth, employment and poverty in the Lisbon era. *Journal of European Social Policy*, *21*(5), 432–449.

Casey, B. H. (2004). Pension reform in the Baltic states: Convergence with 'Europe' or with 'the world'? *International Social Security Review*, *57*(1), 19–45.

Cerami, A. (2006). *Social Policy in Central and Eastern Europe: The Emergence of a New European Welfare Regime*. LIT Verlag.

Cerami, A. (2011). Ageing and the politics of pension reforms in Central Europe, South-Eastern Europe and the Baltic states. *International Journal of Social Welfare*, *20*, 331–343.

Cerami, A., & Vanhuysse, P. (2009). Introduction: Social policy pathways, twenty years after the fall of the Berlin Wall. In A. Cerami & P. Vanhuysse (Eds), *Post-Communist Welfare Pathways: Theorizing Social Policy Transformations in Central and Eastern Europe* (pp. 1–16). Palgrave Macmillan.

Chandler, A. (2001). Globalisation, social welfare reform and democratic identity in Russia and other post-communist countries. *Global Social Policy*, *1*(3), 310–337.

Daly, M. (2010). Lisbon and Beyond: *The EU Approach to Combating Poverty and Social Exclusion in the Last Decade*. Working Paper – Methods Series No. 3. PSE UK.

Deacon, B. (1992). East European welfare: Past, present and future in comparative context. In B. Deacon (Ed.), *The New Eastern Europe: Social Policy Past, Present and Future* (pp. 1–31). Sage.

Deacon, B. (1997). International organizations and the making of post-communist social policy. In B. Deacon, M. Hulse, & P. Stubbs (Eds), *Global Social Policy International Organizations and the Future of Welfare* (pp. 91–153). Sage.

Deacon, B. (2000). Eastern European welfare states: The impact of the politics of globalisation. *Journal of European Social Policy*, *10*(2), 146–161.

Esping-Andersen, G. (1990). *The Three Worlds of Welfare Capitalism*. Polity Press.

Eurostat (2020). Fertility statistics. 1 November. https://ec.europa.eu/eurostat/statistics -explained/index.php/Fertility_statistics#The_birth_rate_in_the_EU_decreased_at _a_slower_pace _between_2000_and_2017_than_before.

Fajth, G. (1999). Social security in a rapidly changing environment: The case of the post-communist transformation. *Social Policy and Administration*, *33*(4), 416–436.

Fenger, H. J. M. (2007). Welfare regimes in Central and Eastern Europe: Incorporating post-communist countries in a welfare regime typology. *Contemporary Issues and Ideas in Social Sciences*, *3*(2), 1–30.

Ferge, Z. (1997). The changed welfare paradigm: The individualization of the social. *Social Policy and Administration*, *31*(1), 20–44.

Ferge, Z. (2001). Welfare and 'ill-fare' systems in Central-Eastern Europe. In R. Sykes, B. Palier, P. M. Prior, & J. Campling (Eds), *Globalization and European Welfare States: Challenges and Changes*. (pp. 127–153). Red Globe Press.

Fodor, E., Glass, C., Kawachi, J., & Popescu, L. (2002). Family policies and gender in Hungary, Poland and Romania. *Communist and Post-Communist Studies*, *35*(4), 475–490.

Frejka, T., & Gietel-Basten, S. (2016). Fertility and family policies in Central and Eastern Europe after 1990. *Comparative Population Studies*, *41*(1), 3–56.

Genelyte, I. (2019). (Ine)quality of life: Lithuanian labor migration to Sweden during the economic crisis and its aftermath, 2008–2013. *Journal of Baltic Studies*, *50*(1), 79–104.

Golinowska, S., Hengstenberg, P., & Žukowski, M. (2008). *Diversity and Commonality in European Social Policies: The Forging of a European Social Model*. Friedrich Ebert Stiftung.

Haggard, S., & Kaufman, R. R. (2008). The legacy of the socialist welfare state, 1990–2005. In S. Haggard & R. R. Kaufman (Eds), *Development, Democracy, and Welfare States: Latin America, East Asia, and Eastern Europe* (pp. 305–345). Princeton University Press.

Hobson, B., Fahlén, S., & Takács, J. (2011). Agency and capabilities to achieve a work–life balance: A comparison of Sweden and Hungary. *Social Politics*, *18*(2), 168–198.

Horvath, B., Ivanov, A., & Peleah, M. (2012). The global crisis and human development: A study on Central and Eastern Europe and the CIS region. *Journal of Human Development and Capabilities*, *13*(2), 197–225.

Inglot, T. (2008). *Welfare States in East Central Europe, 1919–2004*. Cambridge University Press.

Inglot, T. (2016). Path-dependency versus reform in pensions and family policy re-examined: Dual trajectories of the Polish welfare state since the 1990s. *Social Policy and Administration*, *50*(2), 241–261.

Jahn, D. (2017). Distribution regimes and redistribution effects during retrenchment and crisis: A cui bono analysis of unemployment replacement rates of various income categories in 31 welfare states. *Journal of European Social Policy*, *16*(1), 1–19.

Jahn, D., & Kuitto, K. (2011). Taking stock of policy performance in Central and Eastern Europe: Policy outcomes between policy reform, transitional pressure and international influence. *European Journal of Political Research*, *50*(6), 719–748.

Javornik, J. (2014). Measuring state de-familialism: Contesting post-socialist exceptionalism. *Journal of European Social Policy*, *24*(3), 240–257.

Kangas, O. (1999). Social policy in settled and transitional countries: A comparison of institutions and their consequences. Ministry of Social Affairs and Health. http://pre20031103.stm.fi/english/tao/publicat/tandem/kangas/olli.htm (accessed 05.05.03).

Kuitto, K. (2016). *Post-Communist Welfare States in European Context: Patterns of Welfare Policies in Central and Eastern Europe*. Edward Elgar Publishing.

Kvist, J. (2014). A framework for social investment strategies: Integrating generational, life course and gender perspectives in the EU social investment strategy. *Comparative European Politics*, *13*(1), 1–19.

Leitner, S. (2003). Varieties of familialism: The caring function of the family in comparative perspective. *European Societies*, *5*(4), 353–375.

Lendvai, N. (2008). *Incongruities, Paradoxes, and Varieties: Europeanization of Welfare in the New Member States*. Paper Presented at the ESPAnet Conference, Helsinki, 18–20 September.

Lohmann, H., & Zagel, H. (2016). Family policy in comparative perspective: The concepts and measurement of familization and defamilization. *Journal of European Social Policy*, *26*(1), 48–65.

Manning, N. (2004). Diversity and change in pre-accession Central and Eastern Europe since 1989. *Journal of European Social Policy*, *14*(3), 211–233.

Maslauskaitė, A., & Tereškinas, A. (2020). Quality of non-resident father-child relationships: Between 'caring for' and 'caring about'. In D. Mortelmans (Ed.), *Divorce in Europe, New Insights in Trends, Causes and Consequences of Relation Break-Ups* (pp. 291–311). Springer International Publishing.

Matkovic, T., Sucur, Z., & Zrinscak, S. (2007). Inequality, poverty, and material deprivation in new and old members of European Union. *Croatian Medical Journal*, *48*(5), 636–652.

Medaiskis, T., & Eirošius, Š. (2021). Looking for an adequate and sustainable old-age pension system: Sweden and Lithuania compared. In J. Aidukaite, S. Hort, & S. Kuhnle (Eds), *Challenges to the Welfare State Systems in the Baltic States: Family Policy and Pension Insurance*. Edward Elgar Publishing.

Milanovic, B. (1996), *Income, Inequality and Poverty during the Transition*. World Bank.

Mysikova, M., & Zelinsky, T. (2019). On the measurement of the income poverty rate: The equivalence scale across Europe. *Statistics and Economy Journal*, *99*(4), 383–397.

Oláh, L. Sz. (2015). Changing families in the European Union: Trends and policy implications. Working Paper 44. www.familiesandsocieties.eu/wp-content/uploads/2015/09/WP44Olah2015.pdf

Orenstein, M. A. (2009). Transnational actors in Central and Eastern European pension reforms. In A. Cerami & P. Vanhuysse (Eds), *Post-Communist Welfare Pathways: Theorizing Social Policy Transformations in CEE* (pp. 129–148). Palgrave Macmillan.

Pascall, G., & Manning, N. (2000). Gender and social policy: Comparing welfare states in Central and Eastern Europe and the former Soviet Union. *Journal of European Social Policy*, *10*(3), 240–266.

Piirits, M. (2021). The inequality of public pension benefits of the elderly using Estonian data. In J. Aidukaite, S. Hort, & S. Kuhnle (Eds), *Challenges to the Welfare State Systems in the Baltic States: Family Policy and Pension Insurance*. Edward Elgar Publishing.

Rys, V. (2001a). Introduction. *International Social Security Review*, *54*(2–3), 3–6.

Rys, V. (2001b). Transition countries of Central Europe entering the European Union: Some social protection issues. *International Social Security Review*, *54*(2–3), 177–189.

Saraceno, C. (2016). Varieties of familialism: Comparing four southern European and East Asian welfare regimes. *Journal of European Social Policy*, *26*(4), 314–326.

Saxonberg, S., & Sirovátka, T. (2014). From a garbage can to a compost model of decision-making? Social policy reform and the Czech government's reaction to the international financial crisis. *Social Policy and Administration*, *48*(4), 450–467.

Šileika, A., & Zabarauskaitė, R. (2006). Skurdas, jo matavimas ir tendencijos Lietuvoje [Poverty, its measurement and tendencies in Lithuania]. *Ekonomika*, *74*, 64–77.

Simai, M. (2006). *Poverty and Inequality in Eastern Europe and the CIS Transition Economies*. UN/DESA Working Paper No. 17. www.un.org/esa/desa/papers/2006/wp17_2006.pdf.

Sipos S. (1992). *Poverty Measurement in Central and Eastern Europe before the Transition to the Market Economy*. Child Poverty in Industrialized Countries. UNICEF. www.unicef-irc.org/publications/pdf/eps29.pdf.

Standing, G. (1996). Social protection in Central and Eastern Europe: A tale of slipping anchors and torn safety nets. In G. Esping-Andersen (Ed.), *Welfare States in Transition: National Adaptations in Global Economies* (pp. 225–256). Sage.

Stubbs, P., An, S., & Chubarova, T. (2019). Poverty, inequality and well-being in the global East: Bringing the 'social' back in. In S. An, T. Chubarova, B. Deacon, & P. Stubbs (Eds), *Social Policy, Poverty, and Inequality in Central and Eastern Europe and the Former Soviet Union: Agency and Institutions in Flux*. Columbia University Press.

Szelewa, D. (2016). From explicit to implicit familialism: Post-1989 family policy reforms in Poland. In D. Auth, J. Hergenhan, & B. Holland-Cunz (Eds), *Gender and Family in European Economic Policy* (pp. 129–151). Palgrave Macmillan/Springer Nature.

Szelewa, D. (2020). Recurring ideas? Searching for the roots of right-wing populism in Eastern Europe. *European Journal of Cultural Studies, 23*, 989–997.

Szirka, D., & Tomka, B. (2009). Social policy in East Central Europe: Major trends in the twentieth century. In A. Cerami & P. Vanhuysse (Eds), *Post-Communist Welfare Pathways: Theorizing Social Policy Transformations in CEE* (pp. 17–35). Palgrave Macmillan.

Takács, J. (2019). How involved are involved fathers in Hungary? Exploring caring masculinities in a postsocialist context. *Families, Relationships and Societies, 23*, 1–16.

UNICEF (1994). *Central and Eastern Europe in Transition. Public Policy and Social Conditions: Crisis in Mortality, Health and Nutrition*. Regional Monitoring Report, No. 2, 2 August.

Wehner, C., Abrahamson, P., Murphy, F., Clark, R., Hahighasemi, A., & Hort, E. O. S. (2004). *The Role of the Different Actors in the Development of Social Policy*. Paper Presented at the EU Special Conference, Ghent, 13–16 May.

Yeates, N. (2008). The idea of global social policy. In N. Yeates (Ed.), *Understanding Global Social Policy* (pp. 1–25). Policy Press.

11. Twenty years of social policy research on gender

Trudie Knijn

INTRODUCTION

This chapter aims to understand and discuss the development of social policy research on gender. It therefore avoids reflecting on more complex issues, such as understanding the gendered character of social policy research or discussing the gender bias in social policy research. Nonetheless, arbitrary decisions have to be made.

A first decision concerns academic boundaries. In their introduction to a special issue of the *Journal of Women, Politics and Policy* on policymaking from a gender equality perspective, Lombardo et al. (2016) include multiple academic disciplines. Similarly, research on social policy as represented in ESPAnet is inspired by a broad range of disciplines, the more because it is only a recognized academic sub-discipline in some countries, mostly the United Kingdom, the United States, and Finland. ESPAnet is a multidisciplinary network of scholars, hence this chapter reflects this multidisciplinary character of social policy research on gender.

Second, the editors of this volume define social policy according to Béland (2010: 9), as 'an institutionalized response to social and economic problems'. However, neither Béland nor any other social policy scholar assumes social and economic problems as given. Consequently, a main social policy research topic concerns the construction, prioritization, or neglect of specific social and economic problems. This implies that social policy research looks at both whether gender inequality has been defined as a social and economic problem, and if so, which institutional remedies have been offered.

Third, a related question is whether intersectionality of social policy has become a main issue in the past decades through the acknowledgement that gender is a heterogeneous category. Gender presents itself in many shapes and sub-groups; class, ethnicity, religion, and descent sub-divides as well as coincides with gender.

Fourth, the boundaries of social policy and research on social policy are permeable. Some scholars tend to assume socio-economic problems as income, social security, and employment as the core of social policy research. Although the domain of care had already entered the research agenda in the 1970s (see Chapter 2, this volume), it is often approached from an instrumental socio-economic view to stimulate women's employment (see also Chapter 3, this volume). From a gender perspective, this demarcation is too limited as social policies also construct and influence gender relations in the fields of care, health, sexuality, education, housing, and migration.

Fifth, social policy research on gender does not per definition take a feminist perspective. Clasen and Siegel (2007) plead for defining the outcome of social policies as a starting point of research. What is, or aims to be the result or effect of a social policy reform, regulation, or intervention? Did the policy reform contribute to that aim, to what extent, and why? From a feminist perspective, the answer can only be 'more gender equality'. Presumably, not all social policy research on gender presupposes that aim; one can – against the advice of Clasen and Siegel – ignore gender equality as an outcome, or just analyse gender differences in attitudes, employment, the division of household chores, or the use of childcare services without wondering how it contributes to gender equality.

In sum, in this overview chapter I will discuss social policy research on gender during the timespan 2000–2020. Understanding social policy research as a multidisciplinary academic field, the focus will be on the question of how gender inequality has been defined, as a social and economic problem or otherwise, how it is framed, what causes it, what policy responses are implemented, and what outcomes it generates. Acknowledging that gender is a heterogeneous category, the chapter will also look at intersectionality. Finally, I will go beyond Clasen and Siegel's outcome criterion – defined here as gender equality – to see if and how gender is present in social policy research that does not, per definition, take that outcome for granted.

FROM THE WOMBS OF GIANTESSES

Social policy research on gender is indebted to a long intellectual and political feminist tradition. Over 50 years ago, a second wave of feminist scholarship started to continue the work of scholars whose analyses of women's political underrepresentation, exploitation, and misrecognition had challenged the male-dominated status quo since the nineteenth century. Second-wave feminist scholars explored systemic forms of oppression by theorizing capitalist and patriarchal systems, and their interdependence. Feminist political economists calculated the unpaid reproduction costs of workers and children as a benefit for capitalism, resulting in a debate on claims for a housewife wage or outsourcing care work. Feminist anthropologists and historians analysed the split between the public and the private domains, while scholars in the humanities focused on the imprisoning of the female body and psyche, the pitfalls of celebrating motherhood, the absence of women in policymaking, and the lack of attention to women's contribution to science, production, and art. The common denominator of these second-wave studies is bringing women back in – into society, the academic field, and into politics – by simultaneously pointing at their social, economic, political, and cultural relevance and contesting women's marginalized position.

These ancestors have inspired feminist social policy scholars that emerged in the 1980s and 1990s. Instead of exploring systemic forms of oppression, this generation aimed for a more precise analysis of current mechanisms impeding gender inequality. They still questioned the capitalist patriarchal exploitation of female productive and reproductive work, but now focused on more detailed analyses of social policies producing gender (in)equality in the labour market, on differences and similarities between social policies on gender across different welfare states, and on which (political) parties, institutions, laws, and regulations are involved. Likewise, questioning the imprisoning of the female body and motherhood asked for research on access to health care, on dominant medical institutions and their vision on reproduction, on sex education and prostitution policy. Challenging male political dominance required studying the process of policymaking, thus looking more precisely to masculine power processes, old boys' networks, and the quasi-gender neutrality of politically inspired policy reforms. The Titmuss (1968) questions for analysing social policy[1] entered the studies on gender equality and, with that, social policy research on gender developed.

The renewed orientation to social policy research grew in the 1980s when women in liberal as well as social democratic welfare states entered the labour market, immediately putting the issue of gender equality and care on the social policy research agenda (Balbo, 1987; Leira et al., 2005). In Europe, this renewed social policy approach gained even more strength because the European Union (EU) made gender equality in the labour market one of its core values, immediately followed by a neoliberal spirit when the Berlin Wall came down. The 1990s then revived the 'Wollstonecraft dilemma': women might claim gender equality via the neoliberal spirit of individual economic independence but will do so under conditions that never reach full citizenship, or might claim to be different and take reproductive responsibilities, but these activities will always remain undervalued and underpaid (Pateman, 1989). Policy reforms aimed at encouraging women's employment. Welfare reforms redefined women's position in social security and care, and an awareness of constructed differences between women in various countries emerged. The list of social policy research on gender during the 1980s and 1990s is too extensive to summarize here, but key studies include the path-breaking work on the complexity of care policies and how these define not only women's position but also their feelings (Ungerson, 1990), the straightforward analyses of women's marginalized position on the labour market (Sainsbury, 1994) due to their reproductive work (Folbre, 1994), and Fraser's (1994) articulation of moral and systemic shortcomings of gender regimes. Driven by the intention to understand current and specific social policies on gender, feminist scholars started to explore welfare regimes and citizenship from a gender perspective, from various angles (e.g., Hobson, 1993; Lewis, 1993; Orloff, 1993; Knijn & Kremer, 1997; Lister, 1997; Siim, 2000), to which Esping-Andersen (1999) reacted by presenting the Scandinavian ideal of the outsourcing of care. The question I try to answer in the following sections relates to the work of these pioneers; new insights from the last 20 years in social policy research on gender, and what deeper insights they offer regarding the aims formulated in the introduction.

METHODOLOGY

This chapter is selective given time and space constraints. The enormous richness of English-language books and articles on social policy research on gender imposes selectivity. I do not claim to have read all publications or be on top of all recent research. Rather, this chapter relies on an analysis of English-language journal articles (no books) from the past 20 years, focused on a selection of three journals from the wide range of journals publishing on social policy research.[2] Given the aim of the chapter, I have selected three very different journals, assuming they together represent commonalities and particularities of the field: the *Journal of European Social Policy* (JESP), publishing mainly on (cross-)national European responses to social problems; *Critical Social Policy* (CSP), with a more constructionist than positivist approach, combining a British and global scope; and *Social Politics* (SP), with an explicit gender focus along with historical analyses of politics and policymaking. Together, these three journals published 456 articles with regard to social policy research on gender between 2000 and 2020; 15 to 30 articles annually. I classified all articles into four categories that occasionally overlap. Categorizations were based initially on the abstract, and where necessary, the entire article. Throughout this process, categories were redefined, and articles were moved from one category to another. The final four categories are (1) work and income; (2) care and reproduction; (3) (comparative) welfare regimes and gender policy; and (4) sexual rights, identities, and intersectionality (see Table 11.1 for an overview).

Table 11.1   *Articles on social policy on gender in CSP, JESP and SP (2000–2020)*

Year	Work and income	Care/ reproduction	Regimes/ gender policy	Sexual rights/ identity/ intersectionality
2000/14	4	5	2	1
2001/28	9	7	9	1
2002/25	7	7	7	4
2003/12	0	4	1	6
2004/25	2	6	6	9
2005/23	4	5	9	3
2006/28	2	15	2	8
2007/21	7	4	5	4
2008/23	2	7	7	6
2009/27	4	3	12	4
2010/23	8	4	2	8
2011/21	3	5	9	1
2012/24	5	8	3	6
2013/15	2	5		6
2014/25	6	6	3	7
2015/19	8	2	8	1
2016/22	7	1	6	7
2017/33	5	10	6	9
2018/13	3	4	3	2
2019/25	7	15	1	2
2020/23	5	4	6	6
Total/456	99	133	117	107

SOCIAL POLICY RESEARCH ON GENDER 2000–2020

In the process of categorizing the articles,[3] I have also made two additional decisions on what social policy research on gender implies. First, I have excluded articles that focus on households or families that do not refer to gender relations. Second, articles that only measure differences between men and women as dependent variables without reflecting on its gendered meaning are excluded because analysing social policy research on gender is the objective of this chapter.

Care and Reproduction

Research on care (see also Chapter 2, this volume) and reproduction makes up a significant proportion of the social policy research on gender in *JESP*, *CSP*, and *SP* – respectively 46, 33, and 54 articles. Care for elderly or disabled persons gets less attention than childcare, the latter encompassing availability and accessibility of public and private childcare facilities, parental leaves, and cash-for-care schemes. Gender inequality mostly concerns parents' task divisions and migrant care workers' needs; it is less salient in studies on grandparental care, childcare workers, nannies, and other care workers. Publications on care and gender often take an instrumentalist view on adequate, meaning affordable, accessible, and good-quality public care provisions as conditional for gender equality by contributing to reconciliation of work and family for both genders. Comments on this instrumentalist view come from two sides. On the one hand, as Jane Lewis (2006) states, in referring to the Organisation for Economic Co-operation and Development's (OECD) review of work and family reconciliation policies (Vol. 4) in 13 OECD countries, care policies have a wide range of aims. They may be 'supporting parents in fulfilling their aspirations in terms of fertility; to promote the educational, social and cognitive development of children; to increase female employment; to help to eradicate poverty' (Lewis, 2006: 390). Care policies perform diverse political interests and result in a variety of policies depending on what aim is prioritized. 'Most importantly, these policy aims may be at odds with one another' (Lewis, 2006: 390). On the other hand, the instrumentalist approach to care and gender is incomplete in understanding care as a valuable activity in itself, as a complicated emotional and often hierarchical relation between gendered individuals and as an ethical and moral process of giving and taking. Hence, a series of articles goes beyond the instrumentalist approach to deconstruct the relationship between gender and care, to analyse the gendered framing of care or to dive into the complicated relationship between caregivers and care receivers.

Indeed, the wide-ranging care and gender-related policy agenda is reflected in a variety of studies on all the topics mentioned by Lewis. Research on early childhood education and care and/or parental leaves, for instance, studies whether and under which conditions it contributes to gender equality via women's employment (Morgan & Zippel, 2003; Duvander et al., 2010; Ray et al., 2010; Altintas & Sullivan, 2017; see also Chapter 3, this volume). Other articles articulate that competing policy aims regarding gender and care remain unsolved. Neither neoliberal ideas about market efficiency in childcare nor conservative motherhood ideologies combine well with the aim to eradicate poverty by stimulating mothers' employment and to increase fertility, not to speak of gender equality (Castles, 2003; Bernardi, 2005; Heinen &

Wator, 2006; Kershaw 2006; Avdeyeva, 2011; Geisler & Kreyenfeld, 2011; Lopreite & Macdonald, 2013; Oliver & Mätzke, 2014; Flynn, 2017; Hondarlis, 2017; Akkan, 2018; Hoppania, 2018; Szelewa, 2019; Hufkens et al., 2020). Consequently, only when political ideologies on care and gender equality are congruent, resulting in accessible, affordable, quality, and continuity of care *and* well-paid care work or adequate care leaves for both genders can some gender equality effects be reached.

Social policy research on gender related to care and reproduction also focuses on alternative care configurations: grandparents (i.e., 'maternal inter-generational care') (Souralová, 2019), female migrant care workers, guest parents, nannies, and au-pairs. Cultural preferences or motherhood ideals influence the choice for which care substitutes are hired but each of these alternatives passes the social costs to employees or their unpaid or underpaid substitutes (Kremer, 2006; Búriková, 2019). Most alternatives are problematic. For instance, while grandparents do not mind engaging in childcare in addition to sufficient public care, they tend to abstain from intensive care if public care does not suffice (Igel & Szydlik, 2011). Cash-for-care policies, in contrast, can encourage the willingness and the ability to care (Land, 2002) but, in the absence of public care provisions, such policies bring forward migrant care work, an unacknowledged 'wicked issue' falling between or, in contrast, integrating the policy fields of migration, care, and employment (Shutes & Chiatti, 2012; Williams & Brennan, 2012; Da Roit & Weicht, 2013). Michel and Peng (2012) call it a 'demand and denial' type of work that fills the gaps left by welfare states' failed efforts to provide satisfactory support for a gender equity-based reconciliation of work and family policy. Having only macropositive effects for the receiving countries – no public investments in care workers' training, protection, and reproduction – its negative effects are evident. Sending countries – and the care replacers back home – may benefit from the remittances sent to them but they mainly suffer from a care drain. Migrant care workers themselves are overrepresented in precarious jobs in the lower, unprotected, and unattractive sectors of the paid care economy (Lightman, 2019). An overall conclusion is that migrant care work engenders inequality between women who use the service to combine work and care and those who offer the care, and between sending and receiving countries. Moreover, it does not solve gender inequality because men remain out of the picture (Lutz & Palenga-Möllenbeck, 2012; Boccagni, 2013; Estévez-Abe & Hobson, 2015).

As an alternative to the instrumentalist approach, feminist theorists on care and gender reframed care as a civic virtue, a valuable activity, or a relational moral imperative. CSP offers a forum for this constructionist approach that is inspired by the ethics-of-care approach (Tronto, 1993). It puts wellbeing, capabilities, and people's work/life needs centre stage (Williams, 2001). In the same line of thinking, Henderson and Forbat (2002) plead for incorporating in care policy the notion of care as emotional labour in intimate and personal relationships that is not experienced as care 'work' per se and exists in interdependent reciprocal giving and taking. Taking such a perspective, Dahl (2009) argues that in the context of New Public Governance, different understandings of care intersect, meaning that home helpers are interpreters instead of passive applicants of municipal guidelines. They resign, negotiate, and protest depending on different views of good care. Alternatively, ethics of care inspire scholars to critically evaluate social (development) policies that interpret care as a familialist, gender-neutral, and instrumental resource for economic production, be it in the United Kingdom or South Africa (Sevenhuijsen, 2000; Sevenhuijsen et al., 2003). Gender equality in this strand of social policy research is mainly understood as the upgrading of the inherent value of reproduction for mankind and society to be accomplished by social policies that stimulate a gender-equal sharing of care work, affordable and good-quality care facilities, and well-paid care jobs. In fact, these studies accentuate that care is misinterpreted in a masculine-dominated economic system.

WELFARE REGIMES AND GENDER POLICY

The second main gender-related issue in these three journals is on welfare regimes' gender and family policy. To avoid overlap with the previous paragraph, this heading includes articles explicitly centred on welfare regime differences and similarities. Such articles unavoidably include care policies. Articles in which care is central are included above, and those focused on broader welfare regime policy analyses in which care policies are of minor importance are included here. These studies analyse reconciling work and family life, familialist policies, and welfare reforms impacting gender equality. SP has published 78 articles on this issue, JESP 33, and CSP only six. A preliminary conclusion could be that CSP is more focused on national, regional, and local understandings of gender policies while SP and JESP publish more on comparing (supra-)national tendencies.

Inspired by Esping-Andersen's comparative welfare regime analysis (1990), studies on gender policy initially researched Western European welfare states and the United States. That tendency continued from 2000 onwards while gradually studies on Central and Eastern European countries in the process of reform after the fall of the Soviet Union joined in (Pascall & Manning, 2000; Van der Molen & Novikova, 2005; Gerber 2011; Javornik, 2014; Leschke & Jepsen, 2014; Dobrotić & Blum, 2020; Van Winkle, 2020) as well as studies on Turkey (Seckinelgin, 2006), Israel (Ajzenstadt & Gal, 2001), East Asian (Gottfried & O'Reilly, 2002; Estévez-Abe, 2005; Everett, 2009; Estévez-Abe & Naldini, 2016; Estévez-Abe et al., 2016; León et al., 2016; Saraceno, 2016;

Shire & Nemoto, 2020) and South American countries (Peng, 2001; Gottfried & O'Reilly, 2002; Griffith & Gates, 2002; Mills, 2006; Glass & Fodor 2007; Saxonberg & Szelewa, 2007; Teplova, 2007; Molyneux, 2012; Staab, 2012; Estévez-Abe & Naldini, 2016; Estévez-Abe et al., 2016; León et al., 2016; Saraceno, 2016; Rodríguez Gustá et al., 2017; Nagels, 2018; Shire & Nemoto, 2020).

Besides large-scale comparisons based on international datasets looking for factors explaining gender (in)equality, theoretical debates concern core concepts of familialism as an indicator of welfare regimes' gender equality and Varieties of Capitalism (VOC). The usual suspects in large-scale comparative welfare regime studies on gender are institutionalized family policy models influencing variations in gender role attitudes (Sjöberg, 2004) and policies reducing gender – and class – inequalities (Korpi, 2000). More recently, the economic crises and labour market trends of flexibilization and precariousness affect the earning capacities of both men and women as well as gender equality, also depending on the availability of gender-sensitive parental leave schemes (Dotti Sani, 2017; Dobrotić & Blum, 2020). Comparative research on gender equality in European member states has been further stimulated because of the EU's explicit aim to mainstream gender equality. For this purpose, various versions of a gender equality index have been proposed, such as the one based on Fraser's (1994) universal breadwinner model (Plantenga et al., 2009), in reaction to which Permanyer (2015) argues that the finally agreed upon GEI-index (2013) is unfair to underperforming countries if their achievements to reach gender equality are not embedded in their overall performance. Nonetheless, disagreement on what should be the outcome of gender equality policies (the Clasen and Siegel problem, see the introduction to this chapter) persists. Von Wahl (2005), for instance, claims that because the EU's gender policy only aims for equal access to employment, thus being non-redistributive and regulatory, this supra-national level has been able to force member states to develop a nominally gender-equal playing field. Document-based research, however, critically comments on the direction the EU's gender equality policy has taken since the 1990s. The one-sided focus on the labour market and subsequent degendering of 'family policies' according to these scholars: (a) undermines the original feminist potential of reaching gender equality; (b) takes labour market needs as its main criterion; (c) is too vague in its purposes, presented as a harmonious process thus denying power relations and male privileges to be overcome; and (d) frames core issues like domestic violence as being outside the scope of gender equality (Stratigaki, 2004; Walby, 2004; Verloo, 2005; Lombardo & Meier, 2008). The social investment approach offers an alternative to this neoliberal perspective on gender equality (Morel et al., 2012; Van Kersbergen & Hemerijck, 2012). It assumes the state as investor on behalf of the citizenship rights of the poor and the powerless by investing in the future of children via childcare, education, and anti-poverty measures. Jenson (2009) fears, however, that this approach neglects gender equality by favouring children's interests above those of adult women. Attitudinal research by Busemeyer and Neimanns (2017) shows that among the population, different beneficiary groups compete for such investments, for instance single parents versus the unemployed. Bothfeld and Rouault (2015) signal that this competition is not only imaginary. Social reforms in the name of social investments show a trade-off between the redistributive and investive aspects of social policy, in particular at the cost of families. Effects for gender equality are not clear, however.

The VOC research on gender, initiated by Estévez-Abe (2005, 2009; see also Soskice, 2005) further challenges the scope and influence of policy reforms on gender equality by embedding these in the political economy literature on occupational segregation in either coordinated or liberal market economies. Comparative research shows a trade-off between institutionalized labour protection, occupational gender stratification, and families' income security; a prisoner's dilemma because in liberal market economies solving one issue (gender stratification) unavoidably will be at the cost of another (institutionalized labour protection). In response, McCall and Orloff (2005) and Mandel and Shalev (2009) state that the VOC literature is unable to resolve that dilemma due to a functionalist approach that does not consider politics, ideology, or the history of institutional formation. Moreover, they argue that research on VOC firstly needs to understand intersectionality of class and gender, meaning that different forms of capitalism have different implications for women – and men – in different class positions; class is not only a male issue and higher-educated women might perform well in liberal market economies just because of the lower costs and protection of lower-class and/or migrant women (see Rubery, 2009). Secondly, the VOC literature often neglects the particularities of conservative continental European welfare states that, until recently, avoided policies that supported mothers' employment (by way of paid leaves) and did not assist in integrating paid and unpaid work by offering decent public-sector jobs. Finally, Kleider (2015) shows that skill specificity, the VOC's main claim, is less important for women's employment than policies actively promoting female employment and the absence of social policies that slow down female employment.

Thus, while research dives deeper into the (preferred) outcome of gender policies as well as the complexities of the relationship between political economies and social policies, a core conceptual problem remains 'familialism' and policy reforms that intend to (de)familialize care work.[4] Introduced to critically assess Esping-Andersen's decommodification concept in comparative welfare regime research (Esping-Andersen, 1990) from a gender perspective, it adds women's economic independence and the redivision of care work within the family as conceptual tools (Orloff, 1993; Lister 1994; McLaughlin & Glendinning, 1994). Defamilialization, however, quickly became framed in the EU and its member states, and mainstream social policy research (Esping-Andersen, 1999; Korpi, 2000), as conditional for labour market policy by 'freeing women from care', as if outsourcing family care does not imply that other women will do the job. Lohmann and Zagel (2015), in summarizing theoretical debates on the familialization-defamilialization duality, conclude that feminist scholars instead agree that gender equality implies seeing gender and generational care relations as part of family policies, and understanding care as a reciprocal process between individuals and between the state, the market and the family. As Saraceno and Keck (2010) show, gender equality via defamilialization can fail through state support for familial (feminized) care, or due to a lack of state provisions.

SEXUAL RIGHTS/IDENTITY/INTERSECTIONALITY

A third major research topic concerns the complex issue of gender policies related to sexual rights and gendered identities. Touching upon a late-coming area of institutionalized gender equality policies, these studies focus on the politicized relation between sex and gender identities, body politics, and gender-based violence policy as well as the upcoming theoretical intersectionality approach. SP has published 50 articles on this issue and CSP 55. Interestingly, JESP hardly commits itself to this issue with only two publications. In contrast to the often presumed responsibility of the welfare state and the (labour) market for family and work reconciliation as a means for gender equality, recognition of sexual violence, let alone body diversity and its consequences as a policy domain, came rather late. It was only in 2002 that an updated version of the EU's Directive on Equal Treatment (1976) defined sexual harassment as sex discrimination as the result of transnational advocacy networks (Zippel, 2004). Even while it only contained soft law, its effects were instantaneous in national legislation across different Central and Eastern European countries accessing the EU (Krizsan & Popa, 2010). One stream of research in this area accentuates state responsibility for sexual violence either directly, by targeting indigenous and poor women such as in Peru (Boesten, 2012) and India (Chantler et al., 2018), or indirectly, by diminishing support for abused women or violence against LGBTI persons and organizations representing them. Cuts in support systems (social assistance, housing, social services, etc.) due to neoliberal 'self-sufficiency' (Morrow et al., 2004; Daley, 2006; Ishkanian, 2014) or social-conservative 'family-centred' ideologies (Phillips, 2006) and a lack of adequate policing (McGhee, 2003) have devastating effects as do social services offering victims only criminalization or exit options instead of preventative policies (Paterson, 2009, 2010; Phipps, 2010).

Another stream analyses why and how sexual violence uneasily relates to cultural diversity at each governance level. A critical discourse analysis of EU anti-violence policy by Montoya and Rolandsen Agustín (2013) points to the risk of externalization of sexual violence by its culturalization. Emphasizing a minority cultural conception of gender-based violence and articulating it as an external policy aim, as the Commission does, defines this violence as an 'outsider' problem of 'others' within EU member states and of countries outside the EU. Such an articulation hides majority populations' 'common' forms of domestic gender-based violence and fuels a racially problematic rhetoric with a quasi-feminist approach. At the local level, this culturalist or even racist prejudice prevents social services, health care, or asylum organizations from offering adequate support for battered women (Ahlberg et al., 2004; Burman et al., 2004; Canning, 2013; Giannou & Ioakimidis, 2019).

Self-complacency on gender equality, however, does not suit core EU member states or other liberal democratic welfare states as various studies on discrimination of sexual diversity and conduct-based, identity-based, and relationship-based rights claim (Richardson, 2000; Harder, 2007; Smith, 2010; Rawsthorne, 2012). Public opinion and active religious organizations (Siegel, 2020) stand in the way as does the inability to deal with all kinds of non-binary identities in legal and social procedures (Kuhar et al., 2017; Monro & Van Der Ros, 2017). Moreover, the absence of explicit central government policy on sexual diversity makes such rights very dependent on local political, cultural, historical, and religious contexts (Carabine & Monro, 2004).

Gender equality versus inequality is no longer the main issue in social policy research on gender. The first decades of the twenty-first century increasingly relate to the dichotomy of difference versus sameness, the grounds of exclusion and inclusion depending on policies of othering and sameness based on identities. One theoretical approach suggested by Montoya and Rolandsen Agustín (2013) is to apply an intersectional approach that has already proven its analytical merit at the crossroads of gender, ethnicity, and immigration (see Christie, 2006; Rottmann & Ferree, 2008; Spanger, 2011; Strid et al., 2013; Reisel, 2014). Intersectional policy research focuses on both the individual and institutional levels and covers conflicting interpretations of inequalities among relevant actors. It has the potential to conceptualize differences between groups of women and men as well as contestations emerging from heterogeneity (Rolandsen Agustín & Siim, 2013). In recalling Verloo's comment on a too simple 'one-size-fits-all' EU policy, and the research on it, Lombardo and Rolandsen Agustín (2012) propose a continuous reflection both in policymaking and policy research on all potential intersections without losing sight of the adequacy of potential dimensions in each field, and with a further articulation of the actual effect on the groups at specific intersections or the different ways in which they are or may be affected.

LABOUR, INCOME, AND SOCIAL SECURITY

Effects of gender-based discrimination and policies on gender-based labour market segregation, gendered gaps in income, pensions, and on women's poverty are analysed in 50 articles in SP, 29 in JESP, and 20 in CSP. Leading themes in these first two decades of the twenty-first century are the discursive and actual reconstructions of welfare policies in which gender equality, social welfare, changing labour markets, and neoliberal economic purposes are intertwined. In the context of a massive growth in female labour market participation worldwide (Filgueira & Martínez Franzoni, 2019),[5] a range of family policies (Ferraggina & Seeleib–Kaiser, 2015) have been introduced as well as work-related reforms (pensions) aimed to individualize incomes (Frericks et al., 2007; Marrier, 2007). Research evidence critically assesses the discursive frame and the outcomes of the Adult Worker Model and the welfare-to-work rhetoric underlying welfare state reconstructions from a gender perspective (Annesley, 2007). Regarding the discursive frame, scholars argue it neglects that women and men act according to moral and relational choices rather than according to pure rational choices, and therefore do not just accept policies enforcing them to leave behind their children in exchange for a marginal job (Duncan & Strell, 2004; Pulkingham et al., 2010). Regarding its outcomes, studies show time after time that given the heterogeneous category 'women', gender equality cannot be reached by a one-size-fits-all approach. Whether it concerns employment policies (Crompton & Le Feuvre, 2000), old-age systems (Gough, 2001; Leitner, 2001; Sefton et al., 2011), benefits for lone mothers (Skevik, 2005; Korteweg, 2006; Dodson, 2007), or minimum income benefits (Duncan & Strell, 2004; Frericks et al., 2020), or 'welfare-to-work' policies (Dean, 2001), the conclusion is that mostly better-educated women with continuous work experience benefit, while family carers, lower-skilled women, domestic workers, lone mothers, and women with a migration background remain either poor or in precarious work conditions (Jaehrling et al., 2015; Morel, 2015; Devitt, 2016; Österle & Bauer, 2016; Jokela, 2019). Scholarly attention therefore shifts towards intersectional analysis integrating gender, ethnicity, and class. In reaction to the EU's Lisbon agenda, Lewis et al. (2008; see also Mutari & Figart, 2001) conclude that preferences, cultures of work and care, the sharing of housework, childcare facilities, and adult working hours vary so much in member states that it does not legitimate one European policy model. Moreover, leave policies in most European countries still use the male breadwinner model as a normative reference point or are more conditional for men (Björnberg, 2002; Ciccia & Verloo, 2012; Sigurdardottir & Garðarsdóttir, 2018), while destandardization and individualization of women's working hours do not remedy gender inequality (Plantenga, 2002), nor the still existing wage gap (Evertsson et al., 2009). Aside from falling short in reaching gender equality, Ghysels and Van Lancker (2011) signal risks of implementing the model in a socially selective way, resulting in less redistributive welfare systems. Alternatives are suggested too, such as the Belgian service voucher scheme, of which Raz-Yurovich and Marx (2017) demonstrate positive effects on employment rates of low-skilled and highly skilled women, and the family working time model providing income replacement if both parents work 30 hours per week as proposed by Müller et al. (2018).

Along the road towards gender equality in work and income are many barriers and blockades with obstacles that hinder women in different phases of life, in different households, with different skills and backgrounds, in a wide variety of ways. The policy focus on tempting or enforcing women to join the labour market certainly has improved women's work and income position worldwide. However, the reconstruction of labour markets and welfare regimes along neoliberal lines with more flexibility and precarious work and less security tends to undermine these efforts with severe risks for the most vulnerable women.

CONCLUSION

Is there any relationship between policymaking on gender equality in Europe and forceful attacks on women's sexual and reproductive rights in Europe and elsewhere? Is social policy research on gender meaningful in understanding these parallel and paradox trends? In the end, we can interpret that paradox metaphorically for what Bugra (2014; see also Pateman, 1989; Komter, 1990) sees as the inherent and unsolved problem of a combination of the cultural affirmation of women's difference and the gender-blind economic gender-equality employment approach. Indeed, social policy research on gender shows that, with some exceptions, care work remains defined as *women*'s obstacle to employment to be solved by undervalued and underpaid other *women*. This affirmation of gender difference goes hand in hand with welfare regime reforms that both promote and assume gender equality. With bounded hands, women face benefit cutbacks, flexibilization of labour markets, privatization of public services, and individualized taxes and pensions. 'In other words, the old tension between equality and difference initially highlighted in Wollstonecraft's *A Vindication of the Rights of Woman* (1792/1978) remains with us' (Bugra, 2014: 150). Future social policy research on gender might take inspiration from that dilemma remembering that equality and difference are not opposites: 'The opposite of equality is inequality. To posit it as difference disguises the relations of subordination, hierarchy and consequent disadvantage and injustice, which underlie the dichotomy, and serves to distort the policy choices open to us' (Lister, 2003: 98). Given that dilemma, future social policy research would be served by following Fraser's (1994) proposal to approach welfare regimes from five distinct normative principles: (1) anti-poverty (including anti-exploitation and income equality); (2) leisure time equality; (3) equality of respect; (4) anti-marginalization; and finally (5) anti-androcentrism. Indeed, a lot of work needs to be done.

NOTES

1. What is the nature of entitlement, who is entitled and under what conditions, and what methods are employed in the determination of access, utilization, allocation, and payment?
2. I offer my sincere apologies to the editors, authors, and readers of the following journals for being unable to include their social policy research on gender: *European Journal of Women's Studies, Feminist Review, Gender and Society, International Journal of Sociology and Social Policy, Journal of Social Policy, Journal of Women, Politics and Policy, Social Policy,* and *Administration, Social Policy and Politics.*
3. References to articles in the three journals are not listed in the reference list. These can be found in the selected journals CSP, JESP, and SP volumes 2000–2020 as well as in a thematic list of references provided in the supplemental material to this chapter at https://www.e-elgar.com/textbooks/yerkes.
4. Also labelled as (de)familization.
5. With the exception of some post-socialist European countries (Avlijaš, 2020).

REFERENCES

Balbo, L. (1987). Crazy quilts: Rethinking the welfare state debate from a woman's point of view. In A. Showstack Sassoon (Ed.), *Women and the State: The Shifting Boundaries of Public and Private* (pp. 45–71). Routledge.

Béland, D. (2010). *What Is Social Policy?* Polity.

Clasen, J., & Siegel, N. (Eds). (2007). *Investigating Welfare State Change.* Edward Elgar Publishing.

Esping-Andersen, G. (1990). *The Three Worlds of Welfare Capitalism.* Princeton University Press.

Esping-Andersen, G. (1999). *Social Foundations of Postindustrial Economies.* Oxford University Press.

Folbre, N. (1994). *Who Pays for the Kids? Gender and the Structures of Constraint.* Routledge.

Fraser, N. (1994). After the family wage: Gender equity and the welfare state. *Political Theory, 22*(4), 591–618.

Hobson, B. (1993). Feminist strategies and gendered discourses in the welfare states: Married women's right to work in the United States and Sweden. In S. Koven & S. Michel (Eds), *Mothers of the World: Mothers of a New World: Gender and Origins of Welfare States in Western Europe and North America* (pp. 398–429). Routledge.

Knijn, T., & Kremer, M. (1997). Gender and the caring dimension of welfare states: Toward inclusive citizenship. *Social Politics: International Studies in Gender, State and Society, 4*(3), 328–361.

Komter, A. (1990). *De Macht van de Dubbele Moraal. Verschil en Gelijkheid in de Verhouding tussen de seksen*. Van Gennep.

Leira, A., Tobio, C., & Trifiletti, R. (2005). Kinship and informal support: Care resources for the first generation of working mothers. In U. Gerhard, T. Knijn, & A. Weckwert (Eds), *Working Mothers in Europe* (pp. 74–96). Edward Elgar Publishing.

Lewis. J. (Ed.). (1993). *Women and Social Policies in Europe: Work, Family and the State*. Edward Elgar Publishing.

Lister, R. (1997/2003). *Citizenship: Feminist Perspectives*. Palgrave Macmillan.

Lombardo, E., Meier P., & Verloo, M. (2016). Policymaking from a gender equality perspective. *Journal of Women, Politics and Policy*, *38*(1), 1–19.

Morel, N., Palier, B., & Palme, J. (2012). *Towards a Social Investment Welfare State?* Policy Press.

Orloff, A. S. (1993). Gender and the social rights of citizenship: The comparative analysis of gender relations and welfare states. *American Sociological Review*, *58*(3), 303–328.

Pateman, C. (1989). *The Disorder of Women: Democracy, Feminism and Political Theory*. Polity Press.

Sainsbury, D. (Ed.). (1994). *Gendering Welfare States*. Sage.

Siim, B. (2000). *Gender and Citizenship: Politics and Agency in France, Britain and Denmark*. Cambridge University Press.

Titmuss, R. M. (1968). *Commitment to Welfare*. Allen and Unwin.

Tronto, J. (1993). *Moral Boundaries: A Political Argument for an Ethic of Care*. Routledge.

Ungerson, C. (Ed.). (1990). *Gender and Caring: Work and Welfare in Britain and Scandinavia*. Harvester Wheatsheaf.

Van Kersbergen, K., & Hemerijck, A. (2012). Two decades of change in Europe: The emergence of the social investment state. *Journal of Social Policy*, *41*(3), 475–492.

Wollstonecraft, M. (1792/1978). *A Vindication of the Rights of Woman*. Penguin Books.

12. European labour markets and social policy: recent research and future directions

Jochen Clasen and Daniel Clegg

INTRODUCTION

The state of the labour market is vital for social policy. On the macro level, the sustainability of any system of social protection for those unable to work depends in large part on sufficient people being in employment, contributing to economic output, and paying taxes. On the micro level, the standardization of working relationships into the post-Second World War norm of stable, full-time, and overwhelmingly male employment provided the principal basis for the accrual of rights to social protection in the event of social risks or when reaching the age of retirement. The central social insurance pillar of European welfare states was built on the foundations of full (male) employment and the standard employment relationship.

By the late 1970s, rapid deindustrialization was generating new tensions in the labour market–welfare state relationship. Social policies and regulated labour markets both came to be widely seen as a problem for Europe's economies. Some identified a vicious spiral whereby maintaining a high level of social and employment protection drove up hiring costs, stifling job creation especially in the expanding private services sector. Attempts to address youth unemployment by subsidizing the labour force exit of older workers further aggravated this problem. The age-old critique that social security for the able-bodied poor would discourage work also returned with a vengeance. European social policy seemed to be out of step with socio-economic megatrends such as the growing professional aspirations of women and the demand by both some employers and workers for more flexible employment relations.

The period since around the turn of the millennium has been a new phase of labour market change in Europe. Promoting a high level of private-sector employment has become the overarching objective of most European governments and the European Union (EU), which adopted formal employment rate targets in 2000. While social policy has been largely subordinated to this employment objective, this did not simply lead to retrenchment. Maintaining good health and pension systems in ageing societies has been a key motive for expanding employment, while social policies are also seen as crucial instruments for boosting labour supply. Moreover, increased participation in work is often presented as the best way of combating poverty and social exclusion. But there are also risks to traditional social policy concerns in the pursuit of employment growth at all costs, including the potential to neglect those who can't or don't enter work and the acceptance of a growth in types of employment that may diminish the individual and collective value of work itself and create new social and economic divides.

This chapter discusses the changes in Europe's labour markets in the twenty-first century and reviews some contributions of social policy research to understanding them. It is organized in four main sections. We first provide a brief overview of the development of selected aggregate labour market indicators in the last two decades, illustrating apparently positive trends – the massive negative impact of the financial and Eurozone crises in some European countries notwithstanding – in relation to employment, labour force participation, and unemployment, as well as more adverse ones in relation to the growth of vulnerable employment. The subsequent two sections discuss in turn two broad bodies of pertinent social policy research. The first focuses on the impacts of recent labour market changes on key social outcomes; the second on the macropolitical and institutional process of adapting Europe's varied social protection systems to make them more 'employment friendly'. The next section briefly discusses some themes we believe deserve further attention in future social policy research and through attention to which it can highlight its distinctive contribution to understanding contemporary labour market change.

LABOUR MARKET CHANGE IN EUROPE

A high level of employment is crucially important for welfare states as it raises public revenue, not least for the purpose of social spending, while reducing outlays. Data from the Organisation for Economic Co-operation and Development (OECD) (2021) suggest that across the EU27, and despite the global financial crisis of 2008, employment rates increased by about 5 per cent in the past 20 years or so, reaching record levels in some countries, such as Germany. This has especially concerned women, with female employment increasing by eight percentage points to just over 62 per cent by 2020. By contrast, although male employment has also increased (by about three percentage points to just under 73 per cent on average), in many countries, such as France,

Belgium, and across Southern Europe, it has been rather stagnant or even fallen over the past 20 years.

Reaching a peak of 11.5 per cent in 2013, the EU27 average unemployment rate declined thereafter to slightly over 7 per cent by 2020, which was about two percentage points lower than 20 years earlier. Of course, there are notable cross-national differences. Not least due to the much greater impact of the 2008 global financial crisis, Southern European countries still have higher unemployment than in the year 2000. By contrast, there have been enormous falls in unemployment in some Central and Eastern European countries such as Poland and Slovakia. There is also considerable variation by age cohort. Youth unemployment has, on average, remained high (just under 17 per cent in 2020), although this is much lower than its peak of just under 25 per cent in 2013.

The size of the workforce across the EU27 countries has also grown in the past 20 years. The labour force participation rate of all 15–64 year olds rose from just under 68 per cent in 2000 to 73 per cent in 2020. The main driver for this was a 7 per cent growth in prime age (24–64) labour force participation, and a remarkable increase in labour force participation among those aged 55 to 64 (from just under 38 per cent to about 63 per cent).

An increasingly conventional point of departure in public discourse on contemporary European labour markets is that regular employment is in decline while 'atypical' jobs are becoming ever more widespread. More concretely, traditional patterns of stable (male) labour market participation characterized by continuous full-time work are gradually becoming less common and partly replaced by more fluid, less regular, and more non-standard types of work, including part-time, temporary, and agency work, solo (bogus) self-employment, and recently gig economy and platform work (Eurofound, 2020a). There is ample comparative literature describing and evaluating such trends (e.g., Koch & Fritz, 2013; Hipp et al., 2015).

In some respects the conventional narrative is misleading, however. Standard employment has remained dominant with just under 60 per cent of all jobs across the EU plus the United Kingdom (UK) in 2018 (Eurofound, 2020b). Once labour force composition effects are accounted for, between the early 2000s and 2017 there was only a slight decrease (of 5 per cent) in average job tenure across most of the 26 European OECD countries. In a few countries, such as Latvia and Spain, job tenure actually increased by more than 10 per cent (OECD, 2019: 95). Even in liberal welfare states such as the UK, average job tenure has actually grown (Choonara, 2019). Importantly, however, the picture varies considerably by gender, economic sector, qualification level, and especially age cohort, with younger people more affected by labour market insecurity now than they were 20 or 30 years ago. The analytical perspective matters too. Reviewing labour markets at any particular point in time may suggest that the number of non-standard jobs has risen little, but a life-course perspective shows that a growing proportion of people experience non-standard employment for parts of their working life.

Regarding the composition of non-standard work, the share of temporary jobs had already increased (on average) before the year 2000 (to just under 14 per cent) and continued to grow in the Netherlands, Italy, and Poland thereafter, but stagnated in other EU countries. The exception is young people under the age of 25, for whom temporary jobs have become much more common in the past 20 years, growing close to half of all jobs (OECD, 2021). Perhaps the most remarkable change has been the increase in part-time jobs. Despite a slight decline after 2014, part-time work (conventionally defined as 30 hours or less per week) has grown steadily during the past few decades to, on average, 19 per cent of all jobs by 2018 (Eurofound, 2020b), albeit with considerable variation across countries. In addition, across 26 European countries there was another 6 per cent of workers with 'unstable' employment in the same year (OECD, 2020). The category is defined by the OECD as workers who had at least two spells of unemployment in the past three years, but more broadly captures workers who experience precarious employment independent of a specific contractual status. While unstable employment describes the labour market situation of between 5 and 10 per cent of all employees in most countries, in some Southern European countries the share is more than 10 per cent.

Across the EU, the risk of poverty among those in unstable employment is about six times higher than for those in standard employment (OECD, 2020), while it is three times higher for part-time workers (Eurofound, 2020b; see also Horemans et al., 2016). Potentially affected here are particularly the 11 per cent of all employees (17 per cent of women; 6 per cent of men) who work 'low hours', i.e., less than 20 hours per week, often not out of choice. Since the early 2000s there has been a noticeable rise in the number of involuntary part-time workers. In 2018, about a quarter of all part-time employees (but almost half of all 30- to 50-year-old men) would have preferred to work longer hours (Eurofound, 2020b). Once again national differences need to be noted. In countries with relatively high shares of part-time work (such as the Netherlands, Switzerland, Germany, and Austria), the proportion of involuntary part-time employment is low, and vice versa. Moreover, involuntary part-time work is more common in countries with relatively high unemployment rates, suggesting that both phenomena are affected by business cycles, but also the structural expansion of low-skill service sector employment (OECD, 2019).

Another indicator of increasing flexibility is the growth of intermittent and casual employment. This covers workers in seasonal and project-based work, as well as 'on demand' workers who have no guaranteed hours and are called upon when needed (Eurofound, 2020b). Partly due to differences in legal definitions, there is considerable cross-national variation with between 3 and 10 per cent of all employees reliant on intermittent work. Nevertheless, the number of workers affected seems to have been growing since the early 2000s in countries such as the UK, France, the Netherlands, and Czech Republic (Eurofound, 2020b). While it is particularly younger people who find themselves in these types of precarious employment, there is no firm evidence to suggest that these types of jobs are mere stepping stones to more regular employment relationships.

In sum, despite the impact of the financial crisis, European labour markets have performed increasingly well in creating jobs in the new millennium, with both employment and labour force participation standing at record levels prior to the COVID-19 pandemic. High (youth) unemployment remains a serious problem in many European countries, but EU average unemployment in 2019 was well below its level in 2000. While regular jobs are not in danger of being supplanted by flexible employment, there has at the same time been a trend towards more non-standard and especially part-time work.

THE IMPACTS OF LABOUR MARKET CHANGES AND EMPLOYMENT-PROMOTING SOCIAL POLICIES

One strand of social policy research that has interrogated these changes asks about the impact of higher employment participation on key social outcomes as well as on the situation of different social groups. Employment growth has been presented in European political discourse as the key to tackling a range of social problems, including unemployment, reliance on social benefits, and poverty. Based on an analysis of the 20 years to 2000, de Beer (2007), however, showed that increases in employment reduced unemployment less than might have been anticipated because of parallel changes in labour force participation. He further emphasized that increasing employment was insufficient to combat relative poverty and reduce benefit dependency, as these outcomes also depend crucially on the distribution of paid work across households and the operation of the social benefit system. In a similar vein, the concentration of new job growth in already 'work-rich' households and the declining value of unemployment and minimum income benefits as governments sought to reduce reservation wages were identified as reasons that growing employment in the first decade of the new millennium had not given rise to substantial reductions in poverty (Vandenbroucke & Vlemickx, 2011; Cantillon & Vandenbroucke, 2014). This has led to a lively and ongoing debate around the ability of employment-promoting social policies to reconcile economic performance and social justice (Plavgo & Hemerijck, 2020; Parolin & Van Lancker, 2021).

A related literature has looked more specifically at the issue of in-work or working poverty in Europe (Fraser et al., 2011). A common critique of the encouragement of employment growth via flexibilization of the labour market is that a rise in atypical and low-wage work will lead to increasing poverty among workers, long thought to be more a North American than a European phenomenon (Crettaz, 2013). However, closer empirical inspection has revealed the multiple determinants of working poverty, including not only wages and job quality but also hours of work and the role of social benefit entitlements (Goerne, 2011). While low wages are normally necessary for working poverty, far from all low-wage workers are poor (Nolan & Marx, 2014). The complexities in conceptualizing and operationalizing working poverty illustrate a key theme in research on employment-centred social policy to date, namely the need to situate individual situations and transitions in their household context (Crettaz, 2013). It also highlights the increasingly uncertain boundary between work and unemployment (Halleröd et al., 2015), a point to which we return below.

Alongside objective outcomes like poverty and inequality, another focus of the social policy literature on labour market change has been its impact on subjective insecurity (Chung & Mau, 2014). In principle, welfare state and labour market institutions can mitigate the negative impacts of labour market change on subjective insecurity, though evidence suggests that general economic and employment conditions are at least as important (Erlinghagen, 2008; Chung & Van Oorschot, 2011). Nevertheless, Carr and Chung (2014) found that unemployment benefits and active labour market policies can moderate the relationship between high levels of insecurity and low levels of wellbeing, especially for groups most vulnerable in the labour market.

These types of study tend to operationalize cross-national variations in social policies through aggregates and averages, such as levels of spending and typical replacement rates and periods of benefit receipt. But these indicators may not be very helpful in capturing the actual role social policies play in protecting the groups most exposed to new forms of flexible employment. For example, we know that on average across the OECD less than a third of all unemployed actually receive unemployment insurance benefits, and that the level is far lower for groups with limited contribution records like the young (OECD, 2018). Limited unemployment insurance benefit entitlement may be both a consequence of the growth of vulnerable employment but also contributes to it, if it makes workers less selective as regards to job offers (OECD, 2018). Assessing the implications of the rise in non-standard employment for the effectiveness of unemployment protection and other benefit systems has been a distinct – if surprisingly niche, given its importance for so-called 'flexicurity' (cf. Viebrock & Clasen, 2009) – strand in the social policy literature on labour market change (Buschoff & Protsch, 2008; Leschke, 2008). Interest in this theme has been recently reinvigorated by the principle of access to adequate social protection in the European Pillar of Social Rights (Schoukens et al., 2018; Avlijas, 2019). Non-standard employment of course impacts on the accrual of rights to other forms of social protection, and the case of pensions has also been an important focus of research (Hinrichs & Jessoula, 2012).

While these studies probe the repercussions of labour market change for the effectiveness of 'old' social policies, another focus of evaluative research has been the effectiveness of 'new' employment-focused policies in encouraging more people into work. Though not so new in many countries, work–family or work–care reconciliation policies are a case in point. Focusing on the period 1970–2000, Ferrarini (2006) found a strong relationship between the extent of dual-earner support in family policy and the rate of female paid employment. However, analysing the strong differences in the working hours but also preferences for work and for childcare use across European countries, Lewis et al. (2008) suggest that divergent norms and values around child rearing and family life – even if these are to some extent constrained by existing policy contexts (Kangas & Rostgaard, 2007) – made convergence on the dual-earner or 'adult worker' model unlikely. Of a range of tensions in social policies to help reconcile work and care responsibilities (cf. Pfau-Effinger & Rostgaard, 2011), one which has attracted particular attention is the possible trade-off between the extension of various policies to facilitate female and especially maternal employment and the risk of female occupational segregation (Korpi et al., 2013; Brady et al., 2020). Research has shown that outcomes of policies to promote female employment are significantly stratified by social class, though more for some policies than others (Prince Cooke, 2011).

For already socio-economically disadvantaged groups, employ-ment-promoting policies are often also about reducing (long-term) reliance on out-of-work cash transfers. There is a vast literature focused on the evaluation of active labour market policies and other approaches to 'activat-ing' the unemployed, and this is examined comprehensively elsewhere in this volume (see Chapter 8 by Bonoli). Mention here might, however, be made of related research evaluating adjustments to working-age cash benefits that have allowed them to be cumulated with higher levels of earnings, increasing mon-etary incentives to make transitions from unemployment or inactivity to work. These policies may take the form of more liberal rules on the assessment of eligibility for social assistance benefits (e.g., Hiilamo & Kautto, 2009), or the creation of dedicated new 'in-work' benefits, sometimes paid through the tax system (Cousins, 2014). Much research on the latter has involved simulating the impact of their introduction in different contexts and with different design features (Figari, 2010; Vandelannoote & Verbist, 2020), and highlighted their context-specific effects and the complex trade-offs in policy design and poten-tially gendered effects where household based. More qualitative research, which has to date particularly focused on the impact of such policies on lone parents (Duncan & Strell, 2004; Millar & Ridge, 2020), has added important insights on the complex rationalities at play in the appropriation of these opportunities by individuals as well as on the role of structural constraints, including the availability of suitable employment opportunities.

THE POLITICS OF 'EMPLOYMENT-FRIENDLY' SOCIAL POLICY

A second broad strand of social policy research on labour market change focuses on the adaptation of welfare states to an agenda of employment promotion, deregulation, and increased flexibility. The aim here is less evaluative than in the literature discussed above, with the focus instead on the political and institutional determinants of policy development. As unemployment and activation policies are a big part of the employment promotion agenda, our discussion here again complements the analysis by Bonoli (Chapter 8, this volume).

Because of its role in driving the employment promotion agenda in the European context, one consistent theme of social policy research in this area has been the role of the EU (see also Chapter 9 by De la Porte and Madama, this volume). Research has examined the impact of EU strategies on domestic policy development, often going along with an assessment of the 'soft' governance mechanisms through which EU social and labour market policy has been largely pursued since the late 1990s (Jacobbson, 2004; Mailand, 2008). Though present from some of the earliest work in this area (cf. De la Porte & Pochet, 2004), the emphasis on the interaction of EU social and economic policies and their conjoined effects on social policy development has become stronger since the reforms of the economic governance framework adopted in the context of the Eurozone crisis (De la Porte & Heins, 2016; Bekker & Mailand, 2019). A secondary emphasis in this literature, perhaps because EU politics is its own distinct field of research, has been on the political process by which important EU social policy concepts such as flexicurity have been elaborated (e.g., Mailand, 2010).

An early claim of the literature on the domestic politics of post-industrial welfare states was that in an era of resource constraints the political weakness of their principal beneficiaries militated against the expansion of employment-promoting and flexibility-protecting social policies (Bonoli, 2005). A more differentiated view has, however, gradually come to dominate, emphasizing the electoral logic behind widespread expansion of work–family reconciliation policies, not least as women's votes have become a key electoral battleground in the context of changing class structures (Gingrich & Häusermann, 2015). These policies have also been argued to benefit from the support of businesses concerned about female recruitment, albeit in ways that are shaped by nationally specific skill and production regimes (Fleckenstein & Seeleib-Kaiser, 2011).

By contrast, political support for policies that adapt social protection systems to the new employment and income risks facing the low skilled has generally been assessed as far weaker. Studies have shown that the heightened employment insecurity of part-time and temporary workers makes them more supportive of policies that can mitigate the impact of job loss, for example improved unemployment or social assistance benefits (Burgoon & Dekker, 2010). However, in a context of growing inequality there is evidence that higher-income groups increasingly struggle to identify with those exposed to unemployment, pointing more in the direction of support for retrenchment or stricter benefit conditionality (Carriero & Filandri, 2019). Relatedly, in the last decade or so much scholarship has emphasized a supposed divergence of interests between such labour market 'outsiders' and more securely employed – and electorally significant – 'insiders' (Rueda, 2007; Häusermann & Schwander, 2013). This perspective tends to emphasize that even where wholesale retrenchment of unemployment protection is resisted, it is generally only by the de facto exclusion from coverage of those with the weakest labour market attachments (Palier & Thelen, 2010; Eichhorst & Marx, 2011). This is one instance of a broader focus on changes in the labour market leading to a so-called dualization of social protection between workers with standard and non-standard employment biographies (Emmenegger et al., 2012), in many respects the antithesis of the flexicurity model.

The role of welfare state legacies has been an important theme in the literature on the adaptation of social policy to new trends in the labour market. Social democratic welfare states have been argued to be best able to reconcile the new pro-employment agenda with equitable social protection, in part because they were institutionalized when the post-industrial transition was already well under way (Bonoli, 2007). By contrast, the institutional characteristics of welfare states in Continental and Southern Europe are claimed to make them especially susceptible to dualistic responses to growing differentiation in the realm of employment (Clegg, 2007; Palier, 2010). Research in comparative political economy on 'the new politics of social solidarity' tends to emphasize the interplay of institutional legacies and the organization of economic interests in accounting for distinct national patterns in the articulation of social protection and labour market flexibility (Thelen, 2014).

There are clearly high-profile instances where policy development is difficult to explain with reference to such factors, though. The most obvious case may be the Hartz reforms in Germany, which profoundly attacked the interests of insiders as well as core institutional features of the traditional German welfare state model (Manow, 2020). Here an account of policy development based on learning, the role of ideas, and attempts by governments to move towards solutions to problems – in this case, stubbornly high unemployment – is arguably most convincing (Fleckenstein, 2013). Research on the adoption and adjustment of in-work benefits (Vlandas, 2013; Clegg, 2015; Clasen, 2020) is also noteworthy in this context. This work has shown how these policies have been implemented in very different institutional contexts and despite being targeted towards labour market outsiders, in the absence of obvious electoral or interest group demand. It has also highlighted how policy development has been non-linear, featuring phases of policy reversal as policymakers adjust their preferences in light of new assessments of the costs and benefits of these types of policy instruments. The impression is one of policy being developed under conditions of considerable uncertainty and in the presence of complex trade-offs.

FROM EMPLOYMENT PROMOTION TO REORGANIZING LABOUR MARKETS

The preceding sections have illustrated the considerable role social policy research has played in understanding the implications of, and socio-political processes behind, ongoing changes in Europe's labour markets. It has been well placed to do this not least because labour market change is not an exogenous force, relating to the independent actions of economic agents to which the welfare state must somehow react. Rather, to a large extent, social policy actually creates the conditions for labour market change, by setting a framework of constraints, opportunities, and incentives for economic behaviours. As the figure of William Beveridge reminds us, social policy has always been about organizing labour markets as much as merely compensating for the risks they generate (Whiteside, 2021).

With this in mind, we would argue that it can be analytically fruitful for future research to particularly focus on instances where labour market flexibility poses the greatest regulatory dilemmas for social policy. Sustained patterns of irregular, intermittent, or casual employment of the type discussed above are a case in point, as they blur the boundaries between integration in work and absence of work on which social policy intervention, at least in the form of cash transfers, has historically been mainly premised. Compensating individuals and households for the risks to income security that arise from this mode of flexible work organization carries the evident risk of institutionalizing it (Frade & Darmon, 2005), which might be thought of as the 'dark side' of flexicurity. Comparative research, both quantitative and qualitative, could help shed light on the development and extent of these phenomena by exploring patterns of employment in sectors where highly flexible work scheduling is known to be particularly favoured by companies (e.g., private commercial services) and assessing the role played by access to cash transfers in sustaining and otherwise shaping irregular employment biographies. Given the heavily female nature of many of these occupations, the implications for gender relations of different approaches to organizing flexible employment through social policy must also be a central focus.

How policy development has managed regulatory dilemmas in reorganizing labour markets, and the various trade-offs they entail (cf. Clasen, 2020), is another promising avenue for further research. The creation of new benefits or the redesign of existing ones to incentivize labour market participation has very deliberately boosted labour supply for jobs with low and/or irregular earnings, turning social transfers into temporary and sometimes potentially permanent wage supplements. Employment promotion of this type, however, comes at a cost not only of high public expenditure, but also of creating disincentives for workers to increase their working time (or for employers to offer more regular working schedules). But when do the costs of such policies outweigh the benefits? At what point does the promotion of employment cease to justify the de facto socialization of the costs of some employers' production strategies? Though an easy slogan, 'making work pay' in flexible labour markets also poses some formidable challenges for policy design. For example, it is not easy to assess and adjust benefit entitlement to frequently fluctuating incomes, while policing the moral hazard risks inherent in wage supplements may require highly intrusive and cumbersome administrative monitoring of large numbers of working people (Vandenbroucke & Vleminckx, 2011; Millar & Bennett, 2017).

Given the very technical nature of such questions, it is likely that bureaucratic arenas and actors will be central to their resolution. This is not to say the process of reorganizing labour markets can be reduced to a purely problem-solving exercise free of partisan or interest group instrumentalism, however. Social policies that compensate for risks related to precarious employment have obvious material benefits for some economic actors, perhaps most directly low-skilled workers at the highest risk of precarious employment and the companies that schedule work most flexibly. Conventional political economy approaches would anticipate how far such groups are represented in the electoral and/or interest group arenas relative to less vulnerable workers and/or firms with different production strategies to be a significant factor bearing on policy development. But particularly where social policies generate strong trade-offs and dilemmas, generalizing about policy preferences is dangerous. It is a priori quite unclear whether inclusive organizations representing labour market outsiders should prioritize better benefit support for precarious workers over the re-regulation of atypical work, or under what conditions small businesses in the service sector might put their interest in social policies that can support their flexible human resources practices above their traditional antipathy to social spending in general. In practice, it is likely that pre-existing policies and institutions play a major role in influencing preference formation, as may powerful policy ideas.

The diverse toolkit of contemporary social policy research equips it perfectly to make a major contribution to the understanding of current labour market changes. The policy evaluation strand of such research can, with the help of both quantitative and qualitative methodologies, shed light on the implications of labour market developments for the employment trajectories and incomes of workers and households in varying regulatory contexts. The policy development strand can at the same time help explain variations and changes in regulatory contexts, offering a privileged lens on how political, bureaucratic, and economic actors form preferences and accommodate interests on highly concrete questions concerning the future of work and its social regulation. The erosion of the frontier between work and non-work poses particular challenges for the organization of contemporary labour markets, and offers an especially promising focus for future social policy research in this area.

REFERENCES

Avlijas, S. (2019). *The Dynamism of the New Economy: Non-Standard Employment and Access to Social Security in EU-28*. LEQS Paper No. 141.

Bekker, S., & Mailand, M. (2019). The European flexicurity concept and the Dutch and Danish flexicurity models: How have they managed the Great Recession? *Social Policy and Administration, 53*(1), 142–155.

Bonoli, G. (2005). The politics of the new social policies: Providing coverage against new social risks in mature welfare states. *Policy and Politics, 33*(3), 431–449.

Bonoli, G. (2007). Time matters: Post industrialization, new social risks and welfare state adaptation in advanced industrial democracies. *Comparative Political Studies, 40*(5), 494–520.

Brady, D., Blome, A., & Kmec, J. A. (2020). Work–family reconciliation policies and women's and mothers' labor market outcomes in rich democracies. *Socio-Economic Review, 18*(1), 125–161.

Burgoon, B., & Dekker, F. (2010). Flexible employment, economic insecurity and social policy preferences in Europe. *Journal of European Social Policy, 20*(2), 126–141.

Buschoff, K. S., & Protsch, P. (2008). (A-)typical and (in-)secure? Social protection and 'non-standard' forms of employment in Europe. *International Social Security Review, 61*(4), 51–73.

Cantillon, B., & Vandenbroucke, F. (2014). *Reconciling Work and Poverty Reduction: How Successful Are European Welfare States?* Oxford University Press.

Carr, E., & Chung, H. (2014). Employment insecurity and life satisfaction: The moderating influence of labour market policies across Europe. *Journal of European Social Policy, 24*(4), 383–399.

Carriero, R., & Filandri, M. (2019). Support for conditional unemployment benefit in European countries: The role of income inequality. *Journal of European Social Policy, 29*(4), 498–514.

Choonara, J. (2019). *Insecurity, Precarious Work and Labour Markets: Challenging the Orthodoxy*. Palgrave.

Chung, H., & Mau, S. (2014). Subjective insecurity and the role of institutions. *Journal of European Social Policy, 24*(4), 303–318.

Chung, H., & Van Oorschot, W. (2011). Institutions versus market forces: Explaining the employment insecurity of European individuals during (the beginning of) the financial crisis. *Journal of European Social Policy, 21*(4), 287–301.

Clasen, J. (2020). Subsidizing wages or supplementing transfers? The politics and ambiguity of in-work benefits. *Social Policy and Administration, 54*(1), 1–13.

Clegg, D. (2007). Continental drift: On unemployment policy change in Bismarckian welfare states. *Social Policy and Administration, 41*(6), 597–617.

Clegg, D. (2015). The demise of tax credits. *Political Quarterly, 86*(4), 493–499.

Cousins, M. (2014). In-work benefits: Effective social protection or 'emperor's new clothes'? *European Journal of Social Security, 16*(2), 100–121.

Crettaz, E. (2013). A state-of-the-art review of working poverty in advanced economies: Theoretical models, measurement issues and risk groups. *Journal of European Social Policy, 23*(4), 347–362.

de Beer, P. (2007). Why work is not a panacea: A decomposition analysis of EU-15 countries. *Journal of European Social Policy, 17*(4), 375–388.

De la Porte, C., & Heins, E. (2016). *The Sovereign Debt Crisis, the EU and Welfare State Reform*. Palgrave Macmillan.

De la Porte, C., & Pochet, P. (2004). The European Employment Strategy: Existing research and remaining questions. *Journal of European Social Policy, 14*(1), 71–78.

Duncan, S., & Strell, M. (2004). Combining lone motherhood and paid work: The rationality mistake and Norwegian social policy. *Journal of European Social Policy, 14*(1), 41–54.

Eichhorst, W., & Marx, P. (2011). Reforming German labour market institutions: A dual path to flexibility. *Journal of European Social Policy, 21*(1), 73–87.

Emmenegger, P., Häusermann, S., Palier, B., & Seeleib-Kaiser, M. (2012). *The Age of Dualization: The Changing Face of Inequality in Deindustrializing Societies*. Oxford University Press.

Erlinghagen, M. (2008). Self-perceived job insecurity and social context: A multi-level analysis of 17 European countries. *European Sociological Review, 24*(2), 183–197.

Eurofound. (2020a). *New Forms of Employment: 2020 Update*. Publications Office of the European Union.

Eurofound. (2020b). *Labour Market Change: Trends and Policy Approaches towards Flexibilisation*. Publications Office of the European Union.

Ferrarini, T. (2006). *Families, States and Labour Markets: Institutions, Causes and Consequences of Family Policy in Post-War Welfare States*. Edward Elgar Publishing.

Figari, F. (2010). Can in-work benefits improve social inclusion in Southern European countries? *Journal of European Social Policy, 20*(4), 301–315.

Fleckenstein, T. (2013). Learning to depart from a policy path: Institutional change and the reform of German labour market policy. *Government and Opposition, 48*(1), 55–79.

Fleckenstein, T., & Seeleib-Kaiser, M. (2011). Business, skills and the welfare state: The political economy of employment-oriented family policy in Britain and Germany. *Journal of European Social Policy, 21*(2), 136–149.

Frade, C., & Darmon, I. (2005). New modes of business organization and precarious employment: Towards the recommodification of labour? *Journal of European Social Policy, 15*(2), 107–121.

Fraser, N., Gutiérrez, R., & Peña-Casas, R. (Eds). (2011). *Working Poverty in Europe.* Palgrave.

Gingrich, J., & Häusermann, S. (2015). The decline of the working-class vote, the reconfiguration of the welfare state support coalition and the consequences for the welfare state. *Journal of European Social Policy, 25*(1), 50–75.

Goerne, A. (2011). A comparative analysis of in-work poverty in the European Union. In N. Fraser, R. Gutiérrez, & R. Peña-Casas (Eds), *Working Poverty in Europe* (pp. 15–45). Palgrave Macmillan.

Halleröd, B., Ekbrand, H., & Bengtsson, M. (2015). In-work poverty and labour market trajectories: Poverty risks among the working population in 22 European countries. *Journal of European Social Policy, 25*(5), 473–488.

Häusermann, S., & Schwander, H. (2013). Who is in and who is out? A risk based conceptualization of insiders and outsiders. *Journal of European Social Policy, 23*(3), 248–269.

Hiilamo, H., & Kautto, M. (2009). Does income disregard work? *Journal of Comparative Social Welfare, 25*(1), 3–16.

Hinrichs, K., & Jessoula, M. (Eds). (2012). *Labour Market Flexibility and Pension Reforms: Flexible Today, Secure Tomorrow?* Palgrave Macmillan.

Hipp, L., Bernhardt, J., & Allmendinger, J. (2015). Institutions and the prevalence of nonstandard employment. *Socio-Economic Review, 13*(2), 351–377.

Horemans, J., Marx, I., & Nolan, B. (2016). Hanging in, but only just: Part-time employment and in-work poverty throughout the crisis. *IZA Journal of European Labor Studies, 5*(5), 1–19.

Jacobbson, K. (2004). Soft regulation and the subtle transformation of states: The case of EU employment policy. *Journal of European Social Policy, 14*(4), 355–370.

Kangas, O., & Rostgaard, T. (2007). Preferences or institutions? Work–family life opportunities in seven European countries. *Journal of European Social Policy, 17*(3), 240–256.

Koch, M., & Fritz, M. (Eds). (2013). *Non-Standard Employment in Europe: Paradigms, Prevalence and Policy Responses.* Palgrave.

Korpi, W., Ferrarini, T., & Englund, S. (2013). Women's opportunities under different family policy constellations: Gender, class, and inequality tradeoffs in western countries re-examined. *Social Politics: International Studies in Gender, State and Society, 20*(1), 1–40.

Leschke, J. (2008). *Unemployment Insurance and Non-Standard Employment: Four European Countries in Comparison.* Springer.

Lewis, J., Campbell, M., & Huerta, C. (2008). Patterns of paid and unpaid work in Western Europe: Gender, commodification, preferences and the implications for policy. *Journal of European Social Policy, 18*(1), 21–37.

Mailand, M. (2008). The uneven impact of the European Employment Strategy on member states' employment policies: A comparative analysis. *Journal of European Social Policy, 18*(4), 353–365.

Mailand, M. (2010). The common European flexicurity principles: How a fragile consensus was reached. *European Journal of Industrial Relations, 16*(3), 241–257.

Manow, P. (2020). *Social Protection, Capitalist Production: The Bismarckian Welfare State in the German Political Economy, 1880–2015.* Oxford University Press.

Millar, J., & Bennett, F. (2017). Universal credit: Assumptions, contradictions and virtual reality. *Social Policy and Society*, *16*(2), 169–182.

Millar, J., & Ridge, T. (2020). No margin for error: Fifteen years in the working lives of lone mothers and their children. *Journal of Social Policy*, *49*(1), 1–17.

Nolan, B., & Marx, I. (2014). In work poverty. In B. Cantillon & F. Vandenbroucke (Eds), *Reconciling Work and Poverty Reduction: How Successful Are European Welfare States?* Oxford University Press.

OECD. (2018). *Employment Outlook 2018*. OECD.

OECD. (2019). *Employment Outlook 2019*. OECD.

OECD. (2020). *Employment Outlook 2020: Worker Security and the COVID-19 Crisis*. OECD.

OECD. (2021). *Employment and Labour Market Statistics Database*. OECD.

Palier, B. (2010). The long conservative corporatist road to welfare reforms. In B. Palier (Ed.), *A Long Goodbye to Bismarck? The Politics of Welfare Reform in Continental Europe*. Amsterdam University Press.

Palier, B., & Thelen, K. (2010). Institutionalizing dualism: Complementarities and change in France and Germany. *Politics and Society*, *38*(1), 119–148.

Parolin, Z., & Van Lancker, W. (2021). What a social investment 'litmus test' must address: A response to Plavgo and Hemerijck. *Journal of European Social Policy*, *31*(3), 297–308.

Pfau-Effinger, B., & Rostgaard, T. (Eds). (2011). *Care Between Work and Welfare in European Societies*. Palgrave Macmillan.

Plavgo, I., & Hemerijck, A. (2020). The social investment litmus test: Family formation, employment and poverty. *Journal of European Social Policy*, *31*(3), 282–296.

Prince Cooke, L. (2011). *Gender-Class Equality in Political Economies*. Routledge.

Rueda, D. (2007). *Social Democracy Inside-Out: Partisanship and Labor Market Policy in Advanced Industrialized Democracies*. Oxford University Press.

Schoukens, P., Barrio, A., & Montebovi, S. (2018). EU social pillar: An answer to the challenge of the social protection of platform workers? *European Journal of Social Security*, *20*(3), 219–241.

Thelen, K. (2014). *Varieties of Liberalization and the New Politics of Social Solidarity*. Cambridge University Press.

Vandelannoote, D., & Verbist, G. (2020). The impact of in-work benefits on work incentives and poverty in four European countries. *Journal of European Social Policy*, *30*(2), 144–157.

Vandenbroucke, F., & Vleminckx, K. (2011). Disappointing poverty trends: Is the social investment state to blame? *Journal of European Social Policy*, *21*(5), 450–471.

Viebrock, E., & Clasen, J. (2009). Flexicurity and welfare reform: A review. *Socio-Economic Review*, *7*(2), 305–331.

Vlandas, T. (2013). The politics of in-work benefits: The case of the 'active income of solidarity' in France. *French Politics*, *11*, 114–132.

Whiteside, N. (2021). Beveridge on idleness. *Social Policy and Administration*. https://doi.org/10.1111/spol.12740.

13. Recent advances in understanding welfare attitudes in Europe

Wim van Oorschot, Tijs Laenen, Femke Roosma, and Bart Meuleman

INTRODUCTION: WHERE WE CAME FROM

To have knowledge of people's welfare attitudes and to understand their causes and consequences is generally relevant for social policy experts as it provides them with information about the social legitimacy of welfare provisions, either ex ante, where attitudes say something about the legitimacy that may be expected of planned or aspired policies, or ex post, where attitudes concern policies that are in place.

In European comparative social policy analysis, the scientific study of welfare attitudes is a well-settled discipline. This was different some decades ago. Up to the 1990s, the main lines of findings, as summarized by Svallfors (2012), were that there is a universal and continuous support for the welfare state; that universal programmes tend to have higher legitimacy among the general public than selective programmes; and that along with general support in many countries there were also worries about welfare abuse and cheating, and concerns about bureaucracy and inefficiencies in the public sector. Svallfors also recognized some drawbacks for furthering our understanding of welfare attitudes, particularly the cross-sectional design of many studies, lack of cross-national comparability in measurements, and the restricted set of attitudinal measures employed.

In this chapter, we take Svallfors's analysis of welfare attitudes research until the end of the 1990s as a point of departure and address the general question of *how our knowledge of welfare attitudes of Europeans has developed over the past 20 years*. We note that the data situation changed drastically for the better in these past decades. Data from two welfare attitudes modules in the European Social Survey (ESS) 2008 and 2016 allowed detailed cross-national and over time comparison of a range of welfare attitudes in European countries from all regions. The availability of these data contributed crucially (but not exclusively) to the advancements discussed in this chapter.

We identify at least six major advancements: (a) the multidimensionality of welfare attitudes; the role of contextual factors both as (b) contexts influencing welfare attitudes and as (c) factors in so-called feedback loops; (d) the dynamics of attitude change over time; (e) attitudes towards the welfare deservingness of various target groups; and (f) the attitudinal logics concerning specific social policy domains. We will discuss these advancements below. In our conclusions we will address the gaps and challenges that remain and outline avenues for future research.[1]

MORE THAN A ROSY PICTURE OF WELFARE SUPPORT: MULTIDIMENSIONAL WELFARE ATTITUDES

As mentioned, early welfare opinion studies concluded that public support for the idea that the state should provide welfare for its citizens is considerably high and stable across European countries. However, some of these studies reveal attitudinal ambiguity, as people tend to express both welfare support and critical views on welfare abuse, bureaucracy, and unfair tax distributions (see e.g., Edlund, 1999; Goul Andersen, 1999; Svallfors, 1999). Taking stock of the social legitimacy of the welfare state therefore requires a multidimensional perspective, distinguishing between various attitudinal dimensions (Cnaan, 1989; Sihvo & Uusitalo, 1995a; Roosma et al., 2013).

Theoretical advancement as to which welfare state dimensions should be taken into account in attitudes research was made by Roosma (2016), who defined a model distinguishing four conditions of social legitimacy of the welfare state, based on the work of Rothstein (1998). The welfare state can be socially legitimate if it meets the conditions of *substantive justice* (support for the goals and activities of the welfare state), *redistributional justice* (a fair distribution of contributions and benefits), *procedural justice* (a fair, simple, and cheap way of implementation), and *just outcomes* (outcomes as they are intended). These conditions can be assessed by measuring support for related welfare dimensions. The substantive dimensions of support refer then to people's opinions on the main *goals* of the welfare state (tackling poverty and inequality, providing social security, or promoting social inclusion?), on the *range* of welfare state policies where governments can intervene and on the *degree* of welfare state intervention (in terms of social spending or activities). Regarding the *redistributional design*, two sub-dimensions are crucial: who is deserving of receiving benefits on the one hand and who should contribute to the welfare state on the other hand? Procedural dimensions of support contain opinions regarding the *implementation* of welfare: how efficient and effective is the welfare state in terms of bureaucracy, welfare abuse, and underuse? And finally, dimensions related to the *outcomes* of the welfare state are defined: are the intended outcomes reached in the eyes of the public, how are social policies evaluated, and how are the unintended outcomes (strains for the economy and consequences for moral hazard) perceived?

The extended welfare attitudes module of ESS 2008 made it possible for the first time to analyse the multidimensionality of welfare attitudes in a European cross-national setting and many studies have done so. Four main conclusions can be drawn from applying this multidimensional approach to welfare attitudes. First of all, the welfare state meets the condition of substantive justice. Among Europeans there is strong support for a generous welfare state, especially for the idea that the government should be responsible for different social benefits and services. However, as expected there are critical evaluations too. Second, welfare attitudes differ substantially between different European regions; in general, Eastern and Southern European countries combine high support for a generous welfare state with very critical performance evaluations, while Northern and Western European countries are much more positive about the outcomes of their welfare state and support a strong role for the government too. Third, perceived abuse and underuse of welfare benefits seem to be the Achilles' heel of welfare state legitimacy: Europeans in general are very critical about this dimension of procedural justice, be it less so in the Scandinavian countries. And finally, concerning the perceived unintended economic and moral outcomes, we see a rather balanced picture between pro- and anti-welfare state attitudes. For an overview of support for the various dimensions, see Roosma et al. (2013) for the ESS 2008 data and Roosma (2021) for the ESS 2016 data.

MORE THAN RANKING DESERVING TARGET GROUPS: THE CARIN DESERVINGNESS MODEL

Although the condition of *redistributive justice* was not so much covered in the ESS welfare attitudes modules, the dimension regarding 'who is deserving of benefits' has been a field of study with strong advancement in the past 20 years. This advancement builds upon the seminal articles by van Oorschot (2000, 2006) on the popular welfare deservingness of social target groups. Such deservingness attitudes provide insights in the cultural and normative basis of why in modern welfare states social protection for some groups is more extended and of better quality than that for other groups. They are central to understanding the link between popular solidarity norms on the one hand and how social policies allocate welfare rights and obligations among target groups on the other.

Van Oorschot (2000, 2006) suggested that people apply five specific criteria to assess whether a person or group is seen as deserving of welfare, known as the CARIN criteria. Usually, groups are seen as more deserving to the degree that they are considered not to be in *control* of their neediness, they have a grateful *attitude*, are able to *reciprocate*, or already have reciprocated, have an *identity* closer to 'us', and are in *need* of support. It was with these criteria in mind that van Oorschot (2006) hypothesized that popular solidarity would be highest with elderly, closely followed by sick and disabled people, followed by unemployed people, and solidarity would be lowest with migrants. This rank order of solidarity, or welfare deservingness, was exactly what he found in the data of the European Values Study (EVS) of 1999. And this pattern seems universal, since it showed in all (European) countries included in the EVS 1999 and in subsequent EVS waves, and it showed among all social categories as distinguished by age, gender, work status, religion, educational level, and income level.

These findings have inspired others to study welfare deservingness attitudes, thereby extending our knowledge considerably beyond just popular rank ordering. There are critical analyses of whether the rank order is really universal and dominant (Laenen & Meuleman, 2017), but most studies focus on the deservingness criteria; as such, the CARIN deservingness model has become indispensable in understanding welfare attitudes and social policy support. Meuleman et al. (2019) have evidenced that the five CARIN criteria constitute independent but interrelated dimensions. Others evaluated the relative importance of the different criteria; in some studies control and reciprocity turned out to be dominant in evaluating a target group's deservingness, while in other circumstances identity prevailed as the main discriminating criterion (Reeskens & Van der Meer, 2017).

The CARIN deservingness model showed its relevance in other domains and contexts, and for different individuals and target groups. Studies show that the criteria apply in different areas of the allocation of social rights and health care (Van der Aa et al., 2017); that welfare professionals and policymakers do have deservingness perceptions about social target groups, but often different from general deservingness attitudes (Blomberg et al., 2017); and that the allocation of welfare obligations, instead of social rights, is subjected to a deservingness heuristic (Roosma & Jeene, 2017). It is also shown that media differently frame the welfare deservingness of specific vulnerable groups (Lepianka, 2017), and that deservingness opinions are affected by economic and institutional contexts (Uunk & van Oorschot, 2017; Laenen, 2020).

Two main conclusions can be drawn from the great wealth of studies that build upon the CARIN deservingness model. First, the CARIN criteria prove to be robust predictors of popular ideas about who should get what and why, whether in qualitative research with in-depth interviews and forum groups, in vignette studies with more elaborate sketches of vulnerable groups, or in quantitative social surveys (Kootstra, 2017; Laenen et al., 2019). And second, the relative importance of these CARIN criteria seems to differ across individuals and contexts and varies across target groups (Laenen, 2020). How exactly it does is subject of research. This latter conclusion opens up the field for more fine-grained analyses of *how* the importance of the CARIN criteria differ along these factors.

MORE THAN SUPPORT FOR 'THE WELFARE STATE': SPECIFIC POLICY DOMAINS AND NEW POLICY TRENDS

A further differentiation in welfare attitudes to specific policy domains can yield even more fine-grained insights. Welfare arrangements in the fields of pensions, health care, family benefits, unemployment, and social assistance, for example, are based on fundamentally different logics of social justice and deservingness (Meuleman et al., 2019).

Rather than analysing attitudes towards welfare distribution in general, an increasing number of studies have investigated attitudes towards specific domains of social policy. Most studies have focused on policy domains offering protection against traditional social risks – pensions, unemployment benefits, and health care. Meaningful attitude differences across these domains are found. Irrespective of time and place, a nearly unanimous support is found for the idea that it is the government's responsibility to provide a decent living for the elderly (Deeming, 2018; Ebbinghaus & Naumann, 2020). Welfare support in the area of pensions increases slightly with age (Blekesaune & Quadagno, 2003; Kohli, 2008), but differences are too small to discern a generational divide. Government responsibility and spending in the area of health care enjoys a strong legitimacy base as well (Wendt et al., 2010; Missinne et al., 2013). It illustrates that both target groups are seen as deserving, mainly because of their needy situation, and for not being held responsible for their neediness. Support for policies targeting the unemployed is still relatively strong (van Oorschot & Meuleman, 2014; Buffel & Van de Velde, 2019) but substantially lower compared to support for pensions and health care. The European public is, however, critical about the current standard of living of the unemployed. So, the relatively lower level of support for unemployment benefits does not stem from doubts about the needy situation of the unemployed but seems to be related to the public images of the unemployed. There is a widely spread idea that welfare can make unemployed people lazy, there is doubt whether the unemployed are willing to work, and there is suspicion about benefit abuse across European countries (Larsen, 2002; Furåker & Blomsterberg, 2003; Roosma et al., 2015). Perceptions that the unemployed are not willing to work are especially strong in Eastern European countries and the United Kingdom. As a result, support for the unemployed is rather contentious and volatile and hinges strongly on ideological worldviews.

Despite advancement in studies of attitudes in different policy domains, some domains still lack attention from researchers, like support for invalidity benefits or long-term care arrangements. We do see an increasing number of studies focusing on specific policy trends or features, such as the level of conditionality, activation measures, and/or benefit sanctioning (Kootstra & Roosma, 2016; Buss, 2019; Rossetti et al., 2020b). Moreover, there is an increasing interest in examining support for new policy *proposals* such as support for the Europeanization of social policies (Gerhards et al., 2016; Baute & Meuleman, 2020) and, specifically the idea of introducing a universal basic income (UBI) (Roosma & van Oorschot, 2019; Vlandas, 2019; Rossetti et al., 2020a). Although support for a UBI seems high across Europe, it is unclear from these studies whether Europeans support all features of the suggested policy proposal, as its universality and unconditionality directly oppose the deservingness criteria of need and reciprocity (Rossetti et al., 2020b). When asked, respondents seem to prefer targeted schemes over UBI (Rincón García, 2021). More research is needed to disentangle support for separate policy features.

MORE THAN 'WELFARE REGIMES': CONTEXTUAL FACTORS

The idea that economic, social, institutional, and cultural contexts shape citizens' welfare attitudes is a core tenet of social policy analysis. However, it was only with the arrival of cross-national comparative survey data that systematic empirical tests of this assumption became possible. Inspired by Esping-Andersen's (1990) 'worlds of welfare', empirical studies initially attempted to understand cross-national differences in the light of the different welfare regimes (e.g., Andreß & Heien, 2001; Arts & Gelissen, 2001). Generally speaking, these studies find stronger support for government intervention in the social democratic welfare states and less in the liberal welfare states. However, the patterns of differences between countries are too blurred to conclude that distinct 'worlds of welfare attitudes' exist (Bean & Papadakis, 1998; Gelissen, 2000): attitudinal differences too often cross-cut regimes, and diversity within welfare regimes seems to be more important than the differences between regimes (Brooks, 2012). More recent studies have postulated that international variation can be better captured by a European East–West divide in welfare attitudes, in the sense that Eastern European countries show lower levels of satisfaction with current provisions as well as a stronger demand for government intervention (Lipsmeyer & Nordstrom, 2003; Roosma et al., 2014).

The lack of a convincing relationship between the welfare regimes and popular attitudes might stem from the fact that the regime types conflate

institutional logics with elements of economic, social, and political contexts. An increasing number of studies has therefore started to unpack the
all-encompassing regime types into multiple contextual variables and linking
these to various dimensions of welfare attitudes, with varying degrees of
success (Ervasti, 2012; Meuleman & Chung, 2012; van Oorschot et al., 2012).

Institutional characteristics are arguably of prime interest. We discuss
the complex relationship between institutional context and welfare attitudes
below. Next to institutional arrangements, indicators of the economic context
(including performance of the economy and labour market, as well as indicators of poverty and economic inequality) have attracted attention. Overall,
poorer economic conditions, as well as higher levels of unemployment,
seem to be conducive to support for government intervention (Blekesaune &
Quadagno, 2003; Jeene et al., 2014). Yet at the same time, these unfavourable
economic settings also instigate dissatisfaction with the current provisions.
This pattern of context effects is able to explain the East–West divide in
welfare attitudes mentioned above. Income inequality is another economic
context variable that has been studied intensively. Various studies report that
income inequality encourages support for redistribution, as could be expected
because a larger share of citizens are net beneficiaries of redistribution (Jæger,
2013; Schmidt-Catran, 2014). However, others present evidence for a negative
effect of income inequality on welfare support (Dion & Birchfield, 2010) or
conclude that a significant relationship is absent (Kenworthy & McCall, 2008).

Besides institutional and economic context variables, a host of other context
factors have been scrutinized in welfare attitudes research. Be it in a fragmented form, i.e., with specific studies focusing on specific types of factors
(as, e.g., demographic, migration related, political climate, cultural context,
etc.), which means that it is hard to draw any general conclusions from them.

It should be noted that the bulk of the available research is on how contextual variables at the national level influence welfare attitudes. However,
this 'methodological nationalism' could conceal regional differences within
nation states. Factors that show strong intra-national heterogeneity – such as
economic production and growth, income inequality, or migration numbers
– are especially likely to create regional divides. Eger and Breznau (2017),
for example, find a negative relationship between the regional percentage of
foreign-born, on the one hand, and support for redistribution and a comprehensive welfare state on the other.

Despite the advancements discussed, it should be noted that the multitude
of possible contextual effects and the limited number of welfare state contexts
limits researchers to be able to precisely determine the specific contextual
effects in play.

MORE THAN ONE EFFECT, OR THE OTHER: POLICY FEEDBACK AND RESPONSIVENESS

Following up on this, one widely recognized context factor shaping welfare attitudes is the institutional context. Theoretically, this recognition is central to the policy feedback literature, which argues that public policies, once enacted, tend to influence attitudes of different political actors and the general public. Since the work of Pierson (1993), awareness has grown that welfare policies influence welfare attitudes through (perceptions of) self-interest – which he called 'incentive effects'– as well as through moral ideas about a just society – which he called 'interpretative effects'. However, the reverse effect, that welfare attitudes are themselves an important determinant of welfare policy development, has been argued for as well. This idea is central to the policy responsiveness literature, which argues that most (democratically elected) policymakers have good reasons to draw up policies that are at least to some extent in accord with public opinion (Brooks & Manza, 2006). When integrated, the policy responsiveness and policy feedback perspectives suggest the existence of a loop in which, over time, welfare attitudes and welfare policies exert influence on one another (Laenen, 2020).

In the past 20 years, there has been a proliferation of empirical research studying the relationship between welfare policies and welfare attitudes. Most of these are firmly situated in the policy feedback tradition, thereby leaving the policy responsiveness tradition comparatively underexplored. A broad variety of different types of policy feedback effects have been recognized (see Busemeyer et al. (2021) for a useful typology). Researchers started looking for (1) *short-term* instead of *long-term* feedback effects; and (2) for *specific* instead of *general* feedback effects. As for the first, the most known example of the short-term feedback approach is the thermostat model (Soroka & Wlezien, 2010), which argues for a dynamic relationship between public opinion and public policy, where the public adjusts its preferences in response to policymakers' actions. There have, however, been many other attempts to grasp (shorter-term) feedback effects that welfare policies may have on welfare attitudes (Jeene et al., 2014).

Inspired by the growing insight that welfare regime theory actually masked a great deal of variability *within* welfare states, scholars also began to examine the feedback effects that *particular* welfare policies have on people's attitudes towards those policies (see below). The more fine-grained analyses of how welfare attitudes relate to more specific welfare schemes such as unemployment benefits or old age pensions show considerable feedback effects in several policy domains, working both in a positive, self-reinforcing way and in a negative, self-undermining way (Fernández & Jaime-Castillo, 2012; Jordan, 2013).

Although our knowledge about policy feedback (as well as policy responsiveness) has greatly improved, some important caveats remain. Welfare generosity in attitudinal research is often poorly measured, while the cross-sectional nature of much attitudinal data makes it difficult to analyse feedback loops. Little effort is also put into examining how policy feedbacks vary across social groups. As a result, it remains unclear under which conditions – when, where, and why – policies influence attitudes, and vice versa. To enhance our understanding of their causal connection, we are in need of new empirical strategies (see for a valuable example Breznau, 2017).

MORE THAN SNAPSHOTS IN TIME: CHANGES IN WELFARE ATTITUDES

Welfare attitudes are expected to change over time, but lack of longitudinal data has for a long time prevented adequate studies of this. With such data having become available, studies show a difference in dynamics over the longer and the shorter term. On the one hand, scholars find a high degree of stability in welfare attitudes over the longer term. From the 1980s to the present day, research has shown that popular support for the welfare state and its provisions remains at a very high and stable level (Svallfors, 2011; Laenen et al., 2020). Likewise, more recent evidence suggests that there is also great continuity in other dimensions of welfare state legitimacy. Using data from the ESS waves of 2008 and 2016, both Laenen et al. (2020) and Roosma (2021) examined how such legitimacy evolved after the 2008 financial crisis. Both found a 'striking degree of stability in many popular welfare attitudes between 2008/09 and 2016/17' (Laenen et al., 2020: 258), despite major contextual events, such as the financial and economic crisis and the large influx of migrants in 2015.

On the other hand, however, there is plenty of evidence that welfare attitudes are prone to change in the shorter term. There are a number of studies showing that welfare attitudes turn more positive (or more negative) in times of economic downturn (Sihvo & Uusitalo, 1995b; Jeene et al., 2014). Such changes are usually rather short lived, however, and tend to return to the 'normal' situation of attitude stability in the longer run. Similar observations have been made by scholars examining the impact of changes in individuals' life situations. For example, both Margalit (2013) and Naumann et al. (2016) report that citizens increase their support for welfare provisions after experiencing personal economic hardships. However, while the former claims that the shift in attitudes is 'short lived', the latter maintain that it is 'persistent' in their case.

Although big steps have been made, thanks to the availability of new survey data, it is especially at the level of the individual that further research is needed to examine under which conditions – when, where, and why – people change their welfare attitudes in response to changes that happen in their personal lives and in the contexts in which they live.

CONCLUSION: THE ROAD AHEAD

In this chapter, we have touched upon six major advancements in the field of welfare attitudes research. Since Svallfors (2012) outlined his 'major drawbacks', our understanding of welfare attitudes has been truly enriched by more detailed analyses, new insights, and novel perspectives, largely due to the availability of more and better (survey) data.

Within these major advancements, however, we still identify several challenges, gaps, and future lines of research. First of all, while some dimensions in the multidimensional framework have been studied in greater detail, other dimensions remain more or less untouched. For instance, studies about the perceived efficiency of welfare state bureaucracies, about perceptions of the affordability of welfare state provisions, and about the preferred contributors to welfare redistribution, are welcomed to get a more complete picture of the social legitimacy of the welfare. Second, studies focusing on the perceived deservingness of target groups could further explore how the importance of the CARIN deservingness criteria differs across individuals, contexts, and target groups. Cross-national studies, in particular, are necessary to examine if the CARIN criteria are as stable in their relative weight, as the universal rank order of deserving target groups is. Third, as for some policy domains, support has been largely mapped, but the social legitimacy of, for instance, invalidity benefits or long-term care arrangements has almost completely been ignored. Moreover, the more recent characteristics of welfare policies, such as conditionality of welfare benefits, activation policies, or support for social investment perspectives, lack attention from scholars, although societal and political debates seem to focus upon the legitimacy of these types of policy features. Fourth, studies about support for alternative welfare proposals, like a UBI, or European-level social benefits, are still in their infancy. New lines of research lie in examining support for new types of social policies, not only the UBI proposal, and especially whether respondents *prefer* these new policies over the existing ones (see the pioneering work of Rincón García, 2021). Fifth, regarding contextual and policy feedback effects, there is a lot of work to be done in theorizing and studying effects of different elements of contexts on welfare attitude formation. However, as we mentioned above, there are serious limitations in our data to properly examine the (causal!) effects of specific contexts. A regional perspective (instead of a national one) could provide some more comparative power (Eger & Breznau, 2017). Moreover, the impact of contexts on specific sub-groups within the population is a field largely untouched. Finally, real panel data that trace the welfare attitudes of individuals during their life course would largely advance the dynamic perspective on welfare attitudes.

On top of these suggestions there are more pathways in exploring the field of welfare attitudes, including the attitudinal position of different types of stakeholders and how prior knowledge or experience influence attitudes. Two important conditions need to be fulfilled for research to move in these uncharted directions. First, continued investments are needed to collect high-quality and preferably cross-national and/or longitudinal attitudinal data. Second, new or underused methodological techniques should continue to be applied to attitudinal research, including qualitative assessments (Taylor-Gooby et al., 2017; Laenen et al., 2019; Rossetti et al., 2020a), vignette studies, and conjoint/survey experiments (Kootstra & Roosma, 2016; Naumann et al., 2020). More diverse empirical strategies are necessary to obtain a full perspective of complex and multidimensional attitudes that welfare opinions have turned out to be.

We can conclude that, although big steps have been made, a number of new pathways have opened up for scholars of welfare attitudes. We hope many of them feel invited to explore the multiple roads that lie ahead.

NOTE

1. Of course, a chapter with space restrictions as the one here does not allow a complete discussion of the state of the art in the field of welfare attitudes. Among the major specific areas not covered here are people's welfare attitudes in relation to migration, and in relation to political trust, voting, and processes. As for the first, this area is captured in Chapter 17 by Breidahl, Hedegaard and Seibel, in this volume. As for the second, the lack of political science focus reflects our mainly sociological backgrounds. More pronounced political science perspectives on welfare attitudes can be found in, e.g., Brooks (2012) and Kumlin & Stadelmann-Steffen (2014).

REFERENCES

Andreß, H. J., & Heien, T. (2001). Four worlds of welfare state attitudes? A comparison of Germany, Norway, and the United States. *European Sociological Review, 17*(4), 337–356.

Arts, W., & Gelissen, J. (2001). Welfare states, solidarity and justice principles: Does the type really matter? *Acta Sociologica, 44*(4), 283–299.

Baute, S., & Meuleman, B. (2020). Public attitudes towards a European minimum income benefit: How (perceived) welfare state performance and expectations shape popular support. *Journal of European Social Policy, 30*(4), 404–420.

Bean, C., & Papadakis, E. (1998). A comparison of mass attitudes towards the welfare state in different institutional regimes, 1985–1990. *International Journal of Public Opinion Research*, *10*(3), 211–236.

Blekesaune, M., & Quadagno, J. (2003). Public attitudes toward welfare state policies: A comparative analysis of 24 nations. *European Sociological Review*, *19*(5), 415–427.

Blomberg, H., Kallio, J., Kangas, O., Kroll, C., & Niemelä, M. (2017). Social assistance deservingness and policy measures: Attitudes of Finnish politicians, administrators and citizens. In W. van Oorschot, F. Roosma, B. Meuleman, & T. Reeskens (Eds), *The Social Legitimacy of Targeted Welfare* (pp. 209–224). Edward Elgar Publishing.

Breznau, N. (2017). Positive returns and equilibrium: Simultaneous feedback between public opinion and social policy. *Policy Studies Journal*, *45*(4), 583–612.

Brooks, C. (2012). Framing theory, welfare attitudes, and the United States case. In S. Svallfors (Ed.), *Contested Welfare States: Welfare Attitudes in Europe and Beyond* (p. 193). Stanford University Press.

Brooks, C., & Manza, J. (2006). Why do welfare states persist? *Journal of Politics*, *68*(4), 816–827.

Buffel, V., & Van de Velde, S. (2019). Comparing negative attitudes toward the unemployed across European countries in 2008 and 2016: The role of the unemployment rate and job insecurity. *International Journal of Public Opinion Research*, *31*(3), 419–440.

Busemeyer, M. R., Abrassart, A., & Nezi, R. (2021). Beyond positive and negative: New perspectives on feedback effects in public opinion on the welfare state. *British Journal of Political Science*, *51*(1), 137–162.

Buss, C. (2019). Public opinion towards targeted labour market policies: A vignette study on the perceived deservingness of the unemployed. *Journal of European Social Policy*, *29*(2), 228–240.

Cnaan, R. A. (1989). Public opinion and the dimensions of the welfare state. *Social Indicators Research*, *21*(3), 297–314.

Deeming, C. (2018). The politics of (fractured) solidarity: A cross-national analysis of the class bases of the welfare state. *Social Policy and Administration*, *52*(5), 1106–1125.

Dion, M. L., & Birchfield, V. (2010). Economic development, income inequality, and preferences for redistribution. *International Studies Quarterly*, *54*(2), 315–334.

Ebbinghaus, B., & Naumann, E. (2020). The legitimacy of public pensions in an ageing Europe: Changes in subjective evaluations and policy preferences, 2008–2016. In T. Laenen, B. Meuleman, & W. van Oorschot (Eds), *Welfare State Legitimacy in Times of Crisis and Austerity* (pp. 159–176). Edward Elgar Publishing.

Edlund, J. (1999). Progressive taxation farewell? Attitudes to income redistribution and taxation in Sweden, Great Britain and the United States. In S. Svallfors & P. Taylor-Gooby (Eds), *The End of the Welfare State? Responses to Retrenchment*. Routledge.

Eger, M. A., & Breznau, N. (2017). Immigration and the welfare state: A cross-regional analysis of European welfare attitudes. *International Journal of Comparative Sociology*, *58*(5), 440–463.

Ervasti, H. (2012). Is there a religious factor involved in support for the welfare state in Europe? In H. Ervasti, J. Goul Andersen, T. Fridberg, & K. Ringdal (Eds), *The Future of the Welfare State: Social Policy Attitudes and Social Capital in Europe* (p. 214). Edward Elgar Publishing.

Esping-Andersen, G. (1990). *The Three Worlds of Welfare Capitalism*. Polity Press.

Fernández, J. J., & Jaime-Castillo, A. M. (2012). Positive or negative policy feedbacks? Explaining popular attitudes towards pragmatic pension policy reforms. *European Sociological Review, 29*(4), 803–815.

Furåker, B., & Blomsterberg, M. (2003). Attitudes towards the unemployed: An analysis of Swedish survey data. *International Journal of Social Welfare, 12*(3), 193–203.

Gelissen, J. (2000). Popular support for institutionalised solidarity: A comparison between European welfare states. *International Journal of Social Welfare, 9*(4), 285–300.

Gerhards, J., Lengfeld, H., & Häuberer, J. (2016). Do European citizens support the idea of a European welfare state? Evidence from a comparative survey conducted in three EU member states. *International Sociology, 31*(6), 677–700.

Goul Andersen, J. (1999). Changing labour markets, new social divisions and welfare state support: Denmark in the 1990s. In S. Svallfors & P. Taylor-Gooby (Eds), *The End of the Welfare State? Responses to State Retrenchment* (pp. 13–33). Routledge.

Jæger, M. M. (2013). The effect of macroeconomic and social conditions on the demand for redistribution: A pseudo panel approach. *Journal of European Social Policy, 23*, 149–163.

Jeene, M., van Oorschot, W., & Uunk, W. (2014). The dynamics of welfare opinions in changing economic, institutional and political contexts: An empirical analysis of Dutch Deservingness opinions, 1975–2006. *Social Indicators Research, 115*(2), 731–749.

Jordan, J. (2013). Policy feedback and support for the welfare state. *Journal of European Social Policy, 23*(2), 134–148.

Kenworthy, L., & McCall, L. (2008). Inequality, public opinion and redistribution. *Socio-Economic Review, 6*(1), 35–68.

Kohli, M. (2008). Generational equity: Concepts and attitudes. In C. Arza & M. Kohli (Eds), *Pension Reform in Europe: Politics, Policies and Outcomes*. Routledge.

Kootstra, A. (2017). Us versus them: Examining the perceived deservingness of minority groups in the British welfare state using a survey experiment. In W. van Oorschot, F. Roosma, B. Meuleman, & T. Reeskens (Eds), *The Social Legitimacy of Targeted Welfare: Attitudes on Welfare Deservingness*. Edward Elgar Publishing.

Kootstra, A., & Roosma, F. (2016). *Changing Public Support for Welfare Activation Policy in Britain and the Netherlands: A Persuasion Experiment*. ESPAnet Annual Conference.

Kumlin, S., & Stadelmann-Steffen, I. (2014). *How Welfare States Shape the Democratic Public: Policy Feedback, Participation, Voting, and Attitudes*. Edward Elgar Publishing.

Laenen, T. (2020). *Welfare Deservingness and Welfare Policy: Popular Deservingness Opinions and Their Interaction with Welfare State Policies*. Edward Elgar Publishing.

Laenen, T., & Meuleman, B. (2017). A universal rank order of deservingness? Geographical, temporal and social-structural comparisons. In W. van Oorschot, F. Roosma, B. Meuleman, & T. Reeskens (Eds), *The Social Legitimacy of Targeted Welfare: Attitudes on Welfare Deservingness*. Edward Elgar Publishing.

Laenen, T., Meuleman, B., & van Oorschot, W. (2020). *Welfare State Legitimacy in Times of Crisis and Austerity: Between Continuity and Change*. Edward Elgar Publishing.

Laenen, T., Rossetti, F., & van Oorschot, W. (2019). Why deservingness theory needs qualitative research: Comparing focus group discussions on social welfare in three welfare regimes. *International Journal of Comparative Sociology, 60*(3), 190–216.

Larsen, C. A. (2002). Unemployment and stigmatization: The dilemma of the welfare state. In J. Goul Andersen & K. Halvorsen (Eds), *Unemployment and Citizenship: Marginalization and Integration in the Nordic Countries* (pp. 55–72). Policy Press.

Lepianka, D. (2017). The varying faces of poverty and deservingness in Dutch print media. In W. van Oorschot, F. Roosma, B. Meuleman, & T. Reeskens (Eds), *The Social Legitimacy of Targeted Welfare: Attitudes to Welfare Deservingness* (pp. 127–145). Edward Elgar Publishing.

Lipsmeyer, C. S., & Nordstrom, T. (2003). East versus West: Comparing political attitudes and welfare preferences across European societies. *Journal of European Public Policy, 10*(3), 339–364.

Margalit, Y. M. (2013). Explaining social policy preferences: Evidence from the Great Recession. *American Political Science Review, 107*(1), 80–103.

Meuleman, B., & Chung, H. (2012). Who should care for the children? Support for government intervention in childcare. In H. Ervasti, J. Goul Andersen, T. Fridberg, & K. Ringdal (Eds), *The Future of the Welfare State: Social Policy Attitudes and Social Capital in Europe* (pp. 107–133). Edward Elgar Publishing.

Meuleman, B., Roosma, F., & Abts, K. (2019). Welfare deservingness opinions from heuristic to measurable concept: The CARIN deservingness principles scale. *Social Science Research, 85*.

Missinne, S., Meuleman, B., & Bracke, P. (2013). The popular legitimacy of European healthcare systems: A multilevel analysis of 24 countries. *Journal of European Social Policy, 23*(3), 231–247.

Naumann, E., Buss, C., & Bahr, J. (2016). How unemployment experience affects support for the welfare state: A real panel approach. *European Sociological Review, 32*(1), 81–92.

Naumann, E., De Tavernier, W., Naegele, L., & Hess, M. (2020). Public support for sanctioning older unemployed: A survey experiment in 21 European countries. *European Societies, 22*(1), 77–100.

Pierson, P. (1993). When effect becomes cause: Policy feedback and political change. *World Politics, 45*(4), 595–628.

Reeskens, T., & Van der Meer, T. (2017). The relative importance of welfare deservingness criteria. In W. van Oorschot, F. Roosma, B. Meuleman, & T. Reeskens (Eds), *The Social Legitimacy of Targeted Welfare: Attitudes to Welfare Deservingness.* Edward Elgar Publishing.

Rincón García, L. (2021). *The Paradox of Universality: Preferences for Universal Basic Income in Finland and Spain.* Doctoral thesis, Universitat de Barcelona.

Roosma, F. (2016). *A Multidimensional Perspective on the Social Legitimacy of Welfare States in Europe.* Doctoral thesis, Tilburg University.

Roosma, F. (2021). The social legitimacy of European welfare states after the age of austerity. In B. Greve (Ed.), *Handbook on Austerity, Populism and the Welfare State* (pp. 110–129). Edward Elgar Publishing.

Roosma, F., & Jeene, M. (2017). The deservingness logic applied to popular opinions on work obligations of benefit claimants. In W. van Oorschot, F. Roosma, B. Meuleman, & T. Reeskens (Eds), *The Social Legitimacy of Targeted Welfare: Attitudes on Welfare Deservingness.* Edward Elgar Publishing.

Roosma, F., & van Oorschot, W. (2019). Public opinion on basic income: Mapping European support for a radical alternative for welfare provision. *Journal of European Social Policy, 30*(2), 190–205.

Roosma, F., Gelissen, J., & van Oorschot, W. (2013). The multidimensionality of welfare state attitudes: A European cross-national study. *Social Indicators Research*, *113*(1), 235–255.

Roosma, F., van Oorschot, W., & Gelissen, J. (2014). The preferred role and perceived performance of the welfare state: European welfare attitudes from a multidimensional perspective. *Social Science Research*, *44*, 200–210.

Roosma, F., van Oorschot, W., & Gelissen, J. (2015). The Achilles' heel of welfare state legitimacy: Perceptions of overuse and underuse of social benefits in Europe. *Journal of European Public Policy*, *23*(2), 177–196.

Rossetti, F., Roosma, F., Laenen, T., & Abts, K. (2020a). An unconditional basic income? How Dutch citizens justify their opinions about a basic income and work conditionality. *Journal of International and Comparative Social Policy*, *36*(3), 284–300.

Rossetti, F., Abts, K., Meuleman, B., & Swyngedouw, M. (2020b). 'First the grub, then the morals?' Disentangling the self-interest and ideological drivers of attitudes towards demanding activation policies in Belgium. *Journal of Social Policy*, *50*(2), 346–366.

Rothstein, B. (1998). *Just Institutions Matter: The Moral and Political Logic of the Universal Welfare State*. Cambridge University Press.

Schmidt-Catran, A. W. (2014). Economic inequality and public demand for redistribution: Combining cross-sectional and longitudinal evidence. *Socio-Economic Review*, *14*(1), 119–140.

Sihvo, T., & Uusitalo, H. (1995a). Attitudes towards the welfare state have several dimensions. *International Journal of Social Welfare*, *4*(4), 215–223.

Sihvo, T., & Uusitalo, H. (1995b). Economic crises and support for the welfare state in Finland 1975–1993. *Acta Sociologica*, *38*(3), 251–262.

Soroka, S. N., & Wlezien, C. (2010). *Degrees of Democracy: Politics, Public Opinion, and Policy*. Cambridge University Press.

Svallfors, S. (1999). The middle class and welfare state retrenchment. In S. Svallfors & P. Taylor-Gooby (Eds), *The End of the Welfare State? Responses to State Retrenchment* (pp. 34–52). Routledge.

Svallfors, S. (2011). A bedrock of support? Trends in welfare state attitudes in Sweden, 1981–2010. *Social Policy and Administration*, *45*(7), 806–825.

Svallfors, S. (2012). *Contested Welfare States: Welfare Attitudes in Europe and Beyond*. Stanford University Press.

Taylor-Gooby, P., Leruth, B., & Chung, H. (2017). *After Austerity: Welfare State Transformation in Europe after the Great Recession*. Oxford University Press.

Uunk, W., & van Oorschot, W. (2017). How welfare reforms influence public opinion regarding welfare deservingness: Evidence from Dutch time-series data, 1975–2006. In W. van Oorschot, F. Roosma, B. Meuleman, & T. Reeskens (Eds), *The Social Legitimacy of Targeted Welfare: Attitudes on Welfare Deservingness*. Edward Elgar Publishing.

Van der Aa, M., Hiligsmann, M., Paulus, A., & Evers, S. (2017). Healthcare deservingness opinions of the general public and policymakers compared: A discrete choice experiment. In W. van Oorschot, F. Roosma, B. Meuleman, & T. Reeskens (Eds), *The Social Legitimacy of Targeted Welfare: Attitudes to Welfare Deservingness*. Edward Elgar Publishing.

van Oorschot, W. (2000). Who should get what, and why? On deservingness criteria and the conditionality of solidarity among the public. *Policy and Politics*, *28*(1), 33–48.

van Oorschot, W. (2006). Making the difference in social Europe: Deservingness perceptions among citizens of European welfare states. *Journal of European Social Policy*, *16*(1), 23–42.

van Oorschot, W., & Meuleman, B. (2014). Popular deservingness of the unemployed in the context of welfare state policies, economic conditions and cultural climate. In S. Kumlin & I. Stadelmann-Steffen (Eds), *How Welfare States Shape the Democratic Public: Policy Feedback, Participation, Voting, and Attitudes* (pp. 244–268). Edward Elgar Publishing.

van Oorschot, W., Reeskens, T., & Meuleman, B. (2012). Popular perceptions of welfare state consequences: A multilevel, cross-national analysis of 25 European countries. *Journal of European Social Policy*, *22*(2), 181–197.

Vlandas, T. (2019). The politics of the basic income guarantee: Analysing individual support in Europe. *Basic Income Studies*, *14*(1).

Wendt, C., Kohl, J., Mischke, M., & Pfeifer, M. (2010). How do Europeans perceive their healthcare system? Patterns of satisfaction and preference for state involvement in the field of healthcare. *European Sociological Review*, *26*(2), 177–192.

14. Methodologies for comparative social policy analysis

Emanuele Ferragina and Christopher Deeming

INTRODUCTION

This chapter reviews and takes stock of the research effort and the methodology employed in comparative social policy analysis reported in the *Journal of European Social Policy* (JESP). We trace the evolution and development of comparative methodology, empirically analysing trends in JESP since the first issue was published in February 1991, while situating comparative analysis within the broader theoretical trends and European social policy debates. We focus on methods and substance, looking at how major techniques and approaches have been applied in comparative social policy over time. The key questions driving our analysis are: What is the scholarly use of comparative methods in social policy over the last three decades? How has the comparative methodology helped us to better understand the role, nature, and outcomes of European social policy? Where is comparative methodology heading for the future? JESP is the leading European journal in the field of social policy (with close ties to ESPAnet), and is therefore well suited for such an empirical review of comparative methodologies for social policy analysis.

The purpose of this chapter is to highlight and focus on the main trends in the use of the comparative method, using comparative research articles published in JESP to guide us. The first part sets the scene; it does so by providing an outline of the comparative turn in social policy research, and defines what we mean by the comparative method. For the literature review we have developed a Comparative Journals Database of research articles that includes the work published in JESP, from which data for JESP are extracted to support our analysis set out below. Here we examine how the comparative method has been used in the pages of JESP before going on to consider how the comparative methods helps us to better understand the role, nature, and outcomes of European social policy. We include a qualitative analysis of the comparative articles, and then focus on the methodological characteristics of the most cited comparative articles – the 'greatest hits' of JESP. We conclude by highlighting potential future trends on the basis of our analysis.

THE COMPARATIVE TURN

We find that interest in comparative analysis has grown in the social sciences, with the appearance of new outlets and books, as well as the increasing number of courses designed to equip students with the theoretical, analytical, and methodological tools necessary to engage in comparative analysis. By comparative methodology we refer to a general system of thinking – methodology is 'thinking about thinking'; while the term comparative methods indicates different techniques and approaches that have been developed in the social sciences over the last half century (on the distinction between 'methodology' and 'methods', see Sartori, 1970).

The use of the comparative method has been at the centre stage of social policy analysis. One can perhaps indicate some of the foundational texts that have contributed massively to the expansionary trend in the use of the comparative method in our discipline, for example, Harold Wilensky's (1975) *The Welfare State and Equality* and Gøsta Esping-Andersen's (1990) *The Three Worlds of Welfare Capitalism*. Inspired by the philosophical and epistemological reflection of John Stuart Mill, scholars have refined the use of comparative method (Moore, 1966; Sartori, 1970; Lijphart, 1971; Smelser, 1976; Skocpol, 1979; Ragin, 1987; Collier, 1993) with historical and case-based approaches, and the growing application and development of qualitative and quantitative techniques (see, for example, the pioneering work of Almond and Verba, 1963).

A major comparative turn is certainly associated with Esping-Andersen's seminal work. In *The Three Worlds of Welfare Capitalism*, Esping-Andersen attempted to link a specific type of institutional arrangement to specific political determinants on the one hand, as well as to particular social impacts and outcomes on the other. Adopting a (comparative) political economy perspective, he devised indices for the 18 nations included in his study relating to some of the core principles and functions of the welfare state relating to social citizenship rights. For example, he constructed a decommodification index derived from data on pensions, sickness, and unemployment benefits, stratification, and the public-private mix of welfare provision represented by the distinctive configuration of market, state, and family. The welfare state is the principal institution in the construction of different models of post-war capitalism. Infamously, he argued that the world is composed of three qualitatively different welfare state logics associated with different political movements of the twentieth century: liberalism, conservativism, and socialism.

It is not a coincidence that JESP launched in 1991. While one cannot imply a causal relationship between the work of Esping-Andersen and its arrival, it is certainly possible to conclude that social policy as a discipline or field of study definitely turned more comparative in the 1990s. *The Three Worlds of Welfare Capitalism* and the birth of JESP are representative of this comparative *zeitgeist*. There are, of course, many other influential articles in JESP discussing and reviewing the seminal work of the Danish scholar (in 2015, a whole issue in JESP was dedicated to this task, Vol. 25, No. 1; see also Ferragina & Seeleib-Kaiser, 2011; Deeming, 2017).

DEFINING THE COMPARATIVE METHOD

Thinking without comparing is a Sisyphean task. To a large extent, every intellectual enquiry demands some form of comparison. Even the analysis of natural phenomena usually includes implicit or explicit forms of comparison. The construction of a measurement scale, for example, has to take into account the existence of specific ideal types and/or prototypes (e.g., the absolute range of possible values assumed by the variables under scrutiny). Despite the inherently comparative nature of scientific enquiry, Ragin (2014) pointed to the fact that, while all research methods are comparative in a broad sense, in the social sciences, the idea of comparative research is mostly used to refer to research involving the use of large macrosocial units. Ragin's definition has proved influential in comparative social enquiry.

It is not universally accepted, however. Other scholars in the past proposed different boundaries to delimit the domain of comparative social inquiry. On the one hand, those more geared towards the use of quantitative and multivariate techniques have defined the comparative method simply by considering studies which include comparative data from different societies (see Andreski, 1965; Armer, 1973) or, even more restrictively, they have only included within this category the works based on multiple levels of analysis (see Rokkan, 1966; Przeworski & Teune, 1970). On the other hand, scholars more versed in qualitative/historical analysis, such as Moore (1966) and Skocpol (1979), have counterposed with the case-oriented and the variable-oriented comparative method (such thinking is directly derived from the founding fathers of sociology and political sciences: Tocqueville, Durkheim, and Weber).

These views are too restrictive, and for this reason, we choose to follow Ragin defining the comparative method on the basis of its goals rather than specific methodological orientations. The analysis of macrosocial units is a 'meta-theoretical category', which basically distinguishes comparative social scientists from the others, because they use 'macrosocial units in explanatory statements' (Ragin, 2014: 5). Indeed, the vast majority of scholars working in the field, and the studies reported in JESP, often do not explicitly define the nature and the role of the macrosocial units, but rather use them implicitly as 'observation' and/or 'explanatory' units of analysis (Ragin, 2014: 8).

Comparative social inquiry is a quintessential locus to analyse significant methodological issues for at least two reasons. First, the split between quantitative and qualitative analysis has a long tradition that is evident in JESP. This is mainly because the existence of a vital qualitative tradition has not been completely superseded by the development of increasingly advanced quantitative techniques, evident in JESP. Second, the challenging nature of the task to compare relatively dissimilar macrosocial units has accrued the interaction between theory and practice. As clearly highlighted by Sartori (1970), the constant variation in the level of abstraction and analysis used by researchers in comparative work signals the complexity of the comparative social enquiry endeavour.

THE COMPARATIVE JOURNALS DATABASE

The work presented here forms part of a larger research project and review of comparative method in the social sciences. For our project we have created an original database – the Comparative Journals Database – that allows us to quantitatively and qualitatively map the use of comparative method in research articles published in leading social policy, sociology, and political science journals. The data presented here focus on JESP for the period 1991–2015.

Much of the review involved hand searching, which is a manual method of scanning the selected journals, each issue from cover to cover, page by page. Each article in the database was sorted, reviewed manually, and cross-checked in order to identify and separate the comparative articles from the non-comparative contributions. Relevant details were extracted from the comparative articles only. Along with basic bibliographic information, including the DOI, year of publication, authors, journal, and discipline, we coded methods into seven categories: (1) descriptive statistics only (i.e., no use of formal methods beside simple descriptive statistics); (2) case studies and comparative historical analysis; (3) qualitative comparative analysis/fuzzy-sets; (4) regression techniques; (5) structural equation modelling and factorial analyses; (6) cluster analysis; and (7) other techniques. The other techniques category includes methodologies that are used infrequently, such as diagonal reference models, sequence analysis, scale construction, thematic analysis, propensity score matching, optimal matching, Krippendorff's Alpha, and event history. Moreover, we included the number of methods used, the main macrogeographical unit of analysis (state, lower institutional entity, historical institutional entity), and the number of macrounits considered in the analysis. Finally, in the case of cross-national research, we also collected country-level details.

The coding process was run in four steps over a 36-month period:

1. We calibrated the measurement by coding a random sample of 50 articles from each journal. Each article was coded by the two authors and three research assistants.
2. We then discussed the results, identifying any inconsistencies according to our definition of comparative method.
3. The three research assistants then coded all the articles in the entire database.
4. Finally, a sample comprising 50 articles was then independently coded and checked by the two authors to ensure reliability.

We are also interested in the relative importance of top-cited articles in the database. For this reason, we employed as a proxy measure the number of citation counts extracted from Google Scholar (on 18 July 2019). Google Scholar has a number of distinct advantages, it is freely available and we were able to extract all of the citation data relating to the DOI records over a one-day period, a 'snap-shot' in time in a highly dynamic environment. We developed a search command written in R to capture the citation counts associated with each record contained in the database. Thanks to this device, all the database records were carefully checked, missing citation entries were entered manually, and any errors were corrected. The top-cited comparative articles in JESP (and elsewhere) were extracted using this citation count.

ANALYSING THE USE OF THE COMPARATIVE METHOD IN JESP

JESP has been a highly comparative journal from the outset, with the first issue appearing in 1991. While most other journals in the social sciences present a minority of comparative articles, JESP has consistently published a large number of comparative articles. This trend has been continuous (with the exception of a drop in the period 1998–1999), rising from 40 per cent of all articles in 1993 to more than 50 per cent of all articles since 2012 (Figure 14.1). The strong start and steady growth may not surprise as JESP set out with the objective to provide a focus on comparative analysis in Europe, as noted in the first issue: 'The Journal will therefore give priority to articles on social policy that deal with comparative developments within Europe' (Editorial foreword, 1991: 1). Since 1991, the journal has clearly pioneered new ways of doing social policy – more comparative and progressively geared towards empirical analysis.

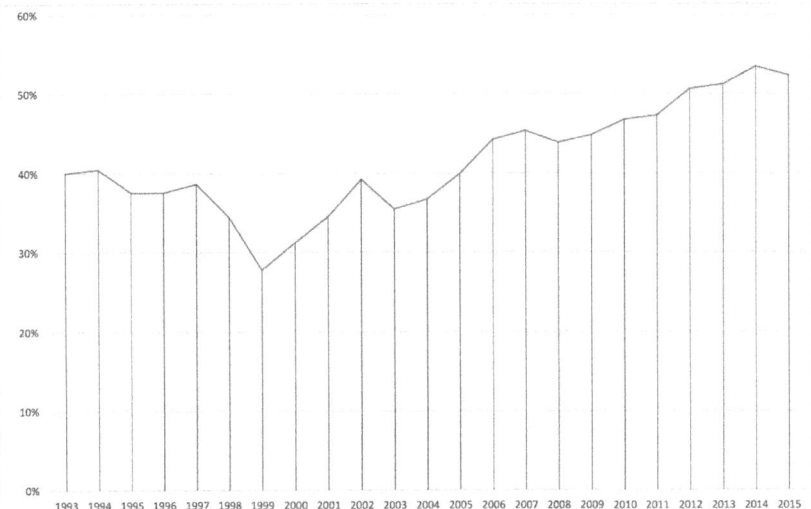

Note: Comparative research articles published in JESP as a percentage of the total articles published in JESP, showing the three-year moving average.
Source: Comparative Journals Database, 1970–2015.

Figure 14.1   Comparative research publishing trends in JESP articles

Moving on to the use of methods, here we observe some interesting features and trends. New data initiatives and the creation of several databases allowed scholars to progressively broaden the variety of techniques employed in comparative analysis from those traditionally embraced, i.e., case-based method, comparative historical analysis, and simple correlations, towards more sophisticated regression techniques and the growing influence of multilevel modelling across the social sciences with large-N. So, for example, comparativists expanded:

- Their capacity to formulate theoretically driven taxonomies with different clustering techniques (i.e., K-Means, hierarchical clustering, principal component analysis, multiple correspondence analysis, latent class analysis), going beyond the use of descriptive statics proposed in comparative social policy by the seminal work of Esping-Andersen (1990).
- The case-based method, combining 'quality and quantity' with the development of qualitative comparative analysis and the fuzzy-set qualitative analysis.
- The potential of regressions, using more systematically time and space with pooled time series cross-section analysis and hierarchical or multilevel modelling since the 1980s. Moreover, major investment in panel

surveys helped to capture important family dynamics and life-course events and transitions (understood with panel regressions).
- Their ability to take advantage of 'natural experiments' and harness 'big data', as well as formalizing the use of mixed methods in a more systematic way.

Figure 14.2 shows that comparative researchers embraced all these methods, but the use of regression techniques has steadily become dominant, particularly during the 2000s, and has progressively superseded the initial prevalence of the case study approach. This is an important trend that now seems stable, an interesting feature in the literature. This trend links to two other important trends that we observe in JESP. Firstly, the fact that articles employing at least one formal method have progressively become more numerous than those relying on descriptive statistics only (Figure 14.3), and secondly, large-N analysis has increased exponentially and is now dominant in JESP, accompanying the rise in regression techniques and formal quantitative methods (Figure 14.4). The influential work by Wim van Oorschot is illustrative of this trend, especially his work on public perceptions of the relative deservingness of welfare beneficiaries, drawing on data from the European Values Study (EVS) wave 1999/2000 for 23 European countries (van Oorschot, 2006); also, the test of the crowding-out effect of the welfare state on people's trust and social capital more generally, again drawing on the data from the EVS wave 1999/2000 for 23 European countries (van Oorschot & Arts, 2005).

Put simply, while in the 1990s the typical comparative article published in JESP was descriptive and mostly based on a case study approach, since the early 2000s, the increasing tendency has been to publish articles based on large-N and the use of regression analysis. Quantitative trend statistics and charts do not tell the whole story, however, and need to be supported by a more qualitative 'outlook'. If we now turn to the influence or impact of the original articles published in JESP, we observe that the four most cited articles – and eight in the top ten — are based on case studies and descriptive statistics, while only two are based on regression analysis (shown in Table 14.1). This is certainly an effect of time – older articles can carry more citations perhaps – but also a reminder that methodological sophistication is not a guarantee of influence in the comparative social policy field. The depth of small-N comparative case study scholarship has certainly been illuminating and has stood the test of time, illustrated by the works of Lewis (1992), Ferrera (1996), and Bettio et al. (2006). Then there are influential comparative studies that are rich in description. Anttonen and Sipilä (1996) consider social care service arrangements in 14 European countries, while Pavolini and Ranci (2008) consider long-term care provision in six European countries.

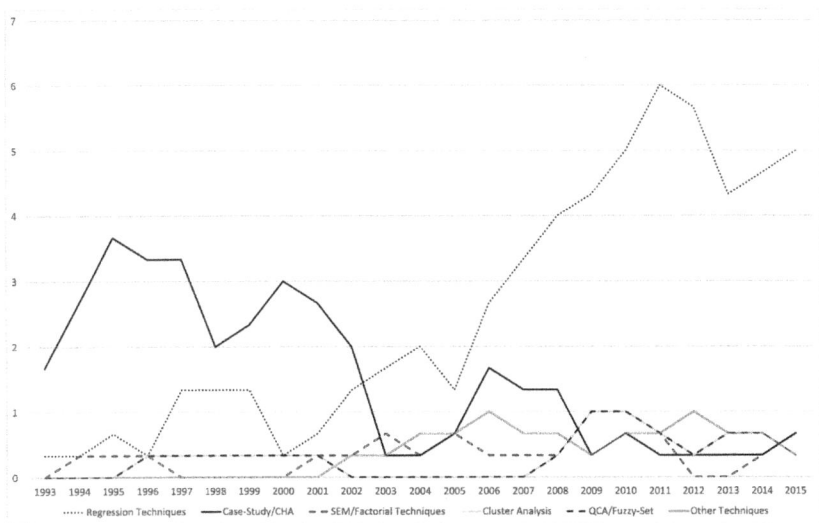

Note: Total number of published comparative articles, showing the three-year moving average.
Source: Comparative Journals Database, 1970–2015.

Figure 14.2   The use of comparative method in JESP articles

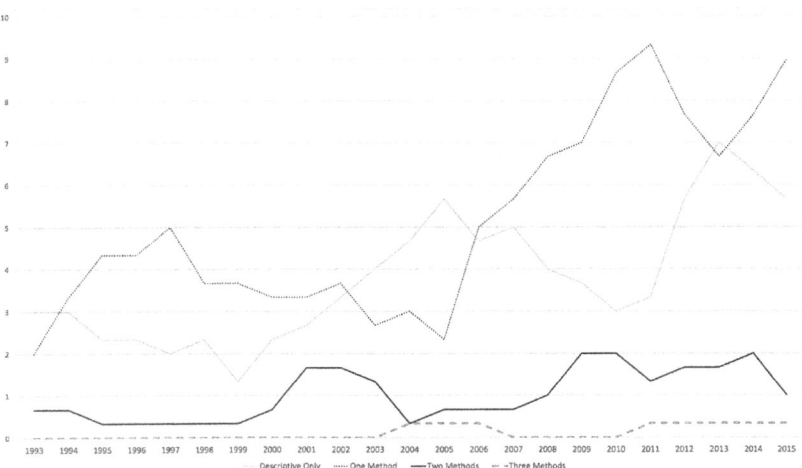

Note: Number of published comparative research articles published in JESP using mixed and multimethods in JESP, three-year moving average.
Source: Comparative Journals Database, 1970–2015.

Figure 14.3   Trends in the use of mixed and multimethods in JESP

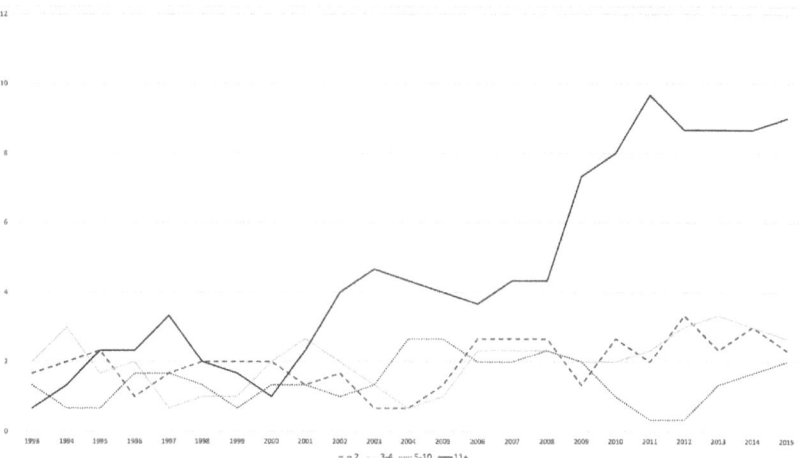

Note: N-size trends over time in JESP, three-year moving average.
Source: Comparative Journals Database, 1970–2015.

Figure 14.4   *Number of comparative units of analysis in JESP research*
                designs

An important dichotomy exists in the field between comparative research primarily geared towards establishing causation and studies that seek to provide a parsimonious or more accurate description of social phenomena. Of course, establishing causation and providing better descriptions of social reality can go hand in hand. In JESP during 1991–2015, we find that 69 research articles explicitly mention the issue of causality. Few, however, really deal with causality and welfare development in any detail (cf. Ganghof, 2006). Recently, despite the strong preference for causation in mainstream academic journals, a renewed interest for 'mere description' is gaining ground (for an excellent discussion of this point see Gerring, 2012). In this respect, the great success of Esping-Andersen's (1990) *The Three Worlds of Welfare Capitalism* is also grounded in the capacity to provide a taxonomy based at the same time on an established macropolitical economy framework and the use of a specific set of indicators, measuring 'decommodification' and 'social stratification' and the public-private mix of welfare.

Table 14.1   Most cited comparative studies published in JESP

Rank	Authors	Year	Citations	Unit of analysis	Number of units	Methods	EA*
1	Ferrera	1996	3,738	Nations	4	Case study, descriptive statistics	Yes [1990]
2	Lewis	1992	3,098	Nations	4	Case study, descriptive statistics	Yes [1990]
3	Anttonen & Sipilä	1996	945	Nations	14	Descriptive statistics/correlation techniques	Yes [1990]
4	Gornick et al.	1997	816	Nations	14	Descriptive statistics	Yes [1990]
5	van Oorschot	2006	745	Nations	23	Regression techniques	Yes [1996]
6	Bettio et al.	2006	728	Nations	4	Case study, descriptive statistics	Yes [1990]
7	Albertini et al.	2007	593	Nations	10	Regression techniques	Yes [1990]
8	Scruggs & Allan	2006	545	Nations	18	Descriptive statistics	Yes [1990]
9	Castles	2003	543	Nations	21	Descriptive statistics/correlation techniques	Yes [1996, 1999]
10	Deacon	2000	540	Nations	8	Descriptive statistics	No
11	van Oorschot & Arts	2005	503	Nations	23	Regression techniques, factor analysis	Yes [1999]
12	Pavolini & Ranci	2008	426	Nations	6	Descriptive statistics	Yes [1999]
13	Alber	1995	395	Nations	3/12**	Case study, descriptive statistics	Yes [1990]
14	Sainsbury	2006	361	Nations	3	Case study, descriptive statistics, social indicators	Yes [1990, 1999]
15	Aassve et al.	2002	336	Nations	10	Regression techniques	Yes [1999]

Note: Measured using Google Scholar on 18 July 2019. * EA: Esping-Andersen (1990) is cited in the work. We also added to the column when Esping-Andersen (1996) and/or (1999) is cited. ** Here the main focus is on explaining the different levels of social service supply in Germany, Denmark, and the Netherlands, within the wider context of other European nations.

COMPARATIVE METHOD AND EUROPEAN SOCIAL POLICY

In this section, we briefly consider how comparative methodology has helped to provide a better understanding of the role, nature, and outcomes of European social policy. Much of the comparative research effort in JESP emerges out of the interaction of national European societies and the study of European political development – 'social Europe' – in the context of changing social policy paradigms and methodological innovations (Room, 2008).

Clearly, the concept or lens of the welfare 'regime' associated with the work of Esping-Andersen (1990, 1999) has been influential for critically engaging with – and for understanding – regional, temporal, and cross-national diversity, trends, and outcomes in European social policy. The highly influential works of Jane Lewis (1992) and Maurizio Ferrera (1996) show how the debate about welfare regimes opened by Esping-Andersen was expanded and fostered in JESP, adding gender roles and institutional and geographical breadth – Southern Europe (Ferrera, 1996) and Eastern Europe (Deacon, 2000) – to the original welfare regime classification.

Anttonen and Sipilä (1996), in another influential work, question whether the inclusion of social services decisively changes the results of comparative social policy research, and more specifically the welfare state regimes proposed by Esping-Andersen. Further influential comparative work on social service models and care regimes in Europe is expanded on by Anttonen and Sipilä (1996), Bettio et al. (2006), and Pavolini and Ranci (2008).

Gornick et al. (1997) examine the congruence of family policy with welfare regime theory, focusing on employment outcomes for mothers. Sainsbury (2006) focuses on immigrants' social rights employing the welfare regimes framework, while family transfers and welfare regimes are considered by Albertini et al. (2007).

Alber (1995) provides an early rejection of Esping-Andersen's regime approach in favour of Stein Rokkan's comparative welfare state research scheme for thinking about church/state relations in the supply of social services and centre–periphery relations between various levels of government. Esping-Andersen's regime theory had focused on 'decommodification' but 'decommodification' is less of an issue for children and elderly – two groups which are not yet or are no longer in the labour market, as Alber notes.

JESP continues to play a major role in the debate and diffusion of quantitative comparative analysis. At the outset, we might expect to see a strong growth in large-N studies, given major investment in the comparative welfare datasets over the period (e.g., Scruggs, 2004; Nelson, 2007; Huber et al., 2008; Korpi & Palme, 2008; Gauthier, 2011; Brady et al., 2014; Scruggs et al.,

2014), and also the cross-national social surveys (Jowell et al., 2007; Esmer & Pettersson 2012; Haller et al., 2012). JESP researchers have exploited the major investments in cross-national datasets, for example:

- Comparative Welfare Entitlements Dataset: Scruggs and Allan (2006) provided a reassessment of Esping-Andersen's decommodification index using these data on the comparative generosity of welfare state programme entitlements for the period 1971–2002.
- Comparative Family Policy Database: this database was used by Rovny (2014) to examine vulnerability to new social risks and the protective effects of social policies in 18 countries in the Organisation for Economic Co-operation and Development (OECD).
- Social Citizenship Indicator Program: these data were used by Danforth (2014) for his historical reassessment of the three-world typology, covering the original 18 nations in the period 1950 to 2000 for evidence of tripartite clustering.
- Social Assistance and Minimum Income Protection Interim Data-Set: these were used by Nelson (2012) to examine the link between social assistance benefit levels and material deprivation in 26 European countries.

Data and findings from the major cross-national social surveys have been extensively used to guide our understanding of comparative and European social policy reported in JESP, notably, for example:

- European Social Survey (ESS): the ESS data have been used to explore the popular legitimacy of health-care systems in 24 European countries (Missinne et al., 2013), as well as relations between labour market policy and subjective wellbeing in 21 European countries (Wulfgramm, 2014).
- European Community Household Panel (ECHP): the ECHP was used to analyse the impact of employment and income on young people's decision making to leave the parental home in 10 European countries (Aassve et al., 2002).
- European Union Statistics on Income and Living Conditions (previously the ECHP): these data were used to examine at-risk-of-poverty rates for the working population in 26 European countries (Lohmann, 2011).
- Luxembourg Income Study (LIS): LIS data have been used to assess the effectiveness of means-tested benefit programmes in terms of poverty alleviation in Britain, Germany, and Sweden (Behrendt, 2000), while Hook (2015) used LIS and ESS data to examine how two-parent families combine work and care in 16 European countries.
- European Values Study (EVS): the EVS data were used by van Oorschot and Arts (2005) to consider whether or the extent to which the welfare state crowds out social capital (networks, trust, and norms) in 23 European

countries. Van Oorschot (2006) also used the EVS data to examine the public perceptions of the relative deservingness of needy groups (elderly people, sick and disabled people, unemployed people, and immigrants) in 23 European countries.

• International Social Survey Programme (ISSP): these data were used to examine gender role attitudes and family policy models (Sjöberg, 2004) and age-related differences in welfare state preferences in 14 OECD countries (Busemeyer et al., 2009).

CONCLUSION: WHERE IS COMPARATIVE RESEARCH HEADING?

This chapter has shown the variety of techniques employed under the broad label of comparative method, and has documented the uses of comparative method within the pages of JESP. Despite recent trends towards mixed and multimethods, we note the existence of major methodological divides that have long characterized the field of comparative social inquiry – and are likely to do so in the future. One example is the distinction between case-oriented and variable-oriented studies, reflected in Table 14.1.

The existence of a dichotomy between case-oriented and variable-oriented studies underlines (more or less implicitly) a different orientation towards the use of the comparative method. In the first instance, the principal aim is the interpretation and understanding of the patterns of a few cases, while in the second, the scope is rather hypothesis testing and generalization. Broadly speaking, case-oriented analysis tends to assume the existence of a large causal complexity, presupposing, on the one hand, a very detailed knowledge of the cases analysed; and, on the other, variable-oriented studies start from simplified assumptions and use variables nested within macrosocial units to prove or disprove a theory or a causal nexus. It is important to note that this distinction is not perfect; at times case-oriented studies clearly seek to make powerful generalizations, such as understanding gender divisions and the development of welfare regimes (Lewis, 1992), rather than stay within the confines of the study sample and the interpretation of results for the specific cases under consideration (i.e., Moore, 1966). Both strategies have important limits and strengths that make them more or less suitable for certain research tasks. Clearly, in recent years the second kind of approach has become more preeminent, in JESP and in other social science journals. This is underpinned by the exponential growth of medium and large-N studies, employing regression techniques to analyse the growing number of cross-national datasets.

However, despite the prominence of these types of studies, in numerical terms, it is important to emphasize once again that at the qualitative level, the most cited articles from JESP are based on the case study approach that is associated with deep description and analysis, often inspired by *The Three Worlds of Welfare Capitalism*. While scholarship seems to be geared more and more towards studies based on causation and more sophisticated techniques, the case study approach is foundational and continues to occupy a prominent place in the literature. However, it is near impossible to identify true causal effects with so few welfare states that can be compared. Despite the increasing volume of comparative studies in JESP attempting to identify what causes social policy divergence, and what effect this has in terms of outcomes. We really do not know the answers to either.

In the future, it is highly likely that an increased methodological sophistication and the larger availability of different kinds of data, including 'big data' and administrative data, will give way to comparative articles increasingly based on large-N, mixed, and multimethods, and perhaps a return to comparative inquiry to shed new light on causal mechanisms. However, case studies will probably continue to occupy a prominent place in the comparative social policy literature, since they are well suited to theoretical development and the understanding of policy change.

ACKNOWLEDGEMENTS

We are grateful to the research assistants based at Sciences Po Paris and the University of Strathclyde in Glasgow who assisted with development of the database, downloading all of the articles, creating a library, and conducted the initial reviews by hand, they are Taysheona Denise Brodie, Edouard Crocq, Federico Plantera and Emmaleena Käkelä. Also, to Yannick Savina who wrote the syntax command in R. We thank the reviewers, editors, and Graham Room and Gøsta Esping-Andersen for their thoughts, reflections and comments on earlier drafts of this chapter

REFERENCES

Aassve, A., Billari, F. C., Mazzuco, S., & Ongaro, F. (2002). Leaving home: A comparative analysis of ECHP data. *Journal of European Social Policy*, *12*(4), 259–275.
Alber, J. (1995). A framework for the comparative study of social services. *Journal of European Social Policy*, *5*(2), 131–149.
Albertini, M., Kohli, M., & Vogel, C. (2007). Intergenerational transfers of time and money in European families: Common patterns – different regimes? *Journal of European Social Policy*, *17*(4), 319–334.
Almond, G., & Verba, S. (1963). *The Civic Culture: Political Attitudes and Democracy in Five Countries*. Princeton University Press.
Andreski, S. (1965). *The Uses of Comparative Sociology*. University of California Press.
Anttonen, A., & Sipilä, J. (1996). European social care services: Is it possible to identify models? *Journal of European Social Policy*, *6*(2), 87–100.

Armer, M. (1973). Methodological problems and possibilities in comparative research. In M. Armer & A. Grinmshaw (Eds), *Comparative Social Research* (pp. 49–79). Wiley.

Behrendt, C. (2000). Do means-tested benefits alleviate poverty? Evidence on Germany, Sweden and the United Kingdom from the Luxembourg Income Study. *Journal of European Social Policy*, *10*(1), 23–41.

Bettio, F., Simonazzi, A., & Villa, P. (2006). Change in care regimes and female migration: The 'care drain' in the Mediterranean. *Journal of European Social Policy*, *16*(3), 271–285.

Brady, D., Huber, E., & Stephens, J. D. (2014). *Comparative Welfare States Data Set*. University of North Carolina and WZB Berlin Social Science Center.

Busemeyer, M. R., Goerres, A., & Weschle, S. (2009). Attitudes towards redistributive spending in an era of demographic ageing: The rival pressures from age and income in 14 OECD countries. *Journal of European Social Policy*, *19*(3), 195–212.

Castles, F. G. (2003). The world turned upside down: Below replacement fertility, changing preferences and family-friendly public policy in 21 OECD Countries. *Journal of European Social Policy*, *13*(3), 209–227.

Collier, D. (1993). The comparative method. In A. Finifter (Ed.), *Political Science: State of the Discipline II* (pp. 105–119). American Political Science Association.

Danforth, B. (2014). Worlds of welfare in time: A historical reassessment of the three-world typology. *Journal of European Social Policy*, *24*(2), 164–182.

Deacon, B. (2000). Eastern European welfare states: The impact of the politics of globalization. *Journal of European Social Policy*, *10*(2), 146–161.

Deeming, C. (2017). The lost and the new 'liberal world' of welfare capitalism: A critical assessment of Gøsta Esping-Andersen's *The Three Worlds of Welfare Capitalism* a quarter century later. *Social Policy and Society*, *16*(3), 405–422.

Editorial Foreword (1991). *Journal of European Social Policy*, *1*(1), 1–2.

Esmer, Y., & Pettersson, T. (2012). *Measuring and Mapping Cultures: 25 Years of Comparative Value Surveys*. BRILL.

Esping-Andersen, G. (1990). *The Three Worlds of Welfare Capitalism*. Princeton University Press.

Esping-Andersen, G. (Ed.). (1996). *Welfare States in Transition: National Adaptations in Global Economies*. Sage.

Esping-Andersen, G. (1999). *Social Foundations of Postindustrial Economies*. Oxford University Press.

Ferragina, E., & Seeleib-Kaiser, M. (2011). Thematic review: Welfare regime debate: past, present, futures? *Policy and Politics*, *39*(4), 583–611.

Ferrera, M. (1996). The 'Southern model' of welfare in social Europe. *Journal of European Social Policy*, *6*(1), 17–37.

Ganghof, S. (2006). Tax mixes and the size of the welfare state: Causal mechanisms and policy implications. *Journal of European Social Policy*, *16*(4), 360–373.

Gauthier, A. H. (2011). *Comparative Family Policy Database*, Version 3. Netherlands Interdisciplinary Demographic Institute and Max Planck Institute for Demographic Research.

Gerring, J. (2012). Mere description. *British Journal of Political Science*, *42*(4), 721–746.

Gornick, J. C., Meyers, M. K., & Ross, K. E. (1997). Supporting the employment of mothers: Policy variation across fourteen welfare states. *Journal of European Social Policy*, *7*(1), 45–70.

Haller, M., Jowell, R., & Smith, T. W. (2012). *The International Social Survey Programme 1984–2009: Charting the Globe.* Routledge.

Hook, J. L. (2015). Incorporating 'class' into work–family arrangements: Insights from and for Three Worlds. *Journal of European Social Policy*, *25*(1), 14–31.

Huber, E., Stephens, J. D., Mustillo, T., & Pribble, J. (2008). *Social Policy in Latin America and the Caribbean Dataset, 1960–2006.* University of North Carolina.

Jowell, R., Roberts, C., Fitzgerald R., & Eva, G. (Eds). (2007). *Measuring Attitudes Cross-Nationally: Lessons from the European Social Survey.* Sage.

Korpi, W., & Palme, J. (2008). *The Social Citizenship Indicator Program.* www.sofi .su.se/spin/about-the-project/social-citizenship-indicatorprogram-scip-1930-2005-1 .202043

Lewis, J. (1992). Gender and the development of welfare regimes. *Journal of European Social Policy*, *2*(3), 159–173.

Lijphart, A. (1971). Comparative politics and the comparative method. *American Political Science Review*, *65*(3), 682–693.

Lohmann, H. (2011). Comparability of EU-SILC survey and register data: The relationship among employment, earnings and poverty. *Journal of European Social Policy*, *21*(1), 37–54.

Missinne, S., Meuleman, B., & Bracke, P. (2013). The popular legitimacy of European healthcare systems: A multilevel analysis of 24 countries. *Journal of European Social Policy*, *23*(3), 231–247.

Moore, B., Jr. (1966). *Social Origins of Dictatorship and Democracy: Lord and Peasant in the Making of the Modern World.* Allen Lane.

Nelson, K. (2007). *Introducing SaMip: The Social Assistance and Minimum Income Protection Interim Dataset* (S-WoPEc No. 11/2007). Swedish Institute for Social Research.

Nelson, K. (2012). Counteracting material deprivation: The role of social assistance in Europe. *Journal of European Social Policy*, *22*(2), 148–163.

Pavolini, E., & Ranci, C. (2008). Restructuring the welfare state: Reforms in long-term care in Western European countries. *Journal of European Social Policy*, *18*(3), 246–259.

Przeworski, A., & Teune, H. (1970). *The Logic of Comparative Social Enquiry.* Wiley-Interscience.

Ragin, C. (1987). *The Comparative Method.* University of California Press.

Ragin, C. (2014). *The Comparative Method: Moving beyond Qualitative and Quantitative Strategies.* University of California Press.

Rokkan, S. (1966). Comparative cross-national research: The context of current efforts. In R. Merritt & S. Rokkan (Eds), *Comparing Nations: The Use of Quantitative Data in Cross-National Research* (pp. 3–26). Yale University Press.

Room, G. (2008). Social policy in Europe: paradigms of change, *Journal of European Social Policy*, *18*(4), 345–352.

Rovny, A. E. (2014). The capacity of social policies to combat poverty among new social risk groups. *Journal of European Social Policy*, *24*(5), 405–423.

Sainsbury, D. (2006). Immigrants' social rights in comparative perspective: Welfare regimes, forms in immigration and immigration policy regimes. *Journal of European Social Policy*, *16*(3), 229–244.

Sartori, G. (1970). Concept misformation in comparative politics. *American Political Science Review*, *64*(4), 1033–1053.

Scruggs, L. (2004). *Welfare State Entitlements Data Set: A Comparative Institutional Analysis of Eighteen Welfare States*, Version 1.1. University of Connecticut.

Scruggs, L., & Allan, J. (2006). Welfare-state decommodification in 18 OECD countries: A replication and revision. *Journal of European Social Policy, 16*(1), 55–72.

Scruggs, L., Detlef, J., & Kuitto, K. (2014). *Comparative Welfare Entitlements Dataset 2*, Version 2014-03. Dataset, University of Connecticut and University of Greifswald.

Sjöberg, O. (2004). The role of family policy institutions in explaining gender-role attitudes: A comparative multilevel analysis of thirteen industrialized countries. *Journal of European Social Policy, 14*(2), 107–123.

Skocpol, T. (1979). *States and Social Revolutions: A Comparative Analysis of France, Russia and China.* Cambridge University Press.

Smelser, N. J. (1976). *Comparative Methods in the Social Sciences.* Prentice Hall.

van Oorschot, W. (2006). Making the difference in social Europe: Deservingness perceptions among citizens of European welfare states. *Journal of European Social Policy, 16*(1), 23–42.

van Oorschot, W., & Arts, W. (2005). The social capital of European welfare states: The crowding out hypothesis revisited. *Journal of European Social Policy, 15*(1), 5–26.

Wilensky, H. L. (1975). *The Welfare State and Equality: Structural and Ideological Roots of Public Expenditures.* University of California Press.

Wulfgramm, M. (2014). Life satisfaction effects of unemployment in Europe: The moderating influence of labour market policy. *Journal of European Social Policy, 24*(3), 258–272.

PART III

Social policy research challenges

15. Social policy research and climate change

Bjørn Hvinden and Mi Ah Schoyen

INTRODUCTION

Climate change is highly relevant to social policy and the welfare state as it more and more frequently affects people's private spheres like homes and livelihoods. In that sense, climate change is an important and growing source of social risks in the twenty-first century. Despite the many points of intersection between climate change and social policy, the research agenda on the intersections of the two spheres is relatively young. Research has focused on the social and welfare implications of the global climate crisis, and more recently, on the actual and potential roles of social policy in contributing to the necessary transformation to a net-zero or low-emissions world. Much of the evolving research adopts a concept of 'sustainability', inspired by but also to some extent challenging the definition put forward by the United Nations (UN). This chapter will outline the main positions in the debate on the inter-actions between social policy and climate change and discuss research in this area, focusing on the different roles of social policy in addressing specific risks associated with climate change.

In particular, the chapter focuses on the risks associated with the shift towards a net zero-emission society and research issues related to these risks. First, we consider the discourse on risks in relation to climate change, and research bridging analyses on social policy and climate change. Our discussion starts here because the protective element of social insurance and related programmes for income redistribution and service provision is likely to become increasingly important because of global warming and the associated transition to a zero-emission society, not least because of changes in the com-position and distribution of social risks. However, more far-reaching forms of social regulation are probably also needed as a just transition to carbon neutrality in most likelihood will require behavioural changes related to how key non-governmental actors deal with social risks. In the sections that follow, we therefore turn to the potential roles of social regulation and social policy (in the form of social investment) in the transition to net-zero societies, before addressing the political prospects of reaching carbon neutrality by drawing on some recent evidence from attitudinal research. The concluding section highlights the uneasy relationship between expensive and growth-dependent advanced welfare states and the need to find solutions to counter the overwhelming ecological challenges of this century.

A 'NEW SOCIAL RISKS' DISCOURSE APPLIED TO CLIMATE CHANGE

As discussed in other chapters in this volume (e.g., Chapters 7 and 17), social policy and welfare state research has long debated the distinction between 'old' social risks (e.g., sickness, disability, old age retirement, and infirmity) and 'new' social risks associated with developments such as increased labour market participation, higher incidence of divorce, separation/end of cohabitation, and lone carerhood, as well as growing shares of the elderly population needing care from others (Taylor-Gooby, 2004). Risks associated with climate change have been growing over many years and are in this sense not 'new'. However, the increase and severity of such risks creates additional challenges for welfare states and, potentially, competition regarding the spending of limited public resources. Research indicates that it is essential in this debate to be sensitive to the issues of *who* are the most vulnerable groups and *where* the most disadvantaged countries and regions in the ecosocial transition are.

Ecological risks associated with climate change are likely to spill over into the social domain, thereby affecting the livelihood of citizens for the foreseeable future. This recognition in research has inspired scholars to discuss the social dimension of ecological degradation, often in close connection with the broader debate on old and new social risks. In the context of European welfare states, it will be crucial from a social cohesion perspective to develop policies that help protect already vulnerable groups from falling further behind. If some vulnerable groups end up being systematically worse off than the rest of the population, the outcomes from the ecological transition we are now witnessing will be questionable from a social justice standpoint (Bal & Stok, forthcoming).

For many social policy scholars, the discourse on ecological and social risks related to climate change can be traced back to the sociologist Ulrich Beck. Through his book *Risk Society: Towards a New Modernity* (1992), Beck was ahead of his time in anticipating such 'new risks' related to climate change. He (1992: 56) refers to the production of new risks, both in the commercial market and through the intervention and expenditure of the welfare state (see also Beck, 1992: 20–24, 189, 229–230). Of particular interest for the current chapter is that Beck combines a focus on social risks *and* on ecological risks (including climate emissions).

Anthony Giddens, inspired by Beck's work, also emphasizes how the late modern world introduces risks that earlier generations did not face. These include the risks of ecological catastrophe and global warming (Giddens, 1991: 4, 22, 137): 'The dangers posed by global warming are high-consequences risks which collectively we face, but about which precise risk assessment is virtually impossible' (Giddens, 1991: 137). Twenty years later, Giddens (2011: 2) referred to this paradox: 'since the dangers posed by global warming aren't tangible, immediate or visible in the course of day-to-day life, many will sit on their hands and do nothing of concrete nature about it'. While there is still some truth in this argument, the increased frequency of extreme climate-related disasters (flooding, wildfires, drought, hurricanes, etc.) during the last decades has undoubtedly enhanced public awareness of the urgency to reduce greenhouse gas (GHG) emissions.

Later research, including the findings of the Stern Review (2007: 25), and Gough et al. (2008: 325), suggests that climate change 'is a new risk that is big, global, long-term, persistent and uncertain'. This research predicts that risks in the (then) coming decades will involve 'increasing risk of droughts and floods, more abrupt and large-scale changes in the climate systems and a rise in sea levels'. This idea on risks was modified in later years (e.g., Gough & Meadowcroft, 2011: 494) to highlight that risks associated with climate change are not new *per se* but the intensity of these risks will likely be new: 'Many of the risks associated with climate change are not new (societies have always had to cope with floods, droughts, violent storms, and so on), but their incidence, severity, and distribution will change, and welfare policies will have to be adjusted to cope'.

Much research on climate-related extreme weather events is concerned with assessing the intensity of these ecological risks. For example, an up-to-date risk assessment by Eckstein et al. (2021) analyses and ranks the extent to which countries across the world are affected by climate-related extreme weather events (storms, floods, heatwaves, drought, etc.). The assessment finds signs of escalating climate change across all continents and regions. However, the occurrence and impact of extreme weather events affect the poorest countries in the world most strongly. These countries, and the citizens living in them, are at particular risk of the damaging effects of climate-related hazards, have lower capacity to cope with the effects, and may need more time and assistance to recover and rebuild. The welfare states in these countries are also less well equipped to provide social protection for citizens' livelihood when it is affected by these ecological risks. At the same time, research on storms in Japan indicates that even high-income countries will experience stronger ecological risks in the coming years (Mori et al., 2021). More effective climate mitigation and adaptation to prevent or minimize the risks and potential damage are needed in all countries (see also BC Sustainability, 2021). The debate around climate change and social policy thus carries an important global dimension and should not be confined to solely the rich countries or Europe (Chancel & Piketty, 2015).

The discourse on risks related to climate change highlights a crucial relationship between the occurrence and intensity of ecological risks and social risks. There is some evidence that taxes on carbon-intensive necessary private energy consumption will be more regressive with an increasing level of income inequality (Andersson & Atkinson, 2020), giving rise to what some commentators have referred to as a 'double' injustice (Gough, 2013, 2019). The 'double' injustice refers to the fact that the socio-economic groups most exposed to the harms of climate change contribute little to its causes as their lifestyles and consumption patterns tend to be associated with small or modest carbon footprints. The double injustice is global in the sense that it is a fundamental issue in the international climate negotiations between Global South and Global North government representatives.

The capacity of countries' welfare states to protect inhabitants against the impact of global warming will generally be least developed in the poorest countries of the world, and hence, will add to the severity of this injustice. Therefore, the Paris Agreement reached at the 21st Conference of the Parties and the follow-up Glasgow Climate Pact from the 26th Conference of the Parties in 2021, both place the main financial burden for climate mitigation and adaptation on countries in the Global North. However, the risk of a double injustice is not only evident in the Global South. It applies to countries at all levels of development (Gough, 2019) and, thus, also *within* European advanced welfare states. Moreover, if the cost of climate mitigation falls disproportionally on socially disadvantaged groups, who are poorly equipped to cope with the consequences of climate change for which they bear little responsibility, the double injustice turns into a 'triple' one.

Past and current research on the risks related to climate change provides key insights for future research. Ultimately, if social inequities are allowed to grow, they risk undermining the political sustainability of climate mitigation efforts and sacrifices necessary to slow down global warming and ensure truly sustainable European welfare states. The potential role for redistribution through welfare policy, e.g., housing or fuel allowances, to as far as possible offset perverse distributional effects of carbon taxes, remains an open question. We need more research to establish whether this is best done through welfare policy (as suggested by the European Commission, 2018), directly in the design of carbon taxes and associated in-built revenue-recycling mechanisms, via more progressive income or luxury consumption taxes, or through other means (for an overview, see Eurofound, 2021). Future research on social policy can play an important role in answering such questions.

FROM RISK TO SOCIAL PROTECTION: THE COMPLEMENTARY ROLES OF REDISTRIBUTION AND REGULATION IN WELFARE STATES

A basic function of welfare states is to provide collective protection against social risks, that is, the likelihood that one might experience something undesirable in the foreseeable future that threatens one's source of income, maintenance, or livelihood. The provision of social insurance (e.g., unemployment insurance) and other forms of financial support to needy persons involves *economic redistribution* from the welfare state financed through contributions and/or taxes (including those paid by employers and employees). Hence, economic redistribution encompasses a reallocation of income that is either 'vertical' (from more affluent persons to less affluent persons) or 'horizontal' (from economically active life phases to economically passive life phases of the same person). Apart from sustaining individuals and their families in periods without paid work (i.e., passive welfare), governments often also seek to reskill affected individuals, and through this, enable them to find a new and relevant job (i.e., active welfare; see Chapter 7, this volume).

There is considerable evidence that existing public provision of income support and employment services will be insufficient in the transition to a net zero-emission society. Many job seekers with relevant qualifications and experience will be unsuccessful in securing a (new) employment contract due to large-scale industrial restructuring and other economic transformations. Groups at particular risk are persons sharing characteristics that employers regard less suitable or relevant, for example in terms of gender or age. Immigrants may also be at greater risk, as employers increasingly may believe that they will not fit in the organization, while disabled or impaired persons may not be called for a job interview because employers assume that they will not be able to perform the job sufficiently well (Halvorsen & Hvinden, 2018).

Common to these examples is that the job applicant becomes the victim of untested assumptions about what he or she is able to or qualified to do. The person is denied the possibility to correct these assumptions, or the opportunity to explain how adjustments or reasonable accommodations in the workplace might make such assumptions even less appropriate. For these reasons, the European Union, the European Economic Area, Canada, and the United States have adopted policies of so-called *social regulation* (Majone, 1993; Levi-Faur, 2014). Social regulation can promote greater substantive equality in labour market participation or other societal objectives that goes beyond mere income redistribution by influencing the behaviour of key non-governmental actors (e.g., employers, service providers, entrepreneurs). Examples of instruments for social regulation include non-discrimination legislation, job subsidies, reduced taxes or social insurance contributions, or having a certain rate of employees with a disadvantaged background as a condition for government tenders. Other social regulation measures include legislative means, financial incentives, and persuasion through information campaigns (Vedung, 2017).

Social policy research demonstrates a long history of social regulation within the welfare state, but the rationale for social regulation is also relevant in the context of climate mitigation. Gough et al. (2008) suggest that there are similarities between social policy and climate policy in terms of the societal forces creating the need for them (industrialization, urbanization, and democratization) because they deal with problems that markets and voluntary actions can only marginally solve, and as they overlap in the means to do so (regulation, fiscal transfers, etc.).

Research further suggests that other social regulation avenues are possible. Nachmany et al. (2019) provide the first global review of climate change adaptation laws and policies. They find that more complex responses like investment in physical and regulatory infrastructures (e.g., economic incentives, taxes, subsidies for encouraging efficient and flexible adaption to climate change) are largely missing. They call for more systematic analysis of current or potential use of instruments like 'regulation' (i.e., standards and obligations, building codes, zoning and spatial planning, disclosure obligations) and 'incentives' (i.e., taxes, subsidies) for encouraging economic actors to adapt to climate change (Nachmany et al., 2019: 3). Such instruments may play important roles in the ecosocial transition by enabling workers in emission-heavy companies and sectors who will have to find new and sustainable jobs. As shown by ILO (2015) and Galgóczi (2019, 2020), the toolbox of social regulation is rich in instruments, both for assisting companies to make the transition towards zero emissions or footprints, and for enabling affected employees to get new jobs and regain fair living standards. In these ways, social regulation can be constructive both in the economic sphere and the social welfare context.

Summing up, welfare states have complementary roles of social regulation and redistribution, which remain important in the face of climate change. In that sense, climate change challenges welfare states to reconsider risk protection in association with vulnerabilities emerging or worsening because of attempts to create a net zero-emission society.

SOCIAL INVESTMENT FOR A JUST TRANSITION TO NET ZERO-EMISSION SOCIETIES

The notion of a 'just transition' builds on the assumption that if one is to achieve the goal of a net zero-emission economy, the process must be balanced and just (Galgóczi, 2020). While the term 'just transition' originated as a trade union demand in a dispute related to uranium mining in Canada, it later became adopted to refer more broadly to reconciling 'efforts to provide workers with decent jobs and the need to protect the environment' (Sabato & Fronteddu, 2020: 369). Similarly, a rich research literature has for a long time used the term 'just transition' in relation to curtailment of the coal industry (Evans & Phelan, 2016; Harrahill & Douglas, 2019). Later, the notion of 'just transition' has been adopted in broader contexts where existing methods of production (e.g., in the steel or car industry) were unsustainable because of high levels of GHG emissions.

Given welfare states' current ambitious emission targets agreed upon in the contexts of the UN and the European Union (Sabato & Fronteddu, 2020), there is a risk for regressive distributional and employment effects. As such, there is a crucial role for the welfare state in organizing a just transition *as well as* ensuring that distributional and employment outcomes are acceptable (e.g., new employment with adequate pay; alternatively offering training for relevant skills; or at least, a fair livelihood in the form of social security benefits for those who do not find a new job or occupation).

Climate change, and the welfare state's shift towards a net zero-emission society, is not unique in creating potentially unjust employment outcomes. Historically, there have been many reasons for the restructuring and close-downs of plants, for instance, a lack of competitiveness, renewal, or modernization, all of which affect the livelihood of citizens. However, with stricter regulations for achieving reduced GHG emissions, climate mitigation regulations are to an increasing extent forcing enterprises to find new platforms for their operations. The practical steps of an adequate just transition will thus often involve substantial costs, and a co-investment between the welfare state and the company in question might be necessary. Such co-investment may help to provide new jobs for affected workers and contribute to diminishing scepticism or resistance to proposals for climate change mitigation.

In short, research on climate change suggests that well-designed packages of measures developed in consultation and dialogue with the communities and actors most directly affected by the changes in question will enhance their effectiveness and robustness against pressures for reversal of changes (Dryzek, 2005: 99–121). Moreover, social protection provisions in a broad sense have an important role in shielding people against both the immediate and potentially long-term adverse consequences of climate-related economic restructuring. ILO (2015: 11–17) spells out in detail the contributions that social policies can make to facilitate a just transition. The contributions include skills development, social protection, active labour market policies, and social dialogue (Galgóczi, 2020). They span what we have referred to as 'redistribution' (through income transfers and social services) and 'social investment' (funding services enabling retraining and employability) to meet the demands of the transition to a climate-neutral economy (see also Sabato & Fronteddu, 2020: 11, 17).

Research points to the fruitfulness of expanding the concept of social investment to include the ecological dimension of wellbeing and welfare. Gough (2017: 174–176) discusses key elements of ecological investment for a post-growth economy more broadly. He emphasizes that the overall reshaping of the economy requires major capital investment in renewable energy supply, energy networks, transport, communications, transformed cities and buildings, retrofitting housing, protection of natural resources, and ecosystems. He highlights that '[t]he necessary eco-investment and subsequent adaptation costs must be paid by society as a whole, whether by higher taxation or subsidised loans' (Gough, 2017: 175). Finally, he anticipates the need for reductions in working time, absolute levels of income, consumption, and emissions (Gough, 2017: 192).

We still need better knowledge about how climate change mitigation affects people's welfare and, thereby, social policy. More concretely, mitigation policies tend to generate direct or indirect risks for people's welfare, creating potentially new demands on the welfare state. Measures such as fuel and energy taxes and carbon emission trading raise the price of carbon for private consumers as well as businesses. For instance, higher energy prices come with an increased risk of energy poverty and industrial restructuring aimed at decarbonization means, by definition, that some jobs will disappear. A key task for future welfare state research will be to identify which of these new contingencies and sources of risk welfare states should treat as 'social' or 'collective', risks that should be met by social protection programmes and whether already existing institutions offer sufficient protection in this regard. Similarly, there are still both theoretical and empirical gaps in our understanding of how the instruments of welfare states (income transfers, provision of health, social and employment services, social regulation) may play constructive roles in enabling the societal transformation to low- or zero-emission societies. Conversely, some authors take a critical approach to economic growth and ask how much economic growth (including some forms of social investment) will contribute to climate change, including the extent to which the welfare state increases people's purchasing power and overall consumption, and through this, lead to higher GHG emissions (Koch, 2020, 2021; Büchs, 2021). Issues like these provide a foundation for future social policy research on climate change.

THE CLIMATE CHANGE AND SOCIAL POLICY NEXUS IN RESEARCH ON POPULAR ATTITUDES

Research on social policy and climate change clearly suggests there is an important role for the welfare state in addressing risks emerging and worsening because of climate change. But to what extent would such attempts to mitigate these risks be politically feasible? In a democratic context, knowledge of public opinions and the degree of acceptance of social policy responses are central to the political dimension of societal responses to climate change. Knowledge of these attitudes is also central to the prospects of an ecosocial transition more generally, whether the goal is ecological modernization in line with contemporary market capitalism or a more radically transformed post-growth society (Bridgen & Schoyen, forthcoming). If subject to strong popular resistance, specific measures are less likely to be implemented.

Outside of social policy research, there is a rich literature on popular preferences and attitudes towards the environment in general and climate change in particular, and of different mitigation strategies (Gelissen, 2007; Scruggs & Benegal, 2012; Franzen & Vogl, 2013). It is beyond the scope of the present chapter to do justice to this research tradition, which will be relatively less familiar to most social policy scholars compared with the 'social policy counterpart' dealing with attitudes and preferences towards the welfare state (see Chapter 12, this volume). However, to give an example of what the climate and environmental attitude literature has to offer, we highlight two recent contributions that are relevant to the issues raised in this chapter.

Based on an innovative international comparative survey of attitudes in China, Sweden, and the United States, Carlsson et al. (2021) show that in the decade 2009–2019, national averages in the recognition of anthropogenic climate change and willingness to pay for mitigation grew more similar. However, the apparent convergence in recognition of anthropogenic climate change at the country level masks considerable and to some extent growing heterogeneity in attitudes and climate policy preferences *within* countries. To explain within-country divergence, they find some evidence of increasing political polarization, i.e., a growing divide in policy preferences, among voters with different political affiliations on the left–right axis. Similarly, Fairbrother et al. (2019) draw attention to another 'political' variable, that of trust in a country's political processes. They find that while a solid majority of Europeans recognize climate change as a challenge, support for fossil fuel taxes is quite limited. However, in countries with a high level of political trust, i.e., 'confidence in the political system and its actors' (Fairbrother et al., 2019: 9), support for fossil fuel taxes is higher and citizens' opinions about such taxes are more closely tied to their view on the anthropogenic character and consequences of climate change.

Furthermore, in recent years, comparative social policy scholars have become increasingly interested in the nexus between social policy and climate or environmental policy preferences. This emerging literature is situated at the intersection between the two rich but traditionally separate research strands. It focuses on attitudes and preferences towards climate and environmental policy on the one hand (see above), and welfare states and social policy on the other hand, in a cross-national, comparative perspective (Koch & Fritz, 2014; Jakobsson et al., 2017).[1] One central question in this literature has been what shapes simultaneous individual-level preferences with regard to goals or specific policies in the social and climate policy domains. Some contributions in this tradition gauge attitudes towards policy goals whereas others address attitudes towards specific policy measures.

At the aggregate level, a key focus has been that of looking for and explaining cross-country similarities and differences in attitudes towards welfare states and environmental policy. Scholars have been particularly interested in investigating whether welfare regimes matter as a driver of variation, that is, whether there is a higher level of simultaneous support for climate mitigation and state responsibility, as well as involvement in welfare provision. A much-cited hypothesis suggests that social-democratic welfare states and coordinated market economies 'are better placed to handle the intersection of social policy and [climate change] than the liberal market economies with more rudimentary welfare states' (Gough et al., 2008: 336). Results from analyses by Fritz and Koch (2019) and Otto and Gugushvili (2020), based on data from round 8 of the European Social Survey collected in 2016, partially but far from unequivocally, confirm the expectation that support for policy efforts to address both ecological *and* social challenges at the same time is strongest in social-democratic welfare states. However, additional research is needed to be more certain about the descriptive patterns as well as to unpack the underlying mechanisms driving these outcomes. These studies also point in the same direction as Fairbrother et al. (2019) and Carlsson et al. (2021) in emphasizing the importance of political (or social) trust and political leaning in explaining differences in attitudes within countries.

AN UNKNOWN FUTURE FOR GROWTH-DEPENDENT WELFARE STATES?

The report of the World Commission on Environment and Development (WCED), *Our Common Future* (World Commission on Environment and Development, 1987), presents a game-changing understanding of sustainability and sustainable development, linking social, economic, intergenerational, territorial, and ecological dimensions. The report is an important reference for subsequent research on these dimensions and essential inspiration for the 2015 UN Agenda 2030 with its 17 Sustainable Development Goals, where Goal 13 states 'Take urgent action to combat climate change and its impact'. The report defines sustainable development in somewhat variable ways, without explaining the reasons for doing so. Most striking is that, in some cases, the authors focus on the extent to which people have equal possibilities to fulfil their *needs*, across generations and territorial space, while they, in other instances, (also) emphasize people's equal opportunities to realize their *aspirations*. While 'need' suggests associations with 'necessity', 'aspirations' rather points towards the possibility of alternative future ways of living and structuring society, different from the current ones. Making such alternative lives and structures of society a reality would require planned individual or collective efforts, joint deliberation, and would depend on the available opportunities in different geographical locations.

Future research on the nexus between climate change and social policy can draw on current debates. For example, Gough (2017: 42–47) provides an important theory of human need in relation to climate change and sustainable wellbeing. He distinguishes between 'basic needs', 'intermediate needs', 'need satisfiers', and 'societal preconditions'. These needs are of significance for the *relationship* between climate policy and social policy, not only the latter.

However, it is possible that the authors of the WCED report have something else in mind with the term 'aspiration' that does not fit any of these elements or individual preferences (Gough, 2017: 39–41) related to need satisfiers (Gough, 2017: 159). Gough expresses reservations about other ways of operationalizing the WCED concept of sustainable development, especially those suggested by Amartya Sen. While praising the WCED overall, Sen criticizes its emphasis on needs: 'Certainly, people do have need, but they also have values and in particular, cherish their ability to reason, appraise, choose, participate and act. Seeing people only in terms of their needs may give us a rather meagre view of humanity' (Sen, 2009: 250, 2013: 7).

Since proponents of the 'sustainable welfare' perspective point to the need for 'degrowth' or 'post-growth' (e.g., Jackson, 2017; Büchs, 2021; Koch, 2021), it is significant that both the WCED and the UN Sustainable Development Goals that were endorsed nearly two decades later embrace economic growth: 'Far from requiring the cessation of economic growth, [sustainable development] recognizes that the problems of poverty and underdevelopment cannot be solved unless we have a new era of growth in which developing countries play a large role and reap large benefits' (World Commission on Environment and Development, 1987: 51).

The problem of how to make welfare states less dependent on future economic growth (Bailey, 2015: 794), while they at the same time must play an active part in helping people cope with and adapt to a societal shift in an ecoso-cial direction, is not easily solved. This problem will likely be on the agenda of decision makers and researchers alike for the next decades. A necessary area of research must focus on the dilemmas arising around a just transition. A just transition requires adequate social protection for risks associated with climate change, such as loss of income due to employment changes in the shift towards a net zero-emission society. Individuals who remain active but are forced to move to another sector must be given access to high-quality labour market services, including affordable education and training programmes. In short, people will need opportunities to pursue paths that are meaningful to them as Europe moves towards the climate targets of 2030 and beyond. How can welfare states resting on post-growth economic principles provide such protection? How can sufficient financial resources be secured?

The debate about climate change and social policy is often performed at fairly high levels of theoretical abstraction, as illustrated not least in our presentation of this important and emerging research field. More research is thus needed in terms of deriving hypotheses about how climate change and social policy intersect, and to test those expectations empirically, especially by means of in-depth policy analyses relying on qualitative as well as quantitative data and methods.

An interesting area for further investigation is the double (or even triple) injustices of climate change, and how social policy can be organized to remedy its most pervasive outcomes. Another issue that deserves more attention in empirical research is how social policy and the welfare state may facilitate a fast transition towards a net-zero carbon emission society, without risking too much political or financial backlash. With the ongoing climate crisis, questions and issues such as these will remain on the future research agenda for years to come.

NOTE

1. Since we assume that many readers of this book will have at least a basic knowl-edge of the key issues raised in the latter, for reasons of space, we do not review this.

REFERENCES

Andersson, J., & Atkinson, G. (2020). The distributional effects of a carbon tax: The role of income inequality. Grantham Research Institute on Climate Change and the Environment Working Paper No. 349. Centre for Climate Change Economics and Policy and Working Paper No. 378. www.lse.ac.uk/granthaminstitute/wp-content/uploads/2020/09/working-paper-349-Andersson-Atkinson.pdf

Bailey, D. (2015). The environmental paradox of the welfare state: The dynamics of sustainability. *New Political Economy, 20*(6), 793–811.

Bal, M., & Stok, M. (forthcoming). Leaving no one behind: Climate change as a societal challenge for social justice and solidarity. In M. A. Yerkes & M. Bal (Eds), *Solidarity and Social Justice in Contemporary Societies: An Interdisciplinary Approach to Understanding Social Inequalities.* Palgrave Macmillan.

BC Sustainability (2021). *Public Consultation 86: New Regulation on Social, Environmental and Climate Risk Disclosures.* Banco Central do Brasil. www.bcb .gov.br/content/financialstability/ruralcreditdocs/BCB_Public_Consultation_86.pdf

Beck, U. (1992). *Risk Society: Towards a New Modernity.* Sage.

Bridgen, P., & Schoyen, M. A. (forthcoming). Sustainability. In B. Greve (Ed.), *Handbook of the Contemporary Welfare State.* Walter De Gruyter.

Büchs, M. (2021). Sustainable welfare: Independence between growth and welfare has to go both ways. *Global Social Policy, 21*(2), 323–327.

Carlsson, F., Kataria, M., Krupnick, A., Lampi, E., Löfgren, Å., Qin, P., Sterner, T., & Yang, X. (2021). The climate decade: Changing attitudes on three continents. *Journal of Environmental Economics and Management, 107*, 102426.

Chancel, L., & Piketty, T. (2015). Carbon and inequality: From Kyoto to Paris: Trends in the global inequality of carbon emissions (1998–2013) and prospects for an equitable adaptation fund. Iddri and Paris School of Economics. http://piketty.pse.ens.fr/files/ChancelPiketty2015.pdf

Dryzek, J. S. (2005). *The Politics of the Earth: Environmental Discourses* (2nd ed.). Oxford University Press.

Eckstein, D., Künzel, V., & Schäfer, L. (2021). *Global Climate Risk Index 2021: Who Suffers Most from Extreme Weather Events? Weather-Related Loss Events in 2019 and 2000–2019.* Germanwatch. www.germanwatch.org

Eurofound. (2021). *Distributional Impacts of Climate Policies in Europe.* Publications Office. https://data.europa.eu/doi/10.2806/44388

European Commission. (2018). *A Clean Planet for All: A European Strategic Long-Term Vision for a Prosperous, Modern, Competitive and Climate Neutral Economy* (COM(2018)773 final). https://eur-lex.europa.eu/legal-content/EN/TXT/PDF/?uri=CELEX:52018DC0773&from=EN

Evans, G., & Phelan, L. (2016). Transition to a post-carbon society: Linking environmental justice and just transition discourses. *Energy Policy, 99*, 329–339.

Fairbrother, M., Johansson Sevä, I., & Kulin, J. (2019). Political trust and the relationship between climate change beliefs and support for fossil fuel taxes: Evidence from a survey of 23 European countries. *Global Environmental Change, 59*, 102003.

Franzen, A., & Vogl, D. (2013). Two decades of measuring environmental attitudes: A comparative analysis of 33 countries. *Global Environmental Change, 23*(5), 1001–1008.

Fritz, M., & Koch, M. (2019). Public support for sustainable welfare compared: Links between attitudes towards climate and welfare policies. *Sustainability, 11*(15).

Galgóczi, B. (2019). Phasing out coal: A just transition approach. Working Paper 2019:04. European Trade Union Institute. www.etui.org/sites/default/files/19 %20WP%202019%2004%20Phasing%20out%20coal%20Galgoczi%20Web %20version.pdf

Galgóczi, B. (2020). Just transition on the ground: Challenges and opportunities for social dialogue. *European Journal of Industrial Relations, 26*(4), 367–382.

Gelissen, J. (2007). Explaining popular support for environmental protection: A multilevel analysis of 50 nations. *Environment and Behavior, 39*(3), 392–415.

Giddens, A. (1991). *Modernity and Self-Identity: Self and Society in the Late Modern Age*. Polity Press.

Giddens, A. (2011). *The Politics of Climate Change* (2nd ed.). Polity Press.

Gough, I. (2013). Carbon mitigation policies, distributional dilemmas and social policies. *Journal of Social Policy*, *42*(2), 191–213.

Gough, I. (2017). *Heat, Greed and Human Need*. Edward Elgar Publishing.

Gough, I. (2019). Necessities and luxuries: How to combine redistribution with sustainable consumption. In J. Meadowcroft, E. Holden, K. Linnerud, D. Banister, O. Langhelle, & G. Gilpin (Eds), *What Next for Sustainable Development?* (pp. 138–158). Edward Elgar Publishing.

Gough, I., & Meadowcroft, J. (2011). *Decarbonizing the Welfare State*. Oxford University Press.

Gough, I., Meadowcroft, J., Dryzek, J., Gerhards, J., Lengfeld, H., Markandya, A., & Ortiz, R. (2008). JESP symposium: Climate change and social policy. *Journal of European Social Policy*, *18*(4), 325–344.

Halvorsen, R., & Hvinden, B. (2018). Youth, diversity and employment in times of crisis and economic restructuring – an introduction. In R. Halvorsen & B. Hvinden (Eds), *Youth, Diversity and Employment* (pp. 1–31). Edward Elgar Publishing.

Harrahill, K., & Douglas, O. (2019). Framework development for 'just transition' in coal producing jurisdictions. *Energy Policy*, *134*, 110990.

ILO. (2015). *Guidelines for a Just Transition towards Environmentally Sustainable Economies for All*. International Labour Organization. www.ilo.org/wcmsp5/groups/public/---ed_emp/---emp_ent/documents/publication/wcms_432859.pdf

Jackson, T. (2017). *Prosperity without Growth: Foundations for the Economy of Tomorrow* (2nd ed.). Routledge.

Jakobsson, N., Muttarak, R., & Schoyen, M. A. (2017). Dividing the pie in the eco-social state: Exploring the relationship between public support for environmental and welfare policies. *Environment and Planning C: Politics and Space*, *36*(2), 313–339.

Koch, M. (2020). The state in the transformation to a sustainable postgrowth economy. *Environmental Politics*, *29*(1), 115–133.

Koch, M. (2021). Social policy without growth: Moving towards sustainable welfare states. *Social Policy and Society*, 1–13.

Koch, M., & Fritz, M. (2014). Building the eco-social state: Do welfare regimes matter? *Journal of Social Policy*, *43*(4), 679–703.

Levi-Faur, D. (2014). The welfare state: A regulatory perspective. *Public Administration*. https://doi.org/10.1111/padm.12063

Majone, G. (1993). The European Community between social policy and social regulation. *Journal of Common Market Studies*, *31*(2), 153–170.

Mori, N., Takemi, T., Tachikawa, Y. et al. (2021). Recent nationwide climate change impact assessments of natural hazards in Japan and East Asia. *Weather and Climate Extremes*, *32*, 100309.

Nachmany, M., Byrnes R., & Surminski, S. (2019). National laws and policies on climate change adaptation: a global review. Policy Brief. Grantham Research Institute on Climate Change, London School of Economics and Political Science and University of Leeds.

Otto, A., & Gugushvili, D. (2020). Eco-social divides in Europe: Public attitudes towards welfare and climate change policies. *Sustainability*, *12*(1).

Sabato, S., & Fronteddu, B. (2020). A socially just transition through the European Green Deal. Working Paper, 2020.08. European Trade Union Institute.

Scruggs, L., & Benegal, S. (2012). Declining public concern about climate change: Can we blame the great recession? *Global Environmental Change*, *22*(2), 505–515.

Sen, A. (2009). *The Idea of Justice*. Penguin Books.

Stern, N. (2007). *The Economics of Climate Change: The Stern Review*. Cambridge University Press. www.cambridge.org/us/academic/subjects/earth-and-envi ronmental-science/climatology-and-climate-change/economics-climate-change-ster n-review

Taylor-Gooby, P. (2004). New risks and social change. In P. Taylor-Gooby (Ed.), *New Risks, New Welfare* (pp. 1–28). Oxford University Press.

Vedung, E. (2017). Policy instruments: Typologies and theories. In M.-L. Bemelmans-Videc, R. C. Rist, & E. Vedung (Eds), *Carrots, Sticks and Sermons: Policy Instruments and Their Evaluation* (1st ed., pp. 21–58). Routledge.

World Commission on Environment and Development. (1987). *Our Common Future*. Oxford University Press.

16. Studying social policy in the digital age

Minna van Gerven

SOCIAL POLICY RESEARCH IN THE DIGITAL AGE

Technological change is hardly a novel phenomenon: humankind has always been exploring new ways to improve human capabilities with technological resources and machines. The modernization of European welfare states centres around contemporary technological advances. The rapid development and popularization of computers and the internet during the late twentieth century have become central catalysts for the third industrial revolution and far-reaching digitalization in the twenty-first century (e.g., artificial intelligence, machine learning, Internet of Things), in combination with big data and machine-based intelligence, creates opportunities and challenges for welfare states. It also creates a rich foundation for social policy research. In the twenty-first-century digital race, governments are keen to replace old methods of welfare provision with automation and datafication, with the aim of developing effective and 'better' public policies. Many new welfare technologies are, however, more invasive, as they 'disrupt' existing systems and practices (Christensen, 1997). For example, automated decision-making technologies – based on algorithmic learning – increasingly circumvent human decision making (Desiere et al., 2018) and thereby considerably challenge the logic of human intervention in giving and receiving public services.

This chapter sets out to explore social policy research on how and to what extent the technological change has affected European welfare states. This research is situated along two key themes: changing digital governance and the impact of digitalization on welfare recipients. Note that while academic interest in digital welfare states is growing, the debate is conceptually fuzzy and requires stronger theoretical embedding. The chapter therefore starts with a discussion of key concepts and their definition in social policy research. It then relates these discussions to classic welfare state discussions, and (levels of) welfare state change (Hall, 1993), to draw attention to two streams of interrelated research on welfare state development: the digitalization of social policy administration (digitalization, automation, and datafication) and the impact of these technological advancements for social policy. The discussion of the latter focuses on two major social policy areas where digitalization efforts are felt the most: welfare policies and labour markets. The chapter concludes with a research road map in this new and quickly emerging field.

WHEN TECHNOLOGY MEETS THE WELFARE STATE

Technological change covers various processes of invention, innovation, and diffusion of technology or processes (Damanpour & Aravind, 2012). It includes the introduction of digitalization and automation technologies (e.g., Eichhorst & Rinne 2017; Thewissen & Rueda 2019), but also wider technological advances in generating knowledge and changing societies as a whole. Digital technologies are ubiquitous and involve various types of electronic tools, systems, or devices (such as artificial intelligence, machine learning, and the Internet of Things[1]) that generate, store, or process digitized data. The terms digitalization and automation are deeply intertwined but they comprise the technological composition of the 'digital welfare state' as regards to its governance as well as its impact on welfare recipients.

Digitalization refers to the 'ways in which social life is organized through and around digital technologies' (Leonardi & Treem, 2020: 1602). It sustains a multitude of technology-driven processes utilizing one or more digital technologies. Standardization and automation are the central aims of many digitalization processes. *Automation* is a modern version of Weberian standardization, where routine tasks are standardized and efficiently organized (Weber, 1968). Modern automation involves the replacement of human action with a technological process, for example, it allows the introduction of (rule-based) decision making, where digital data are processed and all tasks (e.g., organization and assessment) are carried out without human interference (Eurofound, 2020). Automated systems, which involve the processing of enormous volumes of digital big data, are linked to *datafication*: 'the practice of taking an activity, behaviour, or process and turning it into meaningful data' (Ruckenstein & Schüll, 2017: 261; Leonardi & Treem, 2020: 1602). Both automation and datafication open up enormous opportunities for public administration in welfare states. Digital data can potentially deepen knowledge and foster greater efficiency and accessibility of (online) policies. Furthermore, big data, combing various sorts of data, allows the processing of (predictive) profiling and risk scoring and is thereby valuable for designing effective policy interventions for more heterogeneous population groups (see, e.g., Desiere et al., 2018), such as specific training services for a specific group of youth. At the same time, digitalization, automation, and datafication pose serious challenges for welfare governance regarding their impact on policy domains as well as to society. These challenges are further discussed below, since they attract great interest from social policy researchers. As will be shown, technologies can challenge public administrations, by altering both the way that public administration functions as well as how welfare clients interact with administration. Technologies may also strengthen existing inequalities as well as generate new social risks for welfare protection and labour markets.

THEORIZING THE DIGITAL WELFARE STATE

The digitalization of the welfare state attracts significant scholarly attention, yet theoretical reflections on 'digital welfare states' are scarce and the term 'digital welfare state' lacks an explicit discussion of its theoretical foundations. This omission makes it difficult for social policy researchers to evaluate what constitutes a digital welfare state and to what extent welfare states have fundamentally shifted into a new state of being.

Perhaps the most well-known (and used) reference to 'digital welfare states' was provided by United Nations Special Rapporteur for extreme poverty and human rights Philip Alston (2019: 1) in his utterly critical report on the effect of digitalization on society and particularly on vulnerable groups (see, e.g., Dencik & Kaun, 2020; Bekker, 2021). Alston defined digital welfare states as a process where 'systems of social protection and assistance are increasingly driven by digital data and technologies … used to automate, predict, identify, surveil, detect, target and punish'. Without lingering on origins or causes of the digital welfare states, Alston (2019: 1) claims that 'the digital welfare state is either already a reality or is emerging in many countries across the globe'. Van Zoonen (2020) uses a similar process approach to define digital welfare states as a 'transition to data-driven social policy'. Similarly, Dencik and Kaun (2020: 2) have built on Alston's definition as 'a new regime in public services and welfare provision intricately linked to digital infrastructures that results in new forms of control and support'. Also, Pedersen (2019: 301) refers to 'a new model of the provision of public welfare services to citizens'. Neither Pedersen nor Densic and Kaun define what is 'new' in comparison to the 'former' welfare state and both tend to draw a parallel to the development of technological infrastructures and socio-economic development (in a similar fashion as scholars commonly do in Smart City debates, see, e.g., Caragliu et al., 2011). These scholars notably add to this discussion with an explicit outlook towards welfare state tasks, but do little in extending and enriching the welfare state discussion. As commonly done in welfare state studies intersecting economic and social performance, central to this debate is neo-Marxist and critical theory highlighting the linkage between technological advancement and (societal responsibility to safeguarding against) societal harm (e.g., Bär et al., 2020).

The current social policy literature poorly clarifies how welfare states in the digital era have changed. For instance, in terms of a Hallian perspective of change (Hall, 1993), are we witnessing fundamental (i.e., third-order) changes, where digitalization changes the policy paradigm and fundamentally reorients welfare state responses? Or are we witnessing partial developments in certain welfare state institutions, in certain social policy domains, and/or welfare state administration (i.e., second-order change)? Or are we merely witnessing the inclusion of some new welfare state instruments (i.e., first-order change)?

To consider how social policy research on welfare states in the digital era is evolving, this chapter takes a more theoretical approach, returning first to basic theoretical foundations of welfare state research. Although lacking a single definition, welfare states are institutions that protect people's economic and social welfare and wellbeing. In the classic definition given by Therborn (1983), welfare states are state-led institutions servicing the welfare needs of households. Classic scholarship, such as Offe (1984), also claims that welfare states embody an explicit obligation of the state to support citizens with specific needs and risk characteristics. A broader understanding of institutions going beyond the welfare state (see Chapter 1 by Nelson, Nieuwenhuis, and Yerkes, this volume) has given rise to theoretical scholarship on how welfare states (or welfare systems) establish and guarantee social welfare rights and risk protection against the ailments of capitalist market economies (Schubert et al., 2016).

A central concept in this research is the notion of social risks, and the welfare state's collective management of such risks. In the seminal work by Taylor-Gooby (2005), post-war welfare states protected citizens against 'old' social risks, meaning the potential loss of income occurring over a standard industrial life course, e.g., industrial injury, sickness, unemployment, and old age. Welfare state efforts were later extended to cover 'new' social risks arising from post-industrial changes in work and family life, individualized life choices, and also risk rising from globalization (see Chapter 18 by Greve and Paster, this volume; see also Bonoli, 2005; Taylor-Gooby, 2005; Huber & Stephens, 2006). The welfare state and its management of social risks is clearly affected by the technological transformations of the late twentieth and early twenty-first centuries. It creates a need to reorganize and recalibrate welfare state structures and systems to extend social risk protection towards a diverse set of risks, including existing (e.g., changing family structures and labour market participation patterns) and 'new' digitally driven risks (e.g., labour market insecurities induced by platform work and automation). I scrutinize these assumptions below in relation to social policy research on digitalization of the welfare state and welfare state governance as well as digitalization and its impact on specific social policy outcomes.

Digital Welfare Governance

Starting from digitalization of welfare governance and public administration, a key area of social policy research is focused on the impact of technological change on welfare state governance. As argued, digitalization and information and communications technology (ICT) have been an integral part of the modernization of welfare states for decades. For instance, in the Nordic countries, welfare and population management are largely based on administrative databases, which allow standardized, nation-wide assessment of citizens' needs as well as determination of deservingness and just allocation of public resources (Dencik & Kaun, 2020: 2; Larsson & Haldar, 2021). The national register datasets are paramount for 'evidence-based policy', where – in the positivist public administration and social policy research tradition – data are central in assessing and evaluating the impact of public policy and interventions (Crato & Paruolo, 2019). Through datafication and a massive increase of devices connected to the internet, digital technologies produce unprecedented amounts of data. With potential interlinkages to administrative data, the potential of new digital bureaucracies and policy research thus seem endless. Although big data is seen as an opportunity for more accurate and real-time evaluation of social phenomena that social policy researchers are interested in, rising criticism in social policy research is focusing on 'digital governments' who hereby gain technological powers, which enables them to scrutinize and control their citizens. Yeung and Lodge (2018) term this growing reliance on data-driven systems and algorithmic-driven public administration 'new public analytics'. Especially in the field of health, data-driven medical research and public health infrastructures (such as biobanks) allow highly personalized interventions but also undetected surveillance and constant monitoring (Ruckenstein & Schüll, 2017). A similar trend is visible for welfare services, where digitalized processes and machine learning are becoming an integral part of public administration and much scholarly attention is now geared to analysing 'the digital by design' Universal Credit reform, where the United Kingdom's welfare claim and provision was fully automated in 2013 (Millar & Bennett, 2017). Much scholarly attention has also been paid to analysing Denmark, where automated decision-making systems currently process complex tasks, even those requiring in-depth discretion (Henriksen, 2018; Schou & Pors, 2019; Ranerup & Henriksen, 2020). Research shows that although technical systems (are expected) to cut down tedious tasks (Schou & Pors, 2019), they are generally driven by efficiency and budgetary considerations and allow more forceful monitoring and stigmatization. For instance, the British Universal Credit system included 'a fully automated risk' (National Audit Office, 2018: 11). A similar welfare fraud detection system (System Risk Indication) was introduced in the Netherlands. This was recently prohibited by a court decision (https://perma.cc/DS89-K477) on human rights grounds, since it was found to target poor and marginalized neighbourhoods (Bekker, 2021). The high-profile case of automated decision-maker robots (called the robo-debt), used by the Australian government to calculate overpayments and issue debt notices, is another example of what social policy researchers have shown to go wrong with automated decision making (Braithwaite, 2020; Carney, 2020). Cases like this have raised concerns in Europe about machines automating inequalities and currently receive much attention from social policy analysts. United States-based experiences about automation targeting the poor (Eubanks, 2018) and the risks of 'math destruction' inherent in today's algorithmic systems (O'Neil, 2016) have paved the way for increased activism against (un)responsible artificial intelligence also in Europe.

In addition to questions related to human rights, much scholarly work evaluates the effect of digitalization on the nature of public and welfare services. Digital welfare reforms – shifting administrative reorientation – are often fuelled by new public management logics, aiming at improving efficiency and cutting costs (Schou & Hjelholt, 2018). Yet, from a street-level administration's point of view, digitalization may significantly alter existing (human-to-human) work practices by transforming the bureaucracy into 'screen level bureaucracy' (Bovens & Zouridis, 2002) and circumventing human judgement in welfare provision. This may lower the personal biases in decision making (Bullock, 2019), but also blur democratic values such as accountability and transparency (O'Neil, 2016; Eubanks, 2018; Bullock, 2019). Indeed, highly influential scholars see cutting out the human factor from public services as disrupting the very heart of welfare administration (Lipsky, 1980; Simon, 2013). Lipsky's much-quoted claim that 'the nature of service provision calls for human judgement that cannot be programmed and for which machines cannot substitute' (Lipsky, 1980: 161) highlights the view that digitalization is incompatible with some aspects of human-centred work (Hansen et al., 2018; Schou & Pors, 2019; Larsson & Haldar, 2021). The paradox, however, remains that although some public-sector professions, such as social workers drawing on their discretion and holistic understanding of the clients, seem to be ill-suited targets for digitalization, the technological processing is particularly well suited for the public sector, where the workload is high and resources are scarce (Lipsky, 1980).

Challenges to Social Policy Outcomes

The change in governance arising from technological advancements also changes policy outcomes. The digitalization of governance may mean improved targeting of certain benefits and services, and it may solve previously wicked problems, such as the non-take-up of social benefits and the inaccessibility of (online) services. Yet, digitalization can also exclude people based on criteria obfuscated by the black boxes of automated decision making as well as increase the digital divide and digital inequalities in access to, use, and benefits of digital technologies to their users (van Dijk, 2008; Schou & Hjelholt, 2019; Schou & Pors, 2019; Helsper, 2021).

Social policy research has been particularly strong in analysing the challenges arising from technology, in particular in relation to social risks (e.g., how automation transforms and disrupts labour markets and employment). The literature denotes abundant examples of risks relating to technological transformation, including, e.g., the disappearance of routine tasks and higher insecurities among the low skilled (see, e.g., Eichhorst & Rinne, 2017; Thewissen & Rueda, 2019; Lim, 2020). Although more recent forecasts no longer suggest the 'end of work', destruction of jobs or full-fledged human/ machine substitution (Frey & Osborne, 2017), digitalization is believed to cause a creative destruction of jobs and to fundamentally change the nature of work and skills attainment. This is expected to necessitate more effective public policy solutions in education and training policy, social protection, and care policies (see, e.g., Greve, 2019; Palier, 2019; Dermont & Weisstanner, 2020a). Valenduc and Vendramin (2017: 132) recently noted that the relationship between technology and jobs is mediated by various factors, including skills and learning, human resource management social dialogue, as well as economic and social processes of diffusion and adoption of innovations. Some elements of digitalization, such as the rise of platform economies, strengthen labour market precariousness and drive polarization between labour market insiders and outsiders. In a way similar to previous atypical labour forms, platform work may strengthen existing inequalities and magnify social risks (such as workers' exclusion from labour law, social protection, and labour representation) (Drahokoupil & Jepsen, 2017). Platform work can also foster insecurities relating to work and working conditions (Pesole et al., 2018). Some scholars claim that digital labour markets jeopardize the overall functioning of welfare states and labour markets (Degryse, 2016).

These observations have resulted in academic efforts to discuss appropriate welfare state actions in the digital era and the need to renew social protection and social services. Palier (2018: 253–254), for instance, suggests 'a disproportionate increase in resources and security concentrated on one side of modern society, and a growth of low-paid, precariousness and new social risks concentrated on the other'. Palier's observation (see also Palier, 2018; Im et al., 2019; Thewissen & Rueda, 2019) reminds us of the scholarly attention in the early 2000s calling for a rethink of welfare states due to labour market dualism and the recalibration of old institutions into a social investment state (Esping-Andersen & Vandenbrucke, 2002; Ferrera et al., 2007; Jenson, 2010; Hemerijck, 2018). Further scholarly discussions focus on the idea of basic income as a potential answer to technological disruptions in work and income as well as to the problems of social protection of precarious workers and atypical workers (Martinelli, 2019; White, 2019; Dermont & Weisstanner, 2020b).

ROAD MAP TO FUTURE RESEARCH

The welfare state is historically tasked with protecting and investing in people's welfare and wellbeing. In Offe's (1984: 154) words, the welfare state is 'a device, rather than a step in transformation of, capitalist society'. Fundamentally, the welfare states in 2021 still embrace the basic idea of welfare rights and protection. Technological advancements in contemporary societies are great, but the welfare state remains intact. Social policy research shows that differences across Europe remain, but the analysis does not (yet) support the assumption that welfare states have undergone a third-order change (Hall, 1993). As for analysing the nature of welfare states vis-à-vis digitalization, I follow Esping-Andersen by suggesting that it is *not* '*the presence of the battery of typical social programs*' that signifies '*the birth of a welfare state*' (Esping-Andersen, 1989: 20). It is not just the presence of technologies that makes up a digital welfare state. The emerging social policy research discussed in this chapter implicitly suggests that welfare state changes arising from digitalization tend to be 'second-order' changes (Hall, 1993). New institutions such as digital welfare administration (from front-office digitalization to back-office automation) have been introduced and some of these have been 'disruptive', altering the logic of the administration and delivery of social services. Therefore, the digital welfare and automation changes go beyond first-order change.

Regarding policy outcomes, the functioning and legitimacy of welfares are challenged to see to what extent they protect against and mitigate technology-driven risks sustained by the digital era. Again, the empirical evidence remains inconclusive. There is evidence of tech-driven inequalities, such as insecurities in the labour market due to automation. The literature also highlights the inability of existing institutions to safeguard against some of these risks (such as precarious platform workers having no access to social protection). However, to what extent this is fuelled by technology, or other socio-economic factors (globalization, deregulation of labour market) is not clear. Therefore, it is important that the future social policy research agenda gathers and evaluates more empirical evidence of societal and institutional changes caused by technologies and critically analyses its impact on welfare state institutions. This research field remains under-researched, in particular in relation to empirical work. I suggest next some areas and concepts that may prove fruitful for the future research agenda.

A first area of future research should focus on the politics of digitalization. Digital welfare reforms tend to be highly apolitical (Schou & Pors, 2019; see also Löfgren & Sørensen, 2011; Saikkonen & van Gerven, forthcoming), however, these reforms are highly salient and affect the fundamental issues of democratic states, such as equality and legitimacy. Influential research has shown the dangers of automating inequalities on an economy of scale (O'Neil, 2016; Eubanks, 2018). Yet, little empirical work investigates the politics behind digital welfare reforms, the trade-offs making these policies, and the perceived legitimacy of the digital welfare state from a societal perspective (both policy administrators required to use digital systems as well as citizens being subjected to digital reforms). A particularly interesting starting point would be civil society organizations' influence in these areas as they are traditionally important actors in many welfare states. The keynote of Joanna Redden in the ESPAnet 2021 conference, for instance, discussed how these civil society actors draw media attention to digital failures, which can lead to policy change.

A second area needing more research is in welfare administration, for example the impact of digitalization on work for the autonomy and professionalism of welfare administration (Bovens & Zouridis, 2002; Busch & Henriksen, 2018; Bullock, 2019) as well as from the clients' perspective (Hansen et al., 2018; Lindgren et al., 2019). What are the long-term effects of the ICT systems and how multiprofessional organizations construct technology are important areas to understand the long-term effects of digitalization in a broader organizational perspective. Finally, fruitful scholarly advancements can be made by analysing drivers and specific aspects of digital exclusion and interventions against exclusion. Although we know about the risks of exclusion and vulnerabilities in the digital age, we know very little about the mechanisms of digital exclusion and inclusion and how and by whom these can best be mitigated. We also need better empirical evidence of new social risk categories and how technological risks are defined as risks.

CONCLUSION

Coming back to the main puzzle that I started with, what is a digital welfare state and to what extent welfare states have been transformed into new digital welfare states, ample social policy research supports the conclusion that the welfare state's mission to protect citizens against social risks, whether 'old', 'new', or those risks emerging from digitalization, is very much alive. Digitalization can provide useful tools for governing welfare but it also stratifies society and can strengthen marginalization by excluding the vulnerable (Mossberger et al., 2003; Schou & Pors, 2019). In that regard, welfare protection is seen to fall short in many domains. The rapidly growing research agendas around digital exclusion and the existence of a digital underclass (Watling & Rogers, 2012; Helsper & Reisdorf, 2017; Ragnedda, 2020) illustrate stratified inequalities for marginalized groups: old, young, low skilled, migrants, disabled, and work incapacitated.

These research agendas, together with a wide range of social policy scholarship (Greve, 2017; Neufeind et al., 2018; Eichhorst et al., 2020, just to name a few), necessitate a profound rethinking of twenty-first-century welfare states, the impacts of technological change strengthened by the fiscal welfare state, and changing demography and climate change. Emerging social policy research draws inspiration by building on political responses to technological change within the social investment paradigm, encompassing the cross-sectional institutional arenas of the labour market, education policy, and social protection (Hemerijck, 2017; Eichhorst et al., 2020), but also themes of sustainability, city planning, and environmental policies. Technology is part of these discussions and an important research agenda to develop further, but it is not the only challenge welfare states face. We need social policy analysts to engage in the societal, political, and academic debate on the impact of technology on social policy and the welfare state. It is no longer a question of whether technology is a solution for welfare states, but rather *where* technology adds value for welfare and wellbeing and *how* technology should be designed to fight inequality and exclusion.

NOTE

1.   Artificial intelligence in algorithmic technologies imitates human behaviour in applying knowledge in repetitive tasks. Machine learning (or deep learning) is more advanced: it trains algorithms by feeding data to detect patterns or other information. The Internet of Things is a general term for systems of interconnected devices, in a wireless manner, via the internet.

REFERENCES

Alston, P. (2019). *Extreme Poverty and Human Rights.* Ga /74/493, 17564, October, 1–23.   http://statements.unmeetings.org/media2/21999189/sr-extreme-poverty-ga -3rd-cttee-statement-f.pdf
Bär, L., Ossewaarde, M., & van Gerven, M. (2020). The ideological justifications of the Smart City of Hamburg. *Cities, 105,* 102811.
Bekker, S. (2021). Fundamental rights in digital welfare states: The case of SyRI in the Netherlands. In O. Spijkers, W. G. Werner, & R. A. Wessel (Eds), *Netherlands Yearbook of International Law 2019* (Vol. 50, pp. 289–307). T. M. C. Asser Press.
Bonoli, G. (2005). The politics of the new social policies: Providing coverage against new social risks in mature welfare states. *Policy and Politics, 33*(3).
Bovens, M., & Zouridis, S. (2002). From street-level to system-level bureaucracies: How information and communication technology is transforming administrative discretion and constitutional control. *Public Administration Review, 62*(2), 174–184.

Braithwaite, V. (2020). Beyond the bubble that is Robodebt: How governments that lose integrity threaten democracy. *Australian Journal of Social Issues*, *55*(3), 242–259.

Bullock, J. B. (2019). Artificial intelligence, discretion, and bureaucracy. *American Review of Public Administration*, *49*(7), 751–761.

Busch, P. A., & Henriksen, H. Z. (2018). Digital discretion: A systematic literature review of ICT and street-level discretion. *Information Polity*, *23*(1), 3–28.

Caragliu, A., del Bo, C., & Nijkamp, P. (2011). Smart cities in Europe. *Journal of Urban Technology*, *18*(2), 65–82.

Carney, T. (2020). Automation in social security: Implications for merits review? *Australian Journal of Social Issues*, *55*(3), 260–274.

Christensen, C. M. (1997). The innovator's dilemma: When new technologies cause great firms to fail. *Harvard Business Review*. https://doi.org/10.2307/40252749

Crato, N., & Paruolo, P. (Eds). (2019). *Data-Driven Policy Impact Evaluation: How Access to Microdata Is Transforming Policy Design*. Springer.

Damanpour, F., & Aravind, D. (2012). Managerial innovation: Conceptions, processes, and antecedents. *Management and Organization Review*, *8*(2), 423–454.

Degryse, C. (2016). Digitalisation of the economy and its impact on labour markets. ETUI Research Paper, Working Paper 2016.02. European Trade Union Institute. https://doi.org/10.2139/ssrn.2730550

Dencik, L., & Kaun, A. (2020). Datafication and the welfare state. *Global Perspectives*, *1*(1).

Dermont, C., & Weisstanner, D. (2020a). Automation and the future of the welfare state: Basic income as a response to technological change? *Political Research Exchange*, *2*(1).

Dermont, C., & Weisstanner, D. (2020b). Automation and the future of the welfare state: Basic income as a response to technological change? *Political Research Exchange*, *2*(1).

Desiere, S., Langenbucher, K., & Struyven, L. (2018). *Statistical Profiling in Public Employment Services: An International Comparison*. OECD Social, Employment and Migration Working Papers 224. OECD Publishing.

Drahokoupil, J., & Jepsen, M. (2017). The digital economy and its implications for labour, 1: The platform economy. *Transfer*, *23*(2), 103–107.

Eichhorst, W., & Rinne, U. (2017). Digital challenges for the welfare state. *CESifo Forum*, *18*(4), 3–8.

Eichhorst, W., Hemerijck, A., & Scalise, G. (2020). *Welfare States, Labor Markets, Social Investment and the Digital Transformation*. IZA Discussion Paper, 13391. Institute for the Study of Labor. https://papers.ssrn.com/sol3/papers.cfm?abstract_id=3631602

Esping-Andersen, G. (1989). The three political economies of the welfare state. *Canadian Review of Sociology*, *26*(1), 10–36.

Esping-Andersen, G., & Vandenbrucke, F. (2002). *Why We Need a New Welfare State*. Oxford University Press.

Eubanks, V. (2018). *Automating Inequality: How High-Tech Tools Profile, Police, and Punish the Poor*. St. Martin's Press.

Eurofound. (2020). *Impact of Digitalisation on Social Services*. Publications Office of the European Union, Luxembourg. www.eurofound.europa.eu/sites/default/files/ef_publication/field_ef_document/ef19043en.pdf

Ferrera, M., Hemerijck, A., & Rhodes, M. (2007). *The Future of European Welfare States: Recasting Welfare for a New Century*. Oxford University Press.

Frey, C. B., & Osborne, M. A. (2017). The future of employment: How susceptible are jobs to computerisation? *Technological Forecasting and Social Change, 114*, 254–280.

Greve, B. (2017). *Technology and the Future of Work: The Impact on Labour Markets and Welfare States*. Edward Elgar Publishing.

Greve, B. (2019). The digital economy and the future of European welfare states. *International Social Security Review, 72*(3), 79–94.

Hall, P. A. (1993). Policy paradigms, social learning, and the state: The case of economic policymaking in Britain. *Comparative Politics, 25*(3), 275–296.

Hansen, H. T., Lundberg, K., & Syltevik, L. J. (2018). Digitalization, street-level bureaucracy and welfare users' experiences. *Social Policy and Administration, 52*(1), 67–90.

Helsper, E. J. (2021). *The Digital Disconnect: The Social Causes and Consequences of Digital Inequalities*. Sage.

Helsper, E. J., & Reisdorf, B. C. (2017). The emergence of a 'digital underclass' in Great Britain and Sweden: Changing reasons for digital exclusion. *New Media and Society, 19*(8), 1253–1270.

Hemerijck, A. (2017). *The Uses of Social Investment*. Oxford University Press.

Hemerijck, A. (2018). Social investment as a policy paradigm. *Journal of European Public Policy, 25*(6), 810–827.

Henriksen, H. Z. (2018). One step forward and two steps back: E-government policies in practice. In J. Gil-Garcia, T. Pardo, & L. Luna-Reyes (Eds), *Policy Analytics, Modelling, and Informatics: Public Administration and Information Technology* (Vol. 25, pp. 79–97). Springer.

Huber, E., & Stephens, J. D. (2006). Combating old and new risks. In K. Armingeon & G. Bonoli (Eds), *The Politics of Post-Industrial Welfare States: Adapting Post-War Social Policies to New Social Risks* (pp. 143–168). Routlegde.

Im, Z. J., Mayer, N., Palier, B., & Rovny, J. (2019). The 'losers of automation': A reservoir of votes for the radical right? *Research and Politics, 6*(1).

Jenson, J. (2010). Diffusing ideas for after neoliberalism: The social investment in Europe and Latin America. *Global Social Policy, 10*(1), 59–84.

Larsson, K. K., & Haldar, M. (2021). Can computers automate welfare? Norwegian efforts to make welfare policy more effective. *Journal of Extreme Anthropology, 5*(1), 56–77.

Leonardi, P. M., & Treem, J. W. (2020). Behavioral visibility: A new paradigm for organization studies in the age of digitization, digitalization, and datafication. *Organization Studies, 41*(12), 1601–1625.

Lim, S. (2020). Embedding technological transformation: The welfare state and citizen attitudes toward technology. *European Political Science Review, 12*(1), 67–89.

Lindgren, I., Madsen, C. Ø., Hofmann, S., & Melin, U. (2019). Close encounters of the digital kind: A research agenda for the digitalization of public services. *Government Information Quarterly, 36*(3), 427–436.

Lipsky, M. (1980). *Street-Level Bureaucracy: Dilemmas of the Individual in Public Service*. Russell Sage Foundation.

Löfgren, K., & Sørensen, E. (2011). Metagoverning policy networks in eGovernment. In V. Weerakkody, V. (Ed.), *Applied Technology Integration in Governmental Organizations: New E-Government Research* (pp. 298–312). IGI Global.

Martinelli, L. (2019). *Basic Income, Automation, and Labour Market Change*. IPR Report, University of Bath, September. www.bath.ac.uk/publications/basic-income

-automation-and-labour-market-change/attachments/Basic_income-automation -labour-market-change.pdf

Millar, J., & Bennett, F. (2017). Universal credit: Assumptions, contradictions and virtual reality. *Social Policy and Society*, *16*(2), 169–182.

Mossberger, K., Tolbert, C. J., & Stansbury, M. (2003). *Beyond the Digital Divide*. Georgetown University Press.

National Audit Office. (2018). Rolling out Universal Credit. Report by the Comptroller and Auditor General, HC 1123, 15 June. www.nao.org.uk/wp-content/uploads/2018/ 06/Rolling-out-Universal-Credit.pdf

Neufeind, M., O'Reilly, J., & Ranft, F. (2018). *Praise for Work in the Digital Age: Challenges of the Fourth Industrial Revolution*. Foundation for European Progressive Studies.

O'Neil, C. (2016). *Weapons of Math Destruction: How Big Data Increases Inequality and Threatens Democracy*. Crown.

Offe, C. (1984). Some contradictions of the modern welfare state. In C. Offe & J. Keane (Eds), *Contradictions of the Welfare State* (pp. 147–161). Routledge.

Palier, B. (2018). The politics of social risks and social protection in digitalised economies. In M. Neufeind, J. O'Reilly, & F. Ranft (Eds), *Work in the Digital Age* (pp. 1–46). Rowman and Littlefield. https://curis.ku.dk/portal/files/198709895/ Work_in_the_Digital_Age.pdf#page=271

Palier, B. (2019). Work, social protection and the middle classes: What future in the digital age? *International Social Security Review*, *72*(3), 113–133.

Pedersen, J. S. (2019). The digital welfare state: Dataism versus relationshipism. *Big Data*, 301–324.

Pesole, A., Urzì Brancati, M. C., Fernández-Macías, E., Biagi, F., & González Vázquez, I. (2018). *Platform Workers in Europe*. JRC Science For Policy Report, EUR 29275 EN, July. Publications Office of the European Union. https://doi.org/10 .2760/742789

Ragnedda, M. (2020). Traditional digital inequalities: Digital divide. In M. Ragnedda (Ed.), *Enhancing Digital Equity* (pp. 39–60). Springer International.

Ranerup, A., & Henriksen, H. Z. (2020). Digital discretion: Unpacking human and technological agency in automated decision making in Sweden's social services. *Social Science Computer Review*, 1–17.

Ruckenstein, M., & Schüll, N. D. (2017). The datafication of health. *Annual Review of Anthropology*, *46*, 261–278.

Schou, J., & Hjelholt, M. (2018). Digital citizenship and neoliberalization: governing digital citizens in Denmark. *Citizenship Studies*, *22*(5), 507–522.

Schou, J., & Hjelholt, M. (2019). Digitalizing the welfare state: Citizenship discourses in Danish digitalization strategies from 2002 to 2015. *Critical Policy Studies*, *13*(1), 3–22.

Schou, J., & Pors, A. S. (2019). Digital by default? A qualitative study of exclusion in digitalised welfare. *Social Policy and Administration*, *53*(3), 464–477.

Schubert, K., de Villota, P., & Kuhlmann, J. (Eds). (2016). *Challenges to European welfare systems*. Springer.

Simon, H. (2013). *Administrative Behavior*. Simon and Schuster.

Taylor-Gooby, P. (Ed.). (2005). *New Risks, New Welfare: The Transformation of the European Welfare State*. Oxford.

Therborn, G. (1983). *When, How, and Why Does a Welfare State Become a Welfare State?* Sage.

Thewissen, S., & Rueda, D. (2019). Automation and the welfare state: Technological change as a determinant of redistribution preferences. *Comparative Political Studies*, *52*(2), 171–208.

Valenduc, G., & Vendramin, P. (2017). Digitalisation, between disruption and evolution. *Transfer*, *23*(2), 121–134.

van Dijk, J. (2008). The digital divide in Europe. In A. Chadwick & P. Howard (Eds), *The Handbook of Internet Politics*. Routledge.

van Zoonen, L. (2020). Data governance and citizen participation in the digital welfare state. *Data and Policy*, *2*.

Watling, S., & Rogers, J. (2012). *Social Work in a Digital Society*. Sage.

Weber, M. (1968). *Economy and Society: An Outline of Interpretive Sociology*. Bedminister Press.

White, A. (2019). A universal basic income in the superstar (digital) economy. *Ethics and Social Welfare*, *13*(1), 64–78.

Yeung, K., & Lodge, M. (2018). *Algorithmic Regulation*. Oxford University Press.

17. Migrants and social policy: shifting research agendas

Karen N. Breidahl, Troels Fage Hedegaard, and Verena Seibel

INTRODUCTION

New immigration waves gained hold in European countries some 60 years ago. Since then, continuous immigration has increased the ethnic and religious diversity in these countries. These immigration waves reflect a diversity of dynamics, including new opportunities for migrant workers and, not least, how wars and conflicts have displaced an increasing number of people. By the end of 2019, the number reached 79.5 million, meaning approximately 1 per cent of the world's population is displaced according to the United Nations High Commissioner for Refugees. Many of these migrants have looked towards Europe, and around the peak of the 'refugee crisis' in 2015, the total number of annual applications for asylum to the European Union (EU) peaked at over 1.3 million (Eurostat, 2020). Internally, the enlargement of the EU and its common market has caused work-related migration on an unprecedented scale. Among the EU citizens of working age, 3.3 per cent resided in an EU country other than that of their citizenship in 2019 (Eurostat, 2020). Therefore, the topics of migration and social policy are at the top of the political agenda, and many countries have developed policies to deal with this intersection between migration and social policy (Breidahl, 2017; Koning, 2020; Gschwind, 2021).

In this edited volume, social policy is defined as 'an institutionalized response to social and economic problems' (Béland, 2010: 9). Examining social policies in relation to migration and integration therefore raises crucial questions about the rights of migrants within this institutionalized response, the inclusiveness of social protection systems, and how the conditions migrants are facing shape their life conditions (Koning, 2020; Gschwind, 2021). These topics lie at the heart of the social policy discipline as they lay the foundation for migrants' social citizenship, granting entitlement to social rights that guarantee a basic level of socio-economic and cultural wellbeing (Marshall, 1950). These research themes are less concerned about future (worst-case) scenarios and more about how institutionalized social policies influence migrants' formal rights, welfare usage, and attitudes. Consequently, social policy scholars are not only interested in how immigration as a phenomenon influences welfare states and social policies in the future, but also the role that social policies play in migrants' everyday life, wellbeing, life prospects, and attitudes. These topics are of particular concern in a European welfare state context, which is characterized by an elaborate system of redistribution and services in place to mitigate social risks like unemployment, sickness, and old age (Taylor-Gooby, 2004). Before the turn of the century, these questions did not receive much attention among social policy scholars (Sainsbury, 2006). However, migrants' rights to, usage of, and attitudes towards social policies have gained much attention in social policy debates recently, and research findings on these topics have revealed interesting and nuanced insights we wish to highlight.

PRELIMINARY DISCUSSIONS: EXTENSION OR DOWNGRADING OF SOCIAL RIGHTS?

Before going in depth with the current research agenda on the social rights of migrants, we start by providing insights on some of the earliest discussions dating back to the early 1990s. At that time, several important studies showed how a number of European countries became more inclusive in terms of migrants' social rights during the 1970s and 1980s. A citizenship-based model of social protection was weakening, as residence became the main criteria for social rights in many questions (Hammar, 1990). Consequently, social rights became equally available to everyone.

These rather optimistic predictions were followed by studies revealing how a stratification of social rights – between citizens and migrants more broadly – took place during the 1990s and 2000s, despite the weakening of the citizenship-based model (Wenzel & Bös, 1997; Morris, 2002; Andersen, 2007; Breidahl, 2017). These studies provided a new but rather scattered picture of the status of social rights of migrants in Western democracies as they focused on a range of different programmes, including housing policies, labour market policies, education, medical care, etc.

One of the most important preliminary theoretical starting points stems from Sainsbury's 2006 article, which was expanded into a book in 2012. This scholarship has been highly influential in terms of bringing discussions on the social rights of migrants to the front of social policy debates. Among other things, Sainsbury (2006, 2012) argued for the importance of combining insights from comparative welfare state research and international migration literature to fully capture the complex patterns of migrants' social rights. This included a more explicit focus on different categories of migrants (entry categories) as their legal statuses and therefore rights vary considerably across these categories (Söhn, 2013). Asylum seekers and undocumented migrants are the groups that are most vulnerable in terms of social rights. Moreover, newly arrived migrants, most notably refugees, face many additional social rights restrictions compared to other groups (Boucher, 2014; Breidahl, 2017).

THE FORMAL SOCIAL RIGHTS OF MIGRANTS

Fundamentally, the topic of formal social rights of migrants raises the question of the inclusionary capacity of welfare states (Sainsbury, 2006). This research agenda has expanded considerably over the last decades, reflecting how the topic has increasingly entered the political scene. Recently, new indexes have entered the discussion, providing fertile grounds for systematic cross-country comparisons across time and different migrant groups (e.g., Römer, 2017; Koning, 2020). In terms of the current research agenda on formal social rights, three central debates have recently gained prominence.

The first speaks to the debate on the dualization of social policies between 'insiders' and 'outsiders' that has become a prominent topic in the social policy literature (Emmenegger et al., 2012). Following the long line of research on majority welfare chauvinist attitudes, meaning social rights are granted to in-group members only (Sides & Citrin, 2007), it is an intriguing question whether the social rights provided to migrants reflect these attitudes. At the heart of this debate lies the question of the extent to which the social rights of migrants reflect overall institutional logics of different welfare states. For instance, are universal welfare states, which in general are generous towards in-group members, also more generous towards migrants? Or are generous welfare states more likely to exclude migrants from access to welfare benefits due to fiscal pressures and welfare chauvinism (Römer, 2017; Gschwind, 2021)? Basically, this debate has led to two competing hypotheses prominent within social policy research: the so-called 'generosity hypothesis', presuming welfare generosity is positively associated with the social rights of migrants, and the 'dualization hypothesis', presuming that welfare generosity is negatively associated with the social rights of migrants (Römer, 2017).

In a 2017 study based on the Immigration Policies in Comparison index, covering 18 states in the Organisation for Economic Co-operation and Development from 1980 to 2010, Römer mainly finds support for the generosity hypothesis by concluding that 'generous welfare states are more likely to grant immigrants access to welfare benefits, and less generous welfare states are more likely to exclude immigrants from access' (Römer, 2017: 173). These findings are in line with earlier studies (Sainsbury, 2012; Eugster, 2018) pointing to how migrants in generous welfare states tend to have lower poverty risks. Altogether, it is a prominent finding in the social policy literature, showing that migrants generally are more likely to gain access to social benefits in generous welfare states (Schmitt & Teney, 2018). However, studies focusing on specific benefit programmes (e.g., unemployment benefit provision) have also challenged these findings. One example is Gschwind (2021), studying the case of unemployment benefit provision for newly arrived migrants, which points to a *negative* relationship between generosity and social protection. Such findings remind researchers that indexes merging many policy programmes bear the risk of neglecting important nuances within different social policy areas.

The second central topic on the formal social rights of migrants concerns the extent to which welfare states differentiate between migrants and native-born citizens in terms of social rights (Koning, 2020). Despite heterogeneity, migrants face specific barriers due to their migrant status (Lafleur & Vintila, 2020; Gschwind, 2021). Hence, numerous studies point to how welfare states are less inclusive towards different categories of migrants compared to natives – especially when it comes to so-called third-country nationals (Breidahl, 2017; Lafleur & Vintila, 2020). These studies point to specific programmes that are less inclusionary towards these groups, for instance, social assistance programmes, pensions, or unemployment benefits. Can the same pattern be identified when welfare programmes across Western democracies are more broadly considered? This question has recently attracted substantial scholarly attention due to the release of the so-called Immigrant Exclusion from Social Programs Index in 2020. This index pays explicit attention to whether different welfare states differentiate in the benefits provided to migrants compared to native-born citizens. The index relies on a mapping of differentiation in benefit extension across 20 Western welfare states, at four moments in time (1990–2015), based on 25 indicators that span seven different social programmes, including tax-paid pensions, health care, contributory unemployment benefits, contributory pensions, housing benefits, social assistance, and active labour market policy (Koning, 2020). However, in an overview article from 2020, Koning shows that not all Western welfare states have moved in a more exclusionary direction. Rather, the results point to large cross-national differences and striking variation across time, place, and social programmes in the extent to which migrants are excluded from social programmes and services (see also Schmitt & Teney, 2018). Norway and Portugal stand out as the most inclusionary countries, where the differences in social rights between migrants and natives are the smallest. At the other end of the scale, we find countries like the United States and Austria being the most exclusionary.

Third, and not least, the question around the social rights of EU citizens also figures as an important topic. This debate has moved to the centre of political debates in many EU countries (Bauböck, 2019; Seeleib-Kaiser, 2019), reflecting several trends, including the United Kingdom's (UK) Brexit vote, an increase in voters supporting anti-EU populist parties, and how the 'welfare or benefit tourism' debate has entered political decision making. From current research, however, it is difficult to find empirical evidence that intra-EU mobility is driven by widespread 'welfare tourism' (Martinsen & Werner, 2019; Seeleib-Kaiser, 2019). Compared to other migrant categories, migrants from EU countries are privileged in terms of their social rights (Sainsbury, 2012; Koning, 2020), reflecting how EU member states, from the very beginning of European integration, have been obliged to provide the necessary grounds to provide freedom of movement for workers (Hantrais, 2007). This status stems back to the ratification of the Maastricht Treaty whereby 'European Union citizenship has formally become a reality and citizens of European Union Member States are no longer only citizens of the respective Member States, but also "multinational citizens" of the European Union' (Seeleib-Kaiser, 2019).

Despite this formal status, the equal treatment of EU citizens is a contested topic in many EU member states. A number of current studies document how a remarkable stratification of substantial social rights for EU citizens has taken place between different categories of EU citizens (Bruzelius et al., 2017).

WELFARE USAGE AMONG MIGRANTS

As shown above, studies on migrants' formal social rights demonstrate how welfare states differ in the social rights they grant to newcomers. But what do we know about migrants' actual realization of these rights (Söhn, 2013)? To stress the distinction between formal and substantial social rights, Morris (2002) describes the former as 'civic inclusion' and the latter as 'civic gain'. One dominant research topic focuses on the extent to which migrants make more use of welfare benefits and resources than natives, reflecting how the usage of welfare benefits, particularly unemployment benefits and social assistance, is costly. In 2019, the EU spent around 2699 billion euros on social protection schemes, or 19.3 per cent of the EU's gross domestic product. Migrants tend to be overrepresented in these statistics, though usage varies a lot by origin country, which is why migrants are often a group receiving special attention (Breidahl et al., 2021). Moreover, some studies tend to suggest that welfare usage is strongly related to migrants' integration prospects, as non-take-up of social assistance or unemployment benefits (i.e., a significant number of people who are eligible for these welfare benefits do not use them) can contribute to the poverty spiral of certain migrant groups (Lucas et al., 2021). Economists also speak of moral hazard problems, which are typical for welfare states and have specific implications for migrants' integration chances. Following rational choice theory, accessible welfare states might weaken migrants' incentives to take on the costs of integrating into the receiving society. These costs could be time consuming and include difficult tasks like acquiring a new language or adapting to new norms. On the other hand, welfare dependency can be a facilitator of integration as it supports migrants in times of need and enables them to take care of their family, but also pay for language courses, school activities, etc. Concerns about migrants' welfare usage are therefore widespread. Research has extensively studied the extent to which migrants make more use of welfare resources than natives (Brücker et al., 2002; Bruckmeier & Wiemers, 2017; Kornstad & Skjerpen, 2018; Roman, 2019; Yilmaz, 2019; Jakubiak, 2020).

Although sociologists and political scientists have a strong interest in the topic of migration and welfare states, the *interplay* between migration and welfare usage was predominately in the hands of economists until the early 2000s (Boeri et al., 2002; Nannestad, 2007). One of the most prominent theories is the Welfare Magnet Theory, according to which people migrate to countries with the highest levels of welfare (Borjas, 1999). In addition, it has been argued that migration to countries with a well-developed welfare state is predominantly negatively self-selected since generous welfare states reduce earning dispersions in economies, making migration more attractive for low-skilled migrants than for high-skilled migrants. This has led to the assumption that welfare usage should be higher in extended welfare states with high levels of low-skilled migration (Nannestad, 2007).

Whereas Borjas (1999) found that people within the United States tend to move to more generous states, the evidence is more mixed in the European case, likely reflecting how studies vary in terms of the studied time periods, countries, and categories of migrants (Martinsen & Werner, 2019; Ponce, 2019; Agersnap et al., 2020).

A related question in social policy debates concerns whether migrants make more use of the welfare state than natives do. Indeed, in most European countries, the share of migrants receiving unemployment benefits and social assistance is significantly higher than among the native population (Brücker et al., 2002; Jakubiak, 2020). Research conducted in the 1990s and early 2000s explained this ethnic gap mainly with ethnic variation in human capital. In most European countries, migrants are lower educated and less likely to find employment, thereby self-selecting into welfare benefits such as social assistance and unemployment benefits (Brücker et al., 2002). Moreover, the ethnic gap in welfare take-up increased significantly in the early 1990s when several European countries received a significant share of refugees (Riphahn, 1998; Fertig & Schmidt, 2001). However, when looking only at households that are eligible for welfare benefits, the pattern changes: in certain countries such as the UK, Australia, Spain, and most notably in Cyprus, migrants display significantly lower welfare dependency than natives (Giulietti, 2014; Jakubiak, 2020). The literature therefore also speaks of non-take-up of welfare benefits (Bruckmeier & Wiemers, 2017; Dewanckel et al., 2021; Lucas et al., 2021).

Recent political developments, such as Brexit or the 'refugee crisis', have further inspired scholars to look deeper into group characteristics when studying welfare take-up. Yilmaz (2019), for example, looks at the interplay of social policy and the welfare take-up of Syrian refugees in Turkey. Roman (2019) examines the welfare take-up of Eastern European migrants in the UK. The analysis compares migrants from countries belonging to the EU8 enlargement in 2004 (Czech Republic, Estonia, Hungary, Latvia, Lithuania, Poland, Slovakia, Slovenia) to migrants from the EU2 enlargement in 2014 (Bulgaria and Romania). Although different social policies applied to these groups, impacting their labour market chances, Roman (2019) finds no difference between EU8 and EU2 migrants with regards to their welfare behaviour. After establishing the status quo in the early 1990s, follow-up research was interested in whether migrants' welfare dependency changes over time. Whereas research in the late 1990s finds that the longer migrants reside in the host country, the less likely they are dependent on welfare assistance (Brücker et al., 2002), more recent research suggests that this pattern might vary between migrant groups: Kornstad and Skjerpen (2018) also find a decreasing welfare usage over time, however, only for refugees. Labour migrants, on the other hand, are more likely to make use of welfare benefits the longer they stay in the host country. Again, these studies show that welfare behaviour not only depends on the migrant group in question, but also on the context which varies between countries and changes over time.

Altogether, these studies suggest that welfare take-up among migrants is a complex topic and depends on several factors including time, host country, origin country, and several other migrant-specific characteristics such as language skills and education.

MIGRANT ATTITUDES TO AND KNOWLEDGE OF SOCIAL BENEFITS AND THE WELFARE STATE

Studying migrants' attitudes to social benefits and the welfare state is a natural last step after covering formal rights and take-up rates, as this provides insights into how migrants view social benefits and what they know about them. This is a topic that has received increased scholarly attention in recent years. Three streams of research are of particular interest.

The first stream of research focuses on how migrants view the welfare state and aims primarily at testing established theories, such as the self-interest theory on migrant populations, trying to understand what migrants living in Europe think about specific policies or the welfare state in general (Reeskens & van Oorschot, 2015). These studies reflect the significant growth in social policy research around integration and assimilation since the turn of the century (Breidahl, 2017). For instance, several studies are based on the idea that if migrants have different attitudes to what benefits the state should grant to whom and on what basis, then it might challenge the fundamental structure of welfare states (see, e.g., Reeskens & van Oorschot, 2015 for that kind of framing). This is especially relevant in many Western European countries where migrants are becoming a larger part of the population and eventually also the electorate (Eurostat, 2020).

Therefore, studies have looked into general support for the welfare state (Dancygier & Saunders, 2006; Galle & Fleischmann, 2020), the preferred role of government in providing welfare (Reeskens & van Oorschot, 2015; Schmidt-Catran & Careja, 2017; Breidahl et al., 2021), and attitudes towards specific social policies like unemployment, childcare, and health care (Seibel & Hedegaard, 2017; Renema & Lubbers, 2019; Breidahl et al., 2021; Seibel & Renema, 2021). Most of these studies are interested in explaining the differences between migrants and natives in their attitudes towards the welfare state (also see Chapter 13 by van Oorschot, Laenen, Roosma, and Meuleman, this volume). Generally, migrants show greater support for the welfare state than natives do (except for health care; see Seibel & Renema, 2021), which can mainly be explained by their lower socio-economic status. However, migrants' welfare state attitudes converge to the native average over time, supporting the notion that migrants adapt their attitudes to the host country (Breidahl & Larsen, 2016).

The second stream of social policy literature focuses on which social rights migrants think different migrant groups should have. This part of the literature takes its starting point in the debates on 'benefit tourism' or the 'welfare magnet' (Borjas, 1999), referring to the fear that migrants might be attracted by higher levels of benefits in their new receiving countries compared to their origin countries, and therefore be less inclined to work. This debate especially blossomed with the EU enlargements in 2004 and 2007, as it gave the citizens of new Eastern European member countries free movement inside the EU. As migrants are seen to be some of the least deserving of access to social benefits by the majority population (van Oorschot, 2006; Nielsen et al., 2020), this has been argued to lead to welfare chauvinism, suggesting a part of the native population prefers to reserve social benefits for natives, excluding migrants (Andersen, 2007; Bay et al., 2016; see also Chapter 18 by Greve and Paster, this volume). This literature again builds on the current debates within the field, but also turns them on their head by asking whether migrants prefer social benefits for all migrants, or whether they themselves also acquire welfare chauvinistic attitudes.

The general finding is that migrants support what Kremer (2016) calls a 'conditional welfare state' for migrants, where access should depend more on contribution than on need. This is found in studies conducted across Europe, using both qualitative and quantitative methods (Kolbe & Crepaz, 2016;

Degen et al., 2019). The literature further finds that the level of contribution is generally perceived to be high from the migrants' own group, while other migrant groups are viewed as contributing less (Hedegaard & Bekhuis, 2019). Combined, the results thus show that both migrants and natives have, to some degree, what could be described as welfare chauvinistic attitudes, as there seems to be little support for unconditional access.

The third and most recent major debate in the literature concerns what migrants know about social benefits and how to access them. This debate has its roots in welfare domains where migrants, on average, make significantly lower use of welfare benefits than natives, namely health care and childcare (O'Donnell et al., 2007; Migge & Gilmartin, 2011; Seibel, 2019, 2021). One assumption, though hardly tested, is that migrants underuse certain welfare resources because they lack the knowledge to do so (Seibel, 2019, 2021). In addition, one study in the Netherlands also looks at migrants' rights regarding their access to pensions, unemployment benefits, and social assistance and finds that migrants know surprisingly little about these programmes (Renema & Lubbers, 2019). Since migrants' knowledge about their social rights depends very strongly not only on their migrant status but also on the welfare domain, this area of social policy research seems to be more fragmented as the studies focus on different groups of migrants. Some studies focusing on how migrant workers experience the welfare state find that they rarely know much about the welfare state or specific welfare programmes. Instead, knowledge often comes with integration into the host society and changing needs, e.g., losing one's job and needing unemployment benefits or becoming a parent and needing childcare (Seibel, 2019, 2021; De Jong & De Valk, 2020). Yet other studies focusing on asylum seekers find that migrants are quite knowledgeable about welfare programmes, though they are somewhat disappointed about the level of service (O'Donnell et al., 2007; Migge & Gilmartin, 2011). Combined, these studies suggest that future social policy research needs to consider that migrants come from very different countries, have very different socio-economic positions in society, and different legal statuses, in order to assess migrants' knowledge about accessing social benefits adequately.

CONCLUSION AND WAYS FORWARD

The institutional framework of social policies for migrants represents a politically conflicted area filled with inherent dilemmas – competing concerns for the protection of national borders and deterrence on the one hand, and the inclusion of newcomers and ensuring human wellbeing on the other. These concerns are difficult to reconcile. That the social rights of migrants are politically conflicted also reflects the prominence of other key social policy debates on 'benefit tourism' and 'welfare magnets' stating how migration decisions are made based on the relative generosity of the receiving nation's social benefits (Borjas, 1999). As we have shown in this chapter, it is debatable whether this is what motivates migrants. Instead, we have directed attention towards research on migrants' rights to, usage of, and attitudes towards social policies. These areas deserve to be highlighted as they lie at the heart of social policy scholarship on migration and contain a number of interesting and important research insights. Although this research agenda has expanded considerably over the last decades, important questions remain unanswered, which point towards ways of moving social policy research in this area forward.

To start, social policy research is challenged to conclude something definitive about the social rights of migrants, as their social rights differ depending on several factors, including their migration status, the host country, their length of stay, etc. Moreover, the literature measures social rights in different ways and focuses on different welfare programmes. The development of indexes partially tries to solve these issues. However, there seems to be a trade-off between overall standardized indexes that cover a number of social policy areas versus studies that go in depth on specific programmes. Hence, as demonstrated in the empirical findings by Gschwind (2021), the inclusive role of social policy programmes depends on which programmes we are focusing on. Moreover, insights from indexes are not always updated (most indexes end in 2010 and 2015). Therefore, we do not know much about what has happened after the high influx of asylum seekers and refugees from 2015/2016 and onwards. Keeping social policy and migration and integration indexes up to date is thus crucial for future social policy research. Moreover, we are still missing insights into why some migrants refrain from using certain welfare resources, whereas others seem to overuse them. Many studies, mainly conducted by economists, use valuable and extensive data on both the macro and micro levels. These studies, however, often lack an understanding of migrants' own perceptions and rationales behind their decision of whether to make use of certain welfare resources.

Studies of how migrants view the welfare state and social benefits are still in their infancy and there is much work to do in expanding the general understanding in this field. This is especially the case for studies of migrants' knowledge about the welfare state. Another significant scholarly gap is geographical. Most of the studies included here focus on Northern or Western Europe. Therefore, we believe there is much to gain by expanding scholarly attention towards Eastern and Southern Europe, where countries have different migration patterns and attitudes towards migrants are often more sceptical (Senik et al., 2009). Similarly, a more explicit focus on the status of migrants might benefit the social policy research agenda in the future as their rights are influenced by legal status (Sainsbury, 2012). However, more in-depth and nuanced insights on these differences remain absent. Finally, the future social policy research agenda could gain from linking different research areas together, including the extent to which dualization trends within the welfare state might also affect how migrants view the welfare state and their role in it. If the observed dualization trends, more prevalent in some countries than in others, continue to drift apart, how will it affect migrants' views about the welfare state, their national identification, and their role in society in general?

REFERENCES

Agersnap O., Jensen A., & Kleven, H. (2020). The welfare magnet hypothesis: Evidence from an immigrant welfare scheme in Denmark. *American Economic Review: Insights, 2*(4), 527–542.

Andersen, J. G. (2007). Restricting access to social protection for immigrants in the Danish welfare state. *Benefits, 15*(3), 257–269.

Bauböck, R. (2019). Genuine links and useful passports: Evaluating strategic uses of citizenship. *Journal of Ethnic and Migration Studies, 45*(6), 1015–1026.

Bay, A., Finseraas, H., & Pedersen, A. W. (2016). Welfare nationalism and popular support for raising the child allowance: Evidence from a Norwegian survey experiment. *Scandinavian Political Studies, 39*(4), 482–494.

Béland, D. (2010). *What Is Social Policy?* Vol. 1. Polity.

Boeri, T., Hanson, G., & McCormick, B. (2002). *Immigration Policy and the Welfare System: A Report for the Fondazione Rodolfo Debenedetti.* Oxford University Press.

Borjas, G. J. (1999). Immigration and welfare magnets. *Journal of Labor Economics, 17*(4), 607–637.

Boucher, A. (2014). Familialism and migrant welfare policy: Restrictions on social security provisions for newly arrived immigrants. *Policy and Politics, 42*, 367–384.

Breidahl, K. N. (2017). Den danske velfærdsstat og de nye medborgere: Bakker ikke-vestlige indvandrere og efterkommere op om velfærdsstatens centrale værdier. *Politica, 49*(3), 273–291.

Breidahl, K. N., & Larsen, C. A. (2016). The myth of unadaptable gender roles: Attitudes towards women's paid work among immigrants across 30 European countries. *Journal of European Social Policy, 26*(5), 287–301.

Breidahl, K. N., Hedegaard, T. F., Kongshøj, K., & Larsen, C. A. (2021). *Migrant's Attitudes and the Welfare State: The Danish Melting Pot* (1st ed.) Edward Elgar Publishing.

Brücker, H., Epstein, G. S., McCormick, B., Saint-Paul, G., Venturini, A., & Zimmermann, K. F. (2002). Managing migration in the European welfare state. In T. Boeri, G. Hanson, & B. McCormick (Eds), *Immigration Policy and the Welfare System* (pp. 3–168). Oxford University Press.

Bruckmeier, K., & Wiemers, J. (2017). Differences in welfare take-up between immigrants and natives: A microsimulation study. *International Journal of Manpower, 38*(2), 226–241.

Bruzelius, C., Reinprecht, C., & Seeleib-Kaiser, M. (2017). Stratified social rights limiting EU citizenship: Stratified social rights – EU citizenship. *Journal of Common Market Studies, 55*(6), 1239–1253.

Dancygier, R., & Saunders, E. N. (2006). A new electorate? Comparing preferences and partisanship between immigrants and natives. *American Journal of Political Science, 50*(4), 962–981.

De Jong, P. W., & De Valk, H. A. (2020). Intra-European migration decisions and welfare systems: The missing life course link. *Journal of Ethnic and Migration Studies*, *46*(9), 1773–1791.

Degen, D., Kuhn, T., & van der Brug, W. (2019). Granting immigrants access to social benefits? How self-interest influences support for welfare state restrictiveness. *Journal of European Social Policy*, *29*(2), 148–165.

Dewanckel, L., Schiettecat, T., Hermans, K., Roose, R., Van Lancker, W., & Roets, G. (2021). Researching the non-take up of social rights: A social work perspective. *British Journal of Social Work*, 4 June.

Emmenegger, P., Häusermann, S., Palier, B., & Seeleib-Kaiser, M. (Eds). (2012). *The Age of Dualization: The Changing Face of Inequality in Deindustrializing Societies*. Oxford University Press.

Eugster, B. (2018). Immigrants and poverty, and conditionality of immigrants' social rights. *Journal of European Social Policy*, *28*(5), 452–470.

Eurostat. (2020). *Migrant Population Statistics, 2020*. https://ec.europa.eu/eurostat/statistics-explained/index.php?title=Migration_and_migrant_population_statistics

Fertig, M., & Schmidt, C. M. (2001). First- and second-generation migrants in Germany: What do we know and what do people think? SSRN 267223.

Galle, J., & Fleischmann, F. (2020). Ethnic minorities' support for redistribution: The role of national and ethnic identity. *Journal of European Social Policy*, *30*(1), 95–107.

Giulietti, C. (2014). The welfare magnet hypothesis and the welfare take-up of migrants. *IZA World of Labor*, *37*. doi: 10.15185/izawol.37

Gschwind, L. (2021). Generous to workers ≠ generous to all: Implications of European unemployment benefit systems for the social protection of immigrants. *Comparative Political Studies*, *54*(9), 1629–1652.

Hammar, T. (1990). *Democracy and the Nation State: Aliens, Denizens and Citizens in a World of International Migration*. Avebury.

Hantrais, L. (2007). Welfare policy. In C. Hay & A. Menon (Eds), *European Politics* (pp. 292–309). Oxford University Press.

Hedegaard, T. F., & Bekhuis, H. (2019). Who benefits? Perceptions of which migrant groups benefit the most from the welfare state among ten migrant groups in the Netherlands, Denmark, and Germany. *Acta Politica*, *56*(1), 49–68.

Jakubiak, I. (2020). Are migrants overrepresented among individual welfare beneficiaries? *International Migration*, *58*(5), 103–127.

Kolbe, M., & Crepaz, M. M. (2016). The power of citizenship: How immigrant incorporation affects attitudes towards social benefits. *Comparative Politics*, *49*(1), 105–123.

Koning, E. A. (2020). Accommodation and new hurdles: The increasing importance of politics for immigrants' access to social programs. *Social Policy and Administration*, *55*, 815–832.

Kornstad, T., & Skjerpen, T. (2018). Welfare dependency among immigrants to Norway: A panel data study of transfer shares. *Immigration and Development*, 7–30.

Kremer, M. (2016). Earned citizenship: Labour migrants' views on the welfare state. *Journal of Social Policy*, *45*(3), 395–415.

Lafleur, J.-M., & Vintila, D. (2020). *Migration and Social Protection in Europe and Beyond* (Vol. 1). Springer Nature.

Lucas, B., Bonvin, J. M., & Hümbelin, O. (2021). The non-take-up of health and social benefits: What implications for social citizenship? *Swiss Journal of Sociology*, *47*(2), 161–180.

Marshall, T. H. (1950). *Citizenship and Social Class* (Vol. 11). Cambridge University Press.

Martinsen, D. S., & Werner, B. (2019). No welfare magnets: Free movement and cross-border welfare in Germany and Denmark compared. *Journal of European Public Policy*, *26*(5), 637–655.

Migge, B., & Gilmartin, M. (2011). Migrants and healthcare: Investigating patient mobility among migrants in Ireland. *Health and Place*, *17*(5), 1144–1149.

Morris, L. (2002). *Dangerous Classes: The Underclass and Social Citizenship*. Routledge.

Nannestad, P. (2007). Immigration and welfare states: A survey of 15 years of research. *European Journal of Political Economy*, *23*(2), 512–532.

Nielsen, M. H., Frederiksen, M., & Larsen, C. A. (2020). Deservingness put into practice: Constructing the (un)deservingness of migrants in four European countries. *British Journal of Sociology*, *71*(1), 112–126.

O'Donnell, C. A., Higgins, M., Chauhan, R., & Mullen, K. (2007). 'They think we're OK and we know we're not': A qualitative study of asylum seekers' access, knowledge and views to health care in the UK. *BMC Health Services Research*, *7*(1), 1–11.

Ponce, A. (2019). Is welfare a magnet for migration? Examining universal welfare institutions and migration flows. *Social Forces*, *98*(1), 245–278.

Reeskens, T., & van Oorschot, W. (2015). Immigrants' attitudes towards welfare redistribution: An exploration of role of government preferences among immigrants and natives across 18 European welfare states. *European Sociological Review*, *31*(4), 433–445.

Renema, J. A., & Lubbers, M. (2019). Immigrants' support for social spending, self-interest and the role of the group: A comparative study of immigrants in the Netherlands. *International Journal of Social Welfare*, *28*, 179–195.

Riphahn, R. T. (1998). *Immigrant Participation in Social Assistance Programs: Evidence from German Guestworkers*. Centre for Economic Policy Research.

Roman, M. (2019). Work and welfare take-up of enlargement migrants in the United Kingdom. *Applied Economics Letters*, *26*(5), 341–344.

Römer, F. (2017). Generous to all or 'insiders only'? The relationship between welfare state generosity and immigrant welfare rights. *Journal of European Social Policy*, *27*(2), 173–196.

Sainsbury, D. (2006). Immigrants' social rights in comparative perspective: Welfare regimes, forms in immigration and immigration policy regimes. *Journal of European Social Policy*, *16*(3), 229–244.

Sainsbury, D. (2012). *Welfare States and Immigrant Rights: The Politics of Inclusion and Exclusion*. Oxford University Press.

Schmidt-Catran, A. W., & Careja, R. (2017). Institutions, culture and migrants' preference for state-provided welfare: Longitudinal evidence from Germany. *Journal of European Social Policy*, *27*(2), 197–212.

Schmitt, C., & Teney, C. (2018). Access to general social protection for immigrants in advanced democracies. *Journal of European Social Policy*, *29*(1), 44–55.

Seeleib-Kaiser M. (2019). EU citizenship, duties and social rights. In R. Bauböck (Ed.), *Debating European Citizenship*. Springer.

Seibel, V. (2019). Determinants of migrants' knowledge about their healthcare rights. *Health Sociology Review*, *28*(2), 140–161.

Seibel, V. (2021). What do migrants know about their childcare rights? A first exploration in West Germany. *Journal of International Migration and Integration*, *22*(3), 1181–1202.

Seibel, V., & Hedegaard, T. (2017). Migrants' and natives' attitudes to formal childcare in the Netherlands, Denmark and Germany. *Children and Youth Services Review*, *78*, 112–121.

Seibel, V., & Renema, J. A. (2021). Migrants' and natives' attitudes toward public healthcare provision in Denmark, Germany, and the Netherlands. *International Journal of Public Opinion Research*, *33*(1), 118–135.

Senik, C., Stichnoth, H., & Straeten, K. (2009). Immigration and natives' attitudes towards the welfare state: Evidence from the European Social Survey. *Social Indicators Research*, *91*(3), 345–370.

Sides, J., & Citrin, J. (2007). European opinion about immigration: The role of identities, interests and information. *British Journal of Political Science*, *37*(3), 477–504.

Söhn, J. (2013). Unequal welcome and unequal life chances: How the state shapes integration opportunities of immigrants. *European Journal of Sociology*, *54*(2), 295–326.

Taylor-Gooby, P. (2004). *New Risks, New Welfare: The Transformation of the European Welfare State*. Oxford University Press.

van Oorschot, W. (2006). Making the difference in social Europe: Deservingness perceptions among citizens of European welfare states. *Journal of European Social Policy*, *16*(1), 23–42.

Wenzel, U., & Bös, M. (1997). Immigration and the modern welfare state: The case of USA and Germany. *Journal of Ethnic and Migration Studies*, *23*(4), 537–548.

Yilmaz, V. (2019). The emerging welfare mix for Syrian refugees in Turkey: The interplay between humanitarian assistance programmes and the Turkish welfare system. *Journal of Social Policy*, *48*(4), 721–739.

18. Social policy research in times of crisis

Bent Greve and Thomas Paster

INTRODUCTION

Welfare states have historically been argued to be in crisis since at least the oil price changes and their impact on societies in the 1970s (OECD, 1981). During that time, the tide turned against further welfare expansion, driven in part by a critique of the welfare state as being a Leviathan swallowing the market (Hobbes, 1980; Musgrave, 1981) and as a critique of Keynesian demand management, particularly stemming from public choice theory (Niskanen, 1971; Mueller, 1987). In addition, the possibility of a slowdown in productivity growth due to the shift from manufacturing to services, often labelled Baumol's cost disease (Baumol, 1967), heralded the possibility of welfare states becoming financially unsustainable.

Since the 1980s, European welfare states have been exposed to new criticisms related to a number of crises, be they real or perceived: a crisis of financing, a crisis of benefit adequacy, and a crisis of political legitimacy in the face of welfare state criticism (see, for instance, Offe, 1984). Welfare states have also been blamed for contributing to economic and demographic crises: high levels of unemployment, low economic growth, low fertility rates, or deteriorating public finances. During the 1990s, some diagnosed a situation of 'welfare without work', that is, continued high levels of unemployment caused by high levels of wages and payroll taxes (Krugman, 1993; Esping-Andersen, 1996; Scharpf, 2000). Others doubted the capacity of European welfare states to reform, associating European welfare states with 'Eurosclerosis', or likening them to 'immovable objects' or a 'frozen landscape' (Pierson, 1998; Palier & Martin, 2007).

Still, European welfare states have undergone far-reaching changes in response to these diagnoses of crisis, in particular during the last two decades. At the same time, research on the crises of the welfare state has also changed and new themes have emerged that address new perceptions of crisis. While social policy research up to around the 1980s focused on the determinants of welfare state expansion and welfare state typologies, researchers from the 1990s onwards focused increasingly on how welfare states adapted to various old and new challenges, such as globalization, Europeanization, demographic changes, migration, and fiscal pressures.

This chapter discusses how research on welfare state crisis evolved, influenced by empirical developments as well as theoretical innovations. It builds upon the understanding that ideas matter (Béland, 2016). It analyses changes in research and attempts to link these with changes of mainly Western European welfare states since the turn of the millennium. The chapter identifies four research themes that have emerged in this field since the 2000s: new social risks, populism and welfare chauvinism, austerity, and social investment. The first three of these four themes deal with dimensions of welfare state crisis: a crisis of benefit adequacy (new social risks), a crisis of political legitimacy of the welfare state (populism and chauvinism), and a crisis of financing (austerity). In relation to the first crisis, we discuss research related to social risks and the crisis arising in benefit adequacy through increased conditionality.[1] The second crisis, related to political legitimacy, highlights how research on populism and legitimacy can help us understand why changes in social policy have (or have not) occurred, and what direction changes took. To understand the crisis of austerity, the chapter presents basic data on average annual growth rate of expenditures on social protection benefits alongside research on this topic. These expenditure data are at the background of understanding the changes in research, as they have been used by researchers to analyse and show how social policy has changed.

The last theme, social investment, contrasts with the three sections on welfare state crises. It emerged as a proposal for a policy approach intended to overcome crisis by redirecting social spending towards policy measures intended to support productivity and competitiveness, while at the same time strengthening social cohesion. The social investment approach thus offered an ideational tool that appears suitable to overcome the legitimacy crisis of the welfare state as well as economic crises. In the view of its protagonists, social investment would also ameliorate existing fiscal pressures by raising employment.

CRISIS OF BENEFIT ADEQUACY: RESEARCH ON NEW SOCIAL RISKS

Social policy research has focused significantly on the crisis of benefit adequacy in relation to new social risks – that is, social risks that result from societal changes, such as changes in labour markets and family structures that have occurred since the 1980s. To exemplify, they include new and a higher degree of precarious work and single parenthood. New social risks have changed welfare states not only due to a need for new income transfers, but also for new welfare services (especially in relation to children and the elderly). At the same time, citizens are still exposed to old social risks, like sickness or old age, and expect better security provisions by the welfare state also on these risks (OECD, 2018b, 2021).

The stronger role of social policy related to risk was seen as a consequence of globalization, the use of new technology, demographic shifts, as well as weakened trade unions. This was combined with a stronger focus on gender equality and equality in opportunities and how to combine work and family life, and was also argued to have led to strong changes in the structure of the welfare states (Taylor-Gooby, 2013).

The academic debate about new social risks was also a response to the insight that the classical income transfers for old age, occupational disability, sickness, and unemployment were no longer sufficient to cover newly emerging needs for the social protection of citizens, such as needs of single parents, and needs to combine work and family life (e.g., service issues such as childcare), but also the need for reskilling through active labour market policy. These new needs may have shifted spending from those most in need to the middle class, who are also affected by new social risks. This raises the long-standing issue about the position of the middle class for support for welfare states (Brady & Bostic, 2015; Korpi & Palme, 1998), while the middle class is precisely the group that has been squeezed the most in recent years (OECD, 2019).

At the same time, a crisis in benefit adequacy arises because questions around the ability to finance protection against new social risks (in the form of cash benefits and welfare services) can result in stronger means testing and benefit conditionality for old social risks. This might imply a worry among citizens in many countries that living standards will be strongly reduced in case of sickness and unemployment (OECD, 2018b). These concerns around old social risk protection reflect not only a gradual change in the level of benefits, but also the fact that only a minority of jobseekers (less than one in three across countries) has access to unemployment benefits (OECD, 2018a). The rise in the number of solo self-employed and those in precarious employment might entail an even larger number of people without coverage in the future (Greve, 2019; Palier, 2019). Thus, even if new social risks have come on the agenda and influenced social policy development, old social risks remain important; growing inequality and changes in benefit rules have increased the consequences of old social risks and are likely to continue to do so as replacement rates today are often at a lower level than what they were 15–20 years ago.

More recent social policy research on the crisis of benefit adequacy focuses on two aspects: protection for risks related to automation and the need to understand electoral risks related to the crisis of benefit adequacy. First, technological changes, like automation, may reduce the number of jobs in some occupations and thereby may require new social policy measures for those either unemployed or those who left the labour market (Frey & Osborne, 2013; Arntz et al., 2016, 2017). Further, and clearly related to this change, is the issue of what social protection is needed for those outside the labour market for shorter or longer periods of time, including life-long learning. Second, research on voter preferences points towards electoral competition, inducing a spending trade-off between new and old social risks. Studies find that leftist parties are more supportive of social investment policies, which may help to address new social risks, as we discuss below (Abou-Chadi & Immergut, 2019). Still, social investment spending could be an electoral risk as many voters continue to support spending on old social risks. For example, voters consistently see pension spending for retired workers to be legitimate. Reducing pension spending has therefore not been central, and even in liberal welfare states, previous pension policies have been reversed (Bridgen, 2019, 2021).

A CRISIS OF LEGITIMACY? RESEARCH ON WELFARE POPULISM AND CHAUVINISM

Voter support is important for the sustainability of welfare states, an issue that has generated a new strand of research that focuses on the perceived political legitimacy of welfare state programmes. This research on political legitimacy includes studies on changes in welfare attitudes in general (see also Chapter 13 by van Oorschot, Laenen, Roosma, and Meuleman, this volume) as well as studies on the policy positions of populist parties, including welfare populism and chauvinism.

Overall, attitudinal research shows support for the elderly and health care, but less so for the unemployed, and, especially less so for migrants (Meuleman et al., 2018, 2020). Arguments that scroungers take our jobs, benefit recipients are lazy, etc. have long influenced the debate on the role of social policy (Greve, 2020b). Even though there is no clear indication that austerity has been the main development in most European welfare states (Greve, 2020a), as discussed next, chauvinism and changed legitimacy might be a reason why the diversification and changes of social policy have taken place. Welfare chauvinism can be one reason for stronger benefit conditionality for old social risks (alongside the need to finance the costs of new social risks, as discussed in the previous section).

As research in this area suggests, welfare populism and welfare chauvinism are not clear and precise concepts. Still, we know there is a long history of populist traits in welfare state decision making, perhaps most famously linked to the argument of the impact of the median voter (Downs, 1957; Romer &

Rosenthal, 1979). This early research suggests that if support for populist parties increases, this leads other parties to move closer to the viewpoints of populist parties. It is also linked to the issue of who deserves what benefits, which influenced and even paved the way for a new research field on benefit conditionality (Watts & Fitzpatrick, 2018). Research further shows that voters might be negative towards specific benefits (such as social assistance) even without having a clear idea about benefit levels (Geiger, 2017, 2018). Populists might use this lack of knowledge by voters to cut back benefit levels.

Populism can be witnessed in the form of a stronger focus on the condition-ality of benefits (Sacchi & Roh, 2016; Watts & Fitzpatrick, 2018; McGann et al., 2019). Researchers characterize populism as a thin-centred ideology, which stipulates an antagonism between two social groups – the people and the elite (Mudde & Kaltwasser, 2017), and also between those seen as having legitimate social policy demands and those who do not. This understanding of who has legitimate needs is then used by populists to try to change social policy towards those perceived to be legitimate recipients. Debates like these centred on the legitimacy of the welfare state are not new. Historically, in the 1970s, legitimacy was related to the ability to finance the welfare state and concerns that the growth of the public sector had been too strong (Offe, 1984; Klein, 1993). However, the combination of welfare chauvinism and challenged legit-imacy has implied a stronger focus on who should get what and under what conditions as there appears to mainly be support for benefits and services to nationals, as supported by populists, and less support for benefits and services to non-nationals (Ennser-Jedenastik, 2018; Ejrnæs & Greve, 2019).

The focus of policy on reducing social spending in combination with higher levels of migration also fuelled a debate on who should be given benefits, leading to further research in the area. Subsequently, research focuses on what was once labelled welfare tourism, especially related to the free movement of workers within the European Union (EU) (Wasserfallen, 2010; Mantu & Minderhoud, 2016), but also migrants coming to Europe from countries outside the EU. The free movement of workers and increase in migrants has been part of the analysis on welfare chauvinism as an indicator for how countries and debates tried to restrict the use of benefits primarily to natives. This research further shows that in many European countries, we see a trend of targeting social services and benefits towards citizens of the nation state, who are seen to be deserving of support, and of excluding migrants, who are often seen as undeserving. Deservingness is not a new social policy topic but might have changed with respect to the understanding of the legitimacy of the welfare state.

These populist and welfare chauvinistic elements combined with popular voter support for more spending on long-term care, pensions, and health care imply pressure on the political system, related to the legitimacy debate

(Roosma et al., 2016; Ferrera, 2017). At the same time, citizens are not willing to pay more in taxes, and there is a perception that many people receive benefits that they do not deserve (OECD, 2018b, 2021). Recent data from the Organisation for Economic Co-operation and Development (OECD) (2021) confirms the existence of such cleavages in voter preferences on social policy. These data also suggest that variations in the legitimacy across social policy fields might influence the development of social policy in welfare states, with no support for increasing taxes to improve unemployment or pension benefits, except among men in Lithuania. This absence of support for increased taxation might further reflect that many citizens feel that people receive benefits they do not deserve, although it is not clear which benefits people do not deserve. Future research aimed at understanding the crisis of legitimacy can use these data as a starting point. For example, is it the case that these OECD data are an indicator of non-deservingness? If so, this would suggest it is more likely that populist parties can gain voters by supporting lower social protection in certain areas, but also that there might be better options for support if arguing for higher levels of economic resources for areas such as long-term care, pensions, and health care. Moreover, these data suggest a potential link to be studied between the crisis of legitimacy and the crisis of financing, with attention for differing policy programmes as a way of explaining why research on austerity comes to different conclusions, an issue we now turn to next.

AUSTERITY: A CRISIS OF FINANCING?

In addition to new social risks, populism, and welfare chauvinism, fiscal sustainability poses a challenge to welfare states. Policymakers during the 1980s and 1990s considered the size of the welfare state to be part of the problem, not part of the solution to crises. However, the financial crisis in 2007–2009 and the COVID-19 crisis in 2020–2021 illustrated the need for social policy for crisis management. These two crises have also shown variation in how social policies function as mitigators of economic crises. The response to these two crises illustrates fundamentally different approaches across countries, variation which is evident in research on social policy.[2] Following the global financial crisis and a short period of demand stabilization, several countries (but not all) focused on reducing public spending. Following COVID-19, there has been a greater focus on investment and various forms of financial income support for people affected by the crisis, although it is too early to assess any long-term policy consequences of the increase in spending.

Fiscal sustainability can thus be seen as a recurring crisis of the welfare state, leading to a rich scholarly literature. In particular, criticism of the role of the welfare states arising after the oil price crisis, as well as in the wake of the global financial crisis in 2007–2009, has led to research on austerity and its impact on welfare state development. Understood as a reduction in financial resources available for social policy purposes (Greve, 2020a, 2021), the main focus of austerity studies is on the austerity measures that have reduced the level of spending on social policy, including as a core issue the role of generous benefits and the impact on incentives to work (Starke, 2006; Petmesidou, 2013; Matsaganis & Leventi, 2014; Papadopoulos & Roumpakis, 2018). The changes in social policy in the wake of COVID-19 may look slightly different, although this is too early to say.

Some argue that austerity is permanent (Pierson, 1994, 2001); or that it is part of a neoliberal project of reducing the size of the welfare state (Blyth, 2013). Despite policy cutbacks, research does not suggest austerity is everywhere, even though benefit and service reductions did happen in some policy areas in some countries. Additionally, some research suggested welfare state pressures such as globalization, demographic challenges, and fiscal crisis would lead to a race to the bottom, albeit, as Castles points out, 'evidence is now beginning to emerge, with neither the "race to the bottom" predicted by the globophobes nor the expenditure blowout predicted by the gerontophobes apparently taking place on anything like the scale assumed by the crisis scenarios' (Castles, 2004: 7). At the same time, opposition by policymakers resisting change is seen by other researchers as hindering welfare state reforms following the global financial crisis (Diamond & Lodge, 2013).

A crucial research question underlying austerity practices is whether austerity reflects a crisis of welfare state financing. Research suggests that when looking at what is financially available for social policy purposes, the overall picture is that more money is available in constant prices, also when taking into consideration the change in the size of the population. The same picture can be found in most European countries, and in most sub-sections of the welfare state and in most countries since 2000 (Greve, 2020a). Researchers often have difficulty obtaining an accurate picture of what is available for welfare state purposes when relying on percentages of gross domestic product (GDP), as these percentages are not only influenced by the level of money available, but also changes in GDP, a classical dependent variable problem in social policy research (Clasen & Siegel, 2007). At the same time, GDP data indicate whether spending over time within a policy field has followed the general increase in spending available for welfare state purposes as a proportion of a society's wealth. If benefits lag behind GDP growth, benefit recipients might have a sense of relative deprivation compared to average citizens (Runciman, 1966).

Table 18.1   *Average annual growth rate of expenditure on social*
protection benefits in EU27, 2009–2018 (%)

All functions	Old age and survivors	Sickness/health	Disability
1.2	1.5	1.2	1.3
Family/children	Unemployment	Housing/soc. excl.	
1.3	-2.9	2.8	

Note: Based on 2010 prices.
Source: Average annual growth rate of expenditure on social protection benefits, 2009–2018,
Statistics Explained, www.europa.eu.

Research further demonstrates that austerity can take place in more indirect ways as well. A gradual relative reduction in benefits is what has been labelled 'welfare reform by stealth', as decision makers can do this to make such decisions less visible. For example, even if benefits keep their real value, the level compared to the change in median income implies a relative reduction if labour market incomes rise in real terms (Jensen et al., 2018; Otto & van Oorschot, 2019). Naturally, even if the same amount of money is available, there might be change within different parts of the welfare state regarding conditions, eligibility, and the size of individual benefits, depending, for example, on the viewpoint related to who is seen as deserving. Still, as will be discussed more below, there is still no strong support for a hypothesis of retrenchment even when looking into minimum benefit, strictness of activation requirements, or an increase in spending on means-tested benefits (Greve, 2020a).

Future research might therefore also investigate whether spending in specific fields of social policy has developed differently. An initial look at European data (see Table 18.1) indicates that spending on housing and social exclusion have seen the highest increase, albeit still limited compared to other policy fields. In accordance with a populist and chauvinistic approach (see above), there has been an increase in spending on old age and survivors' benefits as the groups targeted by these policies are seen as legitimate and deserving, which naturally is influenced by demographic developments, although this is not the only explanation (Greve, 2020a). Further research would do well to focus on the various mechanisms behind this ambiguity in austerity, for example by comparing and contrasting interrelated policy fields.

While research on austerity and welfare retrenchment comes to different conclusions depending on which country or social policy field is under consideration, we do not observe an overall reduction of welfare spending in Europe since the turn of the millennium. With the exception of Central and Eastern Europe, minimum benefits have not declined relative to median incomes. This is puzzling given the ongoing changes towards a stronger focus in many countries and thus needs further reflection and research.

SOCIAL INVESTMENTS: AN APPROACH TO OVERCOME CRISIS?

Several response strategies to the multiple crises of the welfare state are available, including, in particular, the retrenchment of social benefits or maintenance of the status quo. Some welfare state researchers advocate for what is called social investment as a way to overcome crisis and cope with new social risks. Social investments are social policy measures that promise a future return in the form of a better-skilled work force and higher labour productivity as a result of enhanced skills. Institutional childcare, preventative health care, education and training, and active labour market policy are policies that follow this logic. Social investments are a key component of the EU's Lisbon Strategy and its successor, the Europe 2020 strategy, which are broad reform agendas for promoting growth, jobs, and social cohesion by way of voluntary coordination of member state social and economic reform plans. Protagonists of the social investment approach advocate a redesign of the architecture of the welfare state with the purpose of using welfare policies as tools to enhance labour productivity and skills development over the life course (Nolan 2013; Smyth & Deeming, 2016; Midgley et al., 2017).

Given limited fiscal resources, a strengthening of social investments will often require a shift of spending away from cash benefit programmes, and thus a restructuring of spending programmes, rather than an expansion of overall public social spending. Further, changes in social risks, often labelled new social risks (see above), have been central concepts in social policy research and part of the argument for social investment of the welfare state (Taylor-Gooby, 2013). Extant studies show, however, that outside of the Nordic countries, the shift of social spending to social investments has so far been patchy. A study by Ronchi (2018) on changes in spending on multiple types of social policy in 27 EU countries finds that spending on social investments expanded in many EU countries in the period 2000–2008, but that expansion came to a halt with the onset of the Great Recession in 2008. At the same time, Southern European and Central and Eastern European welfare states are particularly lagging behind in terms of social investment spending (Ronchi, 2018; Bengtsson et al., 2017).

Further analysis relying on quantitative and qualitative data for eight EU countries for the period 2004 to 2013 finds little evidence of an increased social investment orientation in active labour market policies. Spending on upskilling did not increase during the period studied, while work incentives were reinforced, and spending on job placement assistance, which is not about enhancing skills but about marketing skills, accounted for the largest spending item in active labour market policy in all eight countries (Bengtsson et al.,

2017). Overall, the implementation of social investment is uneven across European welfare states, with Nordic countries in the lead and Southern and Central and Eastern European countries lagging behind.

Alongside the uneven implementation of social investment, we can question whether the Keynesian-style interventions developed during the COVID-19 crisis in many countries will continue to be accepted social policy interventions. However, the change within the EU of establishing investment and loan facilities, with most having stronger pressure on social policy spending,[3] might at least be seen as an indication of a higher focus on social investment, and what can be labelled a Hamiltonian solution (Feás, 2021). Thus the COVID-19 crisis might imply a change towards a greater role for social policy, whereas the result of previous crises was often cost containment and benefit cuts. It therefore remains an empirical issue for future social policy research whether social investment is an approach to overcome crisis as well as what the impact of these investments are on the structure and focus of social policy. This empirical issue arises alongside more conceptual questions, such as those raised in other chapters (see, for instance, Chapter 2 by Daly and León, this volume).

CONCLUSIONS

Since the 1990s, European social policy research has shifted from a focus on welfare state expansion to a focus on the welfare state in crisis. New social risks, austerity, and populism/welfare chauvinism have emerged as new research fields dealing with developments that challenge existing social policies, while the social investment approach has emerged as a new ideational paradigm intended to reframe social policy as being part of the solution to crisis rather than part of the problem.

Research on social policy reforms has shown that crisis developments did not result in a general dismantling of social policies, but rather an adaptation and reorientation of social programmes to address the challenges of new social risks, fiscal constraints, and populism and welfare chauvinism. Research and data do not lend support to the thesis of general retrenchment in welfare states in Europe, neither do they lend support to a thesis of permanent austerity, understood as a decline in social spending. However, they do show that spending priorities have changed, and sub-sections of the welfare state have seen reduced levels of available resources. Social policy developments during the last two decades are characterized by a combination of increases in real spending, with no overall movement towards stricter activation requirements, more means testing, or lower minimum benefits, combined with a sustained high level of spending. At the same time, populism, welfare chauvinism, and a restriction of spending towards natives has also taken place. Still, the ability of welfare states to cope with poverty and inequality has been dealt with only in a limited way given the continuous low level of minimum income benefits. At the same time, the strictness of activation requirements does not show a uniform type of development across Europe. Thus, inequality and poverty will remain important aspects of social policy research in the years to come.

Research highlighted in this chapter shows that welfare states are undergoing a continuous flux of changes. At the same time, there is stability in spending and, in some countries, even continued expansion as societies become richer, with societies being nevertheless unable to cover and fulfil all the expectations that citizens have. Social policy will still be an important element for ensuring social inclusion, and to help in sustaining social cohesion. Pressures on the future of the welfare state are thus still there, and more research is needed in order to understand and interpret these developments. Future research should focus on how and to what degree a reorientation of social policy towards social investments will take place. At the same time, new challenges, such as automation and digitalization of work, will create new social risks once again, and require further adaptation of social policies, for instance to facilitate the transition of individuals to new types of work and to ensure adequate coverage of the solo self-employed and of gig workers in the platform economy. Future research on the welfare state will need to investigate the role of social programmes in managing and mitigating these challenges.

NOTES

1. A variety of types of conditionality exist: Clasen and Clegg define category, circumstances, and conduct as the main ones (2007). Category refers to whether benefits are based on the principle of social assistance or insurance, circumstances to why individuals have a need, and conduct to the behaviour required by benefit recipients when receiving the benefit.
2. See, for example, multiple articles in the special issue of *Social Policy and Administration*, 55(2), Special Issue: Social Policy in the Face of a Global Pandemic: Policy Responses to the COVID-19 Crisis.
3. See Recovery and Resilience Facility, European Commission, www.europa.eu.

REFERENCES

Abou-Chadi, T., & Immergut, E. M. (2019). Recalibrating social protection: Electoral competition and the new partisan politics of the welfare state. *European Journal of Political Research*, 58(2), 697–719.

Arntz, M., Gregory, T., & Zierahn, U. (2016). *The Risk of Automation for Jobs in OECD Countries: A Comparative Analysis*. OECD Publishing.

Arntz, M., Gregory, T., & Zierahn, U. (2017). Revisiting the risk of automation. *Economics Letters*, 159(C), 157–160.

Baumol, W. J. (1967). Macroeconomics of unbalanced growth: The anatomy of urban crisis. *American Economic Review*, 57(3), 415–426.

Béland, D. (2016). Ideas and institutions in social policy research. *Social Policy and Administration, 50*(6), 734–750.

Bengtsson, M., De la Porte, C., & Jacobsson, K. (2017). Labour market policy under conditions of permanent austerity: Any sign of social investment? *Social Policy and Administration, 51*(2), 367–388.

Blyth, M. (2013). *Austerity: The History of a Dangerous Idea*. Oxford University Press.

Brady, D., & Bostic, A. (2015). Paradoxes of social policy: Welfare transfers, relative poverty, and redistribution preferences. *American Sociological Review, 10*(2), 268–298.

Bridgen, P. (2019). The retrenchment of public pension provision in the liberal world of welfare during the age of austerity – and its unexpected reversal, 1980–2017. *Social Policy and Administration, 53*(1), 16–33.

Bridgen, P. (2021). Have pensioners been protected during the age of permanent austerity? Evidence from needs-based expenditure and net replacement rate data, 1980–2015. In B. Greve (Ed.), *Research Handbook of Austerity and Retrenchment*. Edward Elgar Publishing.

Castles, F. G. (2004). *The Future of the Welfare State: Crisis Myths and Crisis Realities*. Oxford University Press.

Clasen, J., & Clegg D. (2007). Levels and levers of conditionality: Measuring change within welfare states. In J. Clase & N. A. Siegel (Eds), *Investigating Welfare State Change: The 'Dependent Variable Problem' in Comparative Analysis* (pp. 166–197). Edward Elgar Publishing.

Clasen, J., & Siegel N. A. (2007). Comparative welfare state analysis and the 'dependent variable problem'. In J. Clase & N. A. Siegel (Eds), *Investigating Welfare State Change: The 'Dependent Variable Problem' in Comparative Analysis*. Edward Elgar Publishing.

Diamond, P., & Lodge, G. (2013). European welfare states after the crisis: Changing public attitudes . Policy Network Paper, Policy Network.

Downs, A. (1957). An economic theory of political action in a democracy. *Journal of Political Economy, 65*(2), 135–150.

Ejrnæs, A., & Greve, B. (2019). Populism, welfare chauvinism and hostility towards immigrants. In B. Greve (Ed.), *Welfare, Populism and Welfare Chauvinism* (pp. 137–152). Policy Press.

Ennser-Jedenastik, L. (2018). Welfare chauvinism in populist radical right platforms: The role of redistributive justice principles. *Social Policy and Administration, 52*(1), 293–314.

Esping-Andersen, G. (1996). Welfare states without work: The impasse of labour shedding and familialism in continental European social policy. In G. Esping-Andersen (Ed.), *Welfare States in Transition: National Adaptations in Global Economies* (pp. 66–87). Sage.

Feás, E. (2021). The state of fiscal union in the Euro zone: Are we closer to a 'Hamiltonian' moment. *The Euro In*, 219–238.

Ferrera, M. (2017). The Stein Rokkan Lecture 2016, mission impossible? Reconciling economic and social Europe after the euro crisis and Brexit. *European Journal of Political Research, 56*(1), 3–22.

Frey, C., & Osborne, M. (2013). *The Future of Employment: How Susceptible Are Jobs to Computerisation?* Oxford University Press.

Geiger, B. B. (2017). False beliefs and the perceived deservingness of social security benefit claimants. In W. van Oorschot, F. Roosma, B. Meuleman, & T.

Reeskens (Eds), *The Social Legitimacy of Targeted Welfare: Attitudes to Welfare Deservingness* (pp. 73–92). Edward Elgar Publishing.

Geiger, B. B. (2018). Benefit 'myths'? The accuracy and inaccuracy of public beliefs about the benefits system. *Social Policy and Administration, 52*(5), 998–1018.

Greve, B. (2019). The digital economy and the future of European welfare states. *International Social Security Review, 72*(3).

Greve, B. (2020a). *Austerity, Retrenchment and the Welfare State: Truth of Fiction?* Edward Elgar Publishing.

Greve, B. (2020b). *Myths, Narratives and Welfare States*. Edward Elgar Publishing.

Greve, B. (2021). *Research Handbook of Austerity, Retrenchment and Populism*. Edward Elgar Publishing.

Hobbes, T. (1980). *Leviathan*. Penguin.

Jensen, C., Arndt, C., Lee, S., & Wenzelburger, G. (2018). Policy instruments and welfare state reform. *Journal of European Social Policy, 28*(2), 161–176.

Klein, R. (1993). 'O'Goffe's tale'. In C. Jones Finer (Ed.), *New Perspectives on the Welfare State in Europe* (pp. 14–23). Routledge.

Korpi, W., & Palme, J. (1998). The paradox of redistribution and strategies of equality: Welfare state institutions, inequality, and poverty in the Western countries. *American Sociological Review, 63*(5), 661.

Krugman, P. (1993). *Inequality and the Political Economy of Eurosclerosis*. CEPR Discussion Papers.

Mantu, S., & Minderhoud, P. (2016). Exploring the limits of social solidarity: Welfare tourism and EU citizenship, *Revista Lusófona de Estudos Culturais, 2*, 4–19.

Matsaganis, M., & Leventi, C. (2014). The distributional impact of austerity and the recession in Southern Europe. *South European Society and Politics, 19*(3), 393–412.

McGann, M., Nguyen, P., & Considine, M. (2019). Welfare conditionality and blaming the unemployed. *Administration and Society, 53*(3), 466–494.

Meuleman, B., van Oorschot, W., Gugushvili, D., Baute, S., Delespaul, S., Laenen, T., Roosma, F., & Rossetti, F. (2018). *The Past, Present and Future of European Welfare Attitudes: Topline Results from Round 8 of the European Social Survey*. European Social Survey.

Meuleman, B., van Oorschot, W., & Laenen, T. (2020). Welfare attitudes in times of crisis and austerity. In T. Laenen, B. Meuleman, & W van Oorschot (Eds), *Welfare State Legitimacy in Times of Crisis and Austerity* (pp. 3–22). Edward Elgar Publishing.

Midgley, J., Dahl, E., & Wright, A. (Eds). (2017). *Social Investment and Social Welfare: International and Critical Perspectives*. Edward Elgar Publishing.

Mudde, C., & Kaltwasser, C. R. (2017). *Populism: A Very Short Introduction*. Oxford University Press.

Mueller, D. C. (1987). The growth of government: A public choice perspective. *Staff Papers, 34*(1), 115–149.

Musgrave, R. (1981). 'Leviathan cometh – or does he?' In H. Ladd & N. Tideman (Eds), *Tax and Expenditure Limitations*. Urban Institute.

Niskanen, W., Jr. (1971). *Bureaucracy and Representative Government*. Aldine-Atherton.

Nolan, B. (2013). What use is 'social investment'? *Journal of European Social Policy, 23*(5), 459–468.

OECD. (1981). *The Welfare State in Crisis*. OECD Publishing.

OECD. (2018a). *OECD Employment Outlook 2018*. OECD Publishing.

OECD. (2018b). *Risks That Matter.* OECD Publishing. www.oecd.org/social/risks-that-matter.htm%0D

OECD. (2019). *Under Pressure: The Squeezed Middle Class.* OECD Publishing.

OECD. (2021). *Main Findings from the 2020 Risks That Matter Survey.* OECD Publishing. https://doi.org/https://doi.org/https://doi.org/10.1787/b9e85cf5-en

Offe, C. (1984). *Contradictions of the Welfare State.* Routledge.

Otto, A., & van Oorschot, W. (2019). Welfare reform by stealth? Cash benefit recipiency data and its additional value to the understanding of welfare state change in Europe. *Journal of European Social Policy, 29*(3), 307–324.

Palier, B. (2019). Work, social protection and the middle classes: What future in the digital age? *International Social Security Review, 72*(3), 113–133.

Palier, B., & Martin, C. (2007). Editorial introduction: From 'a frozen landscape' to structural reforms: The sequential transformation of Bismarckian welfare systems. *Social Policy and Administration, 41*(6), 535–554.

Papadopoulos, T., & Roumpakis, A. (2018). Rattling Europe's ordoliberal 'iron cage': The contestation of austerity in Southern Europe. *Critical Social Policy, 38*(3), 505–526.

Petmesidou, M. (2013). Is social protection in Greece at a crossroads? *European Societies, 15*(4), 597–616.

Pierson, P. (1994). *Dismantling the Welfare State? Reagan, Thatcher and the Politics of Retrenchment.* Cambridge University Press.

Pierson, P. (1998). Irresistible forces, immovable objects: Post-industrial welfare states confront permanent austerity. *Journal of European Public Policy, 5*(4), 539–560.

Pierson, P. (2001). Coping with permanent austerity: Welfare state restructuring in affluent democracies. In P. Pierson (Ed.), *The New Politics of the Welfare State.* https://doi.org/10.1109/TELSKS.2011.6143211

Romer, T., & Rosenthal, H. (1979). The elusive median voter. *Journal of Public Economics, 12*(2), 143–170.

Ronchi, S. (2018). Which roads (if any) to social investment? The recalibration of EU welfare states at the crisis crossroads (2000–2014). *Journal of Social Policy, 47*(3), 459–478.

Roosma, F., Van Oorschot, W., & Gelissen, J. (2016). A just distribution of burdens? Attitudes toward the social distribution of taxes in 26 welfare states. *International Journal of Public Opinion Research, 28*(3), 376–400.

Runciman, W. G. (1966). *Relative Deprivation and Social Justice: a Study of Attitudes to Social Inequality in 20th Century England.* University of California Press.

Sacchi, S., & Roh, J. (2016). Conditionality, austerity and welfare: Financial crisis and its impact on welfare in Italy and Korea. *Journal of European Social Policy, 26*(4), 358–373.

Scharpf, F. W. (2000). Economic changes, vulnerabilities, and institutional capabilities. *Welfare and Work in the Open Economy, 1*, 21–124.

Smyth, P., & Deeming, C. (2016). The 'social investment perspective' in social policy: A longue durée perspective. *Social Policy and Administration, 50*(6), 673–690.

Starke, P. (2006). The politics of welfare state retrenchment: A literature review. *Social Policy and Administration, 40*(1), 104–120.

Taylor-Gooby, P. (2013). The double crisis of the welfare state. In P. Taylor-Gooby (Ed.), *The Double Crisis of the Welfare State and What We Can Do about It* (pp. 1–25). Springer.

Wasserfallen, F. (2010). The judiciary as legislator? How the European Court of Justice shapes policy-making in the European Union. *Journal of European Public Policy*, *17*(8), 1128–1146.

Watts, B., & Fitzpatrick, S. (2018). *Welfare Conditionality*. Routledge.

19. Where to from here? Social policy research in future European societies

Kenneth Nelson, Rense Nieuwenhuis, and Mara A. Yerkes

INTRODUCTION

The purpose of this edited volume, as set out in the introduction, was to take stock of major developments in social policy research from the last two decades and set a research agenda for the future. Three research questions were central to this stock-taking exercise: (1) What is the state of the art regarding research about social policy in Europe? (2) How has research about social policy in Europe evolved to this point? (3) Where should research about social policy in Europe be headed? Each of the chapters in the book has provided answers to these questions, showcasing the diversity of research on social policy across this multidisciplinary field.

In this concluding chapter, we reflect on future research about social policy in Europe. Based on this rich collection of chapters and their outline of the past, present, and future, we note three key developments. First, research about social policy in Europe is dynamic and shows a strong evolution. The goals, achievements, and challenges of specific and cross-cutting policy themes are in a constant state of flux, and the descriptions of these themes as covered in the book clearly illustrate 20 years of research progress.

Second, research about social policy in Europe clearly shifted away from broad-brush regime-based approaches common during the late 1980s and early 1990s towards analyses of single-policy programmes in narrower parts of the welfare state machinery. This gain in policy detail has provided a solid foundation for much of the current comparative social policy literature. Research includes both large-scale cross-country comparisons as well as more in-depth case studies of single countries, often thematically oriented towards specific policy (sub-)fields.

Third, research on social policy has become increasingly evaluative, whereby the focus is on the outcomes produced by various cash benefit programmes and services. We have therefore learned a great deal about who benefits from social policy. As illustrated in several chapters in this book, European welfare states are, in several instances, associated with Matthew effects, particularly in relation to the provision of services (i.e., subsidized early childhood education and care, active labour market policy, health care, etc.). Matthew effects occur when social policies advantage those who need help the least (e.g., the middle class, higher-educated citizens), thereby reducing the equalizing effects of policies and potentially even widening the gap with more disadvantaged groups in society.

Where do we go from here? Given these three overarching developments in research on social policy in Europe, we offer three suggestions for moving forward. First, the diverse set of chapters in this book illustrate the need for research to broaden its view on social policy once again. The movement away from welfare regimes towards detailed comparisons of distinct areas of social policy in an increasingly thematic way has been fruitful. We now have detailed knowledge of how countries have organized individual policies, and how policies in separate areas of the welfare state have evolved over time. However, we believe that research now needs to make space for both specificity and breadth, accounting for the interplay between multiple policies, relating policy development to underlying social, political, and economic structures in society, and recognizing the multiplicity of citizens' identities.

Second, to ensure a robust future of research on social policy, we need greater theoretical development. We suggest social policy scholarship needs a more integrated understanding of policy outcomes, which is placed in the context of the origins of welfare reform. Increased attention is therefore needed for driving forces of policy change, which used to characterize much of social policy research a few decades ago. Specifically, we need to know more about how institutional designs shape future policy developments, for instance mediated by the outcomes they produce. Institutional structures may encourage or discourage new forms of social policymaking, or (re)define our views about future social problems that need to be addressed by policy. Essentially, we argue for research that links determinants of institutions and institutional change to the outcomes produced by the welfare state, as well as attention to the processes underlying these relationships and how these relationships evolve over time. From this perspective, social policy forms an intermediate variable (or factor) between cause (i.e., partisan politics, deindustrialization, population ageing, etc.) and effect (socio-economic stratification, gender equality, interest group formation, etc.). Note that cause and effect will shift place in the causal order over time, whereas the position of social policy as a mediating variable stays constant.

Third, and finally, we see the need to further strengthen and exploit the multidisciplinary nature of our research community, as demonstrated in the various chapters throughout this book. Discovering new trade-offs or complementarities between different types of policies (and beyond) is a challenging endeavour that can hardly be achieved by following the state of the art in single academic disciplines (like economics, political science, or sociology). Fully understanding the complex relationship between causes and consequences of social policy (our second recommendation) also likely requires insights from multiple disciplines. The multidisciplinary character of the ESPAnet community and the scholarship it represents is a crucial advantage that we should cultivate and nourish in this regard. In the remainder of this concluding chapter, we elaborate on these three recommendations, using illustrative examples from the book.

BROADENING THE SCOPE OF RESEARCH TO INTERSECTIONALITY AND POLICY INTERPLAYS

Our first suggestion is that as social policy scholars, we need to broaden our view to incorporate intersectionality more thoroughly at the individual level as well as the interplay of policies at the institutional level. Intersectionality requires social policy researchers to be cautious of the fact that individuals often have complex identities and, crucially, are affected by multiple policies at the same time. Understanding these complex relationships at the institutional level therefore requires looking beyond a single potential source of (dis)advantage, such as those associated with (low) income or educational attainment. As discussed by Daly and León (Chapter 2, this volume), research on care policy shows, for example, how the increased outsourcing of care responsibilities in a neoliberal market context creates social and economic polarization among women along socio-economic, racial/ethnic, and citizenship lines. Similarly, adopting an intersectional approach to analyses of old age pensions and ageing policies will help to illuminate the complex interactions between gender, socio-economic status, caregiving responsibilities, and labour market inequalities, as discussed by Ebbinghaus and Möhring (Chapter 6, this volume).

Intersectionality is not limited to understanding interrelated factors at the individual level. As highlighted by Knijn (Chapter 11, this volume), the increase in intersectional research on gender and social policy links the individual and institutional levels, with the potential for conceptualizing differences between groups as well as contestations that emerge from this heterogeneity. We must therefore do better in terms of analysing not only the interrelationship of factors at individual/family/household levels, but also at institutional/social policy levels, as well as how these different levels connect.

This interplay between different types of social policies is highlighted by multiple chapters in the book. A clear example can be found in Dewilde and Haffner's overview of research on housing policy (Chapter 5, this volume), which not only concerns housing-related welfare benefits and services, but also tenure structures, housing finance, and housing construction. Even more encompassing, they argue that people's housing conditions may also be related to complementarities between what is typically considered housing policy and other welfare state policies. Similarly, Wendt (Chapter 4, this volume) argues for an integrated approach for research on public health that integrates multiple policy fields beyond health care, including family policy, the educational system, and major programmes for income redistribution. Policy interplays should also be part and parcel of any ambitious attempt to understand how social policies and the welfare state affect poverty and income inequality, as noted by Cantillon in Chapter 7. Similarly, Bonoli (Chapter 8, this volume) raises awareness for the combination of different policy instruments in designing effective social investment strategies.

The integrated approach to the study of social policy that we advocate in this concluding chapter is not new. Policy interplays have been addressed before but have not yet become mainstream in research. Moreover, the connections between policies that have been studied often remain within particular policy sub-fields, such as the interplay between different labour market policies, or the well-documented gap between parental leave duration and the starting age of childcare. We believe that there are many virtues of situating individual social policy programmes in a larger institutional context and analysing how policies interact. Essentially, it brings out the complexity of the regime literature that used to characterize our field, without losing sight of the policy details that may also make a difference. The potential of an integrated approach to the study of social policy in generating new path-breaking findings has yet to be demonstrated. Nonetheless, we expect that the approach will increase scholarly understanding of how different types of policies strengthen or weaken each other. It will also help to unpack competing or complementing policy aims and ideas shaping these outcomes.

Our call for greater attention to the interplay of individual social policies comes with at least two qualifications. First, the social policy landscape has become increasingly complex. Policymaking takes place not only at the national level; the introduction of new policies, their governance, and implementation occurs at local, regional, national, and supra-national levels. Interaction within and between these levels can have important implications for social policy. As shown by De la Porte and Madama (Chapter 9, this volume), regulation at the supra-national level of the European Union increasingly affects national redistributive policies in the fields of pensions, health care, unemployment, and labour market regulation. Yet at the same time, even within single regions, vast differences between policy approaches can be found, as is demonstrated by the research on family policy, pensions, and poverty across countries in the Central and Eastern European region (Chapter 10 by Aidukaite and Navicke, this volume).

Second, the interplay between social policies is necessarily linked to broader political, economic, social, and lately also environmental processes, which is evident not in the least by Hvinden and Schoyen's account of social policy research in relation to climate change (Chapter 15, this volume). Similarly, technological change and specifically the digitalization of public services changes the very mechanisms through which the welfare state operates. The changed and automated nature of welfare provision may also reinforce existing, and bring with it new, cleavages in society (Chapter 16 by van Gerven, this volume).

Scholarly attempts to map developments in separate fields of social policy and the increased focus on policy outcomes have, to some extent, made us lose sight – it would seem – of these broader configurations. At the very least, we need to do more to connect policy evaluative research to the wider context in which policies operate. While the shift away from the regime approach towards more detailed accounts of policy and outcomes in separate parts of the welfare state has paved the way for innovative research, we now encourage the scholarly community to complement these analyses by asking how individual policies are interlinked, how they combine to affect living conditions, attitudes, and behaviour, as well as how they relate to the wider contexts of policymaking.

We realize that our recommendation may appear paradoxical. To an important extent, this book itself has been organized based on specific areas of policy. As described in the individual chapters of this book, research about social policy in Europe has become increasingly adept at describing in great depth the complexity of individual policy programmes (or types of policies). These descriptions showcase intricate policy designs, leading to both intended and unintended outcomes that are typically difficult to pinpoint using holistic regime-based approaches. However, we think it is necessary to step back and analyse how individual policies fit within the larger welfare state machinery and other institutional, social, economic, and cultural contexts relevant to the functioning of the welfare state. To use an old and probably overused saying, with an increasingly narrower focus on specific social policy fields, we risk failing to see the forest for the trees. Research on social policy needs to develop strategies to deal with an increasing demand within academia and among policymakers for institutional detail, without losing sight of how the functioning of policies are interrelated and linked to wider societal structures.

THEORIZING SOCIAL POLICY

If our first recommendation presents a paradox, our second recommendation offers a solution: theoretical advancement. Given the multifaceted nature of what we study, it is easy to get lost in institutional details and fail to observe the wider structures that ultimately determine how policies should be judged. Theory may encourage us to analyse policies from different viewpoints, and provide a deeper understanding of the ways in which social policies shape our lives. Let us return to the Matthew effects of many social policies (particularly in the provision of services) observed in several chapters of the book and highlighted above. Narrowly conceived, (often) unintended and (commonly perceived) pervasive outcomes may be considered to reduce the effectiveness of policies in achieving equality. Yet, a broader theoretical perspective would suggest that if larger shares of the population (who may need it less) receive benefits from a policy, this may affect popular support for the welfare state and make future expansions of policy possible, which also benefits the poor. Considered as such, Matthew effects in some parts of social policy may not necessarily be a solely negative development that should always be avoided. Theory would, in this case, encourage us to see the problem of Matthew effects in a different light, and perhaps judge these effects against possible spill-over effects in more pro-poor areas of social policy.

Contemporary research about social policy in Europe excels at describing institutional arrangements in specific parts of the welfare state, and relating these descriptions to various outcomes (i.e., the effects of social policies). However, to move beyond descriptions to a deeper understanding of the effects of social policy for individuals, families, and society, we need to invest in theoretical development. The role of theory is noted in several chapters of the book and seems to be more developed in some fields of social policy compared to others. Whereas Van Lancker and Zagel (Chapter 3, this volume) explicitly discuss the absence of deeper theoretical engagement in much of contemporary research on family policy, Daly and León (Chapter 2, this volume) call for more research applying a capability approach in care policy. In Chapter 7, Cantillon argues for a multilayered understanding of poverty that conceptualizes social policies across time, space, and scale. Notably, policy interplays form a specific part of this schema. As noted above, the intersectional approach described by Knijn (Chapter 11, this volume) provides further motivation for theoretical advancements in this direction.

Without theory, we risk a myopic viewpoint that insufficiently asks questions about institutional diversity, interplays, and outcomes. Theories may be formulated for different reasons and at different levels of abstraction. In particular, we believe that theoretical advancement is needed concerning recursive processes and the forms of two-way causality that characterizes much of social policymaking. Under such conditions, there is no single direction of change, as cause and effect constantly shift positions over time. This dynamic perspective on social policymaking with its close focus on mutually enforcing processes carries great potential in terms of identifying and better understanding why policies work in some areas but not in others. Some of the chapters in this book touch upon this topic and provide promising starting points. Van Oorschot, Laenen, Roosma, and Meuleman (Chapter 13, this volume) point to the reciprocal relationship between social policy and public opinion, whereas Bonoli (Chapter 8, this volume) provides insights in relation to the political economy of active social policies. Along similar lines, Breidahl, Hedegaard, and Seibel (Chapter 17, this volume) show how migration is not only affected by the welfare state, but also helps to reshape it. Dewilde and Haffner (Chapter 5, this volume) raise the concern that home ownership, and the mortgage policies promoting it, may compensate inequalities due to declining wages, but may also undermine support for redistribution.

Recursive processes further relate to welfare state institutional legacies, and how policy choices at critical conjunctures in the past affect policymaking today (see Chapter 12 by Clasen and Clegg, this volume). Essentially, what is at stake are the feedback effects of policies on outcomes, and vice versa. Theoretical advancement along these lines is also directly related to the broader question of who defines what a social problem is, and which social problems are perceived to be important enough to be addressed by social policy. This power of definition is extensively discussed in the literature on gender (in)equality, as described by Knijn (Chapter 11, this volume), but applies to social policy in general. If citizens in general do not agree with the definition of social problems, and how these are addressed by social policies, this absence of recognition could further contribute to the crisis of political legitimacy in contemporary welfare states, as described by Greve and Paster (Chapter 18, this volume). We posit that linking policy outcome feedback effects to the interplay between policies and the intersection of individual identities with attention for who is defining the problem, and how, will provide challenging but fruitful areas for theoretical advancements in research about social policy in Europe.

MULTIDISCIPLINARITY

Our final recommendation is to strengthen one of the core characteristics of the ESPAnet community, and research about social policy in Europe more generally: its multidisciplinarity. Multidisciplinarity is about the need for multiple perspectives on a given issue to allow for a broad understanding; it does not mean everyone has to become interdisciplinary scholars. Several chapters in the book illustrate how a multidisciplinary perspective could move the field forward. In relation to pensions, for example, Ebbinghaus and Möhring (Chapter 6, this volume) highlight the varying ways in which demographers, economists, political scientists, and sociologists contribute discipline-specific perspectives to understand the complex interplay between demographic ageing, driving forces of pension reform, and the outcomes of changing pension systems. Combined insights from two or more of these disciplines (e.g., economics and sociology) can offer balanced views on the financial sustainability of pensions while accounting for an integrated life-course perspective. On the topic of climate change, multidisciplinary approaches are needed to address the combined challenge of social and ecological sustainability, as emphasized by Hvinden and Schoyen (Chapter 15, this volume).

Multidisciplinarity certainly brings with it potential theoretical and methodological challenges. Disciplines often differ in their conceptualization of key terms, as highlighted by the chapter on care policy by Daly and León (Chapter 2, this volume). While some research succeeds in taking an interdisciplinary approach that integrates multiple disciplinary perspectives, the existence of different disciplinary conceptualizations is not necessarily a disadvantage. Varying conceptualizations can offer avenues for future research, as shown by Wendt in the health-care literature (Chapter 4, this volume). Approaching health as a combined individual and population health issue – in essence integrating epidemiology, medical sciences, sociology, public health, and social policy – is likely to move the field of health-care policy several steps forward.

Conceptual differences across disciplines may, however, create methodological challenges, with disciplines differing with respect to the use of quantitative and qualitative approaches for measuring concepts, and the specific methodological tools applied. Nonetheless, as Ferragina and Deeming (Chapter 14, this volume) show, research on social policy, particularly related to comparative analyses, offers room for multiple approaches. Despite the growth in large-N, quantitative studies, small-scale country case studies, generally qualitative in approach, are still prominent in research about social policy in Europe. Their analysis of nearly 20 years of comparative policy analysis in the *Journal of European Social Policy* suggests, moreover, that few social policy scholars are using multiple or mixed methods. In our view, future research on social policy relying on multidisciplinary approaches that combine or use multiple methods offers significant opportunities for moving the field forward.

CONCLUSION

With our contemporary and highly specialized understanding of the welfare state, it is difficult to appreciate how much has been learned during the last 20 years – and thus how superficial our understanding of European social policy perhaps was. Trying to look ahead another 20 years, a number of major challenges can be foreseen for European welfare states, creating new opportunities and needs for social policy research. To start, it is unclear how long the social and economic consequences of the COVID-19 pandemic will last. Recent major challenges, like the Great Recession that started in 2007/2008, shaped social policy research for at least a decade. The need for research on the role of social policies in the pandemic and the amelioration of the consequences of the pandemic will likely remain for at least a decade as well. Moreover, the response to climate change will, in all likelihood, require a fundamental shift in work, production, and consumption in attempts to make the transition to net-zero emissions socially equitable, a question that still remains largely unexplored in research. With Europe's population still ageing, significant challenges also remain that call into question the financial sustainability of European welfare states.

European welfare states will likely also face unforeseen, far-reaching challenges in the next decades that are difficult to predict today. However, we believe that social policy research is well positioned to address these challenges, informing policymakers and the public about the immediate problems at hand, bringing clarity about which policies work and for whom, and showing which alternative policy solutions may be available. This is particularly the case in an increasingly integrated European Union, where countries attempt to learn about and from social policy approaches in other member states.

As demonstrated by the chapters in this book, the vivid landscape of social policy research is not afraid of addressing new and sometimes inconvenient questions about the role, functioning, and outcomes of collective action, irrespective of whether it is organized at the level of the state, market, or family. We believe that the recommendations formulated in this concluding chapter on the future orientations of social policy research in Europe will further strengthen the relevance and significance of social policy research, for academia, policymaking, and the general public alike. Researching interplays between policies and their connection to the wider society provides insights into how social policy is embedded in national contexts, which will help us assess the transferability of policy solutions from one European country to the next. Theorizing social outcomes in relation to institutional change and its driving forces will provide policy guidance, not only in relation to the challenges raised by the recurring crises of the welfare state and social policy, but also in the context of new challenges that have yet to be studied empirically. To examine these complex challenges from a diversity of perspectives, the multidisciplinary and multimethod character of research on social policy in Europe is perhaps the greatest asset to be used and fostered by our academic community.

Index